T0339871

Transportation Cyber-Physical Systems

Transportation Cyber-Physical Systems

Edited by

Lipika Deka
School of Computer Science and Informatics,
De Montfort University, Leicester,
United Kingdom

Mashrur Chowdhury
Glenn Department of Civil Engineering, Clemson
University, Clemson, SC, United States

Elsevier
Radarweg 29, PO Box 211, 1000 AE Amsterdam, Netherlands
The Boulevard, Langford Lane, Kidlington, Oxford OX5 1GB, United Kingdom
50 Hampshire Street, 5th Floor, Cambridge, MA 02139, United States

Copyright © 2018 Elsevier Inc. All rights reserved.

No part of this publication may be reproduced or transmitted in any form or by any means,
electronic or mechanical, including photocopying, recording, or any information storage and
retrieval system, without permission in writing from the publisher. Details on how to seek
permission, further information about the Publisher's permissions policies and our
arrangements with organizations such as the Copyright Clearance Center and the Copyright
Licensing Agency, can be found at our website: www.elsevier.com/permissions.

This book and the individual contributions contained in it are protected under copyright by
the Publisher (other than as may be noted herein).

Notices
Knowledge and best practice in this field are constantly changing. As new research and
experience broaden our understanding, changes in research methods, professional practices,
or medical treatment may become necessary.

Practitioners and researchers must always rely on their own experience and knowledge in
evaluating and using any information, methods, compounds, or experiments described
herein. In using such information or methods they should be mindful of their own safety and
the safety of others, including parties for whom they have a professional responsibility.

To the fullest extent of the law, neither the Publisher nor the authors, contributors, or editors,
assume any liability for any injury and/or damage to persons or property as a matter of
products liability, negligence or otherwise, or from any use or operation of any methods,
products, instructions, or ideas contained in the material herein.

Library of Congress Cataloging-in-Publication Data
A catalog record for this book is available from the Library of Congress

British Library Cataloguing-in-Publication Data
A catalogue record for this book is available from the British Library

ISBN: 978-0-12-814295-0

For information on all Elsevier publications visit our
website at https://www.elsevier.com/books-and-journals

Working together
to grow libraries in
developing countries

www.elsevier.com • www.bookaid.org

Publisher: Joe Hayton
Acquisition Editor: Brian Romer
Editorial Project Manager: Lindsay Lawrence
Production Project Manager: Anusha Sambamoorthy
Designer: Miles Hitchen

Typeset by TNQ Technologies

Lipika Deka: To my husband Dr. Diganta Bhusan Das and son Anuron Bhusan Das.

Mashrur Chowdhury: To my father Manzur Chowdhury.

Contents

List of contributors

Shofiq Ahmed   Department of Civil and Environmental Engineering, West Virginia University, Morgantown, WV, United States

Eduardo S. Almeida   Department of Computer Science, Federal University of Bahia, Salvador, Brazil

Amy Apon   School of Computing, Clemson University, Clemson, SC, United States

Nick Ayres   School of Computer Science and Informatics, De Montfort University, Leicester, United Kingdom

Mashrur Chowdhury   Glenn Department of Civil Engineering, Clemson University, Clemson, SC, United States

Lipika Deka   School of Computer Science and Informatics, De Montfort University, Leicester, United Kingdom

Kakan Dey   Department of Civil and Environmental Engineering, West Virginia University, Morgantown, WV, United States

Huseyin Dogan   Department of Computing & Informatics, Faculty of Science & Technology, Bournemouth University, Poole, United Kingdom

John Fitzgerald   Newcastle University, Newcastle upon Tyne, United Kingdom

Ryan Fries   Department of Civil Engineering, Southern Illinois University, Edwardsville, IL, United States

Carl Gamble   Newcastle University, Newcastle upon Tyne, United Kingdom

Venkat N. Gudivada   Department of Computer Science, East Carolina University, Greenville, NC, United States

Longxiang Guo   Department of Automotive Engineering, Clemson University, Greenville, SC, United States

Michael Henshaw   School of Mechanical, Electrical, and Manufacturing Engineering, Loughborough University, Loughborough, United Kingdom

Yunyi Jia   Department of Automotive Engineering, Clemson University, Greenville, SC, United States

Tony Kenyon Chief Product Officer & SVP Engineering, R&D Guardtime, Guildford, United Kingdom; The De Montfort University Interdisciplinary Group in Intelligent Transport Systems (DIGITS), De Montfort University, Leicester, United Kingdom

Sakib M. Khan Glenn Department of Civil Engineering, Clemson University, Clemson, SC, United States

Peter G. Larsen Aarhus University, Aarhus, Denmark

Martin Mansfield Newcastle University, Newcastle upon Tyne, United Kingdom

John D. McGregor School of Computing, Clemson University, Clemson, SC, United States

Linh Bao Ngo School of Computing, Clemson University, Clemson, SC, United States

Julien Ouy CLEARSY, Aix-en-Provence, France

Roberto Palacin Newcastle University, Newcastle upon Tyne, United Kingdom

Ken Pierce Newcastle University, Newcastle upon Tyne, United Kingdom

Brandon Posey School of Computing, Clemson University, Clemson, SC, United States

Srini Ramaswamy ABB, Inc., Cleveland, Ohio, United States

Roselane S. Silva Department of Computer Science, Federal University of Bahia, Salvador, Brazil

Seshadri Srinivasan Berkeley Education Alliance for Research in Singapore (BEARS), Singapore

Xin Wang Department of Automotive Engineering, Clemson University, Greenville, SC, United States

Paul Whittington Department of Computing & Informatics, Faculty of Science & Technology, Bournemouth University, Poole, United Kingdom

Foreword

I am delighted to provide the forward for this new and timely book on Transport Cyber-Physical Systems.

We are on the cusp of something very exciting and transformational in transport with the advent of new digital and computing technologies, sensing and IoT leading to the potential of an all-seeing, all-knowing transport system and the emergence of key new technologies such as automation, electromobility and the evolution of new business cases of how to do transport through mobility as a service.

Underpinning these transformations are cyber-physical systems that will sense, analyse, make sense of and then manage and control the transport systems and networks of the future. I am delighted that this book tackles this issue and provides some clarity to stakeholders, practitioners and the research community as to what this all means and how such systems will evolve in the future.

The book provides an insight to a panoply of the building blocks of cyber-physical systems, including the architecture, communications, data management, modelling and data processing, real-time control and the privacy and security aspects that underpin this, which are all useful reference materials for future implementers. However, to future proof the material, this book also considers the education and skills needed to deliver such systems in the future and the interaction with the end users through a consideration of human factors.

A provision of case studies that cover many of the modes of transport are an important aspect of the book. It illustrates that, with the underlying digital data and communications architectures we can finally be able to think of transport as a system, rather than a set of loosely connected modes. Moreover, cross-learn from successes and best practices in one mode to another.

In the context of the United Kingdom, as the Government moves towards its Grand Challenge on the Future of Mobility and the support of major transport technologies through the industrial strategy challenge fund, the book has a leading role to play in informing the industry and providing a reference guide to many of the underlying topics of TCPS in one place. Moreover, this book's recognition of synergies is in how we approach this in the United Kingdom and the United States, and the common research questions we have, to deliver smart transportation in smart cities, eloquently frames some medium to long term challenges of the transport sector.

Professor Phil Blythe
Professor of Intelligent Transport Systems and Chief Scientific Adviser,
Department for Transport School of Engineering
Newcastle University, UK
February, 2018

Preface

Transportation is no longer limited by the physical world, as the cyber world is fast becoming an intrinsic part of the transportation ecosystem. It collects vital data from physical elements such as sensors and traffic management centres, controls elements of the system (for example, traffic lights and vehicle brakes) when needed and provides feedback or information, thus enabling the transportation ecosystem to provide safety, security, mobility and environmental services through seamless connectivity. Transportation infrastructure (roads, bridges, tunnels, waterways and rails) and transportation modes (cars, trucks, ships and trains) are interacting with the cyber world to provide increasingly efficient services, and the role of the cyber world will increase exponentially within the next decade and beyond. Such a marriage of the cyber- and the physical world within the transportation sector is termed the Transportation Cyber-Physical System (TCPS).

It is clear that the internet of transportation is on us, but are transportation students and professionals ready? Knowledge of the physical elements of transportation systems alone cannot equip students or professionals properly. Realising this, we embarked on a journey to put together this book on the Transportation Cyber-Physical System, as a collaboration between authors from either side of the Atlantic, to prepare our students and professionals as planners, designers, developers, operators and maintainers of the amazing world of the TCPS. This TCPS world promises safety, efficiency, sustainability, mobility and other benefits that will help our future societies thrive.

Soon TCPS will be mainstreamed in transportation systems operations and business practices around the world. It is where the intelligent transportation systems will meet the smart cities and regions of the future. It is where people will get the most out of their transportation in connected communities. In TCPS, transportation will be an enabler and accelerator for the productivity and sustainability of our societies—never an impediment.

This book is intended to serve as a primary or supplemental textbook for upper-level undergraduate and graduate courses related to TCPS, transportation systems or intelligent transportation systems. This book will also serve as a reference text for multidisciplinary professionals working in transportation-related areas. We are excited to join the journey to all the amazing innovations that will come from the future TCPS to help us live better. We hope this book will contribute to the future exciting world of transportation in our connected societies.

Lipika Deka
Mashrur Chowdury

Acknowledgements

We are delighted to acknowledge the support from the Elsevier staff in the publication of the book. They were always very responsive to our requests and questions. We would also like to thank the chapter authors for their dedication in developing the chapter manuscripts. This book would not have been possible without their outstanding collaborations. We would also like to acknowledge the support of Dr. Diganta Bhusan Das and Farzana Chowdhury—our professional achievements have always been founded on their support.

Transportation Cyber-Physical System and its importance for future mobility

1

Lipika Deka [1], Sakib M. Khan [2], Mashrur Chowdhury [2], Nick Ayres [1]
[1]School of Computer Science and Informatics, De Montfort University, Leicester, United Kingdom; [2]Glenn Department of Civil Engineering, Clemson University, Clemson, SC, United States

1. Introduction of Transportation Cyber-Physical System

Ageing populations, climate change, advent of mega cities, increased energy requirements and overarching need for smart, green and integrated transport have been clearly identified as the key global challenges faced by our modern society [1]. Immense advancement in research and innovation in the field of embedded intelligence systems has shown promise to be the key enabling technological solutions to address these major challenges. Within these systems, physical elements such as sensors and actuators function hand in hand with cyber elements such as software to monitor and initiate physical processes, while the associated cyberspace, records and analyses store data and support decision-making. Further, the simultaneous and equally rapid advancement in the field of communications and the Internet of Things has allowed embedded systems to be equipped with the power of collective knowledge as opposed to functioning in isolation. For example, the collective intelligence gathered from smartphones that act as sensors of the traffic network very quickly and easily enable individuals and authorities to gauge the level of congestion, CO_2 emissions, etc., and hence take near real-time actions towards effective traffic management. The term used to describe such systems that seamlessly integrate computational algorithms and physical components with mutual communication much exceeding the capability of relatively 'humble' embedded systems is Cyber-Physical System (CPS).

The term CPS has been perceived and defined in a number of closely related ways. In particular, there seems to be a noteworthy difference in how the term is used and understood on either side of the Atlantic. In the United States [2], the CPS definition seems to give equal emphasis to the 'cyber' and 'physical' components of CPS [3], whereas the European Union (EU) definition [1] seems to give more emphasis on the 'cyber' component of CPS.

Transportation Cyber-Physical Systems. https://doi.org/10.1016/B978-0-12-814295-0.00001-0
Copyright © 2018 Elsevier Inc. All rights reserved.

Definition of Cyber-Physical System as perceived in the United States:

Cyber-Physical Systems (CPS) are integrations of computation and physical processes. Embedded computers and networks monitor and control the physical processes, usually with feedback loops where physical processes affect computations and vice versa [2].

Definition of Cyber-Physical System as perceived in Europe:

Cyber-Physical System are systems with embedded software (as part of devices, buildings, means of transport, transport routes, production systems, medical processes, logistic processes, coordination processes and management processes), which:

- directly record physical data using sensors and affect physical processes using actuators;
- evaluate and save recorded data, and actively or reactively interact both with the physical and digital world;
- are connected with one another and in global networks via digital communication facilities (wireless and/or wired, local and/or global);
- use globally available data and services;
- have a series of dedicated, multi-modal human-machine interfaces [1].

Nevertheless, as Lee suggests, it would be most appropriate to define CPS without linking it to its varied applications (as is suggested above in the US definition of CPS) by regarding it as a 'fundamental intellectual problem of conjoining the engineering tradition as of the cyber and physical worlds' [4].

CPS has driven innovation across diverse fields including transportation systems within which it is termed as Transportation Cyber-Physical System (TCPS). Compared to a traditional transportation system, TCPS can make the transportation systems achieve higher efficiency and reliability by enabling increased feedback-based interactions between the cyber system and the physical system in transportation. TCPS can be broadly classified into three categories as shown in Table 1.1, which include: (1) infrastructure-based TCPS, (2) vehicle–infrastructure coordinated TCPS and (3) vehicle-based TCPS.

The transportation system is the complex system of systems both enabling and sabotaging societies, trade, politics and environment. Development within the field of TCPS is enhancing efficiency while reducing environmental stress and meeting societal demands across the continually growing air, land and water transport of both humans and goods. Such developments are continually occurring within multiple domains including transportation modelling, big data analytics, real-time control and optimisation, verification and validation, computer networks and cybersecurity. Fig. 1.1 shows the conceptual overview of TCPS, where the decision such as activating emergency braking system is implemented by the TCPS actuators such as the brakes based on the data collected from TCPS sensors such as radars and cameras on cars.

Table 1.1 **Instances of Transportation Cyber-Physical System (TCPS)**

Types of TCPS	Physical Components	Cyber Components	Applications
Infrastructure-based TCPS	Traffic signals, infrastructure sensors such as cameras, computational devices in traffic management Centre, etc.	Wired/wireless communication, software	Real-time infrastructure monitoring, traffic control, etc.
Vehicle—infrastructure coordinated TCPS	Vehicles and their associated sensors such as GPS, traffic signals, computational devices in traffic management Centre, etc.	Wireless communication, software	Transit signal priority, queue warning, etc.
Vehicle-based TCPS	Sensing and computational devices inside the vehicles. Actuators such as gears, brakes, ignitor, etc.	Wireless communication, software such as those embedded in the electronic control units.	Proximity detection, black ice detection, etc.

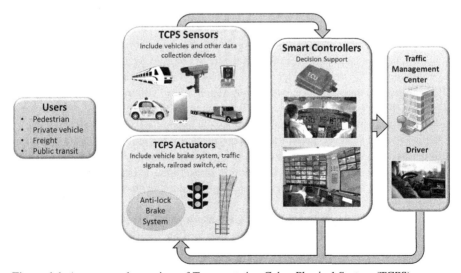

Figure 1.1 A conceptual overview of Transportation Cyber-Physical System (TCPS).

Traditionally, decisions are determined and carried out by vehicle drivers or traffic management centres. Drivers/centres make the decision by evaluating what they observe from the information captured by different sensors and by themselves. Thus, drivers/centres act as the controller. Also, smart controllers can assess existing conditions after analysing data received from the monitoring sensors and then make the decisions and automatically initiate the actuators.

This book is aimed at facilitating the accelerated growth in the research and development of TCPS for the security, reliability and stability of the society at large through contributions from experts and visionaries, bringing the knowledge that lays the multi-disciplinary foundation of TCPS onto a single platform.

2. Transportation Cyber-Physical System examples and its components

TCPS is critical to the safety, security and benefit of society and the environment because they represent some of the most important infrastructure, such as the systems for aviation, rail, road and marine transportation, and its components for the transportation of both humans and goods. The following sections will introduce TCPS within the different transportation modes with examples. It must be noted here that the components and examples listed here are not in anyway an exhaustive list.

2.1 Aviation Transportation Cyber-Physical System

Air transportation has the inherent ability to drive economic and social progress by connecting people, countries, cultures and providing access to the global market, making it the most far-reaching among all the transportation modes. Demand on air traffic from both passenger and cargo is continually rising with 2017 seeing a 31% rise in passenger demand compared to figures in 2012 [5], and consequentially to serve this demand, the number of aircrafts is expected to double in the next 2 decades. Intertwined with its immense socioeconomic benefits and subsequent increase in demand, the aviation sector houses some of the most complex systems to date including the unmanned aerial vehicles. Hence, the earliest and most advanced development of CPS within the transportation sector has taken place within the aviation sector. Modern aerospace systems have the immense potential of tightly coupling cyberspace and the physical space. This is primarily due to the cyberspace technological advances in the area of the internet, networking and information technology, with advances in performance goals such as cyberspace reliability and availability, security and privacy and performance metrics, such as bandwidth, throughput, latency and both software and data size [6], which are all mandatory requirements for the real-time operational environment.

The physical elements of aviation TCPS are widely diverse, ranging from the uncertain natural airspace (such as clouds, pressure, precipitation, storms, wind, air pockets, temperature, solar interference, surrounding wildlife, etc.); infrastructure and hardware (such as the actual aircraft and its numerous electromechanical systems, the air control system, runway, airport, etc.) and the human factor (as facilitators and threats); which are all controlled and monitored through policies, performance goals (e.g., safety, security, privacy, efficiency, carbon neutrality), performance metrics (e.g., speed, weight, fuel burning rate, air quality, passenger throughput) and legal, ethical and existing CPS within the aviation sector [6].

2.1.1 Examples of aviation Transportation Cyber-Physical System

In Europe the developments from the CPS point of view in the Air Traffic Management (ATM) area are happening under the umbrella of the Single European Sky ATM Research (SESAR) programme, which is a collaborative venture between the EU and EUROCONTROL as the main founding bodies together with partners from airports, air navigation service providers, scientific communities and different categories of airspace users. The primary aim of SESAR is to transform European ATM into a more modular and automated system that is safe and environmentally friendly. Fig. 1.2 shows every stage of a flight and SESAR's procedural requirements [6].

In particular automated hazard perception, accurate positioning and navigation, risk identification and mitigation, surveillance, all aspects of air traffic management (with potential from optimisation and control algorithms), flight dynamics and control can be put forward as classical examples of vision of integrating each of these phases into a holistic ATM system.

The ATM system is a combination of a number of CPSs and hence in reality a Cyber-Physical System of systems of which the system supporting a pilot in approach and landing particularly in bad weather conditions is an integral CPS of the ATM system. Most airports use the ground-based augmentation of satellite navigation systems (GBAS) to support pilots during approach and landing in bad weather conditions with precise location information, thus maintaining its capacity needs while ensuring safety. GBAS use four global navigation satellite system reference receivers and a very high frequency broadcast transmitter system to calculate the differentially corrected position and deviation from an aircraft's selected approach path, thus facilitating the aircraft to land automatically and safely in poor visibility conditions [7]. Another example is the automated aircraft collision alerts, where based on the enhanced airborne collision avoidance system (ACAS) aircrafts will automatically change the

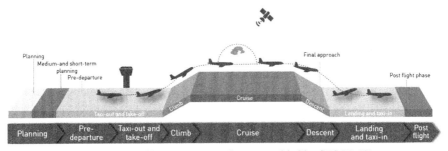

Figure 1.2 Integrated Air Traffic Management System enabled by SESAR [7].

elevation. After implementing the enhanced ACAS, the vertical rate at the approach of the selected flight level will be automatically adjusted to reduce unnecessary flight deck distraction.

The equivalent of SESAR is the Next Generation Air Transportation System (NextGen) in the United States for modernising air traffic control, where its primary aim is to reduce gridlock both in the sky and at airports through gradual replacement of radar-based radio communication and manual processing of data with satellite-based technologies and automation. A prominent example of a CPS within the Next-Gen System is the Automatics Dependent Surveillance-Broadcast (ADS-B) [8] for replacing radar-based surveillance. ADS-B technology involves an aircraft automatically and accurately determining its position through high-integrity GPS-based techniques and periodically broadcasting this position to neighbouring aircraft and ground-based air traffic control through a dedicated data link. This information helps aircrafts to improve situational awareness and judge more accurately the safe self-separation distance. ADS-B technology is seen to replace the task of the secondary radar.

Sampigethaya and Poovendran [6] lay out the vision of the future of an integrated aviation TCPS with self-monitoring and self-correcting aircrafts, a system that autonomously optimises and supports decision-making in all aspects from fuel efficiency, interflight separation during landing, take-off or in-air to optimising operational revenue and providing a personalised experience to passengers which will include their desired relaxing/working environment while on board or at airports. Such a vision is supported through advances in avionics software, which is making a paradigm shift from distributed and isolated onboard system architecture to a more integrated modular avionics-based architecture running on multicore and multiprocessing computers. An integrated architecture allows for consistent and seamless interelement connectivity, with modularity allowing for clean separation between individual processes, which in turn allows for better management and isolation in case of errors or attacks. Modularity is also supporting the inroad of off-the-shelf components, such as sensors, actuators and radio frequency identification tags, which are getting increasingly affordable, efficient and with lower carbon footprints. Advances in avionics software are being supported through a shift in the onboard network to the standardised aircraft data network based on commercial Ethernet. This integration of software and communication is not limited to onboard systems, rather it integrates the onboard systems to off-board systems on the ground, air and space through several dedicated data links [6].

Given all these advances, a simple example of a future aviation TCPS is illustrated in Fig. 1.3 [6]. The altitude sensors, currently used for flight control, together with other flight and individual conditions can be used to control the light transmission properties of the electrochromic aircraft windows. The automation of this process can optimise crew operational performance that would otherwise have to supervise central control or assist individual passengers. Such features though simple are envisaged to improve individual experience and performances of both crew and passenger.

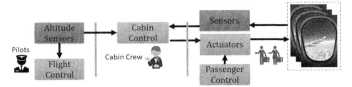

Figure 1.3 Cyber-physical interaction for controlling aircraft windows.
Adapted from K. Sampigethaya, R. Poovendran, Aviation cyber—physical systems: foundations for future aircraft and air transport, Proceedings of the IEEE 101 (8) (2013) 1834—1855.

Despite the obvious technological advancement in the field of aviation, there are plenty of challenges and adversities yet to be conquered, and innovation to overcome these adversities is driven by the huge potential for increased capacity, safety and efficiency while being kind to the environment [9].

2.2 Rail Transportation Cyber-Physical System

Rail transport can be seen as the relatively more orthodox mode of transport with the earliest known form of raillike transport being the wagon ways functioning from the 1500s in Europe primarily in the mines. These early 'trains' were either human or horse pulled. This gave way to steam-powered engines, followed by the diesel and electric engines that we are familiar with today. Recent times have seen advances in the area of communication networks and information technology penetrating into the operations of this orthodox means of transport transforming it into a more efficient, reliable and safe mode of transport aspiring to provide a personalised seamless journey experience to its customers.

2.2.1 Examples of Rail Transportation Cyber-Physical System

The components of the rail TCPS can be explained with that of the train control system. For the European Train Control System (ETCS), Siemens has developed a solution which is known as Trainguard. For level 1 application, Trainguard transmits the variable track vacancy detection information to the onboard antenna. The driver gets the permitted speed, the line profile ahead, speed restrictions and ETCS-specific data through a display. The drivers get a warning once the train exceeds the maximum permitted speed. The actuators become active to decelerate the train to the permitted speed if he fails to respond. Fig. 1.4 shows the Trainguard component of the Siemens solution for the ETCS, where Global System for Mobile communications — Railways, the digital communication system for railways within Europe, facilitates driving by 'electronic sight' through reliable communication of accurate train positions [10].

Similarly as another example, onboard GPS tracking devices accurately track trains in real time as the train runs, thus providing real-time train time tables to

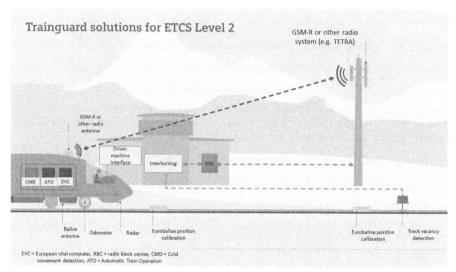

Figure 1.4 Trainguard component for European Train Control System.
Adapted from SIEMENS, European Train Control System, [Online]. Available: http://www.
mobility.siemens.com/mobility/global/en/interurban-mobility/rail-solutions/rail-automation/
train-control-system/european-train-protection-system/Pages/european-train-control-system.
aspx.

customers through station announcements, websites and mobile phone apps.
Such train-tracking technology not only helps train operators to better inform passengers but also envisaged to support operators in planning ahead and performing
strategic decision-making for real-time scheduling changes as in the case of delays
or emergencies. Live train-tracking technology together with advances in communication technology will also help trains and cars in the not-too-distant future
to automatically communicate to each other their position, particularly when
approaching a crossing [11].

Innovations in the cyberspace has not only benefitted the operational and customer
satisfaction aspects of railways but also ushered in CPS developments in efficient management and refurbishment of railways' complex asset base, for example, automatic
condition monitoring of lineside buildings, masonry structures, drainage systems, signalling systems, tracks, etc. There has particularly been a substantial amount of development around wireless sensor networks for automating the process of railway
infrastructure condition monitoring [12], such as those of railway sleepers [13], which
has until recently been performed manually which can be cumbersome, leading to
many faults not being detected in a timely manner. One of the many challenges to
be addressed within this area is the development of an integrated and holistic system
for real-time condition monitoring. This could include combining infrastructure health
monitoring sensor data with GPS and train route data to validate track conditions, such
as validating a track defect through vibrations data monitored by several trains at the
same GPS location [14].

2.3 Road Transportation Cyber-Physical System

The road transport sector is under enormous pressure for being one of the leading contributors for global injuries and deaths, as well as one of the highest contributors of greenhouse gas emissions (17.5% of overall gas emission in Europe in the last decade) [15], whilst facing an ever-increasing demand with the number of cars worldwide predicted to touch 1.6 billion by 2030. Road transport has a huge impact on society, the environment and the economy and is hence one of the primary areas currently undergoing major CPS R&D investment aimed towards increasing safety, reducing congestion and increasing road capacity while meeting strict environmental regulations. We have already seen major advances in embedded intelligence (within vehicles, infrastructure, goods and management), vehicle-to-everything (V2X) communication technologies and applications and automated driver safety systems. Such developments are seen in both public and private transport sector for both humans and goods.

The components of road TCPS can be explained with a perception-based traffic incident management system. Road TCPS includes the three main processes [16] for traffic situation assessment in the cyber-physical space. They are (1) senor-based perception, (2) situation assessment and (3) actuation. As shown in Fig. 1.5, based

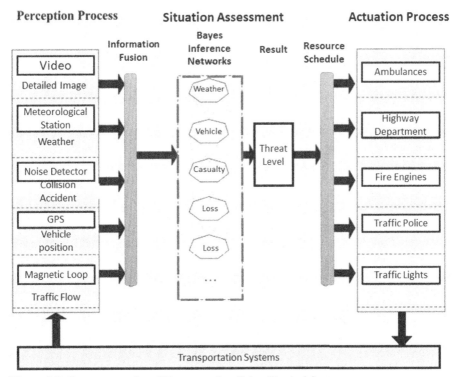

Figure 1.5 Components of road Transportation Cyber-Physical System.
Adapted from Y. Wang, G. Tan, Y. Wang, Y. Yi, Perceptual control architecture for cyber−physical systems in traffic incident management, Journal of Systems Architecture 58 (10) (2012) 398−411.

on heterogeneous multisensory-based data fusion, perception occurs. Information on the traffic situation coming from data fusion supports the assessment process. After the information is processed, the traffic resource scheduling can be optimally distributed to reduce the impact of incidents or to alleviate the traffic emergency situation.

2.3.1 Examples of Road Transportation Cyber-Physical System

From the user/consumer perspective, major inroads have been made in the area of Mobility as a Service (MaaS) where consumers particularly the younger generation are keen on viewing transport as a service that one can buy when needed and less preference is given to ownership, showing a clear shift from the ownership model to the service model. This service business model is also the primary business model seen by businesses and the government as we usher in driverless vehicles. The acceleration in the growth of MaaS is particularly attributed to the prolific use of smartphones and many organisations willing to make database public; this is evident in the way consumers are embracing services such as Uber. Another example of TCPS on the service sector is the availability of numerous journey planner apps. Clearly, providing personalised solutions to every individual's mobility needs is high on the agenda of businesses in this sector, with journey planner apps providing tailored options fitting every individual's need, be it a low-cost route to the most direct route to the most environmentally friendly route [17].

Traffic management worldwide has also seen major benefits from embedding cyberspace solutions. For example, through its Smart Motorway project, Highways England is introducing active traffic management technologies to tackle congestion on highways on its existing road space. The Smart Motorways monitor traffic levels and incidences through roadside sensors including cameras to then actively manage any traffic hiccoughs through changing speed limits, activating warning signs and closing lanes or opening the hard shoulder.

Different vehicle-level applications can be observed as examples of TCPS. One example is dynamic wireless power transfer for electric vehicles, where vehicle power transfer is activated when power transfer coils can sense electric vehicles on top of them. However, the most promising of all paradigm shifts in TCPS this century that we will see is the development and deployment of driverless cars. Every aspect of driverless cars from vehicular health checks, route planning while considering individual preferences and on-route traffic conditions during the prejourney phase to obstacle detection, collision avoidance, trajectory planning and navigation together with dynamic route planning during the journey phase is only possible with the tight coupling of cyberspace solutions, such as intelligent algorithms, effective data analysis, V2X communication, with physical elements, such as the electronic control unit, sensors, actuators, roadside equipment such as traffic lights and most importantly humans inside and outside the car.

All advancements in TCPS are only possible with advancement in infrastructure, and inductive charging for electric cars is one such example among many. Transport for London has introduced wireless charging for buses while they wait at stops — to cite an example among many such initiatives.

2.4 Marine Transportation Cyber-Physical System

Maritime transport is one of the oldest forms of transportation that moved people and goods between cities, countries and across continents and determined the economic success of empires. It still remains a major form of transportation for transporting heavy goods between countries. Maritime transportation means are also important for the strategic military defence infrastructure of a country, and this includes both over- and underwater vehicles. However, water vehicles face some of the most challenging environments to correctly position, detect obstacles, avoid collisions and navigate. CPS technological advancement particularly in the field of accuracy of sensor data acquisition, control and communication has advanced this mode of transport immensely. It is hence no surprise to see that underwater autonomous vehicles have been in existence for some time now, and ships are increasingly being viewed as floating computers on sea.

Similar to aviation, rail and road TCPS, marine TCPS can be described with its own set of sensors, controllers and actuators. Modern ships are fitted with low-cost, reliable smart sensors that allow monitoring of surrounding conditions and systems performance. Ship machinery systems are increasingly being controlled by software. Ship control systems enable integration of both electrical and mechanical actuators, and using these actuators maintain safe and efficient routes.

2.4.1 Examples of Marine Transportation Cyber-Physical System

Various technologies are connecting the water transport sector including Wi-Fi, the cellular network, very high frequency data exchange system and, most importantly, satellite communication. The deployment of very small aperture terminals equipment has dramatically increased, and as seen from Fig. 1.6, the bandwidth utilisation capacity will touch 200 Gbps by 2025. This will make possible a dramatic increase in

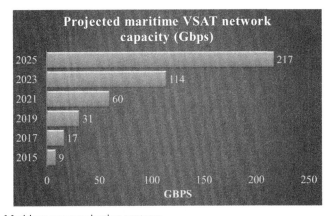

Figure 1.6 Maritime communication systems.
Adapted from Dnvgl, Digitization of Shipping, [Online]. Available: https://to2025.dnvgl.com/shipping/digitalization/.

information communication, thus improving the performance of fleet utilisation, routing, fuel consumption, assets management and to a huge extent automation of many elements of shipping [18].

Some of the areas in which CPSs will be deployed within the marine sector are listed in the following:

1. Dynamic positioning systems that use sensors to accurately position the vessels, as well as detect and position obstacles and hazards in the water, thus calculating a safe trajectory and navigating on it.
2. Vessel management includes monitoring and managing all components of the vessel including position, speed, sensing adverse weather conditions and preparing various aspects of the vessel to face such conditions, monitoring oil stocks and tuning components for optimised fuel utilisation.
3. Remote monitoring and control of propulsion and navigational systems are particularly applicable for underwater unmanned vehicles. It is particularly challenging as GPS signals are low and even nonexistent in some locations. Moreover, communication to such vessels is also unreliable. Using technologies, such as simultaneous localisation and mapping, inertial sensors and beacons support localisation and navigation in challenging environments.
4. Some other areas are fleet management from onshore control centres, automated systems for cargo handling in ports and optimised energy management, taking into account voyage plans, power generation and propulsion systems. Sensors and control systems are also used for noise and vibration reduction through automated detection and tuning.

3. Transportation Cyber-Physical System for the future of mobility: Environmental and societal benefits

Transport is at the heart of all societal and environmental challenges faced by the 21st century world. Transport has the ability to act both as an enabler to tackle such challenges as mobility of the ageing population and disaster management whilst facilitating globalisation and development and as a contributor to such challenges as pollution, climate change, etc. These are but only some examples in which TCPS is envisioned to impact both society and the surrounding environment. Social benefits and environmental befits go hand in hand.

3.1 Environmental benefits of Transportation Cyber-Physical System

The transport sector is a major consumer of fossil fuels and hence a leading contributor to global greenhouse gas emissions, with predictions showing that this sector will contribute to 30%−50% of all emissions by the year 2050. It is also worth noting that road transport is among the highest contributors within transport with the aviation sector following close behind [19]. Minimising the use of fossil fuels and increasing the use of renewable energy in all transport sectors is one way to tackle greenhouse gas emissions, and hence there has been an accelerated move from all sectors including the government to increase the use of alternative energy sources such as electricity, hydrogen and fuel cells.

The European Environmental Agency aims at reducing by 50% the number of vehicles running in conventional fuels such as diesel and petrol by 2030 and eliminating such vehicles by 2050 [20]. This opens up enormous opportunities for TCPS to influence the future of mobility and foster huge environmental benefits, thus effectively lowering overall greenhouse gas emissions. To achieve the full potential of electric vehicles, TCPS solutions are required in all aspects, such as in electric vehicle infrastructure development which includes development of the smart grid and optimised placement of charging points, together with software, hardware and communication interoperability issues between the charging infrastructure and the vehicle; invehicular developments such as automatic and effective monitoring of battery power and development of services, such as scheduling of electric vehicle charging solutions together with automatic route changes depending on charging point availability and current remaining charge on battery, informed by the traffic conditions on the route ahead.

Similarly, alternative fuel sources, such as biofuels, hydrogen cells, natural gases, etc., are being actively looked into in the aviation sector. These solutions bring with them new challenges, such as design, safety and performance challenges, and TCPS is well placed to provide effective solutions to these challenges, thus making the shift to alternative, sustainable fuel sources more feasible.

The average number of hours spent by an American in congestion was 42 h a year (i.e., one full working week) in 2016, and the number of hours is much higher in cities such as New York [21]. Congestion and issues related to congestion, such as pollution, higher energy consumption, alleviated frustration and road rage, are putting a huge burden on our cities and countries, and if left unattended, it shall continue to rise. Introduction of TCPS for detecting and managing congestion is expected to bring immense socioeconomic benefits. Sensors such as cameras and loop inductors detect congestion, and actions are enforced to mitigate congestion through ways such as use of variable speed limits or vehicle rerouting. Future TCPS solutions are looking at dynamic control of traffic signals for more efficient flow of traffic that avoids frequent stop-and-go and controls congestion using vehicle-to-infrastructure communication. The advantage of TCPS as opposed to traditional techniques, such as charging for congestion zones, comes from the fact that connected systems deployed over a large area such as a city or state can globally optimise the traffic flow.

3.2 Societal benefits of Transportation Cyber-Physical System

TCPS is expected to bring forth enormous social benefits facilitating seamless travel, improved accessibility and enhanced safety during transit. Many of the TCPS solutions benefitting society by facilitating seamless travel, improved accessibility and enhanced safety are powered by the easy accessibility of data sources (such as data provided by public transport providers and data passively collected by mobile phone applications such as Google Maps); availability of faster, reliable and higher capacity communication networks; ubiquitous use of mobile phones and easy availability of processing power such as in the cloud. One such example is the proliferation of ridesharing using smartphone applications which integrate databases from multiple sources at the back-end to power the front-end, providing commuters with efficient travel solutions. Based on the rider input, the system decides which nearest available vehicle can serve the rider, and the system actuates the driver. Such applications are benefitted by dynamically updated data sets, made possible through real-time data sensing done by sensors on the phone, location sensors on available vehicles, etc.

The automatic braking system or automatic emergency braking (AEB) system provided by a number of car manufacturers [22] today is an apt example of a TCPS benefitting society directly. AEB system uses a combination of sensors such as GPS, camera, radar and Lidar to detect an imminent crash and either warns the driver to take action or takes over control of the car braking or steering system or both to avoid the crash. Similar such examples are automatic cruise control and automatic parking systems, with more such features being added as vehicles go up in the levels of automation [23] towards a fully automated vehicle. With each level, as the vehicle becomes more aware of the surroundings, reducing the possibilities of human error, the number of accidents and cost associated with accidents are predicted to decrease benefitting the society at large.

The advent of fully autonomous cars is envisioned to redefine mobility and bring forth immense societal and environmental benefits. Advances in the medical field have made it possible for people to live longer. Autonomous vehicles will benefit the growing elderly population by allowing them to continue enjoying life within the larger society by transporting them from their door steps to destinations without the need of driving.

4. Challenges for Transportation Cyber-Physical System adoption and their mapping to book chapters

CPSs are developing very fast, fuelled by the availability of low-cost, low-power, high-quality sensors; abundant communication bandwidth and speed and increasing efficient computing devices. However, this is a field that integrates expertise from a number of fields, such as control systems, communication networks, architecture, modelling and simulation, verification and validation, as well as human factors. This book aims to address the urgent need to facilitate the education and training of future researchers, developers and practitioners in the multidisciplinary field of TCPS with its focus on enhancing safety, security and efficiency while reducing environmental stress and meeting societal demands across the continually growing air, land and water transport of both humans and goods. The following subsections introduce the research and developmental challenges within various aspects of TCPS and maps to the corresponding chapter that addresses some of these challenges.

4.1 Chapter II: Architectures of Cyber-Physical Transportation Systems

Given the safety critical nature of all transport modes, the architectural design of a TCPS is essential for the performance of any given application. A TCPS is a complex integration of heterogeneous elements, which includes but not limited to heterogeneous communication technologies, data or information heterogeneity, multiple terminal devices from different vendors with different processing power, operating systems, security requirements, the communication medium and the presence of humans in the loop. With such diverse heterogeneity, the primary challenge is to design TCPS architectures which are adaptable, scalable and secure, particularly as existing object-oriented architectures and service-oriented architectures are designed based on abstractions that cater mostly to software systems rather than physical systems and even lesser so for tightly coupled software and physical systems [24]. With such cross-domain nondeterministic CPS, the challenges are also to evaluate the architecture and develop test beds allowing for testing of architectural assurance [25]. Including the emerging components of transportation technology, which are mobile (meaning users can leverage the capability of the component from where they are) and rapidly evolving, into architectural models is a challenge. A well thought-out unified architecture is fundamental to the entire life cycle of a TCPS, beginning from TCPS design, verification, security assurance leading on to development, deployment, maintenance and ultimate retirement.

This chapter will introduce the audience to some of the popular architectures for CPS including the quality attributes enhanced and degraded by each architecture and their analysis techniques. This chapter will also discuss about the reference architecture used for TCPS and emerging architectures (i.e., Internet of Things, cloud architecture, smart city architecture) related to TCPS to make the transportation engineer aware of a number of issues to consider when developing a smart transportation system.

4.2 Chapter III: Collaborative modelling and co-simulation for Transportation Cyber-Physical Systems

Models are fundamental to the understanding and development of TCPS. Simulations of these models allow users and developers to study systems behaviour throughout its entire life cycle. Cross-domain (different software domains and different communication mediums) interaction in a multidisciplinary environment makes modelling and simulation challenging. Also, we often need to develop test cases to evaluate models and their interaction with the surrounding environment without fully understanding the environment the TCPS will function in. Once a reliable model for TCPS is identified, it is challenging to find an appropriate simulation methodology to validate the model [26]. Modelling and simulations techniques as well as development platforms vary. In this chapter, the need for multidisciplinary model-based systems engineering approaches in the transport sector is first established. Later some emerging techniques enabling the linking of monodisciplinary, semantically heterogeneous models are identified.

Transportation systems are deemed one of the most safety critical systems because any failure would result in loss of life. Hence, verification and validation of the models and developed TCPS systems are extremely essential. This chapter also includes approaches to co-modelling and co-simulation illustrated through an example on rail interlocking system.

4.3 Chapter IV: Real-time control systems

Safety-critical real-time nature is itself a huge challenge particularly as so many cross-domain components interact with each other. Rigorous testing is required, but many of the scenarios these systems will function in are unknown and in most cases nondeterministic. Another challenge is to develop strict fault tolerant systems, as safety critical systems have a margin for faults. These faults can be software, hardware, communication or human faults.

TCPS control systems such as the vehicle control system rely on components from a myriad of manufacturers, multiple sensors and actuators of various specifications, wireless communication as well as multicore processors. Coordination of these components to act as a unified system in real time is a challenge, and illustrating and addressing these challenges, with the case study for autonomous vehicles, form the content of this chapter.

4.4 Chapter V: Transportation Cyber-Physical System security and privacy

The high degree of connectivity brings with it severe security risks with many possible points of attack. One significant challenge is the unknown nature of such attacks or the absence of cyber-attack profiling. Use of any standard off-the-shelf components to save developing cost and time will bring with it severe security risk. Many of the existing security solutions ignore the 'physical' aspect of the system, and this includes humans within the TCPS.

In Chapter 5, we will address privacy and security issues in TCPS, especially considering the fact that the numerous embedded connected sensors are collecting data continuously. Topics to be covered include intrusion detection in TCPS, network security for TCPS, human factors and human in the loop and its implication towards privacy and security.

4.5 Chapter VI: Infrastructure for Transportation Cyber-Physical Systems

In TCPS, data collected from different transportation modes and data collection devices can be explained using the 'five Vs of big data': (1) volume, (2) variety, (3) velocity, (4) veracity and (5) value. Using traditional database management systems and conventional data processing and delivery systems, the enormous amount of heterogeneous data cannot be processed in real time. To address this challenge, this chapter includes discussion about the architectural design for the modern data infrastructures to support open-source hardware and software technologies, data management systems and data delivery systems. It will also include a discussion of infrastructure as code, which treats infrastructure components as a software system to allow users faster development, modifications and removal/replacement of infrastructure through code.

4.6 Chapter VII: Data management issues in Cyber-Physical Systems

CPS requires a variety of data management solutions depending on the onboard computing power constraints. This chapter will examine the challenges induced by the critical dependency of CPS on data and indicate data management approaches to overcoming these challenges. For TCPS, managing data from numerous devices calls for a special database management system which (1) features flexible and evolving data models, (2) stores high amount of data from multiple static/mobile data sources, (3) offers high availability and elastic scaling of database, (4) provides real-time and near real-time query response times and (5) supports a number of users simultaneously. Based on these requirements, an example NoSQL system (Elasticsearch) for unstructured data processing, analytics and management is described. Finally, this chapter concludes by indicating emerging trends and data-related research issues in CPS.

4.7 Chapter VIII: Human factors in Transportation Cyber-Physical System

Humans show nondeterministic behaviour depending on the situation. Human behaviour changes based on fatigue, complacency and stress level; hence while designing TCPS, one of the major challenges is the inclusion of such human factors, which will have significant impact on the system output. Particular challenges in integrating humans with machines are usability, safety and acceptability.

This chapter will discuss the human factors in TCPS using a smartphone-based system called SmartATRS. SmartATRS is considered as a TCPS that was used to conduct usability evaluations that assessed the suitability of various interaction methods for the user community of people with reduced physical ability. Based on SmartATRS, this chapter includes discussion about human factors and humans in loop consideration during TCPS modelling, systems architecture design and risk analysis in order to measure the safety implications.

4.8 Chapter IX: Transportation Cyber-Physical System as a specialised education stream

TCPS brings together expertise in a number of disparate disciplines, such as transportation engineering, control systems, communication networks, real-time systems, embedded systems, cybersecurity and mechanical engineering, to name a few. There is a serious need for skilled individuals at every level of the TCPS life cycle from modelling and simulation to developing, maintaining and operating such systems.

The challenge is to develop curriculums to fill this skills gap by training individuals in each niche discipline while being able to appreciate and understand all other disciplines interacting within the wider TCPS in question. Chowdhury and Dey reported that current engineering graduate and undergraduate programs are inadequate for preparing future transportation professionals who can develop smart and connected transportation systems [27]. They concluded that multidisciplinary education is essential, beyond the traditional engineering education boundary, to prepare future transportation professionals in TCPS.

Successful TCPS design and operation requires a multidisciplinary skill set. This chapter will look at curriculum designs for specialised TCPS degrees together with opportunities for greater exploitation of mutually exclusive expertise especially for masters' level qualification. Beyond specialised degrees for masters' level qualification, this chapter will identify strategies to train transportation professionals in a synergistic and phased TCPS curriculum that will allow them build their professional capacity in this area.

4.9 Chapter X: Research challenges and transatlantic collaboration on Transportation Cyber-Physical System

CPS has been identified as a research and innovation priority both in Europe and in the United States of America. Both regions have notable technological advancements in this field, but without formal collaborations, advancements are taking place in parallel and in many cases in duplication, resulting in wastage of time and money, while achieving lesser than what could be possible if researcher across the atlantic joint forces.

This chapter will draw on outputs from a recently completed European project of Trans-Atlantic Modelling and Simulation for CPS towards the various means for facilitation of collaborative research advancement [3]. This chapter will also discuss key research challenges (e.g., security, CPS testing and verification, human–TCPS interactions, etc.) for TCPS.

4.10 Chapter XI: Future of Transportation Cyber-Physical System – smart cities/regions

In order to improve the service efficiency and quality of life, 'smart city' includes digitally connected city infrastructure and service systems (e.g., mobility systems, healthcare, public safety) which are deployed with various communication technologies and real-time data collection infrastructure and data analytics. Smart city includes TCPS, and this concluding chapter will discuss how TCPS must be developed in a way so that it can easily be integrated with other smart city components, such as energy CPS, civil infrastructure CPS, home/business CPS and healthcare CPS. This chapter will also layout the future of TCPS, including its potential needs and deployment strategies in developed and developing countries. Examples of smart city deployments will be presented in this chapter along with the future research directions in this area.

Exercises

1. What are the primary differences between the Cyber-Physical Systems definitions perceived in the United States and Europe?
2. How TCPS will benefit society by contributing to meeting future mobility challenges?
3. What are the challenges to TCPS adoption?
4. What are the primary differences between aviation, rail, road and marine TCPS?
5. Based on Fig. 1.1, draw the components of marine TCPS.
6. Give an example of road TCPS related to traffic incident management.
7. Identify at least five research challenges within the area of cybersecurity of TCPS.
8. What are the different capacities humans can be involved in a TCPS? What challenges do you see in each capacity?

References

[1] Acatech, Cyber-physical Systems. Driving Force for Innovation in Mobility, Health, Energy and Production, Springer Berlin Heidelberg, 2011.
[2] E.A. Lee, Computing Foundations and Practice for Cyber-physical Systems: A Preliminary Report, 2017.
[3] M. Henshaw, Trans-Atlantic Modelling and Simulation for Cyber-physical Systems. Deliverable D1.1: Definitional Framework, 2015.
[4] E.A. Lee, The past, present and future of cyber-physical systems: a focus on models, Sensors 15 (3) (2015) 4837–4869.
[5] IATA Press Release, India Sees Highest Domestic Market Growth in 2015, July 5, 2016 [Online]. Available: http://www.iata.org/pressroom/pr/Pages/2016-07-05-01.aspx. (Accessed on 14/04/2018).
[6] K. Sampigethaya, R. Poovendran, "Aviation cyber–physical systems: foundations for future aircraft and air transport, Proceedings of the IEEE 101 (8) (2013) 1834–1855.
[7] SESAR Joint Undertaking, SESAR Solutions Catalogue, 2017.
[8] M. Strohmeier, V. Lenders, I. Martinovic, On the security of the automatic dependent surveillance-broadcast protocol, IEEE Communications Surveys and Tutorials 17 (2) (2015) 1066–1087.
[9] H. Balakrishnan, CPS challenges in NextGen aviation, in: 2014 National Workshop on Transportation Cyber-physical System, 2014. Washington.
[10] SIEMENS, European Train Control System, [Online]. Available: http://www.mobility.siemens.com/mobility/global/en/interurban-mobility/rail-solutions/rail-automation/train-control-system/european-train-protection-system/Pages/european-train-control-system.aspx. (Accessed on 14/04/2018).
[11] GPS, "Rail," NOAA, 2015. [Online]. Available: http://www.gps.gov/applications/rail/.
[12] J.V. Hodge, S. O'Keefe, M. Weeks, A. Moulds, Wireless sensor networks for condition monitoring in the railway industry: a survey, IEEE Transaction of Intelligent Transportation Systems 16 (3) (2014) 1088–1106.
[13] Y. Li, Gould, Peter, Embedding Wireless Sensors in Railway Sleepers, 2014 [Online]. Available, http://www.macltd.com/files/downloads/MAC%20Ltd%20-%20Embedding%20Wireless%20Sensors%20in%20Railway%20Sleepers.pdf. (Accessed on 14/04/2018).

[14] K. Ishida, H. Kitabayashi, M. Nagasu, New train control and information services utilizing broadband networks, Hitachi Review 53 (1) (2004) 21.

[15] EEA, Most Carmakers Must Further Improve Carbon Efficiency by 2015, 2011 [Online]. Available, https://www.eea.europa.eu/highlights/most-carmakers-must-further-improve/. (Accessed on 14/04/2018).

[16] Y. Wang, G. Tan, Y. Wang, Y. Yi, Perceptual control architecture for cyber–physical systems in traffic incident management, Journal of Systems Architecture 58 (10) (2012) 398–411.

[17] Catapult Transport System, Mobility as a Service Exploring the Opportunity for Mobility as a Serice in the UK, July 2016 [Online]. Available, https://ts.catapult.org.uk/wp-content/uploads/2016/07/Mobility-as-a-Service_Exploring-the-Opportunity-for-MaaS-in-the-UK-Web.pdf. (Accessed on 14/04/2018).

[18] Dnvgl, Digitization of Shipping, [Online]. Available: https://to2025.dnvgl.com/shipping/digitalization/. (Accessed on 14/04/2018).

[19] J. Fuglestvedt, T. Berntsen, G. Myhre, K. Rypdal, R.B. Skeie, Climate forcing from the transport sectors, Proceedings of the National Academy of Sciences 105 (2) (2008).

[20] E. E. Agency, Electric Vehicles in Europe, European Union, 2016.

[21] INRIX, INRIX 2016 Traffic Scorecard, INRIX, [Online]. Available: http://inrix.com/resources/inrix-2016-traffic-scorecard-us/. (Accessed on 14/04/2018).

[22] B. Chappell, Automatic Braking Systems to Become Standard on Most U.S. Vehicles, 2016 [Online]. Available, http://www.npr.org/sections/thetwo-way/2016/03/17/470809148/automatic-braking-systems-to-become-standard-on-most-u-s-vehicles. (Accessed on 14/04/2018).

[23] S. International, Automated Driving Levels of Driving Automation are Defined in New sae International Standard j3016, [Online]. Available: http://www.sae.org/misc/pdfs/automated_driving.pdf. (Accessed on 14/04/2018).

[24] E.A. Lee, Cyber-physical systems – are computing foundations adequate?, in: NSF Workshop on Cyber-physical Systems: Research Motivation, Techniques and Roadmap, vol. 2, 2006, pp. 1–9.

[25] S. Hafner-Zimmermann, M.J.D.C. Henshaw, The Future of Trans-Atlantic Collaboration in Modelling and Simulation of Cyber-physical Systems, 2017 [Online]. Available, http://www.tams4cps.eu/wp-content/uploads/2017/02/TAMS4CPS-SRAC-publication_2017.pdf. (Accessed on 14/04/2018).

[26] R. Cartwright, A. Cheng, P. Hudak, M. O'Malley, W. Taha, Cyber-physical Challenges in Transportation System Design, [Online].

[27] M. Chowdhury, K. Dey, Intelligent transportation systems-a frontier for breaking boundaries of traditional academic engineering disciplines, IEEE Intelligent Transportation Systems Magazine 8 (1) (2016) 4–8.

Architectures of Transportation Cyber-Physical Systems

2

John D. McGregor [1], Roselane S. Silva [2], Eduardo S. Almeida [2]
[1]School of Computing, Clemson University, Clemson,
SC, United States; [2]Department of Computer Science, Federal University of Bahia,
Salvador, Brazil

1. Introduction

Transportation systems are usually of sufficient uniqueness and complexity that they are designed specifically for each use. Transportation engineers interact with specialists in electronics, physics and other domains to design and analyse these systems, which increasingly include computational aspects. One important aspect of design is the architecture, the basic structure of the system. The transportation engineer must be able to participate in the design and evaluation of systems that control traffic flow, operate various means of transport and manage the system's interactions with humans. In this chapter we cover some widely used architectures and some of the information used to evaluate them for appropriateness.

Transportation systems are increasingly linked to other systems and to the physical world in which the system is deployed. These systems use sensors to understand the properties of objects and systems with which they interact. Recently, the term 'cyber-physical' has emerged to describe systems that are a blend of physical sensing and computation and that are networked with other similar systems. The collection of these systems is widely touted as the 'Internet of Things (IoT)'. The National Science Foundation of the United States uses the following definition: cyber-physical systems (CPSs) are engineered systems that are built from, and depend upon, the seamless integration of computational algorithms and physical components [1]. The seamless integration is accomplished through carefully structured and rigorously analysed system architecture. The integration makes certain system design problems explicit earlier than in traditional system development.

Architecturally these systems tend to involve the aforementioned sensors, controllers and actuators and some networked infrastructure that often involves the Internet and a cloud infrastructure. This has led to products such as connected vehicles that collect data at the axle level, analyse that data both locally and in the cloud and store the data for further later analysis. The communication of data and commands over various channels has increased the importance of quality attribute analyses, in particular timing and security analyses. This style of architecture has also required the use of architecture patterns that can enhance security and tolerate the loss of Internet connectivity. The ARINC 653 annex to the Architecture Analysis and Design Language

Transportation Cyber-Physical Systems. https://doi.org/10.1016/B978-0-12-814295-0.00002-2
Copyright © 2018 Elsevier Inc. All rights reserved.

(AADL) core language defined a 'partition' pattern which provides isolation and protection in the face of simple failures. Tolerating communication faults requires local storage within the context of the system, schemes for selectively deleting data to prevent overflowing the local storage and approaches for graceful degradation if the disconnect persists.

Popular buzz words such as 'cyber-physical' are often used to justify system and process design decisions whether it is appropriate or not. A CPS architecture is best used when the system controls some physical process where the system must sense the current state of the system in order to command the future behaviour of the system. Systems that simply collect data and store it for later analysis are not cyber-physical, and this chapter does not address their design.

Transportation systems are taking advantage of cyber-physical architectures to define systems that understand more about the environment in which they are operating and to ensure that the computed cyber state of the system stays in synch with the physically controlled side of the system. In this chapter we review some of the architectures of CPSs and explain some of the commonly used architecture analysis techniques. We will give transportation professionals questions to ask when evaluating CPSs for acquisition.

Combining analog and digital representations in one system requires that we understand the interaction between exact versus approximate and discrete versus continuous attributes. The software engineers must be aware of operating in the physical world where objects have physical properties such as momentum compared to the cyber world where objects can be stopped instantaneously. The architecture should describe the types of entities with which we are dealing and define associations between the domains.

Modern architecture practices have evolved to support the representation of architectures in forms that enable reasoning about the properties a design enhances and those properties that it degrades. We will use the AADL and the tools in its infrastructure to represent popular architectures and to illustrate how they can be analysed and tuned to meet the needs of specific applications.

1.1 Networked

CPSs are, by definition, networked together. The usual system has several types of sensors whose signals are propagated using a number of protocols. Network outages and congestion have to be anticipated, and systems must be designed to be robust in the presence of late-arriving data or no data at all. Network links create attack surfaces that must be protected, or at least monitored, for intrusions. This can lead to increasing latencies in processing and can lead to inappropriate interleaving of sensor readings through over- or undersampling. The system architecture must ensure that these asynchronous signals are queued, sequenced and handled correctly.

1.2 Open

The term 'open' refers to how easily new capabilities can be added to a system. Mechanisms such as plug and play allow new capabilities to be added to a system without recompiling. The Integrated Development Environment (IDE) for AADL is based on the Eclipse framework. In that framework, implementations of new components are placed in a particular directory in the product installation. The next time the product is started, the new capability is included in the running product.

Open systems are, by definition, flexible and extensible. This reduces development and maintenance costs and often reduces the time to market. CPSs often evolve over time to allow new capabilities to be implemented and fielded rapidly. This has a multiplying effect, as newly available capabilities are bundled to implement even more sophisticated features. Transportation engineers work with the architects to forecast future feature additions and conditions, such as continuous availability, under which those features can be added to the system.

1.3 Uncertainty

The dividing line between the cyber and physical portions of a system is also the dividing line between exactness and approximation. The sensing of the physical world and its translation into digital values is not exact. Sensors fail in random ways and readings are taken at times which may not accurately reflect the true state of the environment. Successful systems will have mechanisms through which they can control uncertainty.

Another source of uncertainty is the network of organisations that participate in the development of very large CPSs, particularly government-owned systems. In such environments, the government (the customer) provides a high-level set of requirements that are the basis for new, more specific requirements 'derived' from the original set. These are subdivided by capability and provided to subcontractors who will, in turn, derive requirements, at a level of more detail and specificity. It should be possible to follow (trace) an idea from the most abstract level, original set, to the most specific. The uncertainty comes when it is unclear that a new requirement, created by making an existing requirement more concrete, maintains the intent of the higher-level requirement as it adds detail.

Deviation in its expected behaviour is another source of uncertainty. These deviations come from the mistakes of humans during design and operation. For example, during modelling, a connection between two components is misclassified and the actual latency in the physical system does not meet the expectation. Uncertainty also arises from the unanticipated interactions among components as they are integrated. The particular output from one component, which fits within the input range of the second component, produces an unanticipated behaviour in component two because it is in a portion of the second component's input that has not been adequately tested.

The rest of this chapter is structured as follows: the next section provides background necessary to understand the concepts discussed in this chapter; we then describe several widely used CPS architectures; this is followed by a discussion of newly emerging architectures; finally, we summarise the current status and forecast upcoming trends.

2. Background

In this section we present information necessary to understand the rest of the chapter. We first introduce an architecture description language, AADL, intended for embedded, real-time systems. Next, a way of quantifying software quality, in the form of quality attributes, is discussed. Finally, system issues such as differences between analog and digital representations and frameworks are examined.

2.1 Architecture Analysis and Design Language

The AADL is an architecture description language, developed in 2004 by the Society of Automotive Engineers, which contributes to the verification and validation of CPSs [2]. AADL is strongly typed and it can be extended through the use of annex languages. Some examples are an error model annex, which specifies propagation errors, a behaviour annex, which allows us to add behaviour to the architecture using the concept of state machines, and others such as security and safety.

AADL models both software and hardware. Software is represented by process, thread and subprogram constructs while hardware components are represented by device, processor, bus and memory constructs. The language has an integration component typed as 'system' that ties software and hardware together. An example system, a very simple cruise control, represented in AADL can be seen in Fig. 2.1.

In Fig. 2.1, we have a description of a cruise control system that uses data from different sensors as the basis to accelerate/decelerate decisions.

The system has the following *subcomponents*: three *devices* components named radar, gps and camera and a *process* named controller. The *connections* section of the system defines how the subcomponents connect each other. In this example, the data from radar sensor are connected to the input of the controller.

```
system cruise_control
        features
            sensed_speed:        in data port data_types::speed;
            sensed_speed_limit: in data port data_types::speed;

    end cruise_control;


system implementation cruise_control.impl
        subcomponents
            radar:      device radar.impl;
            gps:        device gps.impl;
            camera:     device camera.impl;
            controller: process controller.impl;

        connections
            radar_con:  port radar.data_out->controller.data_in;

    end cruise_control.impl;
```

Figure 2.1 AADL snippet.

Moreover, as we can see in the snippet, AADL components have two definitions. The first definition is a specification where features are added to the component, and each feature is an input or output *port*. These ports can be *event*, *data* or *event/data* ports, each of which requires a data type. The second definition is an implementation of that component specification. Implementations are defined below the respective component specification and are represented by the keyword *implementation*. The main idea of having two separated definitions is that a specification component can have more than one different implementation.

In addition to the core language, AADL has the concept of an annex, a self-contained language that addresses a specific type of behaviour. The behaviour annex goes beyond the structure to define the behaviour of a component under normal conditions. A state machine notation is used to describe the flow of logic in response to incoming stimuli.

The error annex defines a domain-specific language whose concepts allow the modeller to describe the behaviour of a system that has generated an error. A state machine is used to describe the behaviour. Errors that are not handled in the component in which they arose are propagated through designated ports to other components that can handle the error.

2.2 Quality attributes

Transportation systems are partially defined by functional requirements—what the system must do—and by nonfunctional requirements—attributes of the system. These attributes describe the qualities of the system such as reliability, availability and many others. The ISO 9126 standard, which has been replaced by ISO/IEC 25010 [3], provides a categorisation of these attributes. The point of this standard is to take terms that casual observers might use to describe their experience with a product and give a definition that can be objectively quantified and used in design decision-making.

The quality attributes support trade studies in which the different attribute values resulting from different design decisions are compared allowing the architect to choose the design action that will be best, given the objectives of the architecture. For example, assume Design A will result in a reliability of 0.97 and a latency for an important action of 12 s while Design B will result in a reliability of 0.99 and a latency of 20 s for that same action. The architect must decide if the increase in reliability is worth the increase in latency. This decision can be made with greater confidence given these specific values than if the architect knows that increasing reliability slowdowns the system. The transportation engineer provides input about priorities so that the architect can produce an acceptable design.

ISO 25010 defines two quality models: a 'quality in use' model and a 'product quality' model. Each model defines several characteristics and specialisations of those characteristics. We will focus on the product quality model. This model is used during all product evaluation activities including architecture evaluation. The standard identifies eight characteristics of product quality and decomposes each into more specific characteristics, as shown in Fig. 2.2. Reliability is defined as 'degree to which a system, product or component performs specified functions under

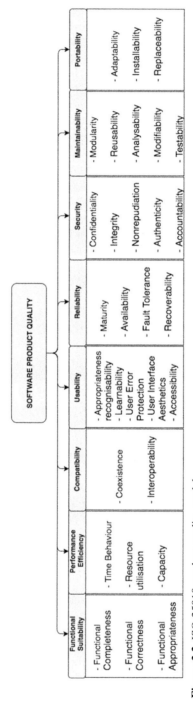

Figure 2.2 ISO 25010 product quality model.

specified conditions for a specified period of time'. For a transportation system, tolerance of defects would be important. ISO 25010 defines fault tolerance as 'degree to which a system, product or component operates as intended despite the presence of hardware or software faults'. Using these standardised terms removes ambiguity in communication.

The transportation engineer participates in the design and evaluation of systems that must exhibit each of these qualities to varying degrees. Part of the early design process is to establish priorities among the eight characteristics, and limitations on these values are captured as nonfunctional requirements. Once that is done, each of the characteristics is evaluated and quantified. Changes are made to the design to enhance those attributes that need improvement. For example, the first draft of a design may not be sufficiently fault tolerant. One way to improve that is to use error modelling to design flows through the system for specific types of errors that could occur. Sufficient error flows could be defined to bring the reliability of the design to the desired level. We discuss more on this in the section on error modelling.

2.3 Analog/digital models

Transportation engineers do not have to understand all of the details of analog to digital (and digital to analog) conversion, but since this is a fundamental factor in CPSs you should at least understand some of the tradeoffs. The dividing line between the part of the system that is analog and that which is digital shifts depending upon the system design, where the A/D conversion is happening more closely to the actual physical process in many sensors. Essentially a sensor changes one form of energy such as blowing wind to another—electrical. For actuators the process is reversed with digital signals being converted into electric current that causes a motor or some other device to perform work. This typically requires more power to process the sensed data. When a very small device is required such as in an automotive component, the analog signal may be communicated back outside the component to a place where there is sufficient power for A/D conversion and data processing.

Both representations have drawbacks and benefits. The analog signal is continuous while the digital is discrete. Each has its own type of uncertainty. Since the analog is continually changing, time of sampling influences the value. The digital signal is more stable, but the representation makes some values impossible to represent exactly. A hardware engineer can assist the system engineer in determining the appropriate hardware building blocks.

2.4 Frameworks

The architect of a CPS has a particular concept in mind when they begin the design of a new system. There are several conceptual frameworks for CPSs that have been created to provide the supporting infrastructure for these concepts. The framework from the National Institute for Standards and Technologies (NIST) is shown in Fig. 2.3. This framework makes obvious the demarcation between the cyber and the physical portions of a device which is embedded in a system. The diagram also shows the system

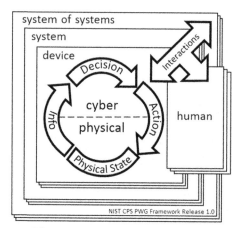

Figure 2.3 NIST conceptual framework.
Ref. [4]. Release 1.0 Reprinted courtesy of the National Institute of Standards and Technology,
U.S. Department of Commerce. Not copyrightable in the United States.

embedded in a system of systems (SoS). SoS is a system that is composed of several
systems, most of which are independently owned, managed and operated. A smart device (CPS) such as a smart thermostat interacts with heating/cooling systems, lighting
systems and security systems. Due to separate ownership, changes may be made to the
lighting system, for example, without the thermostat being aware. Each of the systems
needs to be robust in the context of changes to the other systems.

Most intelligent transportation systems are systems of systems. This architecture requires much more interaction among the owners of the systems and a more collaborative style of architecture design. Both formal standards, such as ISO 13849 standard
for safety in robotics, and ad hoc standards, such as the NIST Framework, have not
only been developed but also continue to evolve at a very rapid pace, at least relative
to the usual pace of standard development.

The NIST Framework provides a reference architecture in which the basic concepts
are decomposed into a matrix of concepts, shown in Fig. 2.4. The three facets of
development—conceptualisation, realisation and assurance—follow closely an
emerging style of development described in [4].

The *aspects* cover concerns that carry across all phases of development. Some
of the aspects correspond to quality attributes discussed in the section on quality
attributes. This framework will provide a basis for some of the rest of this chapter.

3.   Current canonical cyber-physical system architectures

In this section we survey a couple of CPS architectures and describe some criteria for
evaluating architectures.

The canonical feedback/control loop is an architecture that is used in many CPSs.
The main objective of such an architecture is to control some physical process.

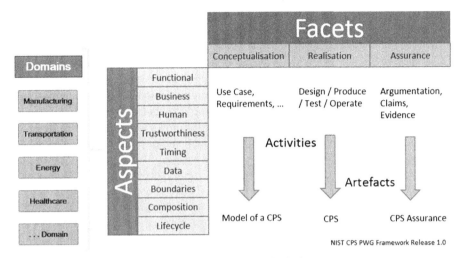

Figure 2.4 Decomposition of concepts. *CPSs*, cyber-physical systems.
Ref. [4]. Reprinted courtesy of the National Institute of Standards and Technology, U.S.
Department of Commerce. Not copyrightable in the United States.

Typically the controlled process is at least partially a physical system such as a jet
engine, automated vehicle or chemical reaction. A commonly used example is controlling the temperature in a house. Fig. 2.5 shows the four major constituent pieces to the
architecture. Below we define the function of each piece of the basic architecture in the
context of the home heating system.

Controlled process — The controlled process is the heating and cooling functions
provided by the system. Its operation is physical and controlled by the amount of
energy/fuel that is being supplied to the heating or cooling unit. When turned on,
the system will blow air into the house. As the system operates, the air temperature

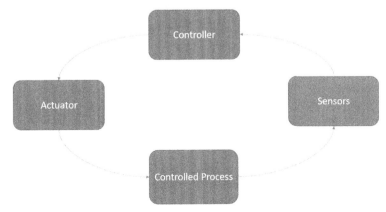

Figure 2.5 Control feedback loop.

will gradually change until it reaches the target temperature. Once the blower shuts off, the unit will continue to radiate hot or cold for some time. Without the unit operating, the temperature will move away from the target temperature toward the ambient temperature due to air circulation in the building. Eventually the deviation from target will be sufficiently great and the system will begin to blow again repeating the cycle.

Controller − The controller is usually a computational engine that takes inputs from sensors and computes the outputs that should be used to command the actuators. Traditionally, the controller for a home furnace simply turns on the current to heat an element or turns it off. When the controller is a computational engine, a more sophisticated controller can be designed that varies the amount of current to be fed to the furnace depending on the mode the system is in. It sends commands to actuators about how much fuel to feed.

Sensor − A sensor measures some characteristics within the system or its environment. For example, inside the house, a temperature sensor, essentially a thermometer, produces an electric current proportional to the temperature of the air. Often this is implemented by a metal spring that expands due to the heat. A digital sensor will convert the current into a discrete value. This value is fed to the controller.

Actuator/effector − The controlled process is modified by one or more actuators. For the house heating example, a rheostat increases/decreases the current flowing in the circuit or a servo motor opens/closes a valve to control the flow of fuel. There are delays (latencies) of varying lengths in opening and closing flows depending on how mechanical the device is.

There are many variations on this architecture. One of the major variations is whether the sensors are analog or digital or a combination. Each signal from an analog sensor runs through an analog to digital converter which sanitises the data, in addition to converting the continuous data signal to a discrete signal. Signals from digital sensors can be fed directly into the controller.

A major issue in these systems is the uncertainty associated with the physical elements of the system. The expansion of metal in a thermostat is not exact and even changes with the repeated expansion and contraction of use over time. Other physical changes also introduce uncertainty. Readings from these sensors must be represented by an interval data value instead of a point value. The interval is sufficiently wide for there to be a 95% probability that the actual answer is within the interval.

An important characteristic of these systems is its sensitivity. Sensitivity is how large a deviation from the target value is permitted before the controller activates an actuator. A larger deviation will take longer to get back on target while a smaller deviation will be quickly corrected but will result in a very choppy operation with system turning on then off again rapidly. The first approach will leave the temperature either above or below the target value longer than the second solution. The second will keep the temperature closer to the target temperature but will produce more wear on the switching circuitry.

One example of a CPS using the control feedback/loop architecture is a collaborating, adaptive cruise control system for a semiautonomous vehicle. We will use this as a continuing example throughout this chapter.

4. Types of architecture models

The architectures presented to transportation professionals are usually either reference architectures or product architectures. A reference architecture is a design for a family of systems. The design includes variation points, with design decisions left unresolved until later in the development process. When all of the reference architecture's variation points are resolved to specific information, the result is a product architecture. The product architecture is the plan for a single system with no design decisions remaining to be made.

The United States Department of Transportation (US DoT) has created reference architectures to capture the essential concepts and semantics of domains within their purview. The Connected Vehicle Reference Implementation Architecture (CVRIA) [5] was an initial effort to frame the domain of connected vehicles. This reference architecture is being used as the basis for some of the research on connected vehicles and the traffic control infrastructure. The more recent effort, Architecture Reference for Cooperative and Intelligent Transportation (ARC-IT) [6], integrates connected vehicle concepts with intelligent transportation systems concepts.

Fig. 2.6 illustrates a portion of the ARC-IT. As a system architecture, the driver is an entity in the system so that the inputs and effects on the driver can be modelled. Attributes of lines such as colour and types of shapes on the ends convey relationship information about how concepts are related. The concepts and relationships become the building blocks of stakeholder-level requirements. The CPS transportation engineer will participate in the conceptualisation and architecting of transportation systems. Using reference architectures such as ARC-IT can speed system development because you are using proven elements and should result in a system design that can be implemented using a high percentage of preexisting implemented parts.

AUTOSAR is a reference architecture for defining vehicles with varying performance characteristics [7]. The reference architecture supports two different platforms: one related to classic designs while the second is intended for autonomous vehicles. Both are built from a common foundation architecture. This modular approach makes the architecture easier to maintain. A number of 2017 automobiles on the market are based on AUTOSAR.

Reference architectures are useful in domains that are immature and changing rapidly. They are particularly successful when they are built under the sponsorship of a body with the power to regulate, such as the US DoT. The architecture sets the research agenda, the vocabulary and the basic decomposition of concepts of the new area. These architecture definitions are versioned to help users understand the progression from initial to more mature constructs and to help users select the most recent thinking as the basis for their work.

While there is not space here for a full examination of one of these architectures, we will discuss the merging of CVRIA and the National ITS Architecture to form the ARC-IT. For example, ARC-IT replaces the three-layer decomposition of the National Architecture with four views as shown in Fig. 2.7. In addition to rearranging concepts within layers, the physical view has been expanded with 30% more object definitions.

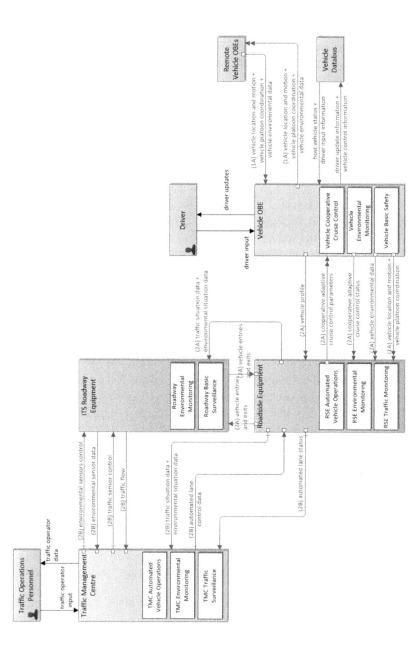

Figure 2.6 Portion of ACT-IT reference architecture-architecture reference for cooperative and intelligent transportation, US DoT, https://local.iteris. com/arc-it/.

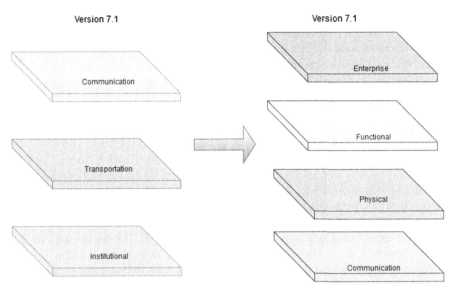

Figure 2.7 Transforming layers into views − architecture reference for cooperative and intelligent transportation, US DoT https://local.iteris.com/arc-it/.

Each object represents a concept and this expansion represents a more fine-grained set of concepts. This redecomposition not only splits some concepts along new fault lines but also causes the system architect to conceptualise their designs differently.

Enterprise − The enterprise view describes the relationships between organisations and the roles those organisations play within the cooperative ITS environment. An enterprise architecture defines the relationships, the data flows and constraints. Any significant smart city transportation system requires the collaboration among several organisations.

Functional − The functional view presents the conceptual functions needed to provide the required system behaviour. This layer includes a set of requirements at an abstract level.

Physical − The physical view presents the physical objects that make up the transportation system. These objects interact as needed to implement the functions defined in the functional level.

Communications − The communications view presents the communication protocols needed to build communication stacks that enable communication among the objects in the physical layer. New stacks can be assembled from the existing protocols and new protocols as they are needed.

A product architecture is simply the structure for a single product. In addition to defining the structure, the architecture also defines the levels of quality attributes the product will possess. If a reference architecture exists that can be used, the product architecture is created by taking structures from the reference architecture and modifying them. If designed without a reference architecture, the product architecture usually is heavily influenced by the interconnections among the hardware elements.

Some large technical systems are referred to as 'federated' when the 'system' is really a combination of several independent systems. The architecture for a federated system describes points in each architecture that will correspond to integration points. A federated system cuts across domains and so is well suited for transportation control systems in which cars, trucks, trains and buses need to be controlled by a single federated system composed of domain-specific control systems.

4.1 Structures

An architecture consists of bundles of computation connected to each other by various mechanisms such as messages or inclusion. The patterns formed by these connections are referred to as architectural patterns. The feedback loop/control system is a classic pattern for CPSs. In this pattern, three of the four elements are mostly hardware with some software while the controller is basically all software. In AADL the *system* is a software component and the *device* is a hardware component. The *connections* among these components are the routes along which data flow through the program.

To understand the operation of a system you need to understand how data flow through the system. CPS transportation programs are usually very complex and tracing through the program is laborious. Building a representation of the flows during architecture design is a less time-consuming process. AADL provides the concept of a *flow*. A flow starts at a flow source, often a port, and follows a connection to a port on another component. It follows into the component and all of the nested components within.

Fig. 2.8 shows an end-to-end error propagation of the error type *LateValue* from our *Cruise Control* example. In this example, the *radar_sensor* component has an error source because it outputs a late data value to *radar_handler* component, and it goes through every connection until it reaches an error sink, which is in the *brake_actuator* component. This end-to-end error propagation leads to a hazard, i.e., a potential condition that can cause injury, damage to or loss of a system, equipment or property [8]. An example of a hazard includes 'component receives late data from the sensor and takes action too late to be effective'. In this case the vehicle might collide with an obstacle because there was insufficient time to decelerate.

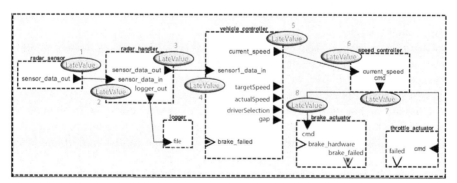

Figure 2.8 Error propagations leading to hazard for cruise control in Fig. 2.1.

4.2   Modelling nominal and error behaviour

A program's structure, as defined in the architecture, defines the routes through which data and control flow. There are nominal (or correct) paths and error paths. The error paths are designed to handle those cases where something is wrong with the operation of the system. These types give four possibilities for the flows through the program. First, the correct data will flow through a path that has the correct structure to correctly compute answers. Second, the correct data will flow through a path with an incorrect structure resulting in incorrect answers. Third, the incorrect data may be placed in an otherwise correct path but the computation will produce answers that are correct with respect to the input but that are inappropriate in the context of the program. Fourth, correct data may be placed in an incorrectly commanded path, which will result in an inappropriate computation and incorrect answers.

Case 1 is obviously the desired situation and all our design and testing efforts are intended to make this the case. Cases 2 and 4 involve architecture defects that should be detected during design using virtual integration and design testing techniques. Case 3 may arise from operational difficulties that happen during execution.

As an example of case 3, where the computation system touches the physical world, runtime errors are possible. A sensor can cease operation while the rest of the system continues to operate. These are possible inputs to the system and the design should accommodate them. AADL defines an annex to the core language that provides a taxonomy of types of errors. The architect examines the taxonomy in the context of the system under development to ensure that the types of errors that can occur are handled by the system. The taxonomy is a set of hierarchies of error types. Fig. 2.9 lists the abstract top of every hierarchy.

AADL defines a taxonomy of types of errors for real-time, embedded systems and provides a language annex that provides a syntax to describe the flow of errors through the system. The taxonomy is a set of classification hierarchies with a general error type as the root and specialisations of that generality filling out the hierarchy. The six general concepts are *ItemValueError, SequenceValueError, ServiceValueErrors, ItemTimingError, SequenceTimingError* and *ServiceTimingError.* The architecture should describe a mapping from the general notions in the error hierarchy to the domain of application.

The error model annex guides the architect and system designers to be certain that they address each important class of error that could occur. Tools such as OSATE can

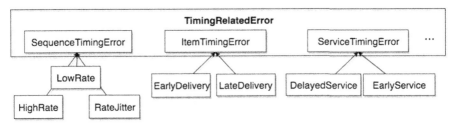

Figure 2.9 Portion of the error ontology.

highlight the error routes through the system. This allows the transportation engineer to participate in verifying that the system will be robust.

5. Issues with the current models

Technologies for command and control are changing rapidly. We discuss two issues and how existing approaches are being changed to address them.

5.1 Mobility

Transportation systems involve the movement of people from one place to another and their smart devices must be sufficiently mobile to move with them while continuing to deliver service. The transportation engineer needs to understand the environment in which the transportation system will be deployed in order to make appropriate design decisions. There are transportation systems which are stationary but many newly emerging capabilities are based on being mobile so that the user can use the capability from exactly where they are rather than going to a spot possibly removed from the events that require attention.

Being mobile requires discoverability, occasional connectivity, access to power and coordination.

Discoverability — As a system moves it needs to discover and potentially be discovered by other capabilities. To be discovered the system must register with a broker. The broker can then match the needs of a system with the capabilities it has registered. This allows a system to move from one infrastructure to another and offer its services or seek services it needs as it moves.

Connectivity — There are a number of communication protocols that can be used wirelessly. The different technologies have different power requirements, and different costs are associated with each one. The design team will probably support multiple communication protocols and have the protocol being used at runtime switchable or at least preruntime configurable. In case study #1 in this chapter we illustrate how adaptability as a way of remaining connected when moving from one location to another increases the amount of radio interference.

Power — Hardware needs energy to run. Transportation engineers are already successful at using certain alternative sources such as solar panels on top of roadway signs in isolated locations where electrical lines are neither available nor easily accessible. New alternative energy sources include the vibrations of bridges as traffic passes over them. These sources have become feasible due to the extremely small demands of most solid state devices.

Coordination — As units move they must recognise each other before working together. Coordination mechanisms provide protocols for exchanging data and analysing data that verify identity. Designing smart transportation systems involves identifying and constraining the spaces in which these systems can move.

Mobile transportation systems must be structured to be adaptive and resilient. As can be seen in case study #2 in this chapter, CPSs need to be able to adapt to environments in which there is interference between the system and another device due to overlapping electromagnetic fields. In the first case study, the system was able to switch between Bluetooth, radio and Wi-Fi radios based on what gave the least interference with broadcasts. These systems must also adapt to the absence of parts of their primary architecture. For example, the system may collect certain types of data which it stores internally until such time as an external system may be located. If the agent is not found in time, then the collector may move to store only a subset of the information in each sensor reading.

5.2 Agility of development

Technologies for intelligent transportation systems are rapidly evolving, but transportation systems are large and development projects associated with these systems are also large and often slow moving. In order to take advantage of the emerging technologies architectures must be modified to allow for faster modification and deployment. DevOps is an emerging organisational technique that merges development and operations responsibilities to facilitate the development to deployment cycle. The basic idea is to ensure that requirements related to deployment are treated as equally important as other capabilities.

The DevOps approach raises the need for rapid development of new capabilities to the same level of importance as the capability itself. It provides an environment in which a continuous development approach could be applied. In that approach each capability is under continuous development. New requirements are accepted by the development team at any time and a roadmap shows a schedule of releases that evolve the capability to its mature state and beyond as maintenance attempts to keep pace with user requests for new capabilities.

One specific architecture being used in this approach uses a microservices style. Service-oriented architectures result in highly modifiable code by keeping the code modular and as many architectural decisions local as possible. A service is a package of capabilities while a microservice represents a single capability. Each microservice uses other microservices to implement its capability. Any one of the services can be replaced by a new service through a dynamic deployment process. Reference architectures such as ARC-IT are too coarse grained for a direct mapping but it does provide an initial decomposition that can be the basis for looking for finer-grained modules.

The popular Docker container technology implements an environment that is a convenient way of defining and using microservices. A container provides an environment in which a complete deployment of a capability can be encapsulated to avoid affecting other microservices running concurrently. These containers are deployed into a runtime environment using an orchestration framework. The orchestration framework handles coordination of use of the physical facilities as well as managing the containers. Containers may need to be started during runtime and some may need to be restarted due to failure at runtime.

The transportation engineer participating in system development as a subject matter expert assists the architects in identifying domain dependencies among actions.

By making these dependencies explicit, they can be allocated to specific service implementations, and interfaces can be defined on each service. Then one service implementation can be replaced with another that also implements that interface without disruption. New technologies can be introduced as long as the effect of the technology can be encapsulated within a single microservice.

A second benefit of this architecture is the ability to assign the implementation of a microservice to a small team. This reduces the need for much ceremony and reduces the number of human-to-human handoffs required. The result is a more dynamic development environment.

One constraint on speeding up development is that many transportation systems are safety critical [9]. Systems that automate driving, flying, traffic management and many other functions are critical to the well-being of humans. Safety critical development projects usually develop requirements specifically about safety and they develop a safety case that gives a logical argument supporting the safe operation of that system. The agile development process can be modified to include safety stories, and the safety case can be incrementally built as the system evolves.

6.   Emerging architectures

6.1   Internet of Things

IoT is one of the new architectural models. As stated above, the IoT comprises context aware applications talking to each other and to the physical world via networked sensors. This first requires a more definite understanding of context. Context is defined by one group as requiring two elements: context situations and context elements [10,11]. That is, we need specific values of specific attributes at a specific time to specify actions that are intended to achieve specific goals: do X if temperature <30. We need time to understand the proximity of events: do X if temperature <30 for the last 5 min. For each new application, which domain attributes are the pertinent ones for an application requires analysis of what rules will be needed to make correct decisions and which are needed to parameterise resulting actions.

Interestingly, this need for domain attributes means an increased reliance on domain analysis. Using ontology building tools, a domain model can be built capturing not only the concepts of an area but also the relationships among concepts. Using standard relationships such as 'is part of' and 'is kind of', the resulting domain model can be used to construct well-formed queries to answer domain-specific queries. The results of these queries lead to actions being performed.

The actual architecture can be thought of as a network that allows 'things' to be arranged in arbitrary ways and talk with each other and the environment in arbitrary ways. The architecture is such that other architectural patterns can be used. For example, cloud architecture could be used to provide a system to compile the data returned by the sensor.

6.2 Cloud architecture

Smart transportation systems generate very large amounts of data from the many sensors. The design of any smart transportation system must include a plan for capturing, storing and analysing large amounts of data. 'Cloud'-based systems are intended for just such a context.

The cloud concept is to have a capability for storing data away from the sites that are generating the data. The intention is to be able to allow access to the data by many stakeholders without regard to their physical location. Recent developments have added a data analytics capability to the cloud-based systems. Cloud systems are intended for situations in which there are large volumes of data collected in real time. The data analytics are used both in real time, for operational decision-making and for long-range planning, and pattern identification.

Cloud-based systems are still a relatively new concept and therefore models are evolving. We will use the NIST cloud reference architecture as the basis for our discussion. Fig. 2.10 shows the fundamental elements.

The NIST conceptual reference architecture defines five roles: cloud consumer, cloud provider, cloud carrier, cloud auditor and cloud broker. The cloud provider, cloud carrier and cloud auditor roles will largely be hidden from the transportation engineer, so we will focus on the consumer and broker roles.

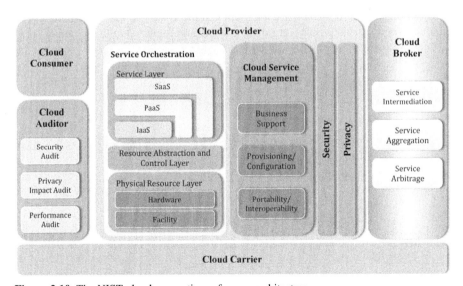

Figure 2.10 The NIST cloud computing reference architecture.
F. Liu, J. Tong, J. Mao, R. Bohn, J. Messina, M. Badger, D. Leaf, Sept 2011. Reprinted courtesy of the National Institute of Standards and Technology, U.S. Department of Commerce. Not copyrightable in the United States.

6.2.1   Cloud consumer

The transportation engineer collaborates with the other roles shown in Figure 2.11. The transportation engineer plays the role of Cloud Consumer. The CPSs used in smart transportation produce very large amounts of data gathered by a spectrum of sensors. Data such as traffic sensing may be analysed in real time to make decisions about setting traffic signals. That same data may be stored for later longitudinal analysis looking for traffic patterns.

6.2.2   Cloud broker

The cloud broker is an intermediary between the cloud consumer (the engineers) and the cloud provider. The broker identifies and bundles sets of services from multiple cloud providers that will provide the consumer the services needed to support their work. The broker sets the service level agreements (allowed latencies and other constraints) that will satisfy the needs of the consumer.

Simple systems may involve the cloud consumer working directly with the cloud provider. The services of the cloud broker become important when the cloud consumer has no one with the technical expertise to interact with the cloud provider. How complicated and how critical the system is will help determine which organisational structure to use.

The initial cloud infrastructure will almost certainly need to be modified due to new services that are requested after the new system stimulates demand. The infrastructure needs to be scalable and modifiable. New versions of existing services and new services that introduce new technologies should be anticipated and be sufficiently modular to allow for unplugging the old and plugging in the new.

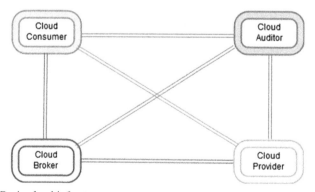

Figure 2.11 Basic cloud infrastructure.
NIST Cloud Computing Reference Architecture. F. Liu, J. Tong, J. Mao, R. Bohn, J. Messina, M. Badger, D. Leaf, Sept 2011. Reprinted courtesy of the National Institute of Standards and Technology, U.S. Department of Commerce. Not copyrightable in the United States.

6.3   Smart city architecture

Large cities tend to face several problems, such as high natural resource consumption, human health concerns, traffic jams, waste management and so on [13]. These issues have become so serious that many cities have been motivated to find smarter ways to handle them. The common thread among their solutions is the use of CPSs. For these cities we use the term Smart City, which brings benefits for the entire city by connecting people, improving citizen's life quality and reducing costs, among other benefits.

Designing smart city software is not an easy task. This architecture must be citizen centric and should handle several aspects of the system such as technology, human—system interaction and cybersecurity. A large number of smart city architectures have been discussed in the literature focussing on these aspects [13—16].

Balancing all these factors to design a complex system, such as a smart city, will be the driving force in addressing many challenges in this context. Challenges related to the security and privacy of citizens are the main issues addressed by these architectures. Cybersecurity architecture is an example of an architecture that supports this issue. Other challenges include scalability, mobility, interoperability, reliability, availability and performance. For example, a smart traffic system is intended to improve road safety and mitigate traffic jams. However, there are levels of quality attributes, which this system must meet to work effectively, that will be very difficult to achieve.

6.3.1   China's smart cities' project

Many cities in Asia, Europe and North America are pursuing smart city architecture projects. Smart city architectures rely heavily on *layered architectures*, providing some benefits of this architectural pattern. Some strengths of this pattern are separation of concerns to reduce complexity and modularity so that multiple applications can share and reuse resources among others. Fig. 2.12 shows a four-layered architecture that China's smart cities' projects have adopted. We use this architecture as an example because its layers correspond to the basic layers that comprise a smart city architecture. Each layer is described below.

Sensing layer — This layer is responsible for identifying objects and collecting data from different types of sensors. IoT is the key of this layer, through which components can interact. This layer must provide advanced infrastructure for data collection in order to provide sufficient data accuracy. The transportation engineer specifies the data sources and data types that will be encountered in this context and participates in the selection of the appropriate types of sensors.

Transmission layer — This layer is responsible for exchanging information and transmitting data through access and transport networks. Wireless is an example of a means of access while the Internet is an example of the transmission network. The transportation engineer identifies potential sources of interference with other devices and designs layouts that avoid interference.

Processing layer — This layer processes and controls information and provides services and other functions to the application layer. It consists of business support,

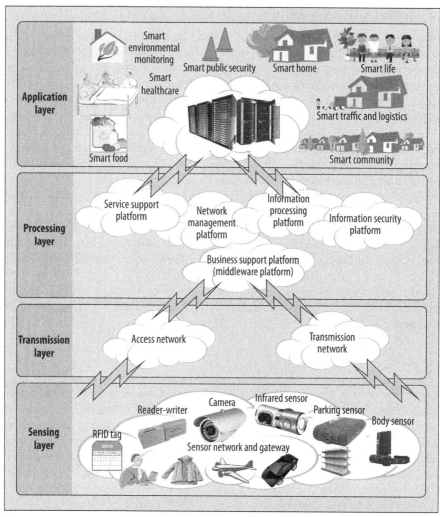

Figure 2.12 China's smart architecture.
Ref. [15]. Reprinted with permission of the IEEE. https://www.researchgate.net/publication/270767244_China%27s_Smart_City_Pilots_A_Progress_Report.

network management, information processing and security, among others. The transportation engineer participates in evaluating issues such as the rate of capacity utilisation.

Application layer – This layer is very important because it is the layer used by citizens who do not necessarily have computer training, and its performance will affect the citizens' experience with smart services. This layer greatly impacts economic and social development. Key challenges here are widespread information resource sharing and the need to provide information security. The transportation engineer acquires and/or specifies applications that will achieve specific transportation goals such as reduced waiting time.

These architectures shape systems that unite various smart city applications into an effective and efficient environment for addressing the issues facing large cities. The layered approach allows the architects of a new smart city application to select the layers to reuse and allows the introduction of new technologies without needless ripples into adjacent layers. These smart city development efforts are using the emerging cyber-physical technologies to bring big data analysis to the automation of many of the functions required to support modern living.

7. Case studies

Case study #1 — In this section we summarise a discussion of a CPS previously published in more detail [17]. The system was developed in response to a request from an industrial client who shall remain anonymous. It soon became obvious that the system could satisfy multiple needs. This is a relatively simple example of a CPS. In the next case study we will explore a more complex system involving mobility issues.

The manufacturing line at the initial target plant was structured in the shape of a horseshoe. Several machines are placed at various positions around the horseshoe. A technician takes a raw part and processes the part at each machine around the horseshoe. After a technician moves to the second machine, another technician begins a new part on machine 1. The organisation wanted to collect data about the manufacturing line by instrumenting the technicians and parts. This system was to be instrumented using accelerometers, gyroscopes, a magnetometer, an environmental sensor and a light intensity sensor. Devices attached to the technician sensed various parameters and used wireless to send the data to a central server. Sensors detected messaging failures and measured signal strength.

The architects were faced with a few basic requirements that had several variations. In particular multiple communication protocols needed to be supported. This was mainly due to different machines being on the different factory floors and having different levels of interference. The requirements allowed each installation to be configured with a set of protocols among which the application can switch. A confounding requirement specified response times, which could be difficult to satisfy for specific combinations of communication protocols. This product line set of requirements evolved as limitations on technologies were revealed during system design. The ALISA toolkit for AADL provided a basis for capturing details of the requirements and relating those requirements to the architecture. During this project one requirement was found to be missing. ALISA was applied to identify that requirement and others.

The manufacturing line was sufficiently large that one position on the line was sufficiently close to one machine and sufficiently far enough away from others to have interference at some points on the line and not at others. The interference was present for certain communication protocols and not others. To be effective the system had to be able to communicate at every point along the manufacturing line.

This architecture illustrates that all CPSs are neither complex nor feedback controlled. A number of sensors were being used to collect data and to forward that data to the base unit; however, the only feedback to the actuators is which communication protocols to use. The workers on the line used their judgement to control the manufacturing process. The controller was a simple processor designed to use two threads. The low-priority thread handles environmental and light intensity sensors. The high-priority thread handles movement sensing such as gyroscopes and accelerometers.

An implicit interaction, signal interference, was a major influence on the architecture definition. The system as originally conceived had a Wi-Fi radio. As the impact of radio interference and the possibility of deploying to multiple manufacturing sites were analysed, it was decided to make wireless communication protocols a major variation point in the architecture. The variation point allowed Bluetooth Low Energy and ZigBee to be added as choices. The system was designed to be dynamically adaptive. Sensors reading the number of transmission failures and signal strengths provided input to the controller that was used to determine when to switch from one protocol to one of the others. At this writing one system has been successfully deployed and other variants have been tested and are ready to deploy.

Case study #2 — In this section we briefly discuss the main findings of a case study on a cyber-physical mobile system (CPMS) in the context of smart city. CPMS is very challenging since it needs to operate within the resource limitations of mobile devices and handle a set of critical smart city requirements that this domain imposes. A case study on RESCUER project [18] was conducted to understand some software architecture aspects of CPMS.

RESCUER stands for 'reliable and smart crowdsourcing solution for emergency and crisis management'. It is an efficient emergency and crisis management system developed to ensure that the people visiting large-scale events, such as the FIFA World Cup, will feel safe.

RESCUER relies on the use of mobile technologies to capture information provided by citizens about crisis scenarios. It uses a crowdsourcing approach, in which citizens contribute to the provision of accurate and updated data on critical scenarios, from a mobile application, helping the stakeholders in the decision-making process. From images, videos and messages shared by crowdsourcing, the application performs multimedia data analysis to aid in the management of emergencies and crises.

Dr. Karina Villela, the European Coordinator of Fraunhofer Institute for Experimental Software Engineering, described their goal for RESCUER as follows: 'We want to develop a solution approach for transmitting information to the right place rapidly and efficiently. To do so, we will focus on new technology trends on global markets, such as the establishment of smart and wireless platforms, larger data sources and automated data analyses'.

Design — In this study, three main areas were investigated: the software architecture, quality attributes for smart city applications and challenges of mobile applications. Since RESCUER's team project used skills related to software engineering, decision support and data analysis systems, it was possible to collect and analyse a rich amount of information about the software engineering process.

Data collection — Several data sources were used in order to limit the influence of one interpretation of a single data source. It consisted mainly of six semistructured interviews with stakeholders who had different roles in the project, administering background questionnaires and archiving data covering all phases of the software development process.

Data analysis — Interviews were recorded and transcribed. Every documentation available was summarised, highlighting the parts that would help to answer the research topics. Then, both data sources (transcripts and notes from documents) were structured into thematic areas to gather and cross-check relevant information.

Main findings — The architecture of RESCUER was analysed and the results described below consider the entire system including the mobile application and the server.

7.1 Software architecture aspects

RESCUER used an adaptive layered architecture, designed in a modular way with several components organised in the layers described in Table 2.1. This model uses the concept of layer isolation, where changes made to one layer do not affect components from other layers. In order to improve performance and communication between the components, the architecture of the system was adapted with the insertion of a vertical layer, named Integration layer, to allow the integration between the components.

Furthermore, aiming to ensure a more efficient communication between the components, the architects implemented another architectural pattern, called *message broker*. It was also used for validation, transformation and routing of messages. This pattern is responsible for receiving a message from one component and making it available to other components.

Table 2.1 Layer Function Mobile Application

Layer	Function
Data transport	Responsible for transporting data between the RESCUER mobile solution and the RESCUER back-end.
Data analysis	Responsible for analysing various kinds of data collected from mobile applications independently and for doing a combined analysis.
Management	Responsible for managing the crowd and workforces. It helps to plan a set of actions based on the current situation.
Visualisation	Responsible for showing analysed data, static emergency plans and the status of the action decided by the command and control centre.
Ad hoc network	Responsible for providing an alternative communication channel in the event of no Internet access.
Data integration	Responsible for integrating components within RESCUER, as well as legacy operating resources.

Moreover, some *architectural styles* were also identified in the case study:

- *Client—Server* — At the client layer, users used a mobile solution (MS) for visitors and work-force members to report an incident and get feedback from the system back-end. At the server layer, the data collection of the several MS and the suitable data analysis provided a good visualisation of the emergency scenario. It also provides integration mechanisms to communicate with external systems, social networks, among others.
- *Publish—Subscribe* — Applying this style, components were able to communicate through asynchronous messages allowing a better integration among them.
- *Peer-to-Peer* (*P2P*) — P2P was implemented for the case in which the Internet connection is low or is off. The components have to adapt their behaviour and communicate over a P2P network.

7.2 Quality attributes for smart city applications

The system was designed taking into account most of the quality attributes that are part of the context of smart cities, in the construction of the architecture. Table 2.2 presents a list of 15 quality attributes in order of importance to the RESCUER project. The project achieved the desired levels for some of the attributes, failed to achieve the levels of some others and simply did not address others. Those results are shown in Table 2.2.

As seen in Table 2.2, the quality attributes were addressed in different ways so that they have been treated differently in each development phase. Thus, for example, some attributes have been fully implemented and others have been considered in the specification or design phase but have not been carried to implementation.

7.3 Challenges of mobile applications

The most critical challenge in the development of the system was being a mobile crowdsourcing application because it carries out a large subset of challenges related to enabling the crowdsourcing for real-time information gathering. An example faced in the project was the high battery consumption due to the frequent use of GPS. It used

Table 2.2 Significance of Quality Attribute

Quality Attribute	Status
Mobility, scalability, reliability, usability, maintainability, performance, robustness	They were successfully specified, designed, implemented and tested.
Availability, portability, reusability, adaptability, interoperability	They have been specified and designed but neither implemented nor tested.
Sustainability, privacy, security	They have been specified but neither designed nor implemented.

GPS for both sending location report information and the crowdsourcing tracking tool through a heat map with people's location information in real time.

The project also had some reliability concerns. Since the people who provide information to the crowdsourcing system are unknown, they had to manage issues like lack of confirmability and data quality. To handle these, the development team used methods to guarantee the reliability of the data. Examples of these methods were algorithms to identify fake GPS locations, procedures for analysis of duplicate reports and creation of different profiles in the application.

Since the project used manual input and several types of data (image, video, text) to collect real-time information, the usability of the app has become a critical factor. To mitigate this risk, several usability tests were conducted during the World Cup in 2014. These events were held to capture feedback from users and the workforces (police, firefighters).

Besides crowdsourcing, several technical challenges related to the development of mobile applications were reported, such as the lack of debugging tools, support for multiple platforms and testing, software development support tools, computational power and network coverage.

8.   Conclusion

Transportation systems are becoming more dynamic with more decisions made during operation. These systems need architectures that can apply traditional control system architectures with the ability to apply autonomy to alter the system dynamically based on different sensing patterns. We have presented a number of aspects of architectural design and discussed the implications of those design aspects in the context of smart transportation systems.

The future for architectures of smart transportation systems can be seen in recent trends. The most significant trend is the reduction in size of the components used to plug together a system architecture. Termed microservices, these components make the system very modular with the ability to replace one behaviour with another at the expense of having many more components to instantiate, configure and deploy. A second trend is to present high-level architectures in a layered format. This style of architecture supports grouping concepts by their degree of concrete representation. That means that the contents of a layer are used at the same point in product development. The relationships between objects in adjacent layers allow the tracing of the evolution of concepts from most abstract to very concrete.

Our presentation is intended to provide the transportation engineer a number of issues to consider when participating in the development of a smart transportation system. We have described the quality attributes that are essential to the success of these systems and some of the architectures needed to achieve the correct attribute values. The transportation engineer can make a valuable contribution to the system development process by combining their transportation knowledge and the information in this chapter.

Exercises

1. Choose a transportation product for which you can get some type of architecture description. (If you cannot find one you want to use, try using a portion of the DoT's reference architecture.) Use the documentation to infer which are the appropriate quality attributes (choose no more than three or four attributes). Briefly describe the structures in the architecture that are intended to enhance the values of these attributes.
2. Using the architecture for the system you chose in Exercise 1, describe several flows through the system. Some of these flows should be nominal (correctly functioning) and some should be error flows (flows due to hardware failure or unanticipated inputs).
3. Find an example of a system that claims to use cloud architecture. Examine the claims made about security and robustness. Determine what features of the cloud architecture as described above contribute to the security and robustness.
4. Take an error defined in one of the flows described in number 2. Determine where in the system the error would occur and describe the units of the system through which the error flows and where the error is handled.

References

[1] National Science Foundation — NSF, Cyber-Physical Systems. (online) Available at: https://www.nsf.gov/funding/pgm_summ.jsp?pims_id=503286. (Assessed on 14/04/2018).
[2] P.H. Feiler, D.P. Gluch, Model-Based Engineering with AADL: An Introduction to the SAE Architecture Analysis & Design Language, first ed., Addison-Wesley Professional, 2012.
[3] ISO/IEC, ISO/IEC 25010-Systems and Software Engineering — Systems and Software Quality Requirements and Evaluation (SQuaRE) — System and Software Quality Models, Technical Report, 2010.
[4] Cyber Physical Systems Public Working Group, Framework for Cyber-Physical Systems Release 1.0, 2016 (online) Available at: https://s3.amazonaws.com/nist-sgcps/cpspwg/files/pwgglobal/CPS_PWG_Framework_for_Cyber_Physical_Systems_Release_1_0Final.pdf. (Accessed on 14/04/2018).
[5] Intelligent Transportation Systems — Communications, Connected Vehicle Reference Implementation Architecture. (online) Available at: https://www.its.dot.gov/factsheets/cvria.htm. (Accessed on 14/04/2018).
[6] United States Department of Transportation, Architecture Reference for Cooperative and Intelligent Transportation, 2017 (online) Available at: http://local.iteris.com/arc-it/. (Accessed on 14/04/2018).
[7] Autosar, AUTOSAR Enabling Innovation, 2017 (online) Available at: https://www.autosar.org/index.php. (Accessed on 14/04/2018).
[8] MIL-STD-882D, Department of Defense Standard Practice for System Safety, 2000.
[9] J. Cleland-Huang, Safety stories in agile development, IEEE Software 34 (4) (2017) 16−19.
[10] D. Karzel, H. Marginean, T. Tran, A Reference Architecture for the Internet of Things, 2016 (online) InfoQ. Available at: https://www.infoq.com/articles/internet-of-things-reference-architecture. (Accessed on 14/04/2018).

[11] D. Karzel, H. Marginean, T. Tran, A Reference Architecture for the Internet of Things (Part 2), 2016 (online) InfoQ. Available at: https://www.infoq.com/articles/internet-of-things-reference-architecture-2?utm_source=infoq&utm_campaign=user_page&utm_medium=link. (Accessed on 14/04/2018).

[12] F. Liu, J. Tong, J. Mao, R. Bohn, J. Messina, M. Badger, D. Leaf, NIST Cloud Computing Reference Architecture, National Institute of Standards and Technology, 2011. Special Publication - 500−292.

[13] N. Zakaria, A.J. Shamsi, Smart city architecture: vision and challenges, International Journal of Advanced Computer Science and Applications 6 (11) (2015).

[14] M. Al-Hader, A. Rodzi, A. Sharif, N. Ahmad, Smart city components architecture, in: 2009 International Conference on Computational Intelligence, Modelling and Simulation, 2009.

[15] P. Liu, Z. Peng, China's smart city pilots: a progress report, Computer 47 (10) (2014) 72−81.

[16] R. Khatoun, S. Zeadally, Smart cities: concepts, architectures, research opportunities, Communications of the ACM 59 (8) (2016) 46−57.

[17] E. McGee, M. Krugh, J. McGregor, L. Mears, Designing for reuse in an industrial internet of things monitoring application, in: Proceedings of the 2nd Workshop on Social, Human, and Economic Aspects of Software − WASHES'17, 2017.

[18] RESCUER., RESCUER PROJECT, 2015 (online) Available at: http://www.rescuer-project.org/. (Accessed on 14/04/2018).

Collaborative modelling and co-simulation for Transportation Cyber-Physical Systems

John Fitzgerald[1], Carl Gamble[1], Martin Mansfield[1], Julien Ouy[2], Roberto Palacin[1], Ken Pierce[1], Peter G. Larsen[3]
[1]Newcastle University, Newcastle upon Tyne, United Kingdom; [2]CLEARSY, Aix-en-Provence, France; [3]Aarhus University, Aarhus, Denmark

1. Introduction

Sustainable transportation, especially in increasingly urbanised environments, relies on mobility being a flexible service that can respond to changes in the environment as well as the behaviour and needs of users. Delivering such responsiveness requires future transportation systems to be 'smart', relying on digital technologies for the acquisition, transmission and analysis of data from physical systems. However, it is also necessary to act on such data, and so transportation systems need to be founded on models that allow stakeholders to analyse the ramifications of interventions, even though they cross digital and physical domains and multiple transport modes. The systems engineering of sustainable transportation is thus inherently cyber physical in character.

The systems engineer working in the transport environment faces many challenges alongside the demands of a complex, multiowner environment. The cyber-physical character of transportation projects means that we must deal with network distributed processes and in integrating the variety of design models and analytic techniques used by the many disciplines that collaborate (intentionally or otherwise) in delivering mobility. In this chapter, we examine progress towards the integration of such diverse models, with the goal of delivering integrative tools that allow holistic analysis of transportation system properties.

We first make a case for multidisciplinary engineering of cyber-physical transportation systems (Section 2) and follow this through to examine technical approaches to the integration of semantically diverse models of the cyber (digital) and physical elements of systems (Section 3). We present an approach to multidisciplinary co-modelling and co-simulation that has been realised in a tool chain (Section 4), and illustrate the potential of the approach by describing a case study undertaken in industry (Section 5). Finally, we look to future research and innovation opportunities in this area (Section 6).

Transportation Cyber-Physical Systems. https://doi.org/10.1016/B978-0-12-814295-0.00003-4
Copyright © 2018 Elsevier Inc. All rights reserved.

2. Transportation Cyber-Physical Systems engineering

Transport systems have been described as the blood system of society [1]. Together with energy, transport is a key driver of our economy and way of life. There is increasing emphasis on adopting more sustainable and clean mobility solutions that would allow us to continue on our path of growth and prosperity. This is particularly relevant in conurbations where the highest proportion of the population and economic activity takes place [2].

Transport is changing through digitalisation. Intelligent systems are providing a shift to user-centric mobility that integrates inadequately connected mode-based systems while allowing system-wide optimisation of networks and resources. Ageing society, energy usage, carbon footprint, network resilience and socioeconomic aspects are all key transport challenges being reimagined through digitalisation. Mulley [3] argues that a major change in technology is sponsoring a new transport paradigm, but rather than the technology itself being the change agent, it is its role in facilitating the paradigm change that is relevant. She goes on citing [4] as they discuss an example of how digitalisation, automation and new business models are revolutionising industries and will end up impacting forever the way in which cars are used.

2.1 New mobility concepts

The transport research community is excited with the prospects that new technologies and digitalisation are bringing, potentially profoundly transforming what we understand by transport in the 21st century. In particular, the discourse around Mobility as a Service (MaaS) is intense among stakeholders, visionaries and academics. There have been many attempts to define MaaS with various degrees of success. Mulley [3] put it very simply by describing MaaS as

> a technology-enabled Mobility Management service where the customer interface and business back office are integrated [...]. MaaS concentrates on resolving the origin and destination requirements of the traveller through providing (usually) a number of options which vary by mode, time and cost.

A recent report by [5] describes MaaS as a concept that 'is built on transport system integration, Internet of Things and sharing economy principles'. Both definitions are valid. At a fundamental level, future transport seems to be moving towards models that are based around access rather and ownership, with the service provision being at the core and the mode used to offer that service being irrelevant. In other words, transport is expected to become modally agnostic, with an integration of private and public transport where digitalisation would make possible to imagine scalable door-to-door services without the need of owning a car.

2.2 Cyber-physical system engineering in transportation

Systems thinking, for example, as described by [6], is fundamental in fulfilling the technical, societal, economic and urban impact that data-driven and digitally enabled technologies and methodologies can have in the future of transport of people and goods. Essential to this new knowledge is an overarching system of connected and co-ordinated systems achieved through synergistic design and optimisation that uses the wealth of opportunities digitalisation has to offer.

Cyber-physical systems (CPSs) use open network technologies, e.g., the Internet with the characteristics that include among others (1) systems of collaborating computational elements controlling physical entities, (2) interconnections between virtual and physical models, (3) systems of systems and (4) ability for autonomous behaviour, e.g., self-control/self-optimisation [7]. These characteristics resonate with current discourse around the revolution of transport facilitated by the advent of autonomous vehicles catalysing a transformation of traffic modelling, network planning and even urban form in the case of road transport.

The above is true for all four transport modes, where next-generation air, road, rail and maritime transport systems are seeking to maximise the potential of novel technologies and digitalisation. For instance, air traffic control could be transformed from current fixed corridor approaches to a more fluid and flexible model allowing for higher capacity. This capacity aspect will also play a fundamental role in the further development of already sophisticated rail traffic management systems where fixed block approaches to traffic and security are giving way to a more dynamic model using intelligent trains that can 'talk' to each other, reducing the distance between them while maintaining the safety critical aspects of the system. On the roads, solutions such as vehicle to infrastructure and vehicle to vehicle (V2V) are key examples of the direction that innovation is taking in this sector.

These systems combine cyber aspects, e.g., wireless communication and computer control with physical aspects, e.g., real-time interfacing with the physical environment, including sensing and actuation, thus forming CPSs [8].

2.3 Multidisciplinary aspects of Transportation Cyber-Physical System

To fulfil the opportunities that new technologies offer to transform transport systems in the digital age, a fundamental approach that is collaborative in nature is essential. Transport systems are complex sociotechnical systems. Schwanen [9] describes a sociotechnical regime as

> A set of rules—cognitive routines, shared beliefs, social norms and conventions, regulations, industry standards, protocols, contracts, laws and so forth—that fulfil a societal function (e.g., everyday mobility) and thereby condition the practices through which the technology, infrastructure, markets, cultural values, user practices, maintenance and repair, regulation and formal knowledge that make up sociotechnical systems are reproduced.

Addressing these physical (e.g., infrastructure, maintenance) and cyber (e.g., technology such as traffic control systems) aspects and their intertwined connections demands a collaborative multidisciplinary approach, which is arguably at its most relevant when attempting to design and apply complex CPS engineering concepts. There is thus a need for methods, tools and guidelines that allow collaborative and multidisciplinary development of CPSs that are applicable in the transport domain. Such approaches should support the sound integration of diverse design models, provide a range of static and dynamic analyses in order to determine holistic system-level consequences of cyber or physical design choices and interventions and be capable of integration into 'chain' of tools deployable in practice.

3. The model-based cyber-physical system engineering context

CPS engineering is a highly active area of research and development. The extensive Road2CPS roadmapping exercise [10] identifies strong drivers for change in the transportation sector, including the rise of artificial intelligence techniques, and increasing computing and network capabilities. However, the report also recognises the need for coordination among diverse systems and disciplines in the sector, particularly the need for networks and applications that 'enable the whole transport ensemble to operate effectively and efficiently'. It states a priority to 'generate improved tool support for heterogeneous modelling techniques, including model management and traceability support, and the ability to consider models of different levels of granularity and abstraction in appropriate relationships to each other'.

While there are well-established methods, such as model-based design, within the disciplines of transportation engineering, they often use diverse formalisms, abstractions and terminology. Mechanical and control engineers typically model in continuous-time (CT) formalisms described through differential equations. These produce high-fidelity physics simulations, which are well suited for mechanical and low-level controller design, but in which it is difficult to analyse supervisory controller behaviours such as mode changes, error detection and response or network messaging. Conversely, software engineers use discrete-event (DE) formalisms to model and analyse these supervisory aspects but often lack the ability to test them against realistic, real-time test data.

It is challenging to integrate diverse approaches because of the need to handle common information in semantically diverse notations which have not been developed to support the common analyses [11]. Current model-based design tools tend to focus on a single formalism [12,13], hindering the integration of heterogeneous models from multiple sources. The design of CPSs clearly requires these methods to be brought together to tackle their inherent heterogeneity (CyPhERS, 2014), and there is an identified 'need to facilitate the integration of models and simulations across multiple domains and disciplines' [6]. Approaches to the challenge of integration include approaches based on hybrid automata [14] and combined modelling techniques, such as Dymola [15]. Common interchange formats have also been used, including Discrete Event System Specification [16]; Modelica [17]. Automated model transformation has also been demonstrated on some platforms.

Collaborative modelling (*co-modelling*) is a promising approach in which diverse models are connected together in a co-model that can be analysed through *co-simulation* [18,19]. This allows individual engineering disciplines to use notations that are well established within their domains, provided they can produce simulators that conform to the interface constraints for the co-simulation framework. Gomes et al. [20] offer a comprehensive survey of the foundations of co-simulation frameworks. Previous work showed the feasibility of co-modelling and co-simulation between CT and DE models in a range of domains [21]. Although the practical benefits of the approach were demonstrated in commercial mechatronics and embedded systems design, in common with other instances of co-simulation (as noted by Gomes et al.), this work was almost exclusively focussed on binary co-simulations of one DE model with one CT: a long way from the scale of distributed CPSs!

From this work, we identified three properties required of successful co-modelling methods and tools. First, the integration of semantically diverse tools should be done on a sound basis so that a full range of analytic techniques from static model checking (MC) to dynamic co-simulation can be applied to the holistic analysis of systems. Second, the tools should form a coherent chain covering a range of design activities and not be confined to abstract designs. Third, the emerging co-modelling and co-simulation methods and tools should be open to the addition of models described in new formalisms. The *integrated tool chain for* CPS (INTO-CPS) described in Section 4 aims to address these three properties.

4. Towards an integrated tool chain for cyber-physical system engineering

In this section we introduce basic concepts of an approach to collaborative modelling and co-simulation for CPS engineering. Section 4.1 briefly describes some core concepts and terms, while Section 4.2 introduces a tool chain that aims to realise the vision set out above. Section 4.3 describes two baseline modelling technologies that are integrated in the tool chain.

4.1 Foundations for collaborative modelling

A *system* is 'a combination of interacting elements organized to achieve one or more stated purposes' [6]. For our purposes, CPSs tightly couple the physical and virtual worlds. They are established from network embedded systems that acquire data from the physical world, interacting with it by implementing instructions from the virtual sphere [10].

4.1.1 Models

We support *model-based* design of CPSs. A *model* is a (potentially partial and abstract) description of a system, limited to those components and properties that are pertinent to the purpose for which the model is being constructed. In a CPS model, we model systems with cyber, physical and network elements. These elements may be modelled in a variety of languages, with different notations, concepts, levels of abstraction and semantics, which are not necessarily easily mapped one to another.

In this chapter, we consider the use of CT and DE models to represent physical and cyber elements as appropriate. A CT model has state that can be changed and observed continuously and is described using explicit continuous functions or implicitly as a solution of differential equations. A DE model has state that can be changed and observed only at discrete intervals [22]. We refer to a collection of DE and CT models describing elements of a CPS as a *co-model*. We refer to the simulation of a co-model as a *co-simulation*.

A *design parameter* is a property of a model that can be used to affect the model's behaviour but remains constant during a given simulation. A *variable* is feature of a model that may change during a given simulation. The activity of creating models may be referred to as *modelling* [21].

4.1.2 System architecture

An architecture 'defines the major elements of a system, identifies the relationships and interactions between the elements and takes into account process' [23]. In a CPS architecture, elements may be either cyber or physical, corresponding to some functional logic or an entity of the physical world, respectively. In our work, we use the SysML notation [24] for giving architectural descriptions of CPS designs. We have defined a profile in SysML [25] to enable the specification of CPS design architectures. It encourages the modeller to provide a decomposition of the system of interest a system into subsystems, each of which is an assembly of cyber and physical components (and possibly other subsystems), each of which may be using one of a range of CT or DE notations as appropriate for the subsystem's domain.

Within an architecture, an *interface* may describe both digital and physical interactions: *digital interfaces* contain descriptions of operations and attributes that are provided and required by components. *Physical interfaces* describe the flow of physical matter (for example, fluid and electrical power) between components.

4.1.3 Analytic techniques

The construction of co-models enables—at least in principle—a wide range of dynamic and static analyses. We describe several important examples below.

Co-simulation is the simultaneous, collaborative, execution of models. The models may be CT, DE or a combination and are regarded as *simulation units* in that they may be executed. A *Co-simulation Orchestration Engine* (COE) is an implementation of a *Master Algorithm* that manages the exchange of data and the progression of time in each of the constituent simulations so that they together deliver a coherent holistic simulation of the CPS. A COE can also allow real software and physical elements to participate in co-simulation alongside models, enabling both *hardware-in-the-loop* (*HiL*) and *software-in-the-loop* (*SiL*) simulation.

Design space exploration (*DSE*) is the process of building and evaluating co-models in order to select a design that satisfies an objective from a space of alternatives [21]. Design alternatives can be defined using either a range of parameter values or different co-models. Objectives will often be holistic properties such as cost or performance that are typically influenced by both cyber and physical elements. Given a collection of alternatives with corresponding objective results, a ranking may be applied to determine the 'best' design alternative.

Test automation (*TA*) is the machine-assisted automation of system tests. In a co-modelling setting, we are able to focus on testing system models against the requirements on the system. In our work, we consider *HiL*, *SiL* and *model-in-the-loop* (*MiL*) TA. In HiL target hardware is involved in the co-simulation; in SiL candidate software is a simulation unit and in MiL, the test object of the test execution is a (design) model.

MC exhaustively checks whether the model of the system meets its specification [26], which is typically expressed in a temporal logic, e.g., [27]. In contrast testing, MC examines the entire state space of the system and is thus able to provide a correctness proof for the model with respect to its specification. If the specification is violated, it provides a counterexample trace that shows how an undesired state of the system can be reached. The price paid for this exhaustive check is of course the computational complexity of potentially covering the entire state space of a system.

4.2   Towards a tool chain for co-modelling

We indicated above that out experience of collaborative modelling and co-simulation led us to identify the need for a well-founded and extensible tool chain, as opposed to focussing on particular co-simulation support for a narrow range of formalisms. Our current work has led us to develop such a tool chain. In this section, we describe its main elements.

Our *INTO-CPS* is founded on a collection of baseline tools that cover requirements analysis and model development in SysML using the Modelio tool, DE modelling in VDM-RT using the Overture tool, CT modelling in 20-sim and OpenModelica and support for TA provided by RT-Tester. Fig. 3.1 gives a graphic overview of the tool chain. At its heart is a COE that orchestrates multiple simulation units that each conform to the open Functional Mock-up Interface (FMI) standard. This allows any number of models to be packaged as Functional Mock-up Units (FMUs) and combined into a co-model for co-simulation. The INTO-CPS COE implements both a standard, fixed time-step master algorithm and a variable time-step algorithm, which can speed up co-simulations and improve the fidelity of results from DE FMUs. Over 30 tools can produce FMUs, and more than 100 have partial or upcoming support (see http://fmi-standard.org/tools/). All of the INTO-CPS baseline tools produce FMI-conformant simulation units.

CPS requirements and architectures may be expressed using SysML, using the profile already mentioned. From each element defined in the profile, we develop a constituent model using the notation and tool of choice. The resulting FMUs can be subjected to a range of analyses, including co-simulation, DSE, MC and TA as described above,

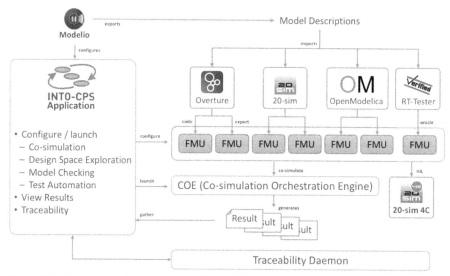

Figure 3.1 The integrated tool chain for CPS (INTO-CPS) tool chain. *FMU*, Functional Mock-up Unit.

as well as code generation. The *INTO-CPS application* (*'the app'*) is a front-end to the tool chain. It allows the specification of the co-simulation configuration and the co-simulation execution itself and provides access to features of the tool chain that do not have a specific user interface (such as DSE and MC).

A set of methods guidelines [28], tutorials and examples [29] support the tool and user manuals. INTO-CPS has been applied to a range of industrial case studies in the agricultural, automotive, building and transport domains. Some 80 companies followed the initial INTO-CPS project, which is succeeded by the INTO-CPS Association (launching in November 2017) to continue development and support work.

Since FMI provides means of co-simulating heterogeneous simulation units derived from constituent models, it forms a good basis for validation, but it does not of itself deliver the capacity formally to verify holistic properties of CPSs. The approach to this adopted in INTO-CPS is to codify the links between the diverse semantics of constituent models. This is done using Hoare and He's Unifying Theories of Programming (UTP) [30,31]. This leads to the potential for practical CPS verification by using the powerful automated proof assistant Isabelle in its instantiation for UTP [32]. Work is ongoing to integrate this with the INTO-CPS tool chain [33].

Multidisciplinary co-modelling and co-simulation naturally generate many design artefacts, including co-models, co-simulation inputs and outputs, requirements, code, etc. Such large design sets are expected to evolve as smart systems and are developed by gradual integration of existing elements and as elements change. The interrelationships between them are vital for allowing validation and third-party assurance. We have used features of the W3C provenance (PROV) model to record the temporal relations between activities, entities and agents within a process, and traceability has been supplied based on the Open Services for Lifecycle Collaboration (OSLC) standard. In INTO-CPS, we have regarded it as a priority to lay foundations for provenance and traceability support in the tool chain; all the baseline tools have been extended with such OSLC support [34]. Together, these provide a capability for impact analysis and traceability in support of verification, for example, of safety properties.

4.3 Modelling technologies

In this section, we briefly introduce two of the modelling technologies used in INTO-CPS and example in the next section: OpenModelica, for CT modelling, and Overture for DE modelling using VDM-RT.

4.3.1 OpenModelica

Modelica is an object-oriented equation-based language for describing physical systems, including, for example, mechanical, electrical and hydraulic phenomena [35]. OpenModelica is an open-source environment supporting models written in the Modelica language. It also supports the graphical of equations through blocks that have input and output ports, which are then connected to form a model of the component or system. OpenModelica provides static checking of Modelica models, including syntax and type checking, and dynamic debugging through breakpoints. It can generate FMUs to be used in co-simulation or export C/C++ code for simulation in custom environment. OpenModelica has a large library of components and is maintained by an activity community, supported by the Modelica Association.

CT models in OpenModelica describe the evolution of variables over time. Fig. 3.2 shows an OpenModelica model that describes of a ball, dropped from an initial height, being accelerated under gravity and bouncing on a surface. The equations on the left and block diagram on the right are equivalent models, which OpenModelica compiles into a common form for simulation and FMU export. Modelica models contain four key elements: variables, equations, parameters and events. Variables are values that change during a simulation. In the bouncing ball example, these are the height of

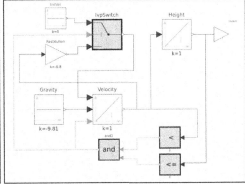

```
model BouncingBall
    parameter g = 9.81;
    Real h; Real v;
initial equation
    v = 0;
    h = 2.0;
equation
    der(h) = v;
    der(v) = -g;
    when h <= 0 and v < 0 then
        reinit(v, -0.8*pre(v));
    end when;
end BouncingBall;
```

Figure 3.2 OpenModelica model of a bouncing ball in equation and graphical form.

the ball, h, and its velocity, v. Equations describe how these variables evolve during a simulation. The equations in Fig. 3.2 state that the derivative of the ball's height (position) is its velocity and that the derivative of its velocity is the acceleration due to gravity, given by the parameter, g. Parameters are properties that are fixed during a simulation but can be changed between simulations to alter the characteristics of a model. Initial equations are evaluated once at the beginning of simulation to initialise variables.

Finally, events allow discontinuous updates to variables, which can occur at a certain time (time events) or in response to a certain state (state events). State events are modelled by detecting when the value of a function crosses zero (changes from positive to negative or vice versa). In the case of the bouncing ball, this occurs when the height and velocity cross zero, as stated in a *when* clause in the equation model. In the case of the bouncing ball, the continuous variables are reinitialised with inverse velocity and a simple damping factor applied.

4.3.2   VDM-RT and Overture

VDM-RT is the real-time dialect of the Vienna Development Method, a well-established formal method for DE modelling. VDM models describe systems and components in terms of their state and how that state changes in response to inputs, such as test data or values from other models during co-simulation. Overture[1] is an open-source tool for writing and analysing VDM models. It provides syntax and type checking, analysis techniques such as combinatorial testing, and simulation of an executable subset of VDM. Overture can also generate FMUs for co-simulation and generate code for deployment on real systems.

VDM-RT is an object-oriented language, where behaviours are divided into objects, which encapsulate functionalities and create manageable hierarchies for complex models. Objects are defined by classes. Fig. 3.3 shows a simple class definition for a controller. The controller should calculate an output, which makes a measured value to reach a given set point, using a proportional control response based on the error between these two. The controller has internal state defined by four instance variables: measured, read from a sensor; set point, the target value; err, the error between them; and output, passed to an actuator. The control behaviour is captured in the Step operation, which calculates the error and sets the output. All operations of VDM-RT take (simulated) time, which the Overture simulator keeps track of. There is a default time for each expression that can be used to estimate execution time. These can be overridden if code is profiled on a target system. In this controller, the Step operation will take 20 (simulated) nanoseconds. The auxiliary function, P, which is called by the Step operation, calculates the proportional response based on a constant gain, Kp. Constants can act as parameters, as in OpenModelica, and be set changed between simulations to alter controller behaviours. Finally, the controller class declares that the Step operation should be called periodically, every 2e7 nanoseconds (at a frequency of 50 Hz).

---

[1] http://www.overturetool.org/.

```
class Controller

instance variables
  private measured: real;
  private setpoint: real;
  private err: real;
  private output: real;

operations
  public Step: () ==> ()
  Step() == duration(20) (
    err := setpoint - measured;
    output := P(err);
  );

functions
  P: real -> real
  P(err) == err * Kp

values
  Kp = 2.0

thread
periodic(2E7, 0 , 0 , 0)(Step);

end Controller
```

Figure 3.3 Simple controller class in VDM-RT.

In addition to a collection of classes defining a controller, a model in VDM-RT should contain two special classes that allow FMU generation. The first is the `system` class, which describes the architecture of the controller in terms of its (simulated) compute units, their speed and connections by buses and how the controller is deployed to these units. This architecture helps estimate execution time. The second is the world class, which provides an entry point for simulation by starting threads in the controller, such as the one defined in the class in Fig. 3.3.

5. An example of co-modelling: railway interlocking system

In this section, we describe a case study in co-modelling and co-simulation, undertaken by ClearSy (http://www.clearsy.com) in France.

5.1 Premise

In railway signalling, an *interlocking* is an arrangement of signal apparatus that prevents conflicting movements through an arrangement of tracks such as junctions or

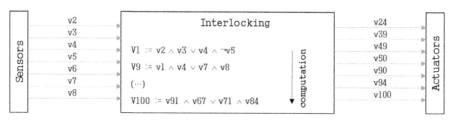

Figure 3.4 Boolean equations lead a signalling system.

crossings. Usually interlocking is in charge of a complete line, computing the status of actuators (switches, signals) based on signalling safety rules that are encoded as so-called 'binary equations'. Overall such a system is in charge of a complete line, where it computes the status of actuators based on signalling safety rules that are encoded as 'Boolean equations' as shown in Fig. 3.4, usually managing 180,000 equations recalculated several times per second. These equations compute the commands to be issued to trackside devices: they encode the safety behaviour that enables trains to move from one position to another through routes that are allocated and then released.

Currently, there are attempts to find the right tradeoff between efficiency of an interlocking system (availability of routes, train delays and system cost) and its safety (collision avoidance, derailment prevention, availability and efficiency of emergency systems). In our case study we will consider an interlocking system that controls part of a tramway, including two platforms and a bidirectional track. It involves 11 track circuits; sensors that detect the absence of a train on a rail track; and three commands that can accept several positions and are activated by the train. Five mechanical switches allow changing direction and must be set in accordance with the route chosen. Three light signals must be red when the train is not allowed on the track, and green when it can pass. The interlocking system also makes use of five mechanical safety relays that externalise the state of a route and allow redundancy between software logic and electronic circuits.

5.2   The challenges of interlocking

A single central interlocking can deal with a complete line, all decisions being made globally. However, the distance between devices distributed along the tracks and the interlocking system may lead to significant delays in updating the status of the devices. Moreover, this architecture, well dimensioned for metro lines, is often overkill for simpler infrastructures like tramway lines. So there is room for a distributed interlocking solution in which a line is divided into overlapping interlocked zones, each controlled by an interlocking system. Such interlockings would be smaller as fewer local devices have to be taken into account and a local decision could be taken more rapidly, resulting in potentially quicker train transfers. However, overlapping zones must be carefully designed (a train cannot appear in a zone without prior notice), and some variable states have to be exchanged between interlocking systems as the Boolean equations have to be distributed over the interlocking systems.

Distribution implies several engineering challenges. An 'optimal distribution' (i.e., the decomposition of the line into overlapping areas such as to minimise delays, availability and costs) requires smart exploration of the design space (decomposition is directly linked with railway signalling rules). It also implies that one has to define what information is to be exchanged between interlocking computers and how many equations have to run on any of them (20,000 equations maximum, for example).

5.3 Accurate train movement simulation and challenges

In order to have a realistic overview of traffic and to deal with safety, train movements along the track map have to be simulated in a realistic way. The greater the fidelity of movement simulation, the more one can ensure that an interlocking system is efficient but safe. Usually, a train receives or considers a Movement Authority Limit (MAL): a stop point that it must never overshoot. Such an MAL is updated in real time by interlocking mechanisms and communication facilities. For an automated train, automatic train operation (ATO) computes the best movement for reaching a stop at the MAL. In parallel, an automatic train protection (ATP) guards against a failure of the 'normal' service mode (e.g., service brakes failure, ATO software/sensor loss of train position). ATP checks that in the worst case, the MAL will never be overshot (see Fig. 3.5). Exploring the behaviour of a 'manual mode' train (with possible rollback movement) and ensuring safe automatic protection are far from being clarified in the rail community. ClearSy has for some years been using the ProB animator (which employs a high-level discrete modelling language with similarities to VDM-RT) on railway use case animations. However, it has not been able to use such DE capabilities to achieve a smart handling of continuous movement, of the maximal assessments of physical

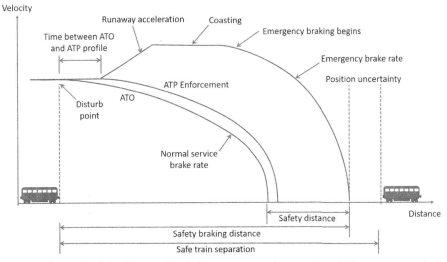

Figure 3.5 Usual safe braking model. *ATO*, automatic train operation; *ATP*, automatic train protection.

parameters, or of the CT problems such as differential equations, Zeno paradox or controlling precision results.

There is thus a strong case for treating the model-based design of interlocking systems as a cyber-physical problem leveraging the benefits of faithful modelling of both computational control and physical train performance. Co-simulating an efficient interlocking system with train movement would enable the enhancement of train performance with respect to delay or availability whilst maintaining safety. In order to gain higher confidence about the safety of the case study, the co-simulation conducted must be accompanied with other techniques such as MC.

5.4 Collaborative model-based design of distributed interlocking

Fig. 3.5 shows an interlocking system. Centralised control would imply a powerful programmable logic controller (PLC) for the many equations and kilometres of wires to connect sensors and actuators to the PLC. A distributed approach might help to reduce the global length of the connections and therefore the cost and the risk of failure. Fig. 3.6 shows a possible division into five zones (ZQ2, ZQ3, ZP, ZV1 and ZV2), each ruled by an interlocking module. Such modules would require less computational power than a global interlocking as fewer local devices have to be handled; local decisions that only involve local devices could be taken more rapidly and potentially yield faster train transfers.

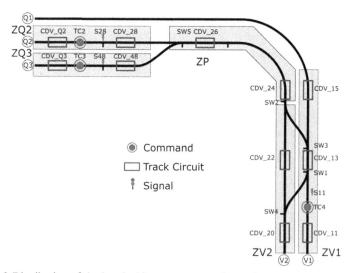

Figure 3.6 Distribution of the interlocking system over the track map.

The distribution has to be carefully designed so that each module can ensure the required local safety properties, and communications have to be introduced so that the global safety properties of the initial interlocking system can be preserved.

5.5 Multidisciplinary co-modelling

5.5.1 Architecture of the co-model

There are many approaches to co-modelling and the choice of which to use depends on the expertise of the organisation(s) involved in the modelling and the perceived challenges of the project. Here we assume a scenario with two teams, one experts in DE modelling, the other with skills in CT modelling and both sharing the goal of constructing a competent model of an existing rail system. In this case the engineers begin by constructing an architecture of the co-model they intend to produce with the purpose of defining the interfaces each model will eventually provide and expect. Following the INTO-CPS process we begin by outlining an architectural structure (see Fig. 3.7). This is the first step in decomposing the CPS into blocks for modelling and simulation. Here we see that the rail system is composed of two blocks: a CT block containing the physical components of the system such as the train, the track switches and the driver, and a DE block containing the Boolean control equations that form the core of the interlock.

It is not the case that physical phenomena are always modelled in CT and cyber phenomena are only modelled in DE. The choice of modelling environment for a particular aspect should be the one that provides the appropriate abstractions and support. In some previous case studies, for example, regarding high-speed machinery,

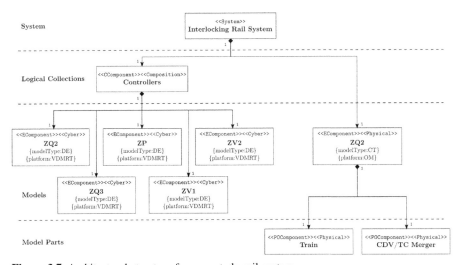

Figure 3.7 Architectural structure for case study rail system.

DE abstractions were found to be most appropriate for describing geometric alignments.

With an overall architecture in place, the development of the CT model of the physical phenomena, the DE model of the interlock controller and the SysML connection diagram (CD) are needed to describe an instance of the co-model.

5.5.2 Continuous-time modelling

Here we present an example in which a CT model of train motion, written with OpenModelica, is co-simulated with DE models of centralised and distributed versions of interlocking, both in VDM-RT. These models have been co-simulated using the INTO-CPS tool chain.

The CT model exists in two flavours. The first version simply models a train following a precalculated route; it can start and stop depending on authorisation signals and can trigger interlocking sensors, command or track circuit. It is decomposed as a driver and an engine; the driver is reading the signal and provides an acceleration (positive or negative), and the engine integrates this acceleration to provide a position, setting the sensors. This version is developed using OpenModelica block representation (Fig. 3.8). This model does not take account of the actual position of the switches and does not simulate derailment.

A more sophisticated CT model reproduces more accurately the behaviour of the train. In this version the driver still reads the signals and provides a set point speed. Then the engine uses its acceleration and braking capability to try to reach the set point speed. The calculation of the position takes account of the track chaining and switch positions. It can detect derailment if a train enters a misconfigured switch from the back. This version of the model is written using equations of OpenModelica.

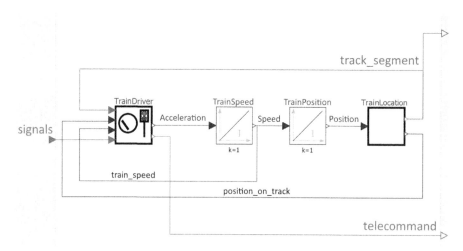

Figure 3.8 Simple continuous-time model of a train.

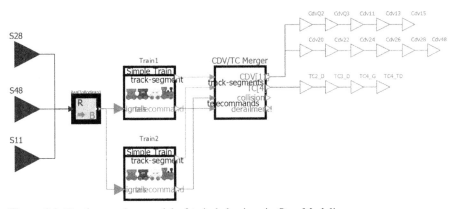

Figure 3.9 Continuous-time model of train behaviour in OpenModelica

Fig. 3.9 shows a closed system in OpenModelica representing two of those full train models and a block called CDV/TC merger that merges track segments and telecommand (remote control) signals coming from the trains and generates CDV and TC signals for the interlocking. A CDV is open (Boolean true) when there is no train on the segment that it protects and closed (Boolean false) when a train is present. Each of the five TC signals is true if one of the train requests the corresponding route.

5.5.3   Discrete-event model of the decentralised controller

The physical components of the interlock CPS have been addressed, and so it remains to model the cyber controller and this is best done in the DE environment. The controller has previously been decomposed into five distributed zonal controllers, and so the challenge for the DE modeller is to model the behaviour of each of those zones. Here the behaviour really means the setting of the track signals in response to routes requested by the trains along with their sensed positions.

Earlier in Fig. 3.5, we saw that the interlock consists of five zones, and those zones could be broken down into two general classes. There are the zones that exist on the periphery of the interlock and are responsible for detecting the approach of trains, obtaining access to the track segments needed by a train and setting the track lights that guard access to the interlock. Zones, ZQ2, ZQ3, ZV1 and ZV2, fall into this category. There is then a special zone, ZP, that is responsible for guarding access to the critical segments of track that are common to many of the routes through the interlock.

The models for each of the controllers follow the structure described earlier in Section 4.3 on VDM-RT. They each contain system and world classes, instantiating the model classes and deploying them to their virtual CPUs, and they also have a hardware interface describing their inputs from and outputs to the physical world. In this model, the hardware interface (Fig. 3.10) includes the inputs and outputs connecting

```
class HardwareInterface

instance variables
-- @ interface: type = output, name="out";
public out : StringPort := new StringPort("");

-- @ interface: type = input, name="iin";
public iin : StringPort := new StringPort("");

-- @ interface: type = output, name="debug";
public debug : StringPort := new StringPort("");

-- @ interface: type = input, name="Cdv11";
public Cdv11: BoolPort := new BoolPort(true);

-- @ interface: type = input, name="Cdv13";
public Cdv13: BoolPort := new BoolPort(true);

-- @ interface: type = input, name="Cdv15";
public Cdv15: BoolPort := new BoolPort(true);

-- @ interface: type = input, name="TC4_G";
public telecommand3 : BoolPort := new BoolPort(false);

-- @ interface: type = input, name="TC4_TD";
public telecommand4 : BoolPort := new BoolPort(false);

-- @ interface: type = output, name="S11";
public signal3: BoolPort := new BoolPort(false);

-- @ interface: type = output, name="SW1";
public switch1 : IntPort := new IntPort(0);

-- @ interface: type = output, name="SW3";
public switch3 : IntPort := new IntPort(0);
values
-- @ interface: type = parameter, name="controllerFrequency";
public static controllerFrequency : RealPort = new RealPort(100);

end HardwareInterface
```

Figure 3.10 The hardware interface model for the ZV1 controller.

the controller to the track elements, such as the track signals, track sensors and train telecommands, but it also includes inputs and outputs from the Ethernet that models the network communications between the distributed zonal controllers.

The control loop of each controller may be then found in its Step method, and this method for zone ZV1 is shown in Fig. 3.11. Here we see that the loop begins by receiving any messages that are incoming from the network and reading the values of any sensors connected to that controller. The loop then acts upon the sensed values by, in this case, setting the trackside lights to red if a train has passed the light. Finally, if the controller receives a telecommand from a train, which requests passage along a route through the interlock, and if the train has not already been granted access to the critical section, then the controller sends a message to the ZP controller to request access.

```
private Step: () ==>()
Step() == cycles(2)
(
  -- synchronise communications and hardware
  dcl incoming: seq of (Messenger`Node * Messenger`Command) := comms.synchronize();
  updateSensors();

  -- close signal as soon as train has passed
  if signal_green and not section3_occupied then update_signal(false);

  -- process external requests
  for all i in set inds incoming do (
    let c = incoming(i) in processMessage(c);
  );

  -- request access to interlock until granted
  if telecommand_request and not signal_green then request_interlock_access();
);
```

Figure 3.11 The step method for the ZV1 zone controller.

```
private Step: () ==>()
Step() == cycles(2)
(
  -- synchronise communications and hardware
  dcl incoming: seq of (Messenger`Node * Messenger`Command) := comms.synchronize();
  updateSensors();

  cases status:
    <free> -> if requests <> [] then (grantAccess(); status := <locked>),
    <locked> -> if interlock_occuppied() then status := <occupied>,
    <occupied> -> if not interlock_occuppied() then status := <free>
  end;

  requests := [];

  for all i in set inds incoming do (
    let c = incoming(i) in processMessage(c);
  );
);
```

Figure 3.12 The step method for the ZP zone controller.

The ZP controller also contains a control loop defined in the periodic Step method (Fig. 3.12). This controller, which acts as the guardian of the critical section, has three states. If it is free and receives a request from a periphery controller, then it grants access to that controller and moves to a locked state preventing further controllers from gaining access. Once it is locked it waits for a train to enter the critical section, at which point it enters the occupied state. While in the occupied state, it waits for the train to leave the critical section at which point it returns to the free state and is ready to grant further access requests from the peripheral controllers.

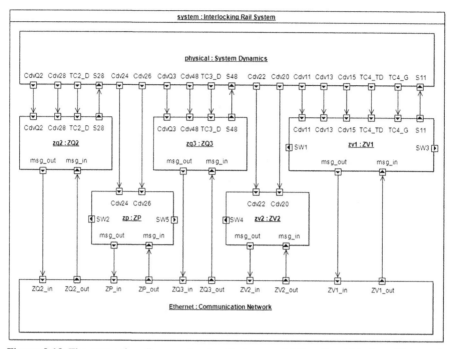

Figure 3.13 The connection diagram showing the two-model Functional Mock-up Units and their port connections.

5.5.4 SysML description of the co-model

With the DE and CT modelling completed, the model behaviours verified individually and the models exported as FMUs, we may then construct the co-model for co-simulation. Here we make use of the INTO-CPS SysML profile to produce a CD where we specify the FMU instances that should exist in the co-model and also the connections between their ports. In this case the CD contains one instance of the CT physical model and one instance of the DE cyber model along with their connections (Fig. 3.13). Since both the centralised and decentralised models use the same FMU interface, their CDs look identical. The CD may then be exported to the INTO-CPS application ready for co-simulation and analysis to take place.

5.6 Running a co-simulation

The INTO-CPS application is used to perform the final configuration of a co-simulation so that it may run. This final configuration can be separated into three parts. In the first (mandatory) part the user describes the duration of the simulation in seconds, optionally adjusting the co-simulation step size. The step size is important as it determines the simulation time that elapses in each FMU between synchronisation events. The second (optional) part describes changes to parameters for each FMU instance, overriding the default values defined when the original model was created.

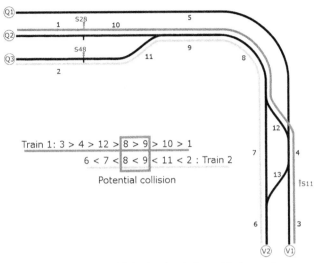

Figure 3.14 The paths of trains 1 and 2 in the simulation with the track segment numbers shown.

Parameters in the rail interlock example include the initial speed of the trains and their maximum speed through the interlock section along with the routes each will take. Varying these allows the user to explore their effects without having to arrange trials over the real interlock system. In the example simulation that follows, train 1 travels from point V1 to Q2 while train 2 travels from Q3 to V2, giving rise to a potential collision on track segments 8 and 9 (Fig. 3.14).

The final (optional) part of the definition indicates what simulation variables are plotted to enable a visual analysis of the results. The user is able to select any variable made available by the FMUs in the co-model and to have them plotted on one or more graphs. In the case of the rail interlock system we are primarily concerned with the safety of the trains passing through, but we could also be interested in confirming that there are no unnecessary delays.

With the configuration completed, running a simulation produces results that allow stakeholders to examine overall system behaviour. These results could represent the physical properties of the system from the CT simulator, the cyber properties of the system from the DE environment or results that represent system-wide properties. In the case of the interlock the user might want to consider the speed profiles of the trains as they pass through. Fig. 3.15 shows both trains slowing down as they approach the interlock. Train 2 then accelerates once it receives a green signal while train 1 comes to a halt. After some time, when train 2 has cleared the critical section, train 1 accelerates to move through.

The user may also wish to examine outputs from the controllers during the simulation. Fig. 3.16 presents three graphs revealing the signals from the distributed controllers that in turn define if the trackside lights are green or red. Here we see that signal S48 goes green early on, letting train 2 enter the interlock, and then goes red again once

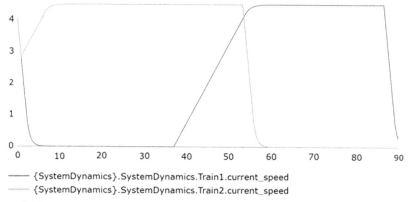

Figure 3.15 The speeds of the two trains as they pass through the interlock.

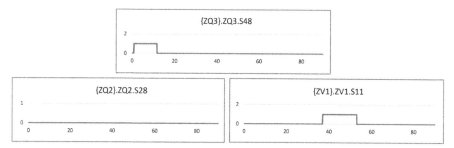

Figure 3.16 The track signal outputs from the controller, a value of 1 equates to a green signal.

it has entered. A little later, when train 2 has left the critical section, signal S11 goes green, letting train 1 accelerate and pass through the interlock.

Finally, the user may want to confirm the system-wide property that no collisions occurred. Fig. 3.17 shows a graph plotting the track segments occupied by each train through the simulation. Here we can see that both trains passed through the interlock from their starting position to their end positions without ever occupying the same track segment at the same time, thus demonstrating the safety property of the interlock in this case.

5.7 Design space exploration

The INTO-CPS tool chain supports automated DSE, where it may autonomously run a campaign of simulations with the goal of optimising or validating a design. These features could be applied to the rail example presented above. DSE may vary one or more of three aspects of the simulations, with different purposes and we will now discuss what that could mean in the context of the rail interlock system described above.

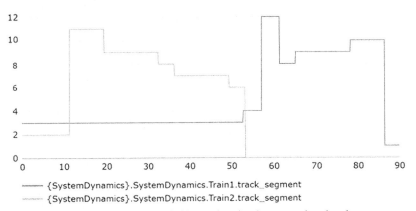

—— {SystemDynamics}.SystemDynamics.Train1.track_segment
—— {SystemDynamics}.SystemDynamics.Train2.track_segment

Figure 3.17 The track segments occupied by each train, demonstrating that they never occupy the same segment.

The first type of DSE involves the sweeping over parameters of the system, where those parameters describe either physical or cyber properties of one or more components. Physical parameters could include the maximum speed of the train at various points on the track or perhaps define the exact position of the signals or sensors. These parameters are not limited to representing physical properties but could just as easily represent properties of the cyber model. Examples of cyber properties in this case could be the frequency at which sensors are read or indeed the clock speed of the processor evaluating those inputs to make decisions, both of which affect the reaction time of the controller.

The second type of DSE is about changing the architecture of the system. By architecture we mean the components in the system and the ports and connectors they use to exchange data. In the case of this rail example the most likely application would be exploring different decompositions of the original centralised controller into two or more distributed controllers. It could also include changes to the components themselves; for example, if there are different types of signals, track sensors or track switches, then we may want to explore the effect of introducing these rather than the original items.

The final type of DSE steps away from what we might consider the design of the system and focusses on the specific conditions posed by the environment around the system under test. We refer to these sets of conditions as scenarios. In the context of the rail example a scenario might include the route each train wants to take, the arrival time of the train or the arrival speed. If the models include fault behaviours, such as the message exchange faults that could be modelled with an Ethernet, the scenario could also describe which faults should be injected into a simulation.

Up till this point we have discussed the different ways the models could be altered to explore the design space, but the closed-loop optimisation algorithms need to be able to compare the results of simulations to function, and so we now introduce the concept of objectives. In this context, an objective is some value we may derive from a simulation result that characterises the behaviour of that simulation in some way.

Examples of numerical objective measures we might produce from the train simulations could be the time for all trains to complete their route or the energy used by the trains during the simulation. Objectives may also be Boolean, and so we could have objectives that report if the model detected a collision or a derailment.

After performing some number of simulations and computing the objective values for each of those simulations, the DSE may then make use of this data to rank the designs in order of preference. One means for ranking designs is to use the Pareto method. In this method, the user specifies two or more of the objectives that they want to 'optimise', where optimisation means to either maximise or minimise the value of an objective. We may then compute a 'nondominated set', which is the set of results where it is not possible to improve the value of one objective without degrading the value of another. The nondominated set then represents the set of best tradeoffs between the objectives that are to be optimised. Fig. 3.18 shows a plot of the results of a simple line following robot where the objectives were to minimise the values of both the lap time and the cross track error for the robot. The nondominated results are shown in blue.

We have already stated that objectives may also return Boolean values, in which case it is not easy to use them directly for ranking. They may, however, be used to filter results. It is clear that in a rail system as described in this example, we would not want to use a design that is known to cause a collision under normal conditions even if it used the least amount of energy, and so the DSE tools may use objective constraints to filter out such results, e.g., collisions detected must equal false.

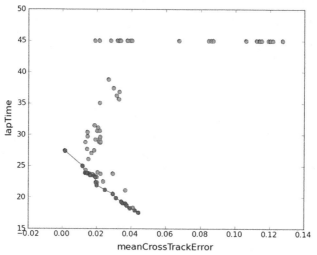

Figure 3.18 Design space exploration results plot comparing lap time and cross track error for a line following robot.

Figure 3.19 A hardware-in-the-loop simulation of the train interlock system, where the controller and Ethernet Functional Mock-up Units are replaced with generated code running on actual hardware. The train dynamics are still represented by the continuous-time model as a simulation.

5.8 Hardware-in-the-loop simulation

As described earlier in Section 4.1, it is possible to perform *HiL* simulations, where selected component that were previously modelled are replaced with suitably instrumented hardware. In the case of the train interlock example, HiL simulations can be performed where the DE controller FMUs, along with the Ethernet FMU, may be replaced with the controller hardware running code generated from DE models. Fig. 3.19 shows an example of such a simulation being performed. Here the code generated from the models is being executed on the target hardware with the outputs controlling that track signals and switches being visualised via coloured lights. The network that was previously represented by Ethernet FMU has been replaced by an actual Ethernet communication board. This hardware interacts with the COE running on computer (not shown) where the CT model of the train dynamics is being simulated. The graphs shown in Section 5.6 are also available when performing HiL simulation, providing the engineer with further evidence supporting claims about the performance of the CPS when components are deployed to the actual hardware.

6. Conclusions and future directions

In this chapter we have argued for a multidisciplinary approach to transportation systems engineering that is CPS based and multidisciplinary, supported by sound, comprehensive and extensible tool chains. We have presented a first such tool chain containing formal foundations that may ultimately deliver static verification; providing coverage from requirements that are traceable to structured co-models and thence to test definitions and results and integrating tools by means of open standards to promote extensibility. We have illustrated the approach on an industry case study undertaken by ClearSy, that has illustrated holistic system-level safety properties that integrate both digital and physical aspects. We have sought to demonstrate some of the potential of co-modelling and co-simulation in DSE and HiL co-simulation.

Our approach has been applied to industry studies in areas as diverse as agricultural robotics, building design and management, automotive advisory systems and manufacturing plant design. These studies lead us to believe that there is considerable opportunity for collaborative modelling and co-simulation in breadth, as well as increasing the depth of analysis that is possible in this framework. However, there is clearly some way to go until we have affordable model-based verification of CPS designs at scale. Key topics for future work include increasing the range of models that may be co-simulated; methods and tools for delivering co-simulations at a wide range of granularities and abstraction levels, provision of traceability over the design artefacts produced in a collaborative approach and combining co-simulation with data analytic and machine learning technologies.

One priority is broadening the range of model types that can be linked into our framework. Agent-based and stochastic models that might be used to approximate human aspects in this process are particularly significant in the transportation domain [10]. We also consider the integration of domain-specific models such as those deployed in building information modelling (BIM), where co-simulation capability would add a dimension of dynamic behaviour to models, as envisaged in the plans for the United Kingdom's 'Digital Built Britain' BIM standard [36].

In application domains such as transportation, where there is a continual interaction between a large-scale infrastructure and individual people and vehicles, co-modelling may be considered at many different scales. Work is required on managing (possibly dynamically) seamless movement between more abstract models of system performance in the large and localised detailed co-modelling of individual cyber-physical interactions.

Models and co-models are often generated during design, but a weakness of model-based design is the risk that models do not accurately reflect the reality of a transportation system as constructed and as used. This can be because the environment or user behaviours after implementation do not match the original design assumptions or because systems as built evolve over time as elements (such as sensor, actuators, software or vehicles) are updated. An important area of future work is to examine how real-time data gathered from instrumented systems and infrastructure can be used alongside data analytics and machine learning technology to tune co-model parameters, bringing the model closer to reality.

Exercises

1. If you would like to experience the technical aspects of co-modelling and co-simulation, download and install INTO-CPS and baseline tools from http://into-cps.github.io/. Use the 'Getting Started' guide to develop your first co-model.

2. Thinking at the overall architectural level (not at the level of individual models in detail), consider how you might update the co-model in our example in Section 5 to describe the throughput of passengers in a section of track. What types of model might we wish to

integrate in order to analyse the performance of the rail network in terms of passenger travel times under varying assumptions about passenger arrival at stations? How might DSE be useful in order to optimise the rail network performance with respect to such metrics?
3. How might you extend the co-model of our example in Section 5 to describe trains that are able to communicate with one another (V2V) in order to maintain safe separation?
4. Consider a multimodal transportation environment with which you are familiar. Thinking about the 'MaaS' concept discussed in Section 2, consider how you would use co-simulation to help decision-making in analysing the effects on power consumption of—say—extending a rail route.

References

[1] M. Givoni, D. Banister, The need for integration in transport policy and practice, in: Integrated Transport: From Policy to Practice, 2010, pp. 1−11.
[2] A.P. Roskilly, R. Palacin, J. Yan, Novel technologies and strategies for clean transport systems, Applied Energy 157 (2015) 563−566.
[3] C. Mulley, Mobility as a Services (MaaS)−does it have critical mass? Transport Reviews 37 (3) (2017) 247−251.
[4] P. Gao, H.W. Kaas, D. Moh, D. Wee, Disruptive Trends that Will Transform the Auto Industry (McKinsey Report), 2016.
[5] M. Kamargianni, M. Matyas, W. Li, Londoners' Attitudes towards Car-ownership and Mobility as a Service: Impact Assessment and Opportunities that Lie Ahead (MaaSLab-UCL Energy Institute Report, prepared for Transport for London. London), 2017.
[6] D.D. Walden, G.J. Roedler, K.J. Forsberg, R.D. Hamelin, T.M. Shortell (Eds.), Systems Engineering Handbook, fourth ed., INCOSE, Wiley, 2015.
[7] D.P.F. Möller, Guide to Computing Fundamentals in Cyber-Physical Systems-Concepts, Design Methods, and Applications, 2016.
[8] A. Platzer, Verification of cyberphysical transportation systems, IEEE Intelligent Systems 24 (4) (2009) 10−13.
[9] T. Schwanen, The bumpy road toward low-energy urban mobility: case studies from two UK cities, Sustainability (Switzerland) 7 (6) (2015) 7086−7111.
[10] M. Reimann, C. Rückriegel, et al., Road2CPS: Priorities and Recommendations for Research and Innovation in Cyber-Physical Systems, Steinbeis-Edition, 2017.
[11] C. Sonntag, Modeling, simulation and optimization environments, in: J. Lunze, F. Lambnabhi-Lagarrigue (Eds.), Handbook of Hybrid Systems Control − Theory, Tools, Applications, 2009, pp. 328−362.
[12] P. Derler, E. Lee, A.S. Vincentelli, Modeling cyber-physical systems, Proceedings of the IEEE 100 (1) (2012) 13−28.
[13] L.P. Carloni, R. Passerone, A. Pinto, A.L. Sangiovanni-Vincentelli, Languages and tools for hybrid systems design, Foundations and Trends in Electronic Design Automation 1 (1) (2006) 1−193.
[14] T. Henzinger, The theory of hybrid automata, in: Proceedings of the Eleventh Annual IEEE Symposium on Logic in Computer Science. New Brunswick, NJ, July 27−30, 1996.
[15] D. Brück, H. Elmqvist, H. Olsson, S.-E. Mattsson, Dymola for multi-engineering modeling and simulation, in: M. Otter (Ed.), Proc. 2nd Intl. Modelica Conference, pp. 55-1−55-8, The Modelica Association, 2002.

[16] B. Zeigler, T. Kim, H. Praehofer, Theory of Modeling and Simulation, Academic Press, 2000.

[17] A. Siemers, P. Fritzson, D. Fritzson, Encapsulation in object-oriented modeling for mechanical systems simulation: comparison of Modelica and BEAST, in: I. Troch, F. Breitenecker (Eds.), Proc. MATHMOD 2009, 2009.

[18] J.S. Fitzgerald, P.G. Larsen, K. Pierce, M. Verhoef, A formal approach to collaborative modelling and Co-simulation for embedded systems, Mathematical Structures in Computer Science 23 (4) (2013) 726−750.

[19] P.G. Larsen, J. Fitzgerald, J. Woodcock, R. Nilsson, C. Gamble, S. Foster, Towards semantically integrated models and tools for cyber-physical systems design, in: T. Margaria, B. Steffen (Eds.), Leveraging Applications of Formal Methods, Verification and Validation: Discussion, Dissemination, Applications, ISoLA 2016. Lecture Notes in Computer Science, vol. 9953, Springer, 2016.

[20] C. Gomes, C. Thule, D. Broman, P.G. Larsen, H. Vangheluwe, Co-Simulation: State of the Art, Technical Report, 2017, http://arxiv.org/abs/1702.00686. (Accessed on 16/04/2018).

[21] J.S. Fitzgerald, P.G. Larsen, M. Verhoef, Collaborative Design for Embedded Systems − Co-Modelling and Co-Simulation, Springer, 2014.

[22] J. van Amerongen, Dynamical systems for creative technology, in: Controllab Products, Enschede, Netherlands, 2010.

[23] S. Perry, J. Holt, R. Payne, J. Bryans, C. Ingram, A. Miyazawa, L.D. Couto, S. Hallerstede, A.K. Malmos, J. Iyoda, M. Cornelio, J. Peleska, Final Report on SoS Architectural Models, Technical Report, COMPASS Deliverable, D22.6, September 2014. Available at: http://www.compass-research.eu/. (Accessed on 16/04/2018).

[24] OMG (Object Modeling Group), OMG System Modeling Language, Version 1.5, 2017. http://www.omg.org/spec/SysML/. (Accessed on 16/04/2018).

[25] N. Amalio, R. Payne, A. Cavalcanti, E. Brosse, Foundations of the SysML Profile for CPS Modelling, 2015. Technical report, INTO-CPS Deliverable, D2.1a. Available from: http://projects.au.dk/into-cps/. (Accessed on 16/04/2018).

[26] E. Clarke, O. Grumberg, D. Peled, Model Checking, The MIT Press, 1999.

[27] A. Pnueli, The temporal logic of programs, in: 18th Symposium on the Foundations of Computer Science, ACM, 1977, pp. 46−57.

[28] J. Fitzgerald, C. Gamble, R. Payne, K. Pierce, Method Guidelines 2, 2016. Technical Report, INTO-CPS Deliverable, D3.2a. Available from: http://projects.au.dk/into-cps/. (Accessed on 16/04/2018).

[29] R. Payne, C. Gamble, K. Pierce, J. Fitzgerald, S. Foster, C. Thule, R. Nilsson, Examples Compendium 2, 2016. Technical Report, INTO-CPS Deliverable, D3.5. Available from: http://projects.au.dk/into-cps/. (Accessed on 16/04/2018).

[30] C.A.R. Hoare, H. Jifeng, Unifying Theories of Programming, Prentice Hall, 1998.

[31] J. Woodcock, A. Cavalcanti, A tutorial introduction to designs in Unifying Theories of Programming, in: E.A. Boiten, J. Derrick, G. Smith (Eds.), Proc 4th Intl. Conf on Integrated Formal Methods, IFM 2004, Canterbury, UK, April 4−7, 2004, Proceedings, Lecture Notes in Computer Science, vol. 2999, Springer, 2004, pp. 40−66.

[32] S. Foster, F. Zeyda, J. Woodcock, Isabelle/UTP: a mechanised theory engineering framework, in: Proc. 5th Intl. Symp. On Unifying Theories of Programming, Lecture Notes in Computer Science, vol. 8963, Springer, 2014, pp. 21−41.

[33] P.G. Larsen, J. Fitzgerald, J. Woodcock, C. Gamble, R. Payne, K. Pierce, Features of Integrated Model-based Co-modelling and Co-simulation Technology, for Cosim-CPS, September 2017 (Trento, Italy).

[34] B. Thiele, T. Beutlich, V. Waurich, M. Sjölund, T. Bellmann, Towards a standard-conform, platform-generic and feature-rich Modelica device drivers library, in: J. Kofránek, F. Casella (Eds.), Proc. 12th International Modelica Conference, Modelica Association and Linköping University Electronic Press, 2017, pp. 713–723.

[35] P. Fritzson, V. Engelson, Modelica – a unified object-oriented language for system modelling and simulation, in: EC-COP '98: Proceedings of the 12th European Conference on Object-Oriented Programming, Lecture Notes in Computer Science, vol. 1445, Springer, 1998, pp. 67–90.

[36] BIM, Digital Built Britain: Level 3 Building Information Modelling – Strategic Plan, H M Government, 2015. Available from: https://www.cdbb.cam.ac.uk. (Accessed on 16/04/2018).

Real-time control systems

4

Yunyi Jia, Longxiang Guo, Xin Wang
Department of Automotive Engineering, Clemson University, Greenville, SC,
United States

1. Introduction

In reviewing the evolution of transport vehicles, innovations are always centred on the safety, power, economy and comfort of vehicles to make them more functional, environment-friendly and 'smart'. The achievement of all these performance relies on a well-designed real-time control system, which is considered as the 'brain' of modern vehicles.

A control system consists of a set of devices that senses, alters or modulates the behaviours or tunable parameters of the controlled plant such that the desirable states of the plant are achieved. In a vehicle, a control system can range from the temperature control of the air conditioner to the stability control of the vehicle motion.

For a traditional vehicle, the driver is the only commander that gives the original orders of accelerating, turning, braking, stopping and parking. Through the communication bus, these orders are sent to the control system as the input signals. At the same time, a series of sensors spreading in the vehicle detects all the important information of the vehicle, including the speed, attitude, engine state and environmental condition, which are also parts of the inputs. Based on all these inputs and the embedded control program, the control system computes and sends the output signal to all the actuators to drive the vehicle according to the driver's order. Typically, the hardware of the control system, namely controller, works in a circular scanning mode. Within one scanning period, it scans all the input ports and sends out the control signal from the output ports. The scanning period is always a few milliseconds and can satisfy the requirements of a real-time control.

With the development of information technology, vehicles are getting smarter with increasing automations with the goal of fully autonomous vehicles on the roadways not in a distant future. By using a variety of techniques, an autonomous vehicle can sense the surrounding environment and navigate itself with limited or without human input. Advanced real-time control systems interpret and analyse sensory information to identify appropriate navigation paths to the desired destination, as well as obstacles and relevant signage, ensuring safe and efficient travel.

Compared with traditional vehicles, an autonomous vehicle encompasses more computational and physical components and is a typical transportation cyber-physical system (TCPS). Therefore, in this book, instead of the control technology of traditional vehicles, we will pay our attention on the real-time control systems of autonomous vehicles.

Transportation Cyber-Physical Systems. https://doi.org/10.1016/B978-0-12-814295-0.00004-6
Copyright © 2018 Elsevier Inc. All rights reserved.

In this chapter, first, the basic concepts of real-time control systems will be introduced and then some examples, including smart traffic lights and autopilots, will be given to illustrate the working principle of a typical real-time control system. Afterwards, we will focus on the basic real-time control technology of an autonomous vehicle. The major content involves the following:

1. The physical components, including the electronic control unit (ECU), sensors and actuators.
2. Functions of the control system and the implementation technology.

The former is mainly about the hardware and the latter is about how to develop the software to realise the whole system.

2. Components in real-time control systems

2.1 Typical real-time control system

A real-time control system is a control system that 'controls an environment by receiving data, processing them, and returning the results sufficiently quickly to affect the environment at that time' [1]. In simulation, the term 'real-time' means that the simulation's clock runs at the same pace as a real clock. In process control, it means 'without significant delay'. In a control system, 'real-time' means the programs run by the controller must be fast enough to generate response within specified time limits, often referred to as 'deadlines'. Such limits or constraints are always in the order of milliseconds or even microseconds. Controlled plants that are critical to the whole system and/or having fast dynamics always require real-time control. For instance, the fly-by-wire system on an aircraft and antilock brakes on a vehicle need real-time control to ensure fast response to avoid catastrophic accidents [2].

For a real-time controller, the hardware scan cycle must be short enough, and the program should be well designed in order that the input scan, program executing and output scan can be completed within a scan cycle. For today's vehicle controller, the scan cycle can be less than 10 ms. Before being used in practical vehicle products, the whole control system must be tested strictly to guarantee the real-time performance.

The following examples can give an outline of how a real-time control system works. They are some typical real-time control systems in different industries, including in the road transportation domain and aviation sector.

2.1.1 Smart traffic light control systems

Smart traffic lights (or intelligent traffic lights) form a real-time traffic control system by combining traditional traffic lights with an intelligent signal control system (Fig. 4.1). The signal control system uses an array of sensors to detect traffic density and adjusts traffic lights via artificial intelligence to increase traffic efficiency and safety [3].

By means of advanced sensors and control technology, the signals of smart traffic lights communicate with both other smart traffic lights and surrounding vehicles to

Figure 4.1 Smart traffic light control systems.

form a real-time control network to manage the traffic in a more efficient way. The major target of this control system is to reduce the amount of time that cars spend idling. It monitors vehicle numbers from different directions through cameras, loop-based detectors and other sensors and makes changes to the schedule of traffic lights in real time to avoid congestion at intersections wherever possible [4]. In some of these systems, lights will change to red to stop the traffic from one direction when a vehicle or cycler is sensed approaching the intersection from another direction without a braking intention to avoid crash. At current stage, some companies, including BMW and Siemens, have developed smart traffic management systems [5]. These systems can warn the automatic start−stop system on many modern vehicles of impending light changes to make them work more intelligently. They will also help those vehicles to schedule upcoming stops according to signal phasing of traffic lights to improve fuel efficiency.

2.1.2   Autopilot systems

An aircraft autopilot (automatic pilot) system controls the aircraft without the pilot directly operating the controls. Such system is developed to reduce the work load of human pilots in order to lessen their fatigue and reduce operation errors during long flights. It handles most of the time-intensive non−decision-making tasks, helping the human pilots to focus on the overall status of the aircraft and flight.

Autopilot systems use computers to generate the control output. The control software reads the aircraft's current speed, pose, height and location and then issues control signal to a flight control system, which is a lower-level actuator controller, to adjust the control surfaces of the aircraft in order to maintain the aircraft's attitude, height and speed while guaranteeing the lateral, vertical and longitudinal stability. One critical ability of the autopilot system is error correction. When the plane fails to follow the desired states, an error occurs. The autopilot system should be able to correct the error and restore the aircraft to the states desired by the flight task automatically. Two basic autopilot structures can realise this. The first is position based and the second is rate based. A position-based autopilot controls the aircraft so that it always follows desired

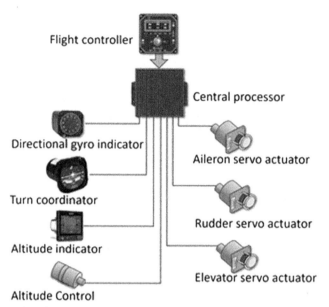

Figure 4.2 An aircraft autopilot system.

position profile. The autopilot system moves the control surfaces so that the aircraft's motion reduces the error between the desired aircraft attitude and recorded actual aircraft attitude. Rate-based autopilots use information about the rate of the aircraft and move control surfaces to counter the speed of change that causes the error [6]. A basic structure of an aircraft autopilot is shown in Fig. 4.2.

2.2 Structure of the real-time control system of autonomous vehicles

The implementation of real-time control for an autonomous vehicle relies on a series of components, and each of these components performs a different role. Some of them act as the 'brain' to coordinate and make decisions and we call them ECUs; some of them are responsible for collecting the external and internal information and we call them sensors; some of them are responsible for executing commands from ECUs and we call them actuators; some of them play as information-transmitting channels and we call them communication bus. Fig. 4.3 shows the functions and the interrelationship of these components.

2.3 Electronic control units

Electric Control Unit (ECU) refers to dedicated vehicular embedded microcontrollers that controls one or more of the electrical systems or subsystems in a vehicle. Types of ECU include central control module, engine control module, powertrain control module, transmission control module, electronic brake control module, speed control unit,

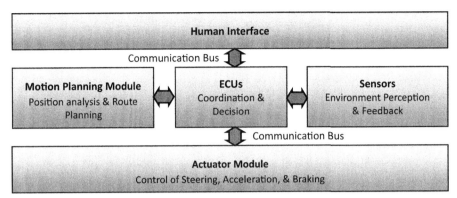

Figure 4.3 Components in real-time control system for an autonomous vehicle. *ECUs*, electronic control units.

body control module, suspension control module, human—machine interface, telematic control unit, brake control module (including Anti-lock Braking System (ABS) and Electronic Stability Control (ESC)), battery management system, door control unit and seat control unit. Some modern motor vehicles have up to 80 ECUs [7].

For an autonomous vehicle, the above ECU functions are mostly unchanged, especially in hardware. However, to realise the autonomous driving, new applications must be added into the real-time control system. As a result, the complexity of the embedded software in ECUs will increase significantly, for many decisions should be made by ECUs independently instead of human drivers. In Section 3, the control functions related to autonomous driving will be introduced in detail.

2.4   Sensors in autonomous vehicles

In order to travel on the roadway safely and obey traffic laws, autonomous vehicles rely on a series of sensors that help the vehicles 'see' and understand the environment where they are travelling. The environment can be digitally mapped out by using a combination of ultrasonic, radio detection and ranging (RADAR), camera, light detection and ranging (LiDAR) sensors, etc., each of which performs one or more unique functions.

So, what sensors do autonomous vehicles require? In this section, we will give a profile of some basic sensors for autonomous vehicles. These sensors include (1) ultrasonic sensors, (2) RADAR sensors, (3) LiDAR sensors, (4) cameras, (5) speed sensors, (6) global positioning system (GPS), (7) acceleration sensors and (8) inertial measurement unit (IMU) (Fig. 4.4).

2.4.1   Ultrasonic sensors

An ultrasonic sensor is a device that can measure the distance by using ultrasonic waves. It works by sending out an ultrasonic wave at a specific frequency and receiving the wave reflected back from the target, as shown in Fig. 4.5. By recording

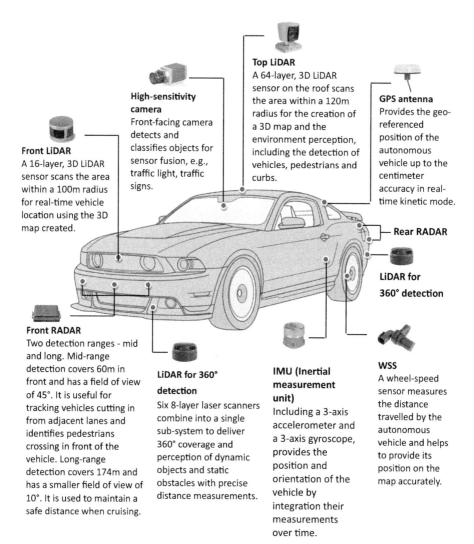

Front LiDAR
A 16-layer, 3D LiDAR sensor scans the area within a 100m radius for real-time vehicle location using the 3D map created.

High-sensitivity camera
Front-facing camera detects and classifies objects for sensor fusion, e.g., traffic light, traffic signs.

Top LiDAR
A 64-layer, 3D LiDAR sensor on the roof scans the area within a 120m radius for the creation of a 3D map and the environment perception, including the detection of vehicles, pedestrians and curbs.

GPS antenna
Provides the geo-referenced position of the autonomous vehicle up to the centimeter accuracy in real-time kinetic mode.

Rear RADAR

LiDAR for 360° detection

Front RADAR
Two detection ranges - mid and long. Mid-range detection covers 60m in front and has a field of view of 45°. It is useful for tracking vehicles cutting in from adjacent lanes and identifies pedestrians crossing in front of the vehicle. Long-range detection covers 174m and has a smaller field of view of 10°. It is used to maintain a safe distance when cruising.

LiDAR for 360° detection
Six 8-layer laser scanners combine into a single sub-system to deliver 360° coverage and perception of dynamic objects and static obstacles with precise distance measurements.

IMU (Inertial measurement unit)
Including a 3-axis accelerometer and a 3-axis gyroscope, provides the position and orientation of the vehicle by integration their measurements over time.

WSS
A wheel-speed sensor measures the distance travelled by the autonomous vehicle and helps to provide its position on the map accurately.

Figure 4.4 Sensors in an autonomous vehicle.

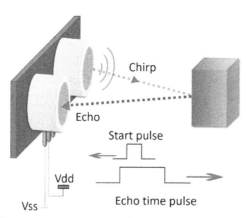

Figure 4.5 Ultrasonic sensor.

the time between the emission and reception, we can obtain the distance between the sensor and the object using the following formula:

$$D = \frac{C_s t}{2} \tag{4.1}$$

where D is the distance, t is the travel time between the emission and reception and C_s is the sonic speed, as we know that sound travels through air at about 344 m/s.

The accuracy of ultrasonic sensors is affected by the temperature and humidity of the air. Some objects might not be detected by ultrasonic sensors because they are shaped or positioned in a way that the sound wave bounces off the object or the object is too small to reflect enough of the sound wave back to the sensor. Other objects, such as cloth, can absorb the sound wave, which means there is no way for the sensor to detect them accurately. These are important factors to consider when using an ultrasonic sensor [8].

The most common applications for ultrasonic distance sensors in vehicles are kerb alert and parking assistance systems.

2.4.2 Radio detection and ranging sensors

RADAR sensors can detect the distances of objects at a very wide range, as well as the speeds they are moving.

2.4.2.1 Distance detection by radio detection and ranging sensor

RADAR utilises the same 'time of flight' rule to detect distances as ultrasonic sensors do, as shown in Fig. 4.6, except for the fact that RADAR uses radio waves

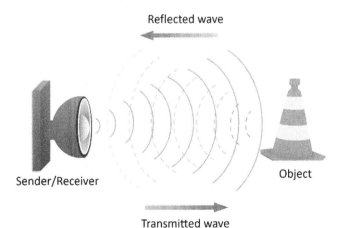

Reflected wave

Sender/Receiver

Object

Transmitted wave

Figure 4.6 Detection by radio detection and ranging sensors.

instead of sonic waves. The distance between the sensor and the object can be calculated by

$$D = \frac{C_R t}{2} \tag{4.2}$$

where D is the distance, t is the time between the emission and reception and C_R is the radio wave travelling speed, approximately 3.00×10^8 m/s.

2.4.2.2 Speed detection by radio detection and ranging sensor

Doppler effect is used to measure speed in RADAR sensors. When the fixed-frequency radio wave sent from the sender continuously strikes an object that is moving towards or away from the sender, the frequency of the reflected radio wave will be changed. This frequency shift is known as Doppler effect, as shown in Fig. 4.7. The presence and the speed of the moving object can be obtained from the difference in frequency between the transmitted and the reflected radio waves [9].

In Doppler effect, the relationship between the received frequency f and the transmitted frequency f_0 is given by

$$f = \left(\frac{c + v_T}{c + v_s}\right) f_0 = \left(1 + \frac{v_T - v_s}{c + v_s}\right) f_0 \tag{4.3}$$

where c is the velocity of radio waves in the medium, v_T is the velocity of the receiver with respect to the medium and v_s is the velocity of the source with respect to the medium. If the speeds, v_T and v_s, are small compared to the speed of the wave c, the relationship between f and f_0 can be approximated by

$$\Delta f = f - f_0 \approx \left(\frac{\Delta v}{c}\right) f_0 \tag{4.4}$$

where $\Delta v = v_T - v_s$. Thus we can acquire the relative speed Δv by the detection of the frequency shift Δf.

2.4.2.3 Different uses of radio detection and ranging sensor in autonomous vehicles

For autonomous driving applications, RADAR sensors can be used for adaptive cruise control (ACC), collision avoidance, etc. Generally, they warn the driver if an imminent

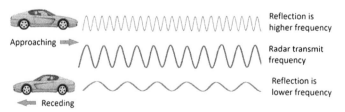

Figure 4.7 Doppler effect.

Table 4.1 **The Different Applications for Radio Detection and Ranging Sensors in Autonomous Vehicles**

Application	Detection Range	Field of View	Technology
Adaptive cruise control (ACC)	150 ~ 200 m	±10 ~ 20 degrees	Single beam, 24 GHz
Forward collision warning and precrash detection	40 ~ 90 m	±35 ~ 45 degrees	Single beam, 76 GHz/24 GHz
Blind spot detection, lane change assist and cross-traffic detection	30 ~ 40 m	±40 ~ 50 degrees	Single beam, 76 GHz/24 GHz
ACC with stop and go	Multiple ranges	Multiple ranges	Multimode electronically scan

collision is detected. If the driver fails to intervene within the stipulated time, the RADAR's input may even engage advanced steering and braking controls to prevent the crash. The high-precision and weather-agnostic capabilities of RADARs make them a permanent fit for any autonomous vehicle, notwithstanding the ambient conditions [10].

Both short- and long-range automotive-grade RADARs are used for autonomous driving applications. Short-range RADARs 'sense' the environment in the vicinity of a car (~ 30 m) especially at low speeds, whereas long-range RADARs cover relatively long distances (~ 200 m) usually at high speeds. Table 4.1 presents the different applications for RADAR sensors in autonomous vehicles.

2.4.3 Light detection and ranging sensors

LiDAR sensor is one of the most important devices in the autonomous vehicles. It can be mounted on the roof, where the corners or the front and rear bumpers of the autonomous vehicle send invisible laser pulses and ascertain their return time to create a 3D profile around the car. LiDAR can scan over 100 m in all directions and generate a comprehensive and precise 3D map of the immediate world around it, as shown in Fig. 4.8 (right). The vehicle can then use the map to navigate and avoid objects. Autonomous cars earn a distinct advantage over conventional vehicles in terms of situation awareness from this type of technology.

LiDAR consists of an emitter (laser source), mirror, rotating housing and receiver, as shown in Fig. 4.8 (left). The emitter shoots out a laser beam that is reflected by a tilting mirror. The mirror along with the housing is rotating, and the rotary encoder records the angular position of current laser beam. After reflected by objects, the laser beam returns to the tilting mirror and is reflected back to the receiver. The distance can be calculated from travel time of the beam, and the position of the object in 2D space can be obtained together with the angular position [11].

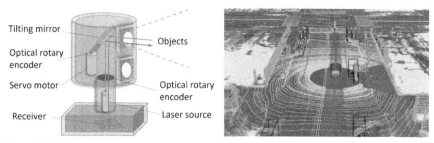

Figure 4.8 Light detection and ranging (left) and laser point map generated by it (right).

2.4.4 Cameras

Cameras convert light to electrical signals which allows autonomous vehicles to perceive its surroundings just like humans do. One unique advantage of cameras is their ability of processing colours, which is very efficient at the classification of textures and makes up for the vacancy other sensors left during interpreting surrounding scenery. Another advantage of cameras is their much better availability and lower price compared to RADAR or LiDAR, which makes them one of the most popular types of sensors being used in autonomous vehicles and one of the top choices for vehicle manufacturers.

There are downsides as well. The powerful processors of some high-definition cameras should be capable of processing millions of pixels for every frame, and some cameras are able to shoot 30−60 frames per second. This requires a very powerful computing platform to ensure the real-time attribute of the control system. Normally, one or more powerful graphics processing units (GPUs) are required and the price can be very costly [12].

2.4.5 Speed sensors

Speed sensors are used in automobiles to determine the speed of wheels, based on which the vehicle speed can be easily calculated, and the speed of other mechanical components. They are usually mounted on the wheels to measure their rotating speed and direction, as shown in Fig. 4.9. These sensors generate input for a variety of

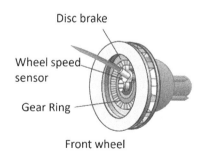

Figure 4.9 Wheel speed sensors.

different automotive control applications such as ACC, antilock brake system and electronic stability control, etc.

Three common wheel speed sensors include the inductive sensors, Hall effect sensors and optical sensors.

2.4.5.1 Inductive sensors

As illustrated in Fig. 4.10 (upper left), a common inductive sensor consists of a permanent magnet on the top of a pole pin which is wrapped by an inductive coil. This assembly is mounted at a short fixed distance from a ferromagnetic rotor teeth along its radical direction. When the rotor rotates, the air gap between the rotor and the pole pin changes, thus changing the magnetic flux in the coil. The flux change generates a voltage pulse across the coil. The vehicle's control module counts the number of voltage pulses within a specific period of time and computes the wheel speed [13].

2.4.5.2 Hall effect sensors

Fig. 4.10 (lower left) shows a typical build of a Hall effect sensor. A permanent magnet is mounted on the top of a Hall effect device. Unlike inductive sensors, the output signal from a Hall effect sensor is not generated by the rate of change of the magnetic field. The Hall effect device is fed with a bias current that is perpendicular to the direction of the magnetic field, and the magnetic field intensity will generate a Hall voltage on the direction that is perpendicular to the directions of both the current and the magnetic field. When the rotor rotates, the air gap between the rotor and the magnet changes, thus changing the Hall voltage and the magnetic field intensity passing through the Hall effect device. The value of Hall voltage is typically in the range of millivolts (mV) and is amplified by integrated electronics. The final output voltage is usually shaped into square waves with amplitude ± 5 V or 12 V. This amplitude remains constant while the frequency of the square wave signal increases proportionally with rpm. Unlike inductive sensors that generate voltage signals by themselves, Hall effect sensors need external voltage supply for integrated electronics [14].

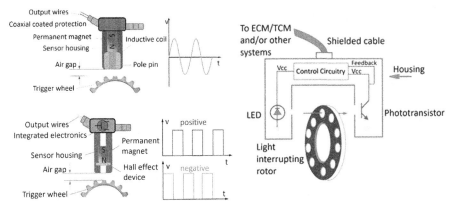

Figure 4.10 Inductive sensor (upper left), Hall effect sensor (lower left) and optical sensor (right). *ECM*, engine control module; *TCM*, transmission control module.

2.4.5.3 Optical sensors

As shown in Fig. 4.10 (right), optical sensors are another type of sensor that generates square wave signals at a frequency in proportion to the rotor's rotation speed. Instead of using a magnet, an optical sensor uses a light interrupting rotor, an LED and a phototransistor. The phototransistor generates a current when either the reflected light or the passed through lights transmitted by the LED is received. When the rotor has bright and dark marks, the phototransistor will be on the same side as the LED and receive the light reflected by the bright marks. When the rotor has a series of slits that allows light passing through, the phototransistor will be on the opposite side of the LED [14].

2.4.6   Global positioning system

The GPS is a global navigation satellite system that provides location and time information to a GPS receiver that is in the line of sight to at least four satellites. It can be applied to air, sea and land transportation. The satellite system of GPS consists of 6 earth-centred orbital planes, each with 4 satellites, i.e., 24 satellites in total. GPS works at almost all time under almost all kinds of weather [15].

2.4.6.1   Basic application of global positioning system in autonomous vehicles

As the most important subsystem of autonomous vehicles, navigation and guidance subsystem must always be active and checking the vehicle location versus the goal. For example, if the 'optimum' route planned originally has any unexpected diversions, the path must be recomputed in real time to avoid going in a wrong direction.

The primary technique used for navigation and guidance is based on the GPS system. GPS receivers are now available as sophisticated system on a chip IC or multi-chip chipsets which require only power and antenna and include an embedded, application-specific computer engine to perform the intensive calculations. The present position of the vehicle is computed based on complex analysis of signals received from at least 4 of the constellations of over 60 low-orbit satellites [16].

Another interesting application of GPS is to measure the vehicle speed. Using GPS signals, the exact location of the vehicle can be determined. Combining with the time information, the speed of the vehicle can be precisely calculated.

2.4.6.2   Real time kinematic global positioning system

RTK (real time kinematic) satellite navigation is a technique used to enhance the precision of position data obtained from standard GPS systems.

The accuracy of the GPS may be affected by many contributing factors like clock difference between satellites, refraction of electromagnetic waves in ionosphere, random noise added to clock in commercialised GPS signal, not enough satellites (less than 8 ~ 9), and signal bounced off buildings or canyons. A good way to correct these variable errors is to set up a fixed GPS receiver as a base station whose position can be measured. The computing unit of this base station can calculate its position from satellite data and compare it with its actual position. The resulting error information can be shared with another moving GPS receiver, called rover, in the vehicle; then the rover GPS can correct its localisation result based on the

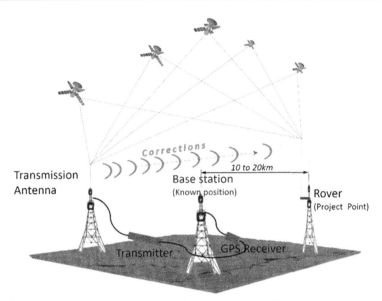

Figure 4.11 Real time kinematic global positioning system (GPS).

correction information sent by the station. This is the basic principle of RTK GPS. Fig. 4.11 shows the working process of RTK GPS.

2.4.7 Acceleration sensors

Acceleration sensors are devices that measure acceleration caused by speed changes, vibration, collision, etc. In autonomous vehicles, acceleration sensors are always applied in collision detection, antilock braking systems, traction control systems, etc. There are different types of acceleration sensors which are based on different physical principles, typically including piezoelectric, piezoresistive, variable capacitance and variable reluctance acceleration sensor.

2.4.7.1 Basic acceleration sensor

The basic physical principle behind the acceleration sensor (accelerometer) is the same as a simple mass spring system, as shown in Fig. 4.12 (left). According to Hooke's law, the restoring force of a spring is proportional to the amount of distance it has been stretched or compressed from the equilibrium point. The equation of such relationship is $F = kx$, where k is the elastic constant of the spring, k is the displacement and F is the force. If we ignore the friction between the mass block and the base (which is reasonable with microelectromechanical systems technology), then by Newton's law, the force from the spring is equal to the resultant force of mass m, which can be written as $F = kx = ma$, where a is the acceleration of mass m. Hence if we observe a displacement of x and we know the mass m, the acceleration can be calculated by $a = kx/m$ [17].

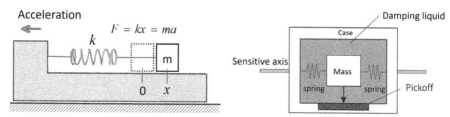

Figure 4.12 Mass−spring system used for measuring acceleration (left) and displacement-type acceleration sensor (right).

2.4.7.2 Piezoelectric acceleration sensor

A piezoelectric acceleration sensor utilises the piezoelectric effect of certain materials to measure acceleration, vibration and mechanical shock.

Piezoelectric material converts mechanical energy into electrical energy and generates an electrical signal in proportion to the applied force. Piezoelectric acceleration sensor consists of a mass attached to a piezoelectric crystal which is mounted on an isolating base inside the case, as shown in Fig. 4.13 (left). When the sensor body is subjected to acceleration along vertical direction, the mass on the crystal accelerates and the resultant force is provided by the piezoelectric crystal (ignoring gravity). This force is proportional to the acceleration according to Newton's second law, $F = ma$, and generates a voltage in the crystal. The final output is then converted into low-impedance voltage with the help of extra electronics. Fig. 4.13 (left) shows the principle of a piezoelectric acceleration sensor [18].

2.4.8 Inertial measurement unit

An IMU is an electronic device that measures and reports the object's linear acceleration, angular angles (roll, pitch and yaw angles) and angular rates, using a combination of accelerometers, magnetometers and gyroscopes.

As illustrated in Fig. 4.13 (right), the IMU consists of a platform fixed to the vehicle, and this platform has three gyroscopes and three accelerometers, one pair

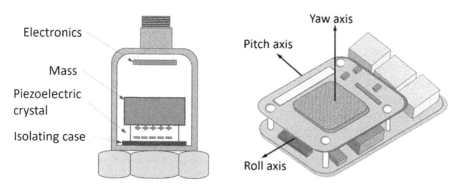

Figure 4.13 Piezoelectric acceleration sensor (left) and inertial measurement unit (right).

oriented each for the orthogonal X, Y and Z axes. These sensors provide data on the rotational and linear motion of the platform, which is then used to calculate the motion and position of the vehicle regardless of speed or any sort of signal obstruction [16].

2.5 Actuators

For any control system, the actuators are the terminal components which are responsible for moving or controlling the system. In modern vehicles, there are various actuators like motors, valves and hydraulic cylinders. These actuators act as 'movers' to execute the steering, gear changing, braking, etc. Because these actuators are universal, i.e., there are no special applications for them in autonomous vehicles; the detail will not be discussed in this book.

3. Real-time control systems in autonomous vehicles

Generally, there are three different modules in a real-time control system for autonomous vehicles, namely the perception module, mission planning module and motion plan and control module (Fig. 4.14). The perception module collects and transforms sensory information into meaningful information and passes it to navigation and behaviour reasoning module and motion plan and control module. The navigation and behaviour reasoning finds the best path from the start to the destination based on map and task information and issues the most appropriate manoeuvre based on perception information. The motion plan and control module executes the issued behaviour based on the perception information.

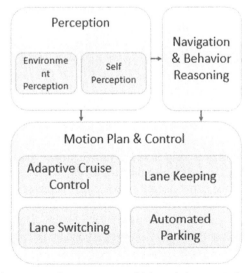

Figure 4.14 General structure of autonomous vehicle real-time control system.

3.1 Perception

The perception system is responsible for converting the sensory information into meaningful information that describes the conditions of the environment and the ego vehicle. It includes the perception of the environment and the perception of the vehicle itself.

3.1.1 Obstacle detection and tracking

Typical obstacles in autonomous driving scenario include moving obstacles, for example, pedestrians and moving vehicles, whose information is not included in any existing map, and static obstacles, for instance, kerbs, bushes and parked vehicles, whose information is included or partially included in an existing map. To avoid collision with these obstacles during driving, the autonomous vehicles need to first detect them, then map the static obstacles and finally track the motion and predict the motion of the moving obstacles in a short future in real time. The detection and tracking of these obstacles are achieved based on the sensory information from vision sensors, LiDARs and RADARs.

3.1.1.1 Feature extraction

The first step here is extracting the useful features from the raw sensory data. Commonly used features include the channels of different colour spaces, for example, RGB (red, green, blue), HSV (hue, saturation, value) and HSL (hue, saturation, lightness) spaces from the camera, the disparity map from the stereo camera, the distance map from the LiDARs and RADARs and the speed map from RADARs. Some higher-level features can be generated from these basic features. For instance, colour histograms can be generated from the RGB space of an image captured by a camera; binary colour maps can be generated from the original colour map by adding threshold to it; depth map can be calculated from the disparity map; histogram of orientated gradients can be generated from a colour map or a depth map. The features will be combined into a final map that has a large depth. This map will help the classifier to categorise the types of the obstacles.

3.1.1.2 Obstacle detection

With the feature map ready, the next task is to find the interested obstacles from the feature map. A straightforward method is using a scanning window to search over the whole feature map and evaluate the scanning window at each step with the classifier to see if there is interested obstacle within the window. To achieve better searching result, the window needs to search over the map multiple times with different size, and they should be overlapped between each search step. That results in a large amount of ROI (region of interest) windows to be classified and reduces the computational efficiency. One way to reduce the computational load is to predict the possible region in the map where an interested obstacle may appear. For example, the sky never needs to be scanned for finding pedestrians and vehicles.

The ROI will be fed into a classifier to determine whether it contains an interested obstacle. Commonly used classifier includes support vector machines [19], Gaussian mixture models (GMM) [20], decision trees [21] and neural networks (NNs) [22] (especially convolutional neural networks (CNNs)). These classifiers are machine learning algorithms that map the input feature to different categories. They need to be trained manually before being used to classify obstacles. In the training process, people need to collect sensory data during driving and manually label the ROIs in the feature map. The classifiers will learn the unique characteristics of different types of obstacles from the training data via machine learning methods. The training of a classifier usually requires very long time data collection and laborious labelling procedure.

3.1.1.3 Moving obstacle tracking

Because of the dynamic and noise in the environment, the detection of the moving obstacles can be unstable and even discontinuous sometimes. Tracking of moving obstacle is needed to stabilise, smoothen and improve the accuracy of the detection of the obstacles so that their motion can be predicted within a short future and the motion control of the ego vehicle can be improved. Two commonly used tracking methods are Kalman filter and particle filter (PF) [23,24].

Kalman filter [25] is a recursive estimator, and it predicts the states at next time step based on the estimated states from the previous time step and the measurement from the current time step. Kalman filter is good at dealing with linear system and Gaussian errors. With a discrete time state space model:

$$x_k = Ax_{k-1} + Bu_k + w_k$$
$$z_k = Hx_k + v_k$$

(4.5)

where x_k is system state(s) at time step k, u_k is system input(s), z_k is system measurement(s), A is system process matrix, B is system input matrix, H is system output matrix, w_k is Gaussian process noise obeying normal distribution $N(0,Q)$, with Q being the variance and v_k is Gaussian measurement noise obeying normal distribution $N(0,R)$, with R being the variance. The process of Kalman filter contains two steps, namely the prediction step:

$$\text{Predicted error covariance } \bar{x}_k = Ax_{k-1} + Bu_k$$
$$\text{Predicted state estimate } \bar{P}_k = Ax_{k-1}A^T + Q$$

(4.6)

and the correction step:

$$\text{Kalman gain } K = \bar{P}_k H^T \left(H\bar{P}_k H^T + R\right)^{-1}$$
$$\text{Update state estimate } \hat{x}_k = \bar{x}_k + K(z_k - H\bar{x}_k)$$
$$\text{Update error coverance } P_k = (I - KH)\bar{P}_k$$

(4.7)

In autonomous driving, the motion model for a vehicle is usually a bicycle model with a fixed shape, as shown in Fig. 4.15A, and the model for a pedestrian is usually a point mass model, as shown in Fig. 4.15B. While the motion models are linear, the observation models may be nonlinear, and the measurement noise does not follow

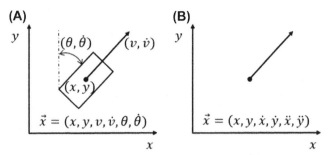

Figure 4.15 Bicycle model for vehicle (A) and point model for pedestrian (B) [31].

Gaussian distribution. To deal with nonlinearity in the state-transition model or the observation model, as shown in Eq. (4.8), extended Kalman filters (EKF) [26] are adopted. v_k is Gaussian observation noise with covariance R_k and w_k is Gaussian process noise with covariance Q_k. f is nonlinear process function and h is nonlinear measurement function.

$$x_t = f(x_{k-1}, u_k) + w_k$$
$$z_k = h(x_k) + v_k \tag{4.8}$$

The process of EKF can be similarly divided into two steps, namely the prediction step:

$$\text{Predicted state estimate } \widehat{x}_{k|k-1} = f\left(\widehat{x}_{k|k-1}, u_k\right)$$
$$\text{Predicted error coveriance } P_{k|k-1} = F_k P_{k-1|k-1} F_k^T + Q_k \tag{4.9}$$

and the correction step:

$$\text{Kalman gain } K_k = P_{k|k-1} H_k^T \left(H_k P_{k|k-1} H_k^T + R_k\right)^{-1}$$
$$\text{Update state estimate } \widehat{x}_{k|k} = \widehat{x}_{k|k-1} + K_k \left(z_k - h\left(\widehat{x}_{k|k-1}\right)\right) \tag{4.10}$$
$$\text{Update error coveriance } P_{k|k} = P_{k|k-1} - K_k H_k P_{k|k-1}$$

where the state transition and observation matrices are expressed by following Jacobians:

$$F_k = \left.\frac{\partial f}{\partial x}\right|_{\widehat{x}_{k-1|k-1}, u_k}$$
$$H_k = \left.\frac{\partial h}{\partial x}\right|_{\widehat{x}_{k|k-1}} \tag{4.11}$$

EKF can only deal with moderate nonlinearity in the system. If the measurement process or the obstacle's motion contains highly nonlinear components or if the noise is not a linear combination of Gaussian components, the effect of EKF can be poor. To deal with this, PF [27] is adopted. PF is a technique for implementing recursive Bayesian filter by Monte Carlo sampling. It represents the posterior density by particles with associated weights and computes estimates based on the samples and wrights. The process of PF is:

Particle generation $x_k^{(m)} \sim p(x_k|x_{k-1})$

Weight computation $w_k^{*(m)} = w_{k-1}^{*(m)} p\left(z_k \Big| x_k^{(m)}\right)$

Weight normalization $w_k^{(m)} = \dfrac{w_k^{*(m)}}{\sum_{m=1}^{M} w_k^{*(m)}}$ (4.12)

Estimation computation $E(g(x_k|z_{1:k})) = \sum_{m=1}^{M} g\left(x_k^{(m)}\right) w_k^{(m)}$

where m is the index of a particle and M is the quantity of particles. $g(x)$ is the system process model.

3.1.2 Localisation

The localisation for autonomous vehicles includes tasks at three different levels: road-level localisation, lane-level localisation and feature-level localisation. The road-level localisation provides the rough estimation of the vehicle position in an existing road map. This level of localisation can be achieved by utilising the position information provided by a GPS system. However, the refreshing rate of civil-level GPS devices (normally lower than 1 Hz) and the accuracy (~ 3 m) are not sufficient for autonomous driving. To achieve lane-level localisation, sensory information from IMUs and wheel speed sensors needs to be fused together with the raw position information to provide higher-positioning refreshing rate (>20 Hz) and accuracy (<0.5 m). Combining this fused position information with an existing road lane map, the vehicle's current lane selection on a road can be identified. The vehicle's position in a lane or in an unstructured environment can be found through feature-level localisation. This level of localisation requires more information from the static obstacle detection and mapping module. Features, for instance, the position of lane markers and kerbs, are further fused with the localisation data to provide more accurate localisation result.

The data fusion in lane- and feature-level localisation is usually done with a Bayesian filter [28]. A typical type of Bayesian filter is PF, as described before.

3.1.3 Vehicle state estimation

Some of the vehicle states cannot be obtained from the sensors directly, or the sensors required to measure certain states are too expensive, and thus the estimation for these states is needed. For instance, in vehicle lateral control, tyre forces and vehicle side-slip are parameters that are critical but difficult to be measured directly. Under this case, a nonlinear model that describes the behaviour of the vehicle states needs to be introduced, and estimation methods, for example, an EKF observer or a sliding mode observer, can be designed based on the structure and the nonlinearity of the model.

3.2 Mission planning

Mission planning module is the higher-level decision-making module in autonomous vehicle control. It takes the information from the perception module and issues the target vehicle poses to the motion planning and control module. Mission planning module has two major parts, the first is path planning and the second is behavioural reasoning.

3.2.1 Path planning

The path planning module finds the optimal route from the vehicle's current location to the requested mission destination using the road network which will be represented as a directed graph with edge weights corresponding to the cost of traversing a road segment. The cost of a road segment varies accordingly to the mission, for example, passenger or cargo delivery. The path planning task can be formulated as finding the optimal path with the least cost on the road network graph. Two commonly used graph search algorithms are Dijkstra's algorithm [29] and A* algorithm [30].

Dijkstra's algorithm is a greedy algorithm that selects the road node from the candidate nodes that has a path with the minimum cost from the starting node. The disadvantage of Dijkstra's algorithm is that it visits too many nodes that are obviously not the best.

A better solution is A* algorithm. The improvement of A* algorithm compared to Dijkstra's algorithm is that an additional term that represents the estimated cost from the next node to the destination node to the cost function $f(n)$ being evaluated at each step:

$$f(n) = g(n) + h(n)$$

$- g(n)$: Actual cost from the starting node to reach the n_{th} node.

$- h(n)$: Estimate of the cost of the cheapest path from the n_{th}

       node to the goal node.

(4.13)

As long as $h(n)$ does not overestimate the actual cost, A* algorithm can always find the optimal path while reducing the computational load compared to Dijkstra's algorithm.

3.2.2 Behavioural reasoning

The behavioural reasoning is responsible for rendering a mission executable based on the route information. More specifically, it needs to decide behaviours from lane keeping, lane changing, lane crossing and free space navigation and generate a set of target goal poses for the motion planner and controller using the perception information and the road map.

Fig. 4.16 shows an example of behavioural reasoning subsystem [31]. The state estimator computes a representation of the vehicle's logical position based on the vehicle's position and the world model. The goal selector takes the logical location from the state estimator to generate the location goals for the motion planner. The lane selector, merge planner, scene reporter, distance keeper and vehicle driver form the lane driving planner and controller. The precedence estimator, pan-head planner and transition manager form the intersection handling planner and controller.

3.3 Motion planning and control

The motion plan and control module creates a path towards the desired goal issued from the mission planning and behaviour reasoning module then tracks this path. The tasks in motion planning and control include ACC, lane keeping, lane switching, intersections and yielding and parking.

3.3.1 Adaptive cruise control

During ACC, the controller controls the longitudinal motion of the vehicle and maintains a proper distance headway from the preceding vehicle based on current

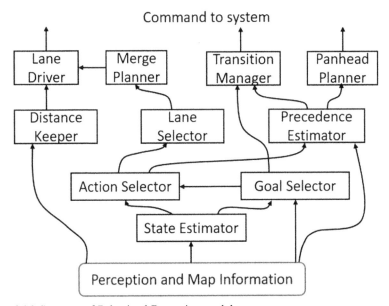

Figure 4.16 Structure of Behavioral Reasoning module.

speed of the ego vehicle, relative distance and relative speed. There are multiple ways to achieve this function.

In traditional analytical model—based control, an analytical model that rules the behaviour of the vehicle is implemented. The input to the model is the information from the perception module and the output is the longitudinal acceleration/throttle and brake pads lift. An example of the analytical ACC model is the Gazis-Herman-Rothery (GHR) model [32]:

$$a_F(t) = cv_F^m(t)\frac{\Delta v(t)}{\Delta x^l(t)} \tag{4.14}$$

where Δv is relative speed, Δx is relative distance. c is the sensitivity coefficient and l and m are the exponents for relative distance and vehicle speed, respectively. Tuning these three parameters can adjust the performance of the ACC controller.

3.3.2 Lane keeping

During lane keeping, the controller controls the lateral motion of the vehicle and keeps the vehicle moving at the centre of the lane.

An example of traditional analytical model—based lane keeping control method is pure pursuit method (Fig. 4.17) [33]. In pure pursuit method an ideal bicycle vehicle model is used. The goal point (g_x, g_y) represents the point on the target path (e.g., the centre line of a lane) that is l_d distance away from the vehicle's rear axle. l_d can be a simple function of vehicle speed, for instance, $l_d = kv$. The vehicle's steering input δ can be computed by using the location of the target point and the angle α between the vehicle's heading direction and the look-ahead direction:

$$\delta(t) = \tan^{-1}\left(\frac{2L\sin(\alpha(t))}{l_d}\right) \tag{4.15}$$

where L is the vehicle's wheelbase.

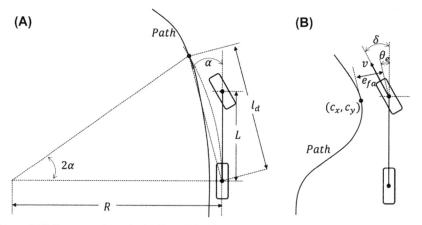

Figure 4.17 Pure pursuit method [40] and Stanley Method [40].

Another analytical model−based lane keeping control method is Stanley method [34]. The vehicle's steering input δ can be calculated with:

$$\delta(t) = \theta_e(t) + \tan^{-1}\left(\frac{ke_{fa}(t)}{v_x(t)}\right) \tag{4.16}$$

where k is a tunable parameter.

3.3.3 Lane switching

During lane switching, the controller needs to decide when to overtake a vehicle in the front and when to merge into another lane (Fig. 4.18). In a traditional rule-based decision-making model, a single longitudinal and a lateral controller are combined with several manually defined criterions to make decisions on lane changing. Typical criterions [35] include safety criterion for deceleration caused to vehicles in the target lane:

$$\widetilde{a}_n \geq -b_{\text{safe}} \tag{4.17}$$

where $\widetilde{a}_n$ is the deceleration of the successor n and b_{safe} is a given safe limit. This criterion avoids collision between the ego vehicle and the successor vehicle in the target lane.

Incentive criterion for double lane changing:

$$\widetilde{a}_c - a_c + p[(\widetilde{a}_n - a_n) + (\widetilde{a}_o - a_o)] \geq \Delta a_{th} \tag{4.18}$$

where $\widetilde{a}_c$ is the acceleration for ego vehicle c after lane change and a_c is the acceleration for ego vehicle before lane change. $\widetilde{a}_n$ is the acceleration for vehicle n after lane change and a_n is the acceleration for vehicle n before lane change. $\widetilde{a}_o$ is the acceleration for vehicle o after lane change and a_o is the acceleration for vehicle o before lane change. p is a tunable weight coefficient. This criterion encourages the traffic to move faster after the prospective lane change.

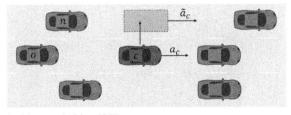

Figure 4.18 Typical lane switching [35].

Incentive criterion for single lane changing:

$$\text{right lane changing}: -a_c + p(\widetilde{a}_o - a_o) \geq \Delta a_{th} - \Delta a_{\text{bias}}$$

$$\text{left lane changing}: a_c - \widetilde{a}_c^{\text{eur}} + p(\widetilde{a}_n - a_n) \geq \Delta a_{th} + \Delta a_{\text{bias}}$$

$$\widetilde{a}_c^{\text{eur}} = \begin{cases} \min(a_c, \widetilde{a}_c) & \text{if } v_c > \widetilde{v}_{\text{lead}} > v_{\text{crit}} \\ a_c & \text{otherwise} \end{cases} \tag{4.19}$$

where v_{crit} is a specified velocity for congested traffic, $\widetilde{v}_{\text{lead}}$ is the velocity of the leading vehicle in the left side lane. Δa_{bias} is a constant bias. This criterion prevents the vehicle from taking a lane change from left to right under normal situation.

3.3.4 Neural network–based advanced control

Besides the traditional control models mentioned above, there are new motion plan and control methods emerging in the past two decades. These methods can have more complex behaviour patterns and better performance.

In NN-based control model, an NN is used to control the motion of the vehicle. The NN needs to be trained with human driving data before it can be used to control the vehicle. A trained NN will mimic the human driver's behaviour in the training data.

The input to an NN can be the same as the analytical-based approach, namely, extracted features from the perception modules [36]. In this case, a normal NN is competent for the control. Correspondingly, in this case, the training data for the NN are the extracted features as well.

The input to an NN can also be the raw sensory data, for example, the video frames from a camera. In this case a deep NN, which is normally a CNN, needs to be adopted (Fig. 4.19). Correspondingly, the training data for the NN is the raw data, and this

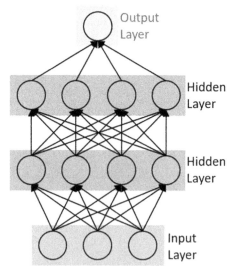

Figure 4.19 Typical architecture of a Neural Network.

specific method is called end-to-end learning [37]. This end-to-end learning based control reduces the load in perception module, but the training process requires much larger amount of training data and computational capacity.

3.3.5 Stochastic model–based control

In this control approach, a probabilistic distribution or a probabilistic state transition process is used to match the perception measurement to vehicle control input. Similarly, to NN-based control, the stochastic model can only be formulated through a machine learning process. A human driver needs to set the expert demonstration for the stochastic model.

One commonly used probabilistic distribution model is the GMM [38]. It can be realised by combining the perception measurements:

$$x_t = \left[v_t, \Delta v_t, \Delta^2 v_t, f_t, \Delta f_t, \Delta^2 f_t, G_t, \Delta G_t, \Delta^2 G_t \right]^T \tag{4.20}$$

and the next time step control output

$$y_t = \left[x_t, G_{t+1} \right]^T \tag{4.21}$$

to formulate a multivariant Gaussian mixture distribution:

$$p(y) = \sum_{k=1}^{M} \alpha_k \phi_k(y) = \sum_{k=1}^{M} \alpha_k N\left(y, \mu_k^y, \sum_k^{yy} \right) \tag{4.22}$$

where v_t, Δv_t, $\Delta^2 v_t$, f_t, Δf_t, $\Delta^2 f_t$, G_t, ΔG_t, $\Delta^2 G_t$ are current vehicle speed, headway distance, control input and their first- and second-order dynamics.

The parameters of the Gaussian components $\phi_k(y)$, including weights α_k, mean value μ_k^y and covariance matrix $\sum_k^{yy}$, will be initialised with random value first and then learnt from training data using iterative statistical model parameter estimation methods such as expectation maximisation method. The next time step control output can be predicted by maximising the conditional probability given by:

$$\widehat{G}_{t+1} = \sum_{k=1}^{M} h_k(x_t) \cdot \widehat{G}_{t+1}^{(k)}(x_t)$$

$$\widehat{G}_{t+1}^{(k)}(x_t) = \arg_{G_{t+1}}^{\max} \{ p(G_{t+1} | X_t, \phi_k) \} \tag{4.23}$$

$$h_k(x_t) = \frac{\alpha_k p\left(x_t | \phi_k^x \right)}{\sum_{k=1}^{M} \alpha_i \cdot p\left(x_t | \phi_i^x \right)}$$

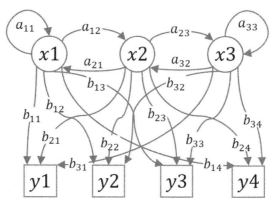

Figure 4.20 Structure of hidden Markov model.

One typical probabilistic state transition process model is hidden Markov model (HMM) (Fig. 4.20). A Markov chain model describes the transition between discrete states with probabilities. An HMM is the Markov chain model with hidden states and observations. In this type of model, the joint distribution between the hidden modes and the observations, which includes the driving situation z_t and control output a_t, can be written as [39]:

$$P(m_{0:t}, z_{1:t}, a_{1:t}) = P(m_0) \prod_{k=1}^{t} [P(m_k|m_{k-1}) \cdot P(z_k, a_k|m_k)] \tag{4.24}$$

where M is the number of the hidden modes, $P(m_0)$ is the initial distribution, $P(z_k, a_k|m_k)$ is the multivariate Gaussian distribution and α_{ij} is the transition probabilities between the ith and j^{th} hidden modes. These parameters will be learnt from human demonstration by using expectation maximisation algorithms. The output will be predicted by calculating the conditional expectation:

$$a_t^{\exp} = E[a_k|z_1, ..., z_t] \tag{4.25}$$

An HMM model can be combined with GMM by assuming Gaussian mixture distribution for the observation probabilities.

3.3.6 Model predictive control

The single model base control methods mentioned above are making decisions only based on current driving situation, without making any predictions. This causes the controller's output to be jerky because the controller is trying to respond to the new environmental measurements at every time step, while some of the responses do not need to be made and some others need to be made earlier. When a good human driver is driving, he/she is considering the current situation

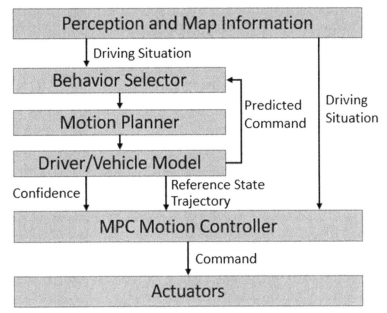

Figure 4.21 The structure of a hierarchical model predictive control (MPC).

and the possible situations in a short future and tries to reduce unnecessary operations and to prevent hazard situation from happening.

A method to make the models behave more like good human drivers is to combine them with MPC and formulate a hierarchical MPC (Fig. 4.21). For instance, in an ACC controller, the states of the car-following system can be expressed with [39]:

$$\begin{cases} d^r_{t+1} = d^r_t + v^r_t \Delta t_d - \frac{1}{2} a_t \Delta t^2_d \\ \\ v^r_{t+1} = v^r_t - a_t \\ \\ v_{t+1} = v_t + a_t \Delta t_d \end{cases} \tag{4.26}$$

where d^r_t and v^r_t are relative distance and speed, v_t is ego vehicle speed and a_t is ego vehicle acceleration. Δt_d is the time step size of the driver model.

The reference trajectory of the longitudinal acceleration can be generated by iterating the state transition model together with the single control model, which can be an analytical model, a stochastic model or an NN model. The safety constraints during the process can be expressed as:

$$\begin{cases} a_{\min} \le a_{k|t} \le a_{\max} \\ \\ v_{k|t} \le v_{\max} \\ \\ d^p_{k|t} - d_{k|t} \ge d_{\text{safe}} \end{cases} \tag{4.27}$$

where $a_{\min}$ and $a_{\max}$ are minimum and maximum possible acceleration limited vehicle physical performance, $v_{\max}$ is maximum allowed speed and d_{safe} is the minimum safe distance. They can be included as a quadratic function $\|\varepsilon\|_S^2 = x^T S x$ in the cost function, where S imposes a high penalty:

$$ J = \sum_{k=t}^{t+P-1} \left[\alpha \left(a_k - a_k^{\text{ref}} \right)^2 + \beta (a_k - a_{k-1})^2 + \gamma (v_k - v_{\max})^2 \right] + \|\varepsilon\|_S^2 \quad (4.28) $$

where P is the total amount of predicting steps in the future, a_k^{ref} is the desired acceleration and α, β, γ are tunable weights. The MPC controller calculates the optimal longitudinal acceleration for all predicting steps such that cost function J is minimised during the prediction horizon.

Similar to ACC, lane keeping controller can be implemented with NN or stochastic models as well (Fig. 4.22). The basic principles are the same, just need to change the input features of the model to steering-related features and model output to steering angle.

To implement an MPC controller for lane keeping, we just need to replace the longitudinal model in ACC to a combined model [40]:

$$ f(z, u) = \begin{cases} \dot{x} = v \cos(\theta) \\[6pt] \dot{y} = v \sin(\theta) \\[6pt] \dot{\theta} = \dfrac{v}{L} \tan(\delta) \\[6pt] \dot{v} = a \end{cases} \quad (4.29) $$

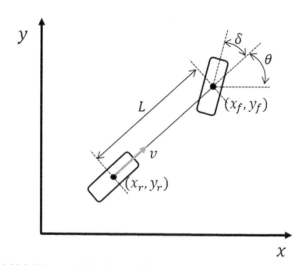

Figure 4.22 Vehicle kinematic bicycle model.

and modify the cost function as well:

$$J = \sum_{k=t}^{t+P-1} \left[\alpha \left(x_k - x_k^{\text{ref}} \right)^2 + \alpha \left(y_k - y_k^{\text{ref}} \right)^2 + \gamma (\delta_k - \delta_{k-1})^2 \right] + \|\varepsilon\|_S^2 \qquad (4.30)$$

where x_k, x_k^{ref}, y_k and y_k^{ref} are vehicle position and reference position along longitudinal and lateral direction. δ_k is vehicle steering and throttle input.

3.4 Autonomous vehicle collaboration in Transportation Cyber-Physical System

All the real-time control systems introduced above are designed for a single autonomous vehicle. However, in the scenario where level 5 fully autonomous driving is achieved, autonomous vehicles will not function as independent individuals but rather form a cyber-physical network where all vehicles and infrastructures are connected. Under this situation, the motion planning and control system may still work similarly, as today, but the perception and mission planning systems will encounter a big reform. The basic methods will not be changed, but the scale and accuracy of the surrounding map built by the perception system will be improved a lot with the help of excessive information exchanged between vehicles and infrastructures.

3.4.1 Communication in Transportation Cyber-Physical System

To form the cyber-physical network of vehicles and infrastructures, special communication methods need to be adopted. Unlike normal networks, vehicles are always moving around and causing the structure of the network to change. The first challenge lies in the communication quality between vehicles and infrastructures. Although there is a dedicated short-range communication system designed for this application, more problems still need to be solved. For instance, when traffic is heavy, a large number of vehicles may transmit information at the same time and that can interfere with each other's communication. Some improved protocols need to be adopted to solve communication overheat and, more specifically, to improve the positioning accuracy by reducing the packet collision [41]. The second challenge lies in the structure of the network. Like mentioned above, it is not realistic to include all vehicles and infrastructures under the same network all the time due to the dynamics in the network. An effective method is grouping the nearby vehicles and infrastructures under a low-level network. In this low-level network, detailed information will be shared among terminals. The low-level network will be connected to a high-level network, in which the general and strategic information of low-level networks is shared.

3.4.2 Vehicle to vehicle collaboration

With the communication system ready, the collaboration between vehicles can be performed by conducting mission planning based on shared perception information between vehicles. This type of collaboration can be very helpful under both highway and urban driving scenarios. For example, during highway driving, the collision prevention system can be both more effective and less intrusive with shared information. By sharing perception information with the leading and following vehicles, a vehicle can expand its perception range by multiple times without the need of adding more expensive sensors. With extra perception information, mission planning system can plan more ahead for potential dangers [42]. Moreover, by sharing mission plan information between each other, a vehicle can learn not only the behaviours but also the reasons for the behaviours of surrounding vehicles, which will significantly reduce unnecessary overshoot or correction in mission plan. Similar collaboration will happen during lane changing manoeuvre. These improvements will bring smoother motion control and better fuel economy on highway. In urban driving scenario, vehicle to vehicle collaboration can also improve driving safety by sharing perceived obstacle information, especially moving obstacles, for example, pedestrians and cyclers. By sharing the perceived traffic light information between each other, vehicles can achieve either least time or minimum energy consumption control strategy in mission planning [43,44]. These targets are not achievable if there is no such TCPS.

3.4.3   Vehicle to infrastructure collaboration

The collaboration between vehicles and infrastructures benefits urban driving. Since infrastructures, for example, traffic lights, RADARs and cameras, are fixed over the road or along the roadside, they can have much more accurate observations of the environment than the moving vehicles. For example, the cameras and RADARs can estimate traffic density in real time and share the information to the cloud [45]. Vehicles that may drive through a congested area can then reschedule its route in advance. Around sharp corners where vehicle onboard sensors may have limited field of vision, cameras mounted on the roadside can help to detect children running across and prevent the happening of accidents by sending a warning to passing-by vehicles. At intersections, the traffic light can share its state to vehicles that are planning to pass it. The vehicles can make adjustment in their mission planner to avoid sudden brake or acceleration. In certain area where human drivers are not presenting, the traffic lights can even be removed to save infrastructure construction cost.

4.   Conclusions and future directions

As a typical CPS system, autonomous vehicles incorporate the three essential factors of computing, communication and control. Among the three factors, the real-time control system is the most sophisticated due to the involvement of various components and functions. Based on the hardware platform constructed by ECUs, sensors and communication buses, each required function is implemented in a form of embedded software. These extendable functions endow the vehicles with intelligence. Instead of a large constellation of sensors working together, future autonomous vehicles will be a real intelligent system, which is the ultimate goal of the autonomous vehicle CPS.

In order to enable autonomous driving functions, the vehicle should rely on the combination of different sensors to perceive the environment with a very high precision and reliability. However, each sensor technology has its own shortcomings and capability limitations, e.g., some of them may be impaired in bad weather scenarios. These shortcomings make it difficult for any of the sensors to be used as a stand-alone system. Moreover, the failure of one or more sensors will possibly result in the malfunction of the autonomous vehicle control system. One way to minimise this is to 'fuse' the data emanating from various sources. This is commonly known as sensor fusion. A fused sensor system combines the benefits of multiple sensors, i.e., RADARs, LiDARs, GPS and cameras, to construct data sources with redundancies. In addition, to make the real-control system more robust, fault diagnosis, tolerance control and the sensorless estimation technology also need to be further researched and applied in the TCPS.

Fully autonomous vehicles and intelligent connected vehicles will be the features of future ground transportation. Human—vehicle interaction and riding comfort will also be the goals of autonomous driving system, as well as of all the autonomous functions addressed in this chapter. As the basic supporting technology, real-time control systems need further fusion with other information technology, such as sensor, communication, cloud computing and big data analysis. At the same time, more advanced control algorithm, e.g., model predictive control, intelligent control, robust control and some machine learning techniques, need to be applied to autonomous vehicles to solve the increasingly complicated and large-scaled control problems.

Exercises

1. What is a real-time control system?
2. What are the required sensors for an autonomous vehicle?
3. How to detect the vehicle speed?
4. What is the basic principle of an acceleration sensor?
5. List three types of distance sensors for an autonomous vehicle and give one application example for each of the three types of distance sensors in an automobile.
6. Why is IMU needed for localisation?
7. What is the difference between Kalman filter and EKF tracking methods?
8. What will happen if the tunable parameter k in Stanley steering control model is larger?
9. What will happen if a NN-based controller is placed in an environment that is totally different from its training environment?
10. In a model predictive controller, which part and how should you modify if you want the vehicle to move as fast as possible without considering the energy consumption?

References

[1] J. Martin, Programming Real-Time Computer Systems, 1965.
[2] K. Kant, Computer-Based Industrial Control, PHI, 2010.

[3] Smart traffic light. [Online]. Available https://en.wikipedia.org/wiki/Smart_traffic_light. (Accessed on 14/05/2018).

[4] X. Xie, Smart and Scalable Urban Signal Networks. [Online]. Available http://www. wiomax.com/team/xie/schic/. (Accessed on 14/05/2018).

[5] M.G. Richard, Networked Traffic Lights Could Save Time, Fuel, and Lives, 2010 [Online]. Available: https://www.treehugger.com/cars/networked-traffic-lights-could-save-time-fuel-and-lives.html. (Accessed on 14/05/2018).

[6] Autopilot Systems in Aircraft Instrument Systems. [Online]. Available http://www.flight-mechanic.com/autopilot-systems/. (Accessed on 14/05/2018).

[7] Electronic Control Unit. [Online]. Available https://en.wikipedia.org/wiki/Electronic_control_unit. (Accessed on 14/05/2018).

[8] What Is an Ultrasonic Sensor? [Online]. Available http://education.rec.ri.cmu.edu/content/ electronics/boe/ultrasonic_sensor/1.html. (Accessed on 14/05/2018).

[9] Doppler Effect, Doppler radar. [Online]. Available http://slideplayer.com/slide/10549388/. (Accessed on 14/05/2018).

[10] What sensors do driverless cars have? [Online]. Available https://www.quora.com/What-sensors-do-driverless-cars-have. (Accessed on 14/05/2018).

[11] Autonomous Vehicles. [Online]. Available http://www.cvel.clemson.edu/auto/AuE835_ Projects_2011/Vallabhaneni_project.html. (Accessed on 14/05/2018).

[12] Three Sensors That 'Drive' Autonomous Vehicles. [Online]. Available https://www. wirelessdesignmag.com/blog/2017/05/three-sensors-drive-autonomous-vehicles. (Accessed on 14/05/2018).

[13] Vehicle Speed Sensor. [Online]. Available http://www.cvel.clemson.edu/auto/sensors/ vehicle-speed.html. (Accessed on 14/05/2018).

[14] Inductive and Hall Effect RPM Sensors. [Online]. Available http://autorepairhelp.us/ inductive-and-hall-effect-rpm-sensors-explained/. (Accessed on 14/05/2018).

[15] J.K. Ravikumar, A. Ravikumar, What Is GPS? 2017. [Online]. Available https://www. geotab.com/blog/what-is-gps/. (Accessed on 14/05/2018).

[16] Automotive Applications. [Online]. Available http://www.mouser.com/applications/ autonomous-car-sensors-drive-performance/. (Accessed on 14/05/2018).

[17] Accelerometer (Analog Devices ADXL50). [Online]. Available http://soundlab.cs. princeton.edu/learning/tutorials/sensors/node9.html. (Accessed on 14/05/2018).

[18] Piezoelectric Accelerometer. [Online]. Available https://en.wikipedia.org/wiki/Piezoelectric_ accelerometer. (Accessed on 14/05/2018).

[19] Z. Sun, G. Bebis, R. Miller, Monocular precrash vehicle detection: features and classifiers, IEEE Transactions on Image Processing 15 (7) (2006) 2019−2034.

[20] C. Premebida, G. Monteiro, U. Nunes, P. Peixoto, A lidar and vision-based approach for pedestrian and vehicle detection and tracking, in: Intelligent Transportation Systems Conference, 2007. ITSC 2007, IEEE, 2007, pp. 1044−1049.

[21] Z. Sun, G. Bebis, R. Miller, On-road vehicle detection: a review, IEEE Transactions on Pattern Analysis and Machine Intelligence 28 (5) (2006) 694−711.

[22] L. Zhao, C.E. Thorpe, Stereo-and neural network-based pedestrian detection, IEEE Transactions on Intelligent Transportation Systems 1 (3) (2000) 148−154.

[23] A. Petrovskaya, S. Thrun, Model based vehicle detection and tracking for autonomous urban driving, Autonomous Robots 26 (2−3) (2009) 123−139.

[24] J. Lou, T. Tan, W. Hu, H. Yang, S.J. Maybank, 3-D model-based vehicle tracking, IEEE Transactions on Image Processing 14 (10) (2005) 1561−1569.

[25] R.E. Kalman, et al., A new approach to linear filtering and prediction problems, Journal of Basic Engineering 82 (1) (1960) 35−45.

[26] M.I. Ribeiro, Kalman and extended kalman filters: concept, derivation and properties, Institute for Systems and Robotics 43 (2004).

[27] P. Del Moral, Non-linear filtering: interacting particle resolution, Markov Processes and Related Fields 2 (4) (1996) 555–581.

[28] J. Levinson, M. Montemerlo, S. Thrun, Map-based precision vehicle localization in urban environments, in: Robotics: Science and Systems, vol. 4, 2007, p. 1.

[29] E.W. Dijkstra, A note on two problems in connexion with graphs, Numerische Mathematik 1 (1) (1959) 269–271.

[30] P.E. Hart, N.J. Nilsson, B. Raphael, A formal basis for the heuristic determination of minimum cost paths, IEEE Transactions on Systems Science and Cybernetics 4 (2) (1968) 100–107.

[31] C. Urmson, et al., Autonomous driving in urban environments: boss and the urban challenge, Journal of Field Robotics 25 (8) (2008) 425–466.

[32] D.C. Gazis, R. Herman, R.B. Potts, Car-following theory of steady-state traffic flow, Operations Research 7 (4) (1959) 499–505.

[33] O. Amidi, Integrated Mobile Robot Control, 1990.

[34] S. Thrun, et al., Stanley: the robot that won the DARPA grand challenge, Journal of Field Robotics 23 (9) (2006) 661–692.

[35] A. Kesting, M. Treiber, D. Helbing, General lane-changing model MOBIL for car-following models, Transportation Research Record Journal of the Transportation Research Board (1999) (2007) 86–94.

[36] R. Fierro, F.L. Lewis, Control of a nonholonomic mobile robot using neural networks, IEEE Transactions on Neural Networks 9 (4) (1998) 589–600.

[37] M. Bojarski, et al., End to End Learning for Self-Driving Cars, arXiv Prepr. arXiv1604.07316, 2016.

[38] Y. Nishiwaki, C. Miyajima, N. Kitaoka, K. Itou, K. Takeda, Generation of pedal operation patterns of individual drivers in car-following for personalized cruise control, in: Intelligent Vehicles Symposium, 2007 IEEE, 2007, pp. 823–827.

[39] S. Lefèvre, A. Carvalho, F. Borrelli, A learning-based framework for velocity control in autonomous driving, IEEE Transactions on Automation Science and Engineering 13 (1) (2016) 32–42.

[40] J.M. Snider, et al., Automatic Steering Methods for Autonomous Automobile Path Tracking, Robot Institute, Pittsburgh, PA, 2009. Tech. Rep. C.

[41] S. Singh, Critical Reasons for Crashes Investigated in the National Motor Vehicle Crash Causation Survey, 2015.

[42] R. Sengupta, S. Rezaei, S.E. Shladover, D. Cody, S. Dickey, H. Krishnan, Cooperative collision warning systems: concept definition and experimental implementation, Journal of Intelligent Transportation Systems 11 (3) (2007) 143–155.

[43] E. Koukoumidis, M. Martonosi, L.-S. Peh, Leveraging smartphone cameras for collaborative road advisories, IEEE Transactions on Mobile Computing 11 (5) (2012) 707–723.

[44] E. Koukoumidis, L.-S. Peh, M.R. Martonosi, SignalGuru: leveraging mobile phones for collaborative traffic signal schedule advisory, in: Proceedings of the 9th International Conference on Mobile Systems, Applications, and Services, 2011, pp. 127–140.

[45] J. Barrachina, et al., V2X-d: a vehicular density estimation system that combines V2V and V2I communications, in: Wireless Days (WD), 2013 IFIP, 2013, pp. 1–6.

Transportation Cyber-Physical Systems Security and Privacy

Tony Kenyon [1,2]
[1]Chief Product Officer & SVP Engineering, R&D Guardtime, Guildford, United Kingdom;
[2]The De Montfort University Interdisciplinary Group in Intelligent Transport Systems
(DIGITS), De Montfort University, Leicester, United Kingdom

1. Introduction

Transportation cyber-physical systems (TCPS) have the potential to generate, process and exchange significant amounts of security-critical, safety-critical and privacy-sensitive information, which makes them attractive targets for cybercriminals. TCPS utilise a wide variety of software, hardware and physical components, interconnected by communications protocols. Computational and physical components (e.g., sensors and actuators) often interface with humans, and include a mix of digital and analog subsystems, with interactions in real time (especially where safety and time-critical functions are needed). Cyber-physical systems will underpin critical infrastructure, intelligent transport systems and autonomous vehicles and form the basis for emerging smart city fabrics.

TCPS integrate a broad range of immature and proprietary technologies, incomplete (or missing) standards, and components that may have little or no security built in by design. Whilst the focus is still very much on safety, the industry is now waking up to the idea that safety cannot be assured without security, and we must incorporate best security practises into TCPS projects from the outset. The complexity, heterogeneity and immaturity of TCPS leave them vulnerable to new classes of cyberthreat, with attacks that have the potential to cause significant physical and economic damage, as well as threaten human lives. The interconnectivity of TCPS and interwoven human dependencies mean that compromises have the potential for major disruption to critical services at unprecedented scale, with serious consequences for all of us.

This chapter will address privacy and security issues in TCPS, paying special attention to the issues raised where large populations of embedded sensors are communicating, interacting and collecting data points continuously. We discuss how security controls will need to be refactored, implications for intrusion detection, vulnerabilities in wireless interfaces and human-in-the-loop implications for privacy and security.

2. Basic concepts

TCPS will become a critical part of national infrastructure, where the risks exposed have the potential to become national or even global issues. It is therefore critical

Transportation Cyber-Physical Systems. https://doi.org/10.1016/B978-0-12-814295-0.00005-8
Copyright © 2018 Elsevier Inc. All rights reserved.

that infrastructures are designed robustly and sufficiently instrumented to detect and mitigate compromises quickly and efficiently, with minimal disruption or compromise to services, and no loss of life.

TCPS overlap with a number of domains and yet introduces new paradigms: however, there are important lessons to be learnt from cybersecurity best practices in traditional infrastructures such as enterprise, Telco and industrial. It would be unwise to ignore these lessons, and we compare and contrast broader cybersecurity practice throughout this chapter, recognising that with any emerging technology these lessons are often ignored in the initial rush to deliver new products and services quickly.

The fundamental security issues raised by TCPS are not necessarily new; however, advances in technology, increased use of low-power components (often with weak security controls) and new service models make it important to employ a different approach to protect data, people and infrastructure against emerging threats. New vulnerabilities will continue to be exposed and exploited, and given the potential attraction of TCPS to adversaries (ranging from lone hackers, organised crime, to nation-state sponsored groups), we should anticipate that ever more sophisticated threats will continue to surface.

2.1 Threats

At a high level we can consider a threat taxonomy that has significant overlap with many other domains. Fig. 5.1 provides a high-level classification for threat classes, partly based on work by the European Union Agency for Network and Information Security [1]. Most of these threat classes are applicable to TCPS, although their relative ease, frequency and implementation will vary depending upon the specific transport domain and systems deployed.

The target of a threat is usually referred to as the 'asset', and the higher the asset value the more attractive it may be for an adversary to attempt compromise. Note that asset value often does not equate directly to monetary value. In TCPS, for example, assets may include systems that hold sensitive information or systems that are mission or safety critical. The scope of any threat will depend on whether the adversary is planning to compromise an entire system (such as a traffic control system) or a more targeted entity (such as a fly-by-wire aircraft or connected vehicle).

2.2 Adversaries

In cybersecurity, adversaries exist in several forms (often referred to as profiles), and they should be considered individually when assessing the scope of risk, vulnerability and threat. We may consider a number of important classifications and attributes when profiling an attacker, such as the following:

- Powerful or weak adversary (e.g., lone actor, computer expert, organised crime, state-sponsored teams of experts)
- Resources available to adversaries (e.g., access to finance, machines, malware tools)
- External or internal to the system (e.g., remote attack or installed keylogger)

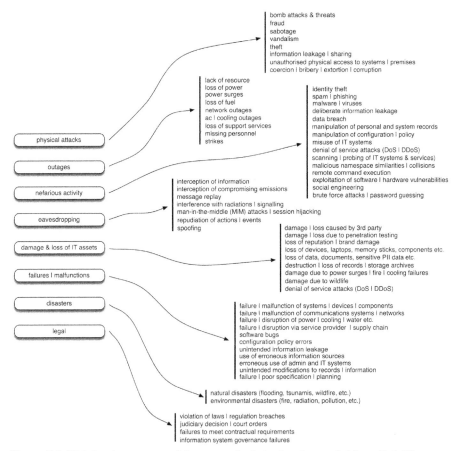

Figure 5.1 High-level taxonomy of threats: partly derived and extended from Ref. [1].

- External or internal to an organisation (e.g., insider threat, social engineering)

We should also consider the possible motivation of potential adversaries:

- Prank or malicious (e.g., peer reputation, boredom)
- Disgruntled employee with access to sensitive data or systems (e.g., air traffic controller)
- Competitor (e.g., reputational damage, intellectual property (IP) theft)
- Ransomware (e.g., threats to disable critical services for financial compensation, often through anonymous accounts using digital currency)
- Diversionary (e.g., disable transport system whilst performing bank robbery)

These loose classifications are not specific to TCPS—in other fields we see the same broad ontologies—however, we must consider these from the new perspective of TCPS in order to fully characterise the range of potential threats and risks. Cybercrime today is extremely well organised and adversaries often display remarkable ingenuity in thwarting security controls and exposing new and subtle flaws. Skill levels range from so-called script kiddies (with basic technology skills using off-the-shelf malware toolkits) through to highly organised, highly qualified and financially sponsored teams. Powerful adversaries may include groups of individuals with postgraduate qualifications in computer science, intimate knowledge of systems and access to sophisticated source code libraries and tools.

2.3 Confidentiality, integrity and availability

In traditional IT information security practise, properties such as confidentiality, integrity and availability (CIA)-the so-called CIA triad-are important concepts used to guide the implementation of security resources — see Fig. 5.2A. These properties represent three dimensions with which to visualise and quantify a system or organisation's security posture. For most real-world scenarios, however, it is near impossible to provide perfect security, and it is rare to place equal weight on each dimension, since there may be pragmatic influences to consider, such as cost, risk, time to market, etc. Fig. 5.2B illustrates a use case where CIA are ranked in descending order of importance; this might, for example, be applicable when determining the security controls required for sensitive data protection.

In information security, *confidentiality* normally takes centre stage, followed by *availability*, whilst *integrity* has remained largely neglected. This may be in part because there are few effective integrity security controls available at scale, although alternative approaches have been proposed in recent years using technologies such as blockchain, which we discuss later. The lack of attention to integrity might seem a little surprising, since we cannot characterise the efficacy of a system's security if we do not fully understand its state. Put more directly, according to Dan Geer, 'Any security technology whose effectiveness can't be empirically determined is indistinguishable from blind luck' [2].

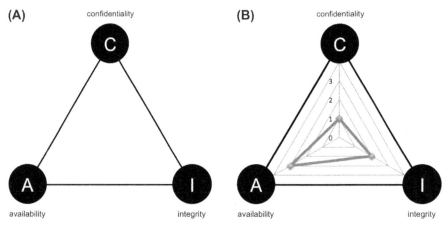

Figure 5.2 In this diagram (A) illustrates the three dimensions of the CIA triad and (B) illustrates an example of how a mapping of each attribute might be applied in a specific security context (1 = high priority, 5 = low priority). *CIA*, confidentiality, integrity and availability.

In TCPS there are security contexts where the CIA triad can provide useful guidance − for example, in allocating security controls for server-side infrastructure and data centres. However, there are scenarios where the limited perspective of CIA is grossly inadequate − such as real-time safety-critical systems, with humans in the loop and poor or nonexistent physical security. Fig. 5.4 illustrates broader dimensions that we might need to consider in TCPS cybersecurity analysis.

2.4 Risk

Cybersecurity is not simply about cryptography; it is about assessing the risk of undesirable actions happening in a given context, and deploying appropriate safeguards and countermeasures (security controls) to militate such risk. Assessing risk in cybersecurity is still more art than science. In enterprise security, for example, we may use a method called annual loss expectancy (ALE) to quantify and manage risk, which broadly follows the methodology listed below:

1. Identity and prioritise assets (e.g., business-and mission-critical systems, intellectual property, personally identifiable information (PII), customer contact lists, etc.). To simplify you may group similar assets.
2. Identify major threats and vulnerabilities. To simplify you may group where appropriate.
3. Estimate the probability of threats against the value of asset being compromised (using probabilities which often rely on domain expertise or industry datasets). This is referred to as the *Single Loss Expectancy* (SLE). SLE is calculated as: *SLE = Asset value × Exposure factor (EF)*. The EF is the estimated percentage damage that a threat would have on a specific asset-if the threat was realised.
4. Estimate the *Annual Rate of Occurrence* (ARO) to determine the likelihood of each class of threat per year.
5. Using the previous two metrics we can determine the *Annual Loss expectancy* (ALE) to estimate the risk exposure for each asset class. ALE is calculated as: *ALE = SLE × ARO*.

Using ALE (or a similar model) and by understanding what level of risk we are prepared to tolerate (the risk appetite), we can estimate (and ideally justify) how much resource should be expended on security controls in order to protect assets and mitigate particular threats.

Ideally this process should be iterative and continually updated. In practice, however, such an exercise is typically resource intensive and may be reviewed periodically (aligned with budget cycles) and tactically in response to significant new threats.

This methodology is asset centric and has a number of flaws − nevertheless, it is arguably the most widely adopted approach we have today for aligning risk and budget in enterprise risk analysis. Perhaps the most serious flaws lie in the calculation of risk itself and level of misplaced confidence we may have in producing metrics with numeric outputs: for example, a model that produces risk score of 87.19% sounds convincingly precise. In fact, accurate risk estimation in cybersecurity is extremely challenging. An organisation's risk profile is also likely to change over time, as new vulnerabilities and threats emerge and as the organisation's attractiveness as potential target fluctuates. Despite advances, it has proven extremely difficult to characterise the true scope and likelihood of threats and vulnerabilities in real-world networked systems, where systems are often highly complex, widely distributed, include multiple access points and trust boundaries, involve human interaction, and where core systems and services are frequently updated, patched and reconfigured. As a consequence, over the last two decades there has been a significant shift towards monitoring and breach detection, given that preventative controls are simply not living up to expectations.

Risk analysis in TCPS is perhaps even more challenging when compared with conventional security domains, when we consider real-time safety-critical aspects together with close human interaction and dependencies. ALE may prove useful for analysing asset risks for back end infrastructure and support services; however, given the complexity and heterogeneity of TCPS, such a model appears inadequate for safety-critical systems. We must consider a different approach, albeit building on some best in prior practice and methodology. In TCPS we should, for example, explore the use of *attack trees* to characterise threats and vulnerabilities, allowing us to consider risk at different levels of abstraction. We may also want to incorporate failure modes and effects analysis (FMEA) [3]: a well-established analytic methodology from reliability engineering. During the risk analysis process it would be highly desirable to incorporate related FMEA recommendations into risk calculations (e.g., where redundant components are included for fault tolerance and might mitigate some risk).

2.5   Attack trees

Attack trees [4] provide a formal method of describing the security of systems by analysing how various threats might be characterised and executed against a target system. Attack trees are frequently used for modelling security risks and threats in complex networked systems. Attack trees may be represented in several different ways; however, the root node typically describes the objective (or goal), and the leaf nodes describe how this goal might be achieved. Attack trees are functionally similar to fault trees used in industrial safety engineering (a form of dependency analysis using directed graphs).

To create an attack tree we typically start by identifying all possible goals and creating separate trees (which may share leaf nodes or some goals may form subgoals for larger objectives). Building attack trees for complex systems can be time-consuming and demands a high level of domain knowledge. Fig. 5.3 shows a highly simplified example, with goals at the top and actions and subgoals in the leaf nodes. In this example the attacker wishes to install malware on the TCPS system, for example, a component that runs critical firmware. The attacker will need to bypass the code repository delivery mechanism (e.g., using interception), exploit preinstalled code (e.g., by exploiting a vulnerability) or install malicious code in the upstream code repository (e.g., by coercing a trusted insider). Note that in the tree there are logical AND and OR paths at each level wherever there are multiple options.

In real-world software supply chains the processes involved in package assembly and delivery can be extremely complex, with thousands of integrated components from many different suppliers, and many more paths to introduce rogue elements into the code. At the base of the tree (the lowest leafs) we will need to do a broad and detailed threat analysis and ensure nothing is missed. There are a number of

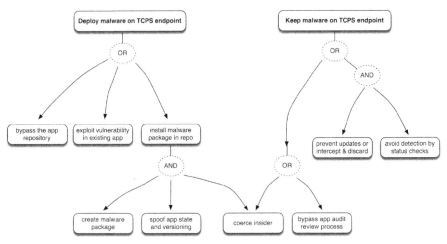

Figure 5.3 Attack tree example. *TCPS*, Transportation Cyber-Physical Systems.

techniques that can be applied but perhaps a useful starting point is the STRIDE classification scheme [5]. STRIDE is used to characterise known threats according to the types of exploit used or motivation of the attacker. The STRIDE acronym is derived from the following categories:

- Spoofing identity
- Tampering with data
- Repudiation
- Information disclosure
- Denial of service (DoS)
- Elevation of privilege

Once the attack tree is complete, you can assign values to each leaf node. These values can be arbitrary depending on the method used. For example, you might assign Boolean, continuous or enumerated values, such as impossible (I) and possible (P), or a specific monetary value. For example, the value of an OR node is possible if any of its children are possible and impossible if all of its children are impossible, whereas the value of an AND node is possible only if all children are possible and impossible otherwise. Once assigned you can make calculations on those nodes and estimate the security of the objective and then analyse whether introducing various security controls mitigates certain attacks to an acceptable level.

Attack trees can reveal surprising insights: often what first appears to be a primary vulnerability concern turns out to be less important − if, for example, analysis reveals a simpler more direct (often unsophisticated) method to compromise the system. This form of analysis should also be a continuous iterative process, since the threat and vulnerability landscape are likely to change over time. It is encouraging to see research initiatives exploring automation in threat and vulnerability analysis, such as the use of artificial intelligence (AI) to autogenerate attack trees for critical infrastructure and transportation systems [6].

2.6 Kill chains

A useful way to view attacks is through a time graph referred to as the kill chain. A kill chain describes how an attack might be broken down over time into a sequence of discrete steps. These steps represent the typical phases of the attack, as adversaries work towards their goal by first surveying and then compromising systems. The theory is that by understanding these steps we can identify and potentially mitigate attacks early by breaking the chain.

The term 'kill chain' has military origins; however, Lockheed Martin have adopted this concept for cybersecurity, identifying seven main phases in the kill chain, using a model referred to as the Cyber Kill Chain [7]. Table 5.1 illustrates the key steps identified.

Whilst kill chains may not be applicable to all scenarios, this technique has been successfully applied to model intrusions on computer networks [8] and has seen some adoption across the information security community. The kill chain methodology offers an alternate approach that could prove useful in modelling certain TCPS threats and use cases and deserves further exploration.

2.7 Security controls

Once we have determined the major threats and vulnerabilities, together with their associated risk, we can set about the task of managing risk. We do this by introducing a range of security controls to mitigate threats and related exposures. In enterprise networks, there is a toolkit of mature security controls, and in some cases, risk can even be transferred (using an insurance policy, for example). Security controls act as safeguards and countermeasures to predict, detect, avoid, mitigate and minimise risk and to take many different forms, including physical, procedural, technical or legal, regulatory compliance directives [9]. In information security, for example, controls

Table 5.1 Key Steps and Actions in Lockheed Martin's Cyber Kill Chain

Step	Title	Description
1	Reconnaissance	Probe and collate addresses, unsecured ports, etc.
2	Weaponisation	Assemble and code malware package and delivery methods
3	Delivery	Deliver weaponised package to victim (e.g., e-mail malware attachment)
4	Exploitation	Exploit vulnerabilities to compromise remote assets
5	Installation	Install malware on target asset(s)
6	Command and control (C2)	Command channel for remote manipulation of target
7	Actions on objectives	Adversaries achieve their goal using C2

are widely used to protect the CIA triad of information described earlier. Security controls fall into the several major categories:

- **Predictive controls:** trend analysis, machine learning (ML) and statistical techniques on historical data, early warning systems
- **Preventative controls:** access controls, firewalls, antivirus (AV) software, intrusion prevention systems (IPS), defensive coding, security policies and processes
- **Detection controls:** intrusion detection systems (IDS), security information and event management systems (SIEM)
- **Corrective controls:** to correct or limit the impact of damage after the event (e.g., disaster recovery, rollback procedures, incident response processes)
- **Privacy controls:** secure channels (encrypted links, virtual private networks (VPNs), etc.)
- **Audit and analytical controls:** logging and reporting tools, laws and regulations, etc.

Technology-based controls (such as firewalls, IDS, AV software) are typically heavily instrumented for monitoring: generating counters, event logs, statistical reports, anomaly reports and 'flow' records, for example. This instrumentation can be used to inform other security controls in a well-architected security solution. For example, an SIEM may correlate events from security appliances and services across the whole network, generating high-level alerts, trend graphs, asset state and audit reports. A highly integrated and well-instrumented security architecture should promote *situational awareness*, enabling security operations staff to visualise the real-time status of critical assets—typically through a risk dashboard—with tools and processes to identify anomalies early and recover from incidents quickly.

In principle these controls and practises are applicable to TCPS; however, there are important differences between cyber-physical systems that must be considered. Enterprise networks rely on mature technologies and standards and are deployed using relatively consistent and well-understood design patterns. TCPS, however, comprises a myriad of new immature components, integrated across a wide variety of deployment contexts, a wide assortment of specifications and processing contexts, a mix of analog and digital components, mobility and human concerns, sensitive telemetry, and stringent timing and safety requirements. This heterogeneity, complexity and lack of mature standards are major challenges when designing secure, safe and performant TCPS infrastructures.

2.8 Extending the confidentiality, integrity and availability triad

When we think about safety-critical control systems in intelligent transportation, such as avionics, automotive and rail, these architectures include many real-time components, demanding functionally correct behaviour within strict time tolerances. The CIA triad introduced earlier (see Fig. 5.2) places emphasis on confidentiality, availability and then integrity. In cyber-physical systems *safety* is often the primary consideration, and we must consider other constraints on performance and privacy, as well as pragmatic concerns on component cost, ease of maintenance, time to market, etc. Whilst the primary importance may be to minimise the risk of fatalities as a result of system failure, the practical realities of commercial deployment, with finite budgets, mean that security becomes a multidimensional trade-off, as illustrated in Fig. 5.4.

Figure 5.4 An example illustrating how the CIA triad might be extended for Transportation Cyber-Physical Systems, with dimensional trade-offs for assessing security priorities (1 = high priority, 5 = low priority). *CIA*, confidentiality, integrity and availability.

In real-world deployments security is almost always a compromise; however, TCPS demand that we consider very carefully how much value we place on safety (and indirectly security) and how to reasonably estimate risk when there are many unknowns and variables. This requires thoughtful and rigorous approaches to design, test, verification, vulnerability assessment, and perhaps new approaches such as *intrusion tolerance*, using a closed feedback loop of instrumentation, integrated heuristics and controls. Advances in AI and software programmable systems are likely to play a major role here, and we discuss this later in this chapter.

3. Threats and vulnerabilities in Transportation Cyber-Physical Systems

Given the scope and diversity in TCPS infrastructures, there are many potential threats and vulnerabilities associated with a broad range of attack surfaces. In this section we review potential attacks and vulnerabilities specific to TCPS.

3.1 Threat scenarios

To gain an understanding of just how broad the potential range of threats is in TCPS, why this differs from conventional cybersecurity and some of the unique challenge raised, it is instructive to consider some examples:

- Disable cameras and/or control traffic control systems on a traffic monitoring system.
- Breach a vehicles' Controller Area Network (CAN) to influence safety-critical systems, provide false readings or activate braking systems, for example.

- Turn off headlights and brake lights, disable the engine or force a vehicle veer off the road.
- Intercept and modify sensor telemetry, manipulating upstream analytics and decision-making control systems.
- Jam vehicle-to-vehicle communications.
- Compromise vehicle audio sensors and eavesdrop on a private conversation.
- Force a drone carrying sensitive intelligence to land in enemy hands.
- Introduce malicious configuration data and malware into an aircraft system.
- Force a ship move to a vulnerable location by affecting its positional awareness.
- Spoof analog signals on physical systems to bypass cryptographic controls.

This list is far from exhaustive, and we are at the early stages of understanding the true scope of the problem space [42]. The unique characteristics of cyber-physical systems, and TCPS in particular, mean we are likely to see new and novel threats emerge that have never been considered previously. Thacker et al. [10] analyses cyber-physical system security threats and the consequences of such attacks, illustrating the differences between cyber-physical systems and traditional IT security and also dynamic security mechanisms more suited for cyber-physical deployment.

3.2 Attack surfaces

TCPS present a broad variety of attack surfaces when we consider the range and complexity of systems in scope: from transport control systems and back end analytical systems to intelligent vehicles (with connected car, fly-by-wire aircraft and fully autonomous trains and cars). This complexity, heavy reliance on wireless communication, mix of analog and digital, often poor physical security and high levels of human interaction and dependence mean that many attack surfaces are inevitably exposed across various abstraction layers (see Fig. 5.5).

- Humans operating TCPS control systems are subject to social attacks, such as phishing and social engineering. There is also the potential for insider threat and fraud.
- Electronics are subject to physical attacks, including invasive hardware attacks, side-channel attacks and reverse engineering.
- Software can be compromised by malicious code, such as Trojans, worms, viruses and runtime attacks, which may in turn lead to privacy breaches and remote control attacks.
- Communication protocols can subject to protocol attacks, including man-in-the-middle attacks, DoS attacks and spoofing.
- Analog systems can be influenced or spoofed to bypass digital security controls (such as access controls and cryptographic safeguards), and emissions leaking sensitive information may be recorded and analysed.

3.3 Reliance on sensors and Wi-Fi

Sensor networks comprising a mixture of digital and analog components present some unique challenges for cybersecurity, and over the next decade we are likely to see a major increase in the reliance sensors and the wireless connectivity in TCPS. This is being driven from a number of different perspectives, for example, to enhance functionality, increase automation, improve maintenance, improve

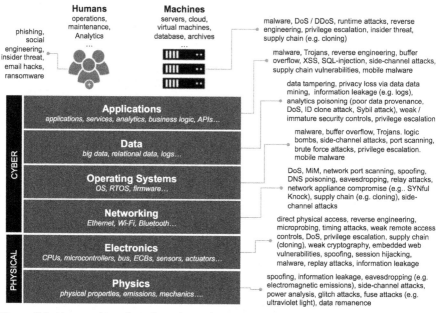

Figure 5.5 Abstracted attack surfaces for Transportation Cyber-Physical Systems. *DoS*, denial of service; *MiM*, man-in-the-middle; *OS*, operating systems.

operational efficiency, and reduce cost. To get an idea of the complexity of these systems, consider the following:

- Modern vehicles currently have an average of 60−100 onboard sensors, and as cars become increasingly intelligent the number of sensors is projected to reach over 200 per vehicle by 2020. Today's systems for semi-autonomous driving use a variety of radar and camera systems. Autonomous vehicles demand complex integration, with sophisticated algorithms running on powerful processors used to make critical decisions from large streams of real-time data, generated by a diverse and complex array of sensors. Fully autonomous driving (security Level 4 or 5) requires multiple redundant sensor systems (typically three for fully autonomous driving − see Table 5.2).
- Modern commercial aircrafts have potentially thousands of onboard sensors, generating terabytes of data per day. Whilst the majority of aircraft engines have fewer than 250 sensors, this is changing quickly: for example, Pratt & Whitney's geared turbofan engine has around 5000 sensors, generating up to 10 GB of data per second. The Airbus A380-1000 will be equipped with 10,000 sensors in each wing alone, with reportedly 250,000 sensors in total. In aviation there is a major shift towards the use of wireless sensors, at least initially for non−safety-critical systems. Wireless sensors have the potential to significantly reduce aircraft weight and cost.

As sensor deployment increases, sensors are themselves becoming increasingly intelligent through enhanced software, computation and connectivity functionality. The increased reliance on low-cost wireless sensors, especially for safety-critical systems, will inevitably lead to additional vulnerabilities and threats.

Table 5.2 **Autonomous Driving Classification Levels**

Level	Description
0	**Driver only:** a human driver controls all functions independently (accelerator, brakes, steering, etc.)
1	**Assisted driving:** assistance systems help a human driver during some vehicle operations (automatic cruise control, anti-lock braking, etc.)
2	**Partial automation:** at least one system in fully automated; however, a human driver must monitor the system at all times (e.g., cruise control and lane centring).
3	**Conditional automation:** a human operator monitors the system and should intervene when required. Safety-critical functions, under certain circumstances, are delegated to the vehicle.
4	**High automation:** vehicles designed to operate all safety-critical functions and monitor road conditions for an entire journey, without intervention by a human driver. Some driving scenarios may not be within the operational scope of the vehicle and a human may need to take over.
5	**Complete automation:** for an entire journey, without any human intervention.

To ensure the correct and safe operation of TCPS systems, it is critical to assure the integrity of the underlying systems and components (in particular embedded code and data) against malicious modifications. Recent studies have revealed multiple security vulnerabilities in embedded systems [11,12], and there are particular challenges in implementing cost-effective secure embedded systems with safety-critical real-time dependencies, and we cover this in more detail in Section 5.

4. Security models for Transportation Cyber-Physical Systems

Whilst there are important lessons to draw from enterprise security best practise, assuring security and privacy in TCPS infrastructures requires a different perspective. In TCPS the consequences of not detecting (and ideally preventing) intrusions and compromises in real time could have serious consequences, resulting in the potential loss of life.

- The cyber-physical world is device-centric and often perimeterless; this is very different from enterprise.
- New protocols and security standards must be defined to support low-power devices, new embedded security controls and best practices specific to intelligent transport systems.
- New regulatory approaches may be required to handle data governance and privacy issues, for example, where sensitive data may be moving across national borders in vehicles.
- Traditional asset-and cost-centric risk models may be inappropriate for many TCPS contexts, especially where safety and real-time response are needed.

- Complex heterogeneous low latency environments mean that new vulnerabilities are inevitable. Solutions may need to be intrusion tolerant, with rapid mitigation and self-healing.
- The heterogeneous nature of TCPS ultimately means that much more cooperation is likely to be required between key stakeholders (manufacturers, government, regulators and users).

Consider a breach of a connected vehicle, where an attacker gains access to critical control systems, affecting steering, acceleration and braking — effectively turning a car into a remote weaponised system. TCPS present new and thought-provoking scenarios for cybersecurity analysts to consider, as well as a whole new set of constraints.

4.1 Challenges

TCPS are inherently complex and heterogeneous, with immature standards and practices, utilising low-cost components that may offer very little resource with which to deploy traditional security controls. Some of the broader challenges in building secure TCPS infrastructures are highlighted in the following:

- Systems are typically complex, heterogeneous and incorporate physical, 'soft', digital and analog components from many different suppliers. This represents a large attack surface and there may be insufficient knowledge, training and skills to design and operate effective security solutions.
- Important technologies used in TCPS are not all publically documented or peer reviewed, which significantly constrains vulnerability analysis and research opportunities and presents opportunities for reverse engineering of potentially weak or obfuscated security features.
- Real-time constraints are particularly challenging when trying to overlay security controls and may require purpose-built operating systems (OS) and refactored security techniques.
- Manufacturers and developers consistently underestimate security risks and vulnerabilities in the race to gain install base and market share.
- The focus on safety, without sufficient attention on security, has the potential to seriously compromise safety itself.
- Existing security and privacy models may be inadequate or even impractical for sensors and microprocessor-based devices with limited resource.
- Traditional perimeter-based approaches to security may be entirely inappropriate in some TCPS contexts, particularly where direct physical access to a system is possible.
- New vulnerabilities will be exposed due to unique deployment and maintenance processes and systemic immaturity.
- Advances in ML may help with TCPS security automation and efficacy may be hampered by lack of training data.

Adam [13] discusses the challenges cyber-physical systems are currently facing with regard to cybersecurity, including the lack of knowledge in dealing with such size and complexity, lack of mature verification and validation (V&V) technologies, lack of mechanisms to meet real time, reliability and security requirements, poor risk awareness and lack of relevant performance indicators.

Arguably one of the largest challenges at present in securing TCPS is the availability of computing resource, particularly in embedded systems. Compactness, ubiquity and cost are important in assuring the success of TCPS initiatives, as they are in and the broader fields such as Internet of Things (IoT) and wearable technology. However, this ability to scale down comes at a cost when we consider cybersecurity: the lack of onboard resource in subsystems to supports de-facto security controls (i.e., lack of processing power, memory, storage, bus width, etc.). This issue is particularly acute where low-end embedded components interact with mission-and safety-critical systems.

Resource constraints mean that the level of security we might typically implement in conventional networked systems may not always be feasible. It is likely (assuming Moore's law and benefits of scale) that increasingly sophisticated and powerful low-cost components will be introduced at much lower cost; however, at present this represents a major challenge for security designers. We can either relax the security posture (and by implication *safety* — which is likely to be unacceptable in many cases) or we must invent new lightweight security controls and enhance system-wide intelligence to cope with this feature gap (for example, by correlating real-time telemetry with known 'normal' operational states across multiple subsystems and components).

As an example, consider Transport Layer Security (TLS), the de facto means to protect channels in conventional network infrastructure, securing everything from online shopping to military signalling. TLS provides privacy and confidentiality by encrypting messaging between interconnected systems via public key infrastructure (PKI). TLS is widely deployed using mature well-tested libraries and is supported by a large active open-source community. In the cyber-physical world, however, it may be infeasible to deploy TLS on low-end systems and components; many small low-power microcontrollers, for example, do not have enough resource to support this sophisticated protocol.

A typical TLS deployment assumes high bandwidth and low latencies in communication channels: for example, PKI certificates are over 1 KB long and require two round trips to establish a secure channel. TLS also requires sufficient processing power to handle computationally expensive cryptography functions (at least 4 KB of RAM, plus memory support for as many as 100 cryptography algorithms). Many of the subsystems and components used in TCPS have low power-constrained bandwidth communications, with tight limits on memory and computational resource. To address some of these challenges, new lightweight standards are being developed by organisations such as the Internet Engineering Task Force (IETF); see Section 4.7.

As with any technology paradigm shift, there is considerable enthusiasm and uncertainty at the outset: we should recognise that we are at the beginning of a long journey in regard to delivering consistently secure, trustworthy and high-availability TCPS infrastructures. Over time both our thinking and the best practices will mature, sharpened by the inevitable consequences of breaches and compromises in these new domains.

4.2 Security architecture

Since we cannot simply transfer existing cybersecurity models and practises onto TCPS in designing new security architectures for TCPS systems and services, we must consider several different perspectives and challenges including the following:

- Identifying and mitigating specific TCPS threats at a domain level (intelligent transport systems, air traffic control, high-speed intelligent rail, autonomous vehicle, etc.)

- Improving and developing new security standards, regulations and protocols that are feasible and applicable in a TCPS context
- Tolerance to faults, noise and intrusion (especially for real-time safety-critical systems), without compromising overall safety and integrity
- The ability to transfer or adapt best-practice security controls in low-power embedded contexts (e.g., embedded firewalls, lightweight security protocols and device attestation techniques)
- How to protect, detect and manage privacy breaches and sensitive data leakage
- Sensor state integrity and end-to-end provenance of telemetry data
- Mobility issues with data portability (e.g., cross-border legislative concerns)
- Protection of interfaces and trust boundaries between the physical environment, sensors and upstream control systems
- Improvements in formal verification, simulation modelling and test in a TCPS security context

TCPS require a security framework that combines both *control* and *information* and deals with the specific implementation constraints and threats, the handling of sensitivity of information, privacy concerns, telemetry provenance, device state and identity, federated trust, as well as classical information system security, certification, audit and regulation. In the fully connected world of TCPS we are only just starting to see the scale of the problem, and equipment manufacturers will need to play a much more active role in designing and delivering products with security built in by design.

4.3   Situational awareness

Situational awareness-in a cybersecurity context-is essentially the ability to visualise and quantify the overall health of a system against a known set of acceptable states; in other words the ability to demonstrate that a system is correctly configured, and operating within acceptable bounds. Situational awareness is achieved by instrumenting systems and processes and applying a range of heuristics, analytics and health checks to determine system state over time, with provenance on information, software and component supply chains. We need to know the active state and trustworthiness of all subsystems, with some qualitative measures on the timeliness and reliability of information generated, especially in complex systems where updates are happening regularly. From a cybersecurity perspective, we want to know the following:

- Is the system in a known acceptable state (software, firmware revisions, configuration files, policies, access control lists, etc.)?
- Is the system behaving as expected, or exhibiting anomalous behaviour?
- Are there indications that the system may have been breached or compromised?
- Is information or telemetry being intercepted, leaked, missed or delayed?
- Are we able to *baseline* what 'normal behaviour' looks like, and is this baseline changing over time?
- Can we predict future failures or additional resource needs using current behaviour and instrumentation?

Situational awareness in TCPS can and should be applicable over many levels of abstraction; for example, an intelligent transport control system may have awareness on the state of a city transport network; an autonomous vehicle should have complete awareness on the state of all its onboard systems; a commercial aircraft should know the health of all onboard sensors and safety-critical systems. State, behaviour and provenance will need to be interrogated all the way down to software, firmware and hardware levels for every key component in the system with full auditability on the supply chain and for every subsequent replacement or revision update.

In TCPS we can achieve situational awareness using a mix of conventional and novel techniques, although a major challenge here is the scale and complexity of sensor deployment and real-time safety constraints. In order to ensure the integrity of sensors and the telemetry coming from those sensors, we need to periodically verify state and infer state through behaviour (assuming some redundancy and profiling of what 'normal' looks like). It may be impractical (or cost prohibitive) to deploy conventional security controls—such as encrypted communications—on low-level embedded systems. Where thousands of real-time sensors are deployed, it may simply be infeasible to poll each sensor for state; we may need to rely on more efficient heuristics and broadcast techniques to assess state and trustworthiness. We can also analyse event logs to periodically audit the state of these systems and look for trends.

4.4 Security controls

Today, cyber-physical security research still relies heavily existing Internet security policies and practises, such as key management and integrity verification. As discussed earlier, whilst we can reuse some concepts from existing security models, because of the specific demands in TCPS this approach may fail to satisfy the requirements of some TCPS systems for real-time capability, reliability and safety. Traditional security controls and practises will neither always transfer comfortably to TCPS nor are likely to satisfy the more demanding levels of scale and automation in embedded systems (where they may be infeasible to deploy). Controls will need to be refactored to handle new security and privacy challenges, for example, in randomly distributed sensor networks, ubiquitous wireless networks, low-power microsystems, etc. In TCPS, security controls fall into three main categories:

- **Reusable:** controls that can be directly reused from existing security domains: for example, the use of security policies, firewalls, IDS, IPS, AV and VPNs. These may be directly transferrable to back-end TCPS control and support infrastructure.
- **Refactored:** controls that must be refactored for application in the constrained environment of TCPS (such as lightweight embedded firewalls and hardware security modules (HSMs)).
- **Novel:** controls designed to deal with the specific challenges and threats in TCPS (such as new models for intrusion tolerance, new methods for large-scale device attestation, etc.)

We discuss in detail how a number of these security controls may be applied in TCPS contexts in Section 5.

4.5 Privacy

Privacy is the special consideration required to protect sensitive information and personally identifiable information (PII) on individuals from exposure or leakage either directly or by using inference. Privacy tends to focus on questions such as the following:

- What information should be collected?
- With whom is this information to be shared?
- What are the permissible uses?
- How long should the information be retained?
- What level of granularity is appropriate for the access control model?
- How can permission to use this information be revoked?

TCPS present some interesting challenges here. For example, in TCPS there may be many sensors deployed, typically small, largely hidden and collectively generating a large number of data points. The invisibility and ubiquity of sensors is a particular concern from a privacy perspective, for example, where humans inside a vehicle are unaware of the presence of sensors capable of recording conversations or interactions. These systems are often communicating remotely in real time and carry a wide variety of information, including geospatial and temporal data. If potentially sensitive data are collated, it may, for example, be difficult for an individual to repudiate having a particular conversation at a particular time and place. Some of the many privacy challenges in TCPS therefore include the following:

- Whether all such data should (or even can) be encrypted?
- Whether data can be intercepted and modified, and if so what controls are in place to detect such events?
- Whether data can be reconstructed or analysed to reveal more sensitive personal information (for example, using big data inferences)?
- Whether a device can be compromised and used maliciously from a remote location (for example, to eavesdrop or leak sensitive information)?
- What regulations and safeguards are being adhered to, especially as TCPS endpoints are often mobile (e.g., vehicles move across national boundaries)?

We discuss these and related points in the following.

Collection and inference of PII: With the increasing number of interconnected sensors and systems in intelligent transport systems, components within TCPS can be used (legitimately or otherwise) for the direct collection of sensitive PII. For example, in connected car we might wish to collect data such as on geolocation, how many passengers are present in a vehicle, who was driving (by identity or inference), average and maximum speed, etc. Without knowing the purpose of collating this information there are clear risks in how it may be processed and passed on to other parties. Such risks are not new; there are similar concerns for mobile Internet and e-commerce, where we already know that such rich data points can be correlated (for example, using big data analytical techniques) to provide insights into shopping habits, frequently visited locations, behavioural habits and trends over time. The difference for TCPS is that there could be many more data points, with potentially deeper insights into behaviour, that allow an interested party to infer sensitive personal information without direct collection of that data. Companies may be tempted to use this personal data to make credit, insurance, health and even employment decisions. Any aggregation of PII data in back end systems would also require adequate governance to ensure it cannot be leaked in the event of a breach.

Insurance companies, for example, may wish to collect data on aspects of individual driving habits — such as the number of hard braking events, miles driven, use of the accelerator and the amount of time spent driving. This data might be processed, with any insights revealed used to set insurance premiums, which could be beneficial to safer drivers and from an industry perspective may lead to the introduction of entirely new products and services (such as dynamic insurance models, for example). However, there is the potential here that such information may be highly detrimental to other drivers, for example, where data might be used to increase premiums or make future decisions on renewals — some drivers may find it hard to get insurance purely based on driving habits, not their accident record. To an extent this is already happening, albeit largely voluntarily; a concern would be that future intelligent vehicles record these data automatically (even if intended for other purposes).

Issues with mobile collected data: An interesting consideration in TCPS is that any sensitive information collected on users may be subject to different legislation in different jurisdictions, and many TCPS entities (cars, trains, ships, aircraft) are self-evidently mobile. It may be legal, for example, to collect and transmit certain PII data in one country, but as a driver crosses a national border, the legislative and regulatory regime may be entirely different. It is important therefore that broad controls are deployed to ensure the widest acceptance, and in some cases users may need to be asked for consent on specific PII transactions.

Potential for breach: In practical terms, all connected systems are vulnerable to breach, and in TCPS we should be designing systems where at least some level of breach is tolerated: it may simply be prohibitively expensive to mitigate entirely. The consequences of breach in TCPS probably require an entire chapter to explore; however, we can imagine the potential consequences if data or sensitive information were to be intercepted, recorded and possibly modified or spoofed. Endpoint vulnerabilities in vehicles together with vulnerabilities in wireless protocols could, for example, enable a skilled adversary direct access to microphones or video feeds, and without supervisory monitoring or alert systems, a driver will be entirely unaware that they were being recorded.

Governance and regulatory issues with collected data: We must also consider the privacy aspects around where data are stored, whether it may be correlated (and possibly enriched) using analytics and how it is governed — especially given the high risk of data breach at present. As a general rule data should not be collected or processed without a driver's consent, and in some jurisdictions such action fall foul of legislation. There are new regulations emerging to legislate on the governance of PII, such as the General Data Protection Regulation (GDPR), which comes into effect on May 2018. These regulations will apply to TCPS security implementations where PII is held and include serious penalties for mishandling such data. It is likely that we will see more regulation in this area in the future.

4.6 Testing and verification

We know that highly complex systems are often hard to test and verify, particularly where there is a lack of uniformity and transparency. Traditionally, the CPS community has focused on well-founded but often incomplete methods to certify operational correctness, with accuracy largely dependent on the quality of abstractions used [14]. One of the major challenges for the V&V process in industrial model-based development design is the scale and complexity of TCPS, and these models may not easily integrate with widely used formal analysis and modelling tools such as Simulink [15]. The physical aspect of TCPS makes verification even more challenging, since existing verification methods are often not transferrable.

This inability to formally verify cyber-physical systems creates security challenges that are not unique; however, the consequence of such complexity and heterogeneity mean that it may be hard, if not intractable, to prove security efficacy. If we consider automotive control systems, for example, these systems comprise cyber-physical discrete-time controllers on embedded hardware, interacting with continuous-time plants, through sensors and actuators. Since the verification problem for standard software systems is undecidable, it can reasonably be assumed that the verification problem for TCPS is unprovable also. Crenshaw and Beyer [16] propose a component-based programmable multinode attack system, using the UPBOT test platform, which can be employed to test cyber-physical security threats and defence (though unfortunately, without a solution for real time).

4.7 Emerging standards

New standards and regulations are required to assist in integration and governance challenges, as well as satisfying some of the unique requirements demanded by TCPS. Perhaps the most obvious area for advancement is the adoption of lightweight protocols and data formats, suitable for implementation in the tightly constrained embedded environments that underpin intelligent transport infrastructures. New standards are being introduced by the IETF, the International Standards Organisation (ISO) and other standards bodies. Examples include the following:

- **Continuous Air Interface for Long and Medium Range:** an ISO initiative defining standard wireless protocols and interfaces for Intelligent Transport System (ITS) services [17].
- **Constrained Application Protocol (CoAP):** a lightweight Hypertext Transport Protocol Secure (HTTPS)-like protocol.
- **Object Security for CoAP:** for securing CoAP messages.
- **Concise Binary Object Representation (CBOR):** human-readable data representation of key−value pairs and array data types (similar to JSON but more compact).
- **CBOR Object Signing and Encryption:** for securing CBOR objects.

This list is not exhaustive, and whilst new standards are developed and ratified, manufacturers will continue to develop and ship products that lack or implement weak security features, and there is likely to be prolonged period of exposure, where TCPS will be particularly vulnerable to a range of relatively trivial attack vectors.

5. Applied security controls in Transportation Cyber-Physical Systems

Current cyber-physical security research tends to rely heavily on existing security controls and design patterns. Due to the specific demands of TCPS this approach may be inappropriate in some key contexts such as large-scale low-end embedded environments, real-time safety-critical environments, and unattended targets with poor physical security. Further research and development is required and it is likely that novel solutions specific to TCPS will be required. Factors such as real-time demands, feedback between network, physical and human actors, distributed command and control, uncertainty around behaviour and threat models, limitations in test and simulation, scalability and geographic distribution must be considered holistically in cyber-physical security design. Neuman [18] discusses security modelling, security of sensors and actuators, system architecture and application security in CPS and offers a design method for integrating security into core system design.

We now discuss some important security controls together with implementation and research challenges specific to TCPS security and privacy. This is a broad and fast-moving field and therefore we cannot explore every initiative here since this would be outside the scope of this chapter. For further information on general security controls, security architecture and practices, refer to Ref. [9].

5.1 Embedded systems security

One of the key challenges in designing effective security controls for TCPS is how to implement such features in embedded contexts. There is a rich body of literature on security architectures for more sophisticated (high-end) embedded systems (typically ARM and Intel architectures, widely used in mobile platforms, for example). For these systems, a number of security architectures have been proposed, including software-based isolation and virtualisation, trusted computing based on secure hardware and processor architectures offering secure execution. These approaches may be applicable in TCPS where larger embedded systems or mobile devices are integrated (for example, in vehicle entertainment systems). This is a highly active research area; for example, Zimmer et al. [19] describe safely restrained code execution time, combining static analysis with the worst-case execution time, with system fault instructions provided where execution time exceeds limits.

Low-end embedded systems are typically designed for specific tasks, optimised for low-power consumption and minimal cost and often required to meet strict real-time requirements. These platforms typically cannot support the feature-rich controls used on high-end embedded systems. Security solutions here are typically based on hardware-enforced isolation of security-critical code and data from other software running on the same platform, for example, by using read-only memory for running tasks, hardware-enforced isolation of tasks, protected data region access, fixed memory layouts, uninterruptable tasks, secure interprocess communication, cryptographic task secrets, configuring task isolation at boot time and real-time scheduling. Examples include SPM [20], TrustLite [21], SMART [22] and SANCUS [23]. As discussed earlier, even basic security controls (such as encryption) may be infeasible to deploy in such environments due to severe resource constraints.

5.2   Access control, encryption and identity

In enterprise security, access to sensitive systems is traditionally managed through security controls such as strong identity, cryptography and role-based access control. These controls may be equally applicable for TCPS infrastructure control systems and back end support services: however, it may be infeasible to deploy even basic access controls in some low-level embedded systems. The installation of encryption may be infeasible due to resource constraints, and the implementation of identity at a hardware level requires careful consideration when one considers scale. Where encryption is not possible this raises issues for data privacy, and as such there are new standards emerging to provide lightweight implementations − see Section 4. In the case of identity, it may be possible to derive unique identities automatically from hardware during manufacturing: for example, *physically unclonable functions* (PUFs) may be applied to integrated circuits and have been widely discussed in both the research community and industry, with several studies demonstrating their use in generating unique hardware fingerprints. PUFs may form the basis for security implementations requiring secure key storage and device authentication [24], for example, as a hardware root of trust for a digital system, to generate and store a system's private master keys [25]. Despite advances, the complexity in many TCPS contexts, lack of basic security controls and presence of physical analog components mean that it may be possible to simply bypass access controls: later in this chapter we discuss the concept of intrusion tolerance.

5.3   Code signing

Code signing is a well-known technique for ensuring that software packages are both built and delivered in a known and trusted state. Essentially we need to verify the authenticity of the publisher when we receive such a package, and for safety-critical systems the value of code signing should be self-evident. Code signing typically employs cryptographic hashes (supported by PKI) to digitally sign a package and potentially all subcomponents of a package, supporting full end-to-end provenance across the entire software supply chain. Code signing enables recipients to challenge (and possibly ignore) suspect packages and helps assure that the system is in a known state and can help simplify post-incident forensic investigation.

5.4   Device attestation

To verify integrity of a system's state we use a mechanism called *attestation*, which enables the detection of differences from a known state. For example, we might wish to know that a particular component is running a specific version of firmware. This becomes especially challenging in environments where large numbers of low-power components are deployed and several approaches to remote attestation have been proposed. Most of these approaches involve the concept of a *prover* and a *verifier*, where the prover periodically sends status reports to the verifier, demonstrating that it is in a known and trustworthy state (without the need to be polled). The verifier validates that the prover's state has not been modified. To mitigate spoofing by malware, the authenticity of reports issued by the prover is normally assured by secure hardware and/or trusted software. Software-based attestation is more suited for low-end embedded devices, since it does not mandate the use of complex hardware or cryptographic secrets (and is therefore likely to be less expensive, albeit with less surety). For safety-critical systems, some basic security features should ideally be implemented in hardware where feasible.

The next generation of embedded systems for topologies such as vehicular ad hoc networks (VANETs) may employ large device swarms (dynamic self-organising heterogeneous networks of embedded devices). Verifying the integrity of such a system requires efficient swarm attestation techniques to collectively verify device states. Current naive applications of remote attestation do not scale to this level, and the design of an efficient attestation scheme is a challenging open research problem.

5.5 Embedded firewalls

Firewalls are invaluable security controls that enforce trust boundaries between security domains. Whilst ubiquitous in traditional networked domains, firewalls are demanding in terms of resources and are therefore applicable for high-level control systems and systems have enough onboard resources to support such features. Implementing stateful firewalls in low-level embedded systems may be infeasible — although it is possible to deploy relatively basic firewall functionality, such as access control rules. Hossain and Raghunathan [26] provide details of a novel lightweight firewall deployment for use in wireless sensor networks.

5.6 Embedded hardware security modules

HSMs are widely used in traditional security to provide embedded hardware support for functions such as cryptography, random number generation and secure key or certificate storage. HSMs are often deployed as rack-mounted security appliances and may include sophisticated antitamper features to mitigate unauthorised physical and remote access. In TCPS, small-scale HSMs are increasingly likely to be embedded directly into safety-critical components — such as low-level control systems and electronic control units (ECUs) in connected vehicles [27].

5.7 Intrusion and fault tolerance

IDS are mature security controls and have been widely employed in data networks. These controls are used to detect and in some cases proactively defend against attack and became increasingly popular after confidence in the traditional layered security model (with a hard security perimeter) attracted increasing scrutiny, and the true scale of the challenges in breach prevention became evident. Most large enterprises today anticipate that a security breach is inevitable, with industry surveys supporting this concern, and IDS controls (and related monitoring solutions) are there to provide an early warning in the event of a breach.

The inevitability of a security breach is instructive for TCPS, where there is very little semblance of a hard security perimeter and in some cases direct physical access to sensitive systems. In the cyber-physical world, IDS are still highly relevant for parts of the back end infrastructure, although significant refactoring of such controls may be needed to cope with low-level constraints and scale in embedded contexts. Given some of the safety implications for TCPS, we need to consider models that are intrusion tolerant, using novel heuristics and AI, with high levels of component and feature redundancy to avoid single points of failure. In TCPS we need methods to detect abnormal behaviour from baseline behaviour and employ self-healing (or exclusion) where components are either misbehaving or compromised. Adam [13] suggests establishing security policy and creating frameworks with safe interfaces to enhance the security of system dynamic behaviours and discusses methods to enable network self-configuring and self-healing, with integrated feedback mechanisms. For further information on intrusion detection in connected vehicles, see Ref. [28].

5.8   Telemetry and message provenance

Information flow is one of the defining characteristics of cyber-physical systems, and TCPS incorporate a wide variety of local and remote wired and wireless technologies. We discussed earlier the use of cryptography and cryptographic signatures in assuring communications provenance, and more recently blockchain has been proposed as a means to assure message provenance (see Section 5.9), although real-time constraints may make these solutions unsuitable for some environments. Tan et al. [29] summarise the safety control problem in cyber-physical systems, describing message integrity, availability and confidentiality issues and analyses deception and DoS attacks on information transfers between physical and control systems, analysing the limitations of existing active defence and passive response mechanisms and problems of automatic control theory in safety control. The study describes challenges and directions in CPS safety control research, applying game theory to intrusion detection models and offering a novel active–passive algorithm for system intrusion. Tang [30] proposes a model for secure information flow, validated by combining it with the flexible AC transmission systems in power systems, and provides a useful reference on security design for future cyber-physical systems. Since it describes only a subset of security incidents there are still some security vulnerabilities that will need to be addressed through further research.

5.9   Other techniques

Research in this field is highly active, with novel approaches being proposed and the extension of work from related cybersecurity domains, as well as the broader field of cyber-physical systems. For example, Little et al. [31] discuss the safety control problem in cyber-physical systems and assesses the feasibility of applying information security and control theory. Kottenstette et al. [32] describe the concept of passivity (based on control theory) and the elastic control of systems under malicious attacks and offers suggestions on how to reduce complexity and improve the accuracy of analysis. More recently blockchain techniques have been proposed as a potential means to support provenance in telemetry, messaging and configuration state between sensors and upstream control systems for use in a variety of contexts such as automotive, industrial and defence. In the latter case blockchain 'signatures' might be used to assure configuration data integrity transmitted between ground systems and military aircraft using calendar hash functions to first register state at source in a time-stamped blockchain and subsequently verify state on receipt: for further information, see Ref. [33].

6. Use case: connected car

Vehicles today contain a mixture of analog and digital components, and to a large extent the driver is still in charge. Automation in vehicles is now receiving a huge amount of attention from both the research community and manufacturers, with product offerings announced by powerful companies such as Google, Apple, Microsoft, Uber and Tesla. As we migrate towards fully connected and ultimately autonomous vehicles, the risk of a serious attack will inevitably increase. Eventually there may be few to no human-accessible controls, as manufacturers move to reduce cost and complexity, with the ability to manually override driver functions removed. If a network of such vehicles was to be compromised, the risk of serious incident at both an individual and macroscale becomes quite probable. It would be unwise to ignore such possibilities, and experience from other fields demonstrates that retrofitting security (as is currently happening in some areas of TCPS) rarely works. Whilst the industry focuses on safety, we need to significantly improve security from the ground up, building in security and privacy controls at the design phase, investing in associated research, improving standards and introducing targeted regulation.

6.1 Key stakeholders

As we discussed in Section 2, it becomes prohibitively expensive to provide near-perfect security in real-world connected systems, and for a number of reasons, achieving perfect security is practically infeasible; it becomes a matter of risk. In order to determine the level of security resources deployed to secure connected vehicles, we should first consider key stakeholders and the assets to be protected. The key stakeholders for connected vehicle are listed as follows; note that this list is partly based on Ref. [28]:

- Private vehicle owners
- Vehicle manufacturers
- Vehicle dealers
- Service providers

- Fleet owners and leasing companies
- Software and hardware companies

The assets that must be protected include a broad range of features including: ownership, privacy, availability, customer satisfaction, intellectual property, liability and reputation − see Ref. [28] for a complete list by stakeholder. This list provides useful guidance on the nature of the goals an adversary might attempt to pursue, and from this we could start to build attack trees (as described in Section 2).

6.2   System and component architecture

Cybersecurity is now a major concern for automotive electronic systems, and vehicles today contain many connected electronic systems that can be orchestrated to deliver control and monitoring on the state of the vehicle. Modern cars may contain between 50 and 120 ECUs, and these embedded computer systems control a wide range of functions, from steering, braking, powertrain and entertainment systems to lighting [28]. Vehicle control systems typically rely on components from many manufacturers with sensors and actuators, multicore processors and wireless communications of varying specifications. The overall safety of the vehicle relies on near real-time communication between ECUs; while communicating with each other ECUs are responsible for predicting crashes, detecting skids, performing anti-lock braking, etc.

For in-vehicle communications, the most widely used message bus is the CAN, although other systems such as MOST busses, LINs, FlexRay and Bluetooth are commonly deployed. Security in these local networks may be weak or nonexistent, and some implementations may be proprietary. CANs are based on a simple packet bus, enabling messages to be broadcast between safety-critical systems. Today there is no implicit support for secure communications in CANs, and there are limitations on bus bandwidth − with short message lengths and timing constraints making it challenging to embed security without adversely impacting safety systems. CANs typically use simple checksums on messages and may implement security features through obscurity with proprietary variations between manufacturers. Due to these undocumented features CANs are vulnerable to reverse engineering and spoofing [34]. CANs therefore represent a significant and attractive attack surface for adversaries.

Connected vehicles communicate externally (typically via gateway ECUs and VANETs) using a wide range of communication technologies such as worldwide interoperability for Microwave Access, wireless access in vehicular environments, dedicated short-range communications (DSRC), universal mobile telecommunications system and long-term evolution. Cellular connections to original equipment manufacturer (OEM) networks are typically employed for over-the-air (OTA) updates to noncritical firmware and software systems − although some manufacturers are already introducing OTA for core ECUs. Smartphone apps have also been developed to provide a range of functions, such as identifying vehicle location, operating door locks

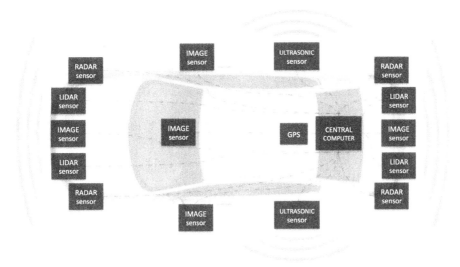

Figure 5.6 Deployment of multiple sensors in a modern connected automobile.

and to start and stop the engine. App functionality is likely to be extended as car manufacturers compete for differentiation.

Connected vehicles increasingly rely on a range of sensors. Fig. 5.6 shows the broad range of sensors required for high levels of automation; these sensors all present attack surfaces to an adversary, and their relative vulnerability depends on whether they are mounted internally or externally, and how well protected associated communications channels are.

Today ultrasonic sensors are used widely for parking; however, these are of limited importance for autonomous driving (see Table 5.2). For higher levels of automation (Level 3 and above), three main groups of sensor systems are required:

- Cameras (mono and stereo)
- Radar (radio detection and ranging)
- LiDAR (light detection and ranging)

Cameras and radar systems are increasingly used in Level 1 and 2 vehicles. When used together, these systems offer accurate feedback on vehicle speed and distance, as well as indicators of obstacles and moving objects. Radar sensors (short-and long range) are located in the front and back of vehicles to monitor traffic and can detect ranges from 1 cm to several hundred metres. At present LiDAR systems are rarely used in production due to cost and limited availability, and the potential of this technology is yet to be fully explored.

Another area to consider is the use of vehicle entertainment systems (often called infotainment systems). The car is quickly becoming a mobile entertainment platform, and as vehicles become increasingly autonomous, infotainment systems will become a key part of the vehicle's function for passengers in transit. Today such systems may be delivered using commercial off-the-shelf software, with OS such as Microsoft Windows Embedded Automotive and QNX (a real time unix-like OS, originally developed by Quantum Software Systems, later acquired by Blackberry Limited), as well as open-source variants of Linux. Whilst commercially attractive, these environments are potentially rich targets for attackers, with well-understood attacks surfaces. Mobile OS often require regular patching to mitigate vulnerabilities, and if these systems interface with in-car control systems, we have the potential for security, privacy and safety concerns, requiring careful scrutiny to sandbox such features.

6.3   Evolution towards autonomy

The various classifications of autonomous driving are listed in Table 5.2. These classifications are the adopted standards: J3016 of the Society of Automotive Engineers (SAE), and in Europe the Federal Highway Research Institute. At the time of writing no commercial production car has achieved Level 3 (although there are a number of demonstration vehicles). Several countries are working on a possible legal acceptance of Level 3 vehicles by 2020.

Fully autonomous vehicles require high level of scrutiny from a security and privacy perspective, and additional safeguards will be required to avoid major incident. We should view autonomous vehicles as an amplification of all of the possible threats and vulnerabilities in today's connected car: the attack surface becomes larger, much more complex and the number of potential vulnerabilities increase significantly. A remotely controlled connected vehicle is a potential terrorist weapon, and the cost of poor security should be viewed from this perspective.

6.4   Threats and vulnerabilities

Modern vehicles present a variety of attack surfaces for adversaries and they are often left unattended for long periods (so physical security may not always be possible). Researchers have already demonstrated that vehicles can be compromised through a number of interfaces, including direct or indirect physical access, short-range wireless communications and long-range wireless communications [35–39]. This is a broad and complex topic and we discuss a sample of common threats and associated research here. For further information, refer to Ref. [28].

Antitheft systems have been routinely compromised, allowing direct physical access to the vehicle and its onboard systems. Such attacks are often surprisingly low tech (such as breaking a lock, finding keys and hot-wiring the ignition), although more sophisticated attacks are now being attempted on high-end cars, using techniques such as relay attacks, radio jamming, DoS and breaking encryption keys [28].

Once inside a vehicle, ECUs may be accessed physically through an on-board diagnostic (OBD-II) port (which is mandated in the United States and present on most vehicles). With this level of access, a malicious adversary can conduct security attacks such as message injection, replay, spoofing and privacy attacks such as eavesdropping. By infiltrating a single automotive ECU, an attacker can gain access to other ECUs over communication buses (such as a CAN) and potentially gain control of features such as the instrument cluster, locks and safety-critical components (such as acceleration and braking systems and the engine). Researchers at the University of Washington and the University of California San Diego [40] have demonstrated how malware might be introduced through physical access to the vehicle or remotely over Bluetooth or the telematics unit. They demonstrated that there are significant threats to accidental failure, where the safety of these systems would be compromised. Note that whilst their research was intended to demonstrate the existence of such threats, the authors did not release exploit code or reveal the identity of the vehicles used in testing.

Researchers have also has shown that it is possible for a malicious adversary to perform remote code execution on ECUs through a number of interfaces, such as the Bluetooth and the telematics unit. Miller and Valasek [41] presented at DEF CON 13 [34] describing various compromises on the CAN busses of two modern automobiles. The authors performed reverse engineering on the CAN bus and demonstrated that connected components can be compromised (or their performance degraded) by either flooding the network (essentially using a DoS attack) or through carefully crafted spoofed packets. Whilst the CAN implementation in these cars precluded some attacks (such as affecting acceleration at speed), others were possible (such as affecting braking at speed). As cars are increasingly connected and automated, the number of safety-critical vulnerabilities will very likely increase.

TCPS employ different sensor types for measuring variables through physical channels [3]; for example, a car may be equipped with both LiDAR and sonar sensors for measuring distance, a magnetic speedometer to measure velocity and sensors to measure tyre pressure. An adversary may attempt to compromise specific sensor types to create specific types of failure: for example, distance-measuring sensors can be compromised to generate false distance readings, which in turn may cause a vehicle's braking functionality to be compromised. Sensors may be more or less trusted depending on whether they are placed internally or externally and whether the adversary (naive or sophisticated) is located inside or outside a vehicle [3].

VANETs may be compromised for a variety of reasons, spanning misuse to terrorism, using a range of attacks from network monitoring, social attacks, timing attacks, application attacks through to DoS attacks. For example, a vehicle owner could mount a so-called Sybil attack, spoofing congestion information from thousands of vehicles either to influence traffic control systems or influence other drivers to take an alternate route [28].

Remote updates to connected car components are often essential, for example, to fix software bugs, upgrade features and maintain a certain risk profile. These updates are increasingly delivered wirelessly OTA and represent a rich attack surface for interception, DoS, eavesdropping and data manipulation.

The supply chain and servicing infrastructure for delivering and maintaining all of the components that make up a connected automobile involve many different OEMs, suppliers and subcontractors. This complexity in the supply chain means that oversight and scrutiny of every aspect of supply may be infeasible, and there is the real possibility for a range of attacks involving insider threat, fraud, sensitive information leakage and implications for safety.

6.5 Threat mitigation

To mitigate the risk of attacks on OTA updates, the associated communication channels need to be encrypted where feasible, ideally with hardware support for cryptographic functions and key storage. The software supply chain will also need to implement end-to-end code signing and regular status checks and version audits to assure system state. If critical components are monitored it should also be possible to implement rollback procedures and to force systems back into a known state, if the active state proves to be inconsistent. A protocol for delivering secure OTA firmware updates is proposed in Ref. [27]; the protocol relies on the use of an HSM for cryptographic functions and random number generation, with each ECU containing an HSM.

For safety-critical functions and fault tolerance (in sensor networks, for example), TCPS may employ multiple different technologies to measure the same variables, providing some redundancy and the ability to detect filter out anomalous readings. For example, vehicles may use sonar with C2C and LiDAR to measure distance. LiDAR is prone to failure fail (e.g., in foggy conditions) and sensor inputs may also be unreliable due to noise, packet loss and other faults. Velocity may be measured using the speedometers and GPS. Since these sensors may be placed internally or externally on a vehicle we should also consider direct physical attacks.

Researchers have proposed the use of message authentication codes to protect against masquerade and replay attacks on CAN networks [35], although these enhancements may be infeasible with the implementation of CAN in today's vehicles, due to limitations in message lengths (64-bits of payload) and real-time constraints. Further details on CAN, LIN and MOST bus vulnerabilities and related exploits can be found in Ref. [28].

Where there are marked discrepancies in sensor readings we may consider the use of introducing signal processing techniques and advanced heuristics (including noise reduction, filters, anomaly detection and consensus algorithms, etc.) to prevent, detect and possibly tolerate a level on unreliability in sensor inputs. These techniques can be used to determine which readings are most trustworthy and which should be excluded − either temporarily or permanently. For example, consensus algorithms may be used that mandate a proportion of sensor inputs to be reporting reliably at a particular time, with any outliers ignored. To evaluate the trustworthiness of sensor readings, it may be possible to apply a number of methods cited in the literature [3].

Cars are often left unattended for long periods, and if the attacker has direct physical access to sensors and safety-critical components, then the scope for vulnerability is far greater. By placing sensors inside the vehicle and where possible removing direct physical access to hardware interfaces in the vehicle (in favour of encrypted Wi-Fi with access controls, for example), such risks may be significantly reduced. The latter may not be feasible where legislation mandates that diagnostic ports—such as OBD interfaces—are easily accessible within the vehicle. As described previously, where sensors are not directly accessible physically, a skilled adversary with intimate knowledge of in-vehicle systems may still be able to remotely compromise a vehicle and manipulate readings in such a way as to influence safety-critical functions.

This is a complex, evolving and important research area. One of the lessons from other security domains is that attacks tend to get more sophisticated over time, as more sophisticated security controls are deployed, especially if the target goal is sufficiently attractive. Such attacks often display intimate system knowledge and high levels of skill. For more detailed analysis of security and privacy issues in smart automobiles, see Ref. [28].

6.6 Summary

Security and privacy challenges should be expected to grow significantly for automotive electronic systems, given the predicted increased use of automation, wireless communications, in particular telematics, OTA updates, especially to core systems, and large-scale sensor deployments. We should assume that interfaces may be vulnerable to breach. It is therefore critical to harden all in-vehicle systems and external communication channels with appropriate security controls that limit the scope for damage and deploy early warning features to alert on anomalous behaviour or unauthorised changes to system state. In parallel we need to explore new security techniques directly suited to low-level embedded devices and large-scale cyber-physical systems. The vulnerability of message busses—with access to safety-critical ECUs—is a particular concern that needs to be addressed in all new vehicles, particularly as we move towards unprecedented levels of automation, connectivity and integration.

7. Emerging technologies

Cyber-physical systems already leverage advances in mobile computing—although there are still a large number of legacy technologies deployed—for example, in critical systems infrastructure. TCPS and the related initiatives such as smart cities are increasingly taking advantage of new and emerging technologies such as dig data, software-defined network (SDN), virtualisation, AI, IoT and blockchain. We now briefly discuss some of these important technologies in the context of TCPS.

7.1 Software-defined networks

Effective cybersecurity remains a hard problem, even in less-complex environments such as enterprise networks; it remains a problem very far from solved. There are simply too many variables and too many dynamics in the threat and vulnerability landscape, including (and often compounded by) interaction with people. The continual arms race in cybersecurity places stress on maintenance processes, with operations staff fighting daily to defend against existing and emerging threats, against a backdrop of frequent patches and updates to core systems and services. As new software development processes are introduced, the speed of change is increasing dramatically (it now takes seconds to deploy new software releases), and we are moving to a new phase in connected systems where the network itself needs to be programmable to maintain pace and make more effective use of limited network resources.

SDNs are essentially a new approach to network orchestration, pushing core routing intelligence out to the edge of the infrastructure, away from traditionally smart switches and routers. The basic idea is that the network should comprise less-intelligent systems at the core, but these can be rapidly reconfigured to respond to changes in the environment through programmable policies. For example, we might choose to implement dynamic *scale-out* of services on detecting a rapid increase in network traffic, without any human intervention or manual reconfiguration. SDNs should prove useful in emerging TCPS control infrastructure (for example, for disaster recovery, rapid response to demand or dynamic traffic routing); however, they come with some risk. With SDN, control becomes highly centralised, and the scope for damage after a compromise is therefore greater. The lack of transparency in virtualised routes may also lead to situations where eavesdropping and manipulation of telemetry and messaging go undetected for long periods. Nevertheless, this is an important field and a promising technology for use in TCPS.

7.2 Virtualisation

Virtualisation is essentially the capability to deploy OS and components inside tightly controlled software containers to be executed over virtual machines, and is proving to be highly advantageous for rapid deployment of so-called *elastic* support infrastructures for data centres and back end support services. Virtualisation speeds up deployment and improves security by assuring consistency across multiple OS instances. Virtualisation is also a fundamental component of the new 'DevOps' approach to software deployment and is likely to be a key enabler for software-defined infrastructures. Virtualisation promotes sandboxing (containing execution of sensitive or risky functions within a container), scale, out and high availability. These properties are very attractive for building cost-effective, secure and agile TCPS infrastructure. Virtualisation is likely to have other benefits in TCPS, such as improved testing and simulation, dynamic rollback of critical systems to a known state and rapid deployment of stable and consistent in-vehicle systems.

7.3 Big data

TCPS infrastructures produce vast quantities of data, and the volume and velocity of these data may be infeasible to store and analyse using traditional relational databases. Big data (in the form of Apache Hadoop, Cassandra and other 'NoSQL' technologies) enables very large unstructured datasets to be held in high-availability processing clusters. With technologies such as Hadoop, large volumes of *unstructured* data can be efficiently queried using specialised techniques such as *MapReduce*, and this ability to span huge amounts of loosely structured data can often reveal surprising insights. In the context of TCPS we should expect to see big data being used heavily in back end support infrastructure, to hold and analyse messaging, telemetry, event logs, geospatial data, even video feeds and images. Where TCPS networks are software programmable, it may also be possible to create feedback loops where insights become actionable with dynamic changes to such networks dynamically orchestrated — in response to changes in demand, for example, or as a result of predictive analytics. Given the previous discussion on telemetry interception and poisoning, we will need to ensure that adequate protections are in place to avoid important decision-making and control systems from being manipulated by downstream sensor data. We will also need to be careful of inadvertently exposing sensitive PII data through correlation or inference.

7.4 Artificial intelligence and machine learning

Since cybersecurity breaches and compromises are practically inevitable and the consequences of these breaches in TCPS are potentially life threatening, we will need to find several advances in improving the intelligent of such networks and systems. TCPS infrastructures are required to be somewhat intrusion tolerant and will need to provide rapid self-healing, alongside new levels of automation. At the analysis phase, ML (together with blended heuristics) is likely to offer important insights and benefits in the automation of threat and vulnerability analysis [6]. Intelligent systems and anomaly detection also have an important roll to play in differentiating normal and delinquent behaviour, both at the control system level and at the sensor—actuator level. ML and techniques such as neural networks (NNs) and fuzzy logic may help differentiate between faulty, failing or misconfigured or compromised components. ML and NNs may also be trained to predict future failures based on existing behaviour. This shift towards a smarter and more proactive security posture could have significant benefits in traditional security contexts such as industrial and enterprise systems.

7.5 Blockchain

Blockchain is a relatively new technology based on well-established concepts (such as Merkle trees and hash codes) and brings together the functions of distributed consensus, immutable state, timestamping and distributed ledgers. Perhaps the best-known implementation of blockchain today is *Bitcoin*, and while Bitcoin is based on blockchain technology it is important to differentiate between *blockchain fabrics* and the implementation of *digital currencies* and tokens on those fabrics. Blockchain fabrics have many potential uses across a wide range of industries and contexts, and research that predates Bitcoin [33] introduces the application of time-stamped calendar blocks that now underpin many blockchain implementations. There have been proposals to use blockchains in many security and privacy contexts, for example, to register immutable asset states, maintain the integrity of audit logs, assure the provenance of sensitive telemetry, protect health records and assure PII transaction integrity for GDPR. The key themes that bind these use cases together are *trust*, *immutability*, *identity* and *scale*. Since blockchain is primarily based on the properties of cryptographic hashes, it may prove useful in TCPS contexts where systems are required to scale to millions of devices and where encryption cannot be deployed (due to resource constraints, for example). Hashing is relatively simple to deploy and is less computationally expensive compared to encryption. An important but subtle distinction is that hash codes promote *integrity*, whereas encryption promotes confidentiality (refer to the CIA triad in Fig. 5.2). Integrated blockchain fabrics may also be used to support situational awareness across millions of assets in connected transport systems: for example, Guardtime [33] has designed blockchain infrastructure that can ingest 10^{12} blockchain registrations per second.

8. Conclusions and future direction

This is a fascinating area and we should recognise that the task of securing TCPS is a journey and we are setting off somewhat unprepared. In all the excitement of setting course, we run the risk of ignoring many of the lessons learnt. After nearly three decades we have arrived at a situation where cybersecurity is widely acknowledged to be in a poor state: cybercriminals are proving to be persistent and extremely resourceful, and breaches are now seen as inevitable-despite all our advances in cybersecurity technology and practices. TCPS represent a unique and broad attack surface for cybercriminals, and by incorporating unprotected technologies into emerging connected designs we run the risk of serious incidents in the future. As we have discussed, in TCPS the consequences of compromise are potentially life threatening and may have significant direct and indirect economic risks, as well as risks to individual privacy.

A holistic cybersecurity approach with multiple abstraction levels is required to address the unique security and privacy risks associated with TCPS. Furthermore, specific domains within TCPS exhibit marked differences in design, implementation and risk appetite and should be treated independently with specialised security controls where appropriate. This approach includes such diverse aspects as risk assessment and modelling; platform security; secure engineering; security management; identity management; sensor integrity; telemetry provenance and PII governance. TCPS mandate a real-time intrusion-tolerant approach, employing novel heuristics, alternate sensor feeds and self-healing to reduce the impact of compromise. We should anticipate and actively promote research and development in techniques that significantly increase levels of automation, efficacy and accuracy in cybersecurity in order to keep pace with emerging threats and deployment scale.

With TCPS there is an opportunity to address some of the fundamental concerns from the ground up by designing in security at the outset, by developing new protocols and standards that incorporate security and privacy, and by developing systems that tolerate some degree of intrusion without compromising safety. This shift towards a more proactive and intrusion tolerant security posture could have major benefits in more traditional security contexts such as industrial and enterprise networks.

There remains a number of significant research challenges that need to be addressed going forward. Risk assessment in TCPS is in its infancy: it is important that we explore how other disciplines such as how ML might be used to offer insights and improve automation in threat and vulnerability analysis (for example, by autogenerating attack trees for critical infrastructure and transportation systems [6]). Work on improving security in real-time message bus design is critically important as we move towards fully autonomous systems. New lightweight security controls are required specifically for TCPS to help mitigate low-level attacks. Intrusion tolerant systems and heuristics are required to deal with anomalous behaviour from compromised or failing components, particularly in areas where physical security is weak. Remote attestation techniques need to be improved to assure correct operational state, especially in core systems that are frequently updated OTA. Current naive applications of remote attestation do not scale and the design of an efficient attestation schemes is a challenging open research problem. Finally, the inherent complexities in supply chain and servicing operations raises major concerns on security and privacy, specifically how we might provide greater transparency and auditability across all components and subcomponents deployed and how we might best simulate and test fully assembled systems with regard to security and privacy.

Exercises

1. Explain the various threats and vulnerabilities in intelligent vehicles.
2. List the main reasons why achieving effective cybersecurity in TCPS differs from the traditional use of security controls.
3. Explain the various ways that privacy can be compromised in TCPS. Give examples.
4. Explain how you might set about testing TCPS for security and privacy vulnerabilities, what tools and techniques might you use.
5. Can any TCPS system be guaranteed to be perfectly secure? Explain your reasoning with examples.
6. Explain the relationship between safety and security in TCPS.
7. Highlight some of the consequences of breach or compromise of TCPS systems Explain your reasoning with examples.
8. Outline potential security attacks on an autonomous vehicle using an attack tree. Describe some of the controls you might deploy to mitigate such attacks.
9. Explain the benefits and issues in using OTA updates for core ECUs in connected vehicles. How might we improve the integrity of the software supply chain.

References

[1] L. Marinos, ENISA Threat Taxonomy: A Tool for Structuring Threat Information, 2016.
[2] Geer's Law; Attributed to Dan Geer, an Internationally Recognised Security Analysts. https://en.wikipedia.org/wiki/Dan_Geer. (Accessed on 18/04/2018).
[3] I. Ruchkin, A. Rao, D. De Niz, S. Chaki, D. Garlan, Eliminating inter-domain vulnerabilities in cyber-physical systems: an analysis contracts approach, in: Proceedings of the First ACM Workshop on Cyber-Physical Systems-Security and/or Privacy, ACM, October 2015, pp. 11−22.
[4] B. Schneier, Attack trees, Dr. Dobb's Journal 24 (12) (1999) 21−29.
[5] Open Web Application Security Project (OWASP) Threat Modelling Web pages. https://www.owasp.org/index.php/Threat_Risk_Modeling. (Accessed on 18/04/2018).
[6] MIT Computer Science and Artificial Intelligence Laboratory (CSAIL) Project Page on the Use of AI to Auto-Generate Attack Trees for Critical Infrastructure and Transportation Systems. https://www.csail.mit.edu/research/automated-attack-tree-generation-critical-infrastructure. (Accessed on 18/04/2018).

[7] Lockheed Martin's Web Page Describing the Seven Phases of the Cyber Kill Chain®. https://www.lockheedmartin.com/us/what-we-do/aerospace-defense/cyber/cyber-kill-chain.html. (Accessed on 18/04/2018).

[8] K.J. Higgins, How Lockheed Martin's 'Kill Chain' Stopped SecurID Attack, 2013.

[9] N.A. Sherwood, Enterprise security Architecture: a Business-Driven Approach, CRC Press, 2005.

[10] R.A. Thacker, C.J. Myers, K. Jones, S.R. Little, A new verification method for embedded systems, in: Proc. IEEE Int. Conf. Computer Design, 2009, pp. 193–200. Lake Tahoe, CA.

[11] A.R. Sadeghi, C. Wachsmann, M. Waidner, Security and privacy challenges in industrial internet of things, in: Design Automation Conference (DAC), 2015 52nd ACM/EDAC/IEEE, IEEE, June 2015, pp. 1–6.

[12] A. Costin, J. Zaddach, A. Francillon, D. Balzarotti, S. Antipolis, A large-scale analysis of the security of embedded firmwares, in: USENIX Security Symposium, August 2014, pp. 95–110.

[13] N. Adam, Workshop on future directions in cyber-physical systems security, in: Report on Workshop Organized by Department of Homeland Security (DHS), January 2010.

[14] X. Jin, J.V. Deshmukh, J. Kapinski, K. Ueda, K. Butts, Challenges of applying formal methods to automotive control systems, in: NSF National Workshop on Transportation Cyber-physical Systems, 2014.

[15] Mathworks' Simulink Web Page (Simulation and Model Based Design). https://uk.mathworks.com/products/simulink.html. (Accessed on 18/04/2018).

[16] T.L. Crenshaw, S. Beyer, UPBOT: a testbed for cyber-physical systems, in: Proc. 3rd Int. Conf. Cyber Security Experimentation and Test, 2010. Washington, DC, Article No. 1–8.

[17] ISO Presentation on Continuous Air Interface for Long and Medium Range (CALM) initiative. https://www.ietf.org/proceedings/63/slides/nemo-4.pdf. (Accessed on 18/04/2018).

[18] C. Neuman, Challenges in security for cyber-physical systems, in: DHS: S & T Workshop on Future Directions in Cyber-physical Systems Security, July 2009.

[19] C. Zimmer, B. Bhat, F. Mueller, S. Mohan, Time-based intrusion detection in cyber-physical systems, in: Proc. 1st ACM/IEEE Int. Conf. Cyber-Physical Systems, 2010, pp. 109–118. Stockholm, Sweden.

[20] R. Strackx, F. Piessens, B. Preneel, Efficient isolation of trusted subsystems in embedded systems, in: Security and Privacy in Communication Networks, Springer, 2010.

[21] P. Koeberl, S. Schulz, A.-R. Sadeghi, V. Varadharajan, TrustLite: a security architecture for tiny embedded devices, in: European Conference on Computer Systems (EuroSys), ACM, 2014.

[22] K. Eldefrawy, A. Francillon, D. Perito, G. Tsudik, SMART: secure and minimal architecture for (establishing a dynamic) root of trust, in: Network and Distributed System Security Symposium (NDSS), 2012.

[23] J. Noorman, P. Agten, W. Daniels, R. Strackx, A. Van Herrewege, C. Huygens, B. Preneel, I. Verbauwhede, F. Piessens, Sancus: low-cost trustworthy extensible networked devices with a zero-software trusted computing base, in: USENIX Conference on Security, USENIX Association, 2013.

[24] A. Schaller, V. van der Leest, Physically unclonable functions found in standard components of commercial devices, in: First Workshop on Trustworthy Manufacturing and Utilization of Secure Devices (TRUDEVICE 2013), May 2013, pp. 1–2. Avignon, France.

[25] R. Maes, V. van der Leest, E. van der Sluis, F. Willems, Secure key generation from biased PUFs, in: International Workshop on Cryptographic Hardware and Embedded Systems, Springer, Berlin, Heidelberg, September 2015, pp. 517–534.

[26] M. Hossain, V. Raghunathan, Aegis: a lightweight firewall for wireless sensor networks, in: Distributed Computing in Sensor Systems, 2010, pp. 258–272.

[27] M.S. Idrees, H. Schweppe, Y. Roudier, M. Wolf, D. Scheuermann, O. Henniger, Secure automotive on-board protocols: a case of over-the-air firmware updates, in: International Workshop on Communication Technologies for Vehicles, Springer, Berlin, Heidelberg, March 2011, pp. 224–238.

[28] J. Deng, L. Yu, Y. Fu, O. Hambolu, R.R. Brooks, Security and data privacy of modern automobiles, in: Data Analytics for Intelligent Transportation Systems, 2017, pp. 131–163.

[29] Y. Tan, M.C. Vuran, S. Goddard, Spatio-temporal event model for cyber-physical systems, in: Proc. 29th IEEE Int. Conf. Distributed Computing Systems Workshops, 2009, pp. 44–50. Montreal, QC.

[30] H. Tang, Security Analysis of a Cyber-physical System (M.Sc. thesis), University of Missouri-Rolla, Rolla, 2007.

[31] S. Little, D. Walter, K. Jones, C. Myers, Analog/mixed-signal circuit verification using models generated from simulation traces, in: Proc. 5th Int. Symp. Automated Technology for Verification and Analysis, 2007, pp. 114–128. Tokyo, Japan.

[32] N. Kottenstette, G. Karsai, J. Sztipanovits, A passivity-based framework for resilient cyber physical systems, in: Proc. 2nd Int. Symp. Resilient Control Systems, 2009, pp. 43–50. Idaho Falls, ID.

[33] Guardtime Website. Guardtime is an Estonian based Company That Offers a Novel Range of Blockchain Solutions to Assist in Remote Attestation, Provenance, Compliance, and Situational Awareness. www.guardtime.com. (Accessed on 18/04/2018).

[34] DEFCON, One of the Longest Running and Best Known Annual Hacker Conventions. https://www.defcon.org/. (Accessed on 18/04/2018).

[35] C.W. Lin, Q. Zhu, C. Phung, A. Sangiovanni-Vincentelli, Security-aware mapping for CAN-based real-time distributed automotive systems, in: Proceedings of the International Conference on Computer-Aided Design, IEEE Press, November 2013, pp. 115–121.

[36] S. Checkoway, D. McCoy, B. Kantor, D. Anderson, H. Shacham, S. Savage, K. Koscher, A. Czeskis, T. Roesner, T. Kohno, Comprehensive experimental analyses of automotive attack surfaces, in: USENIX Security Symposium, August 2011.

[37] P. Kleberger, T. Olovsson, E. Jonsson, Security aspects of the in-vehicle network in the connected car, in: IEEE Intelligent Vehicles Symposium, 2011, pp. 528–533.

[38] K. Koscher, A. Czeskis, F. Roesner, S. Patel, T. Kohno, S. Checkoway, D. McCoy, B. Kantor, D. Anderson, H. Shacham, S. Savage, Experimental security analysis of a modern automobile, in: IEEE Symposium on Security and Privacy, 2010, pp. 447–462.

[39] I. Rouf, R. Miller, H. Mustafa, T. Taylor, S. Oh, W. Xu, M. Gruteser, W. Trappe, I. Seskar, Security and privacy vulnerabilities of in-car wireless networks: a tire pressure monitoring system case study, in: USENIX Conference on Security, 2010.

[40] Centre for Automotive Embedded Systems Security. https://www.autosec.org/publications.html. (Accessed on 18/04/2018).

[41] C. Miller, C. Valasek, Adventures in automotive networks and control units, in: DEF CON, 21, 2013, pp. 260–264.

[42] Y. Liu, Y. Peng, B. Wang, S. Yao, Z. Liu, Review on cyber-physical systems, IEEE/CAA Journal of Automatica Sinica 4 (1) (2017) 27–40.

Infrastructure for Transportation Cyber-Physical Systems

Brandon Posey[1], Linh Bao Ngo[1], Mashrur Chowdhury[2], Amy Apon[1]
[1]School of Computing, Clemson University, Clemson, SC, United States; [2]Glenn Department of Civil Engineering, Clemson University, Clemson, SC, United States

1. Introduction to infrastructure for Transportation Cyber-Physical Systems

We begin with an example of data infrastructure in a traditional data processing or web services environment before describing the more complex data infrastructures needed for Transportation Cyber-Physical Systems (TCPS). In this example, we examine web service stacks, which typically rely on the traditional LAMP architecture [1]. The acronym LAMP stands for the Linux operating system, the Apache HTTP Server, the MySQL relational database management systems (RDBMS) and the PHP programming language. In Fig. 6.1, which provides a graphical representation of the LAMP architecture, we can identify the role of individual components within LAMP. Linux is responsible for providing an open source and reliable operating system on top of the hardware resources. The RDBMS, not necessarily MySQL, is the core data infrastructure, where data are stored and accessed. The Apache HTTP Server provides an interface and supporting platform through which users can invoke applications written using PHP or other programming languages such as JavaScript. These web services will access the RDBMS for data that can be used to create content for users to consume. The data inside the RDBMS can be populated via direct insertion or with information provided by users. To a certain extent, the RDBMS and the corresponding external programs or web-based applications responsible for data collection, insertion and presentation form the data infrastructure within a web service stack.

To meet the complex data challenges of TCPS, standard data infrastructure must evolve to cope with the characteristics of TCPS data which can be described using '5Vs of big data': (1) volume, (2) variety, (3) velocity, (4) veracity and (5) value [2]. A data infrastructure to accommodate these characteristics called lambda architecture (LA) has been proposed [3]. As shown in Fig. 6.2, the data infrastructure in LA is divided into four primary components: the data layer, the batch layer, the stream layer and the serving layer. The concepts presented in LA present a solid foundation to utilise within TCPS. Within the data layer, the data brokering component is a critical element that ties both batch and stream layers together. It provides several critical services to the entire infrastructure. Examples of these services include improving data stream accessibility by duplicating and partitioning data and reducing risk of data loss when data ingestion services on batch and stream layers fail. Like the stream

Transportation Cyber-Physical Systems. https://doi.org/10.1016/B978-0-12-814295-0.00006-X
Copyright © 2018 Elsevier Inc. All rights reserved.

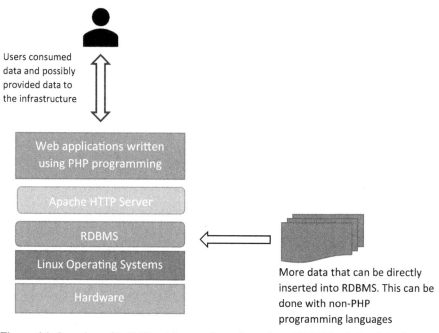

Figure 6.1 Overview of LAMP architecture for web services. *RDBMS*, relational database management systems.

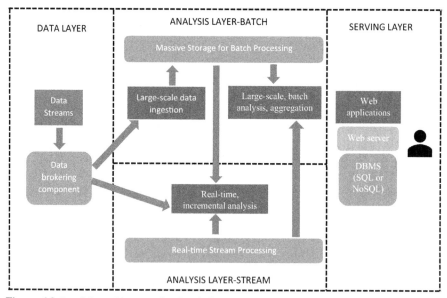

Figure 6.2 Lambda architecture for data infrastructure.

layer, various software frameworks capabilities exist that can provide data brokering. Among them, Apache Kafka is the latest framework whose development and motivation come from a data enterprise production environment [4].

The batch layer is consisted of components that can store and process massive amount of data without a real-time service-level requirement. Unlike traditional DBMS that primarily support data ingestion and data access via query languages, the LA's batch layer must also support the ability to develop complex manipulation and computation tasks on massive amounts of data. To this end, components that separate computation and large-scale storage are not appropriate due to the network bandwidth limitation for transferring data. Currently, one of the most popular software ecosystems that is being used in the batch layer is the Hadoop ecosystem, which includes the Hadoop Distributed File System (HDFS) [5] for large-scale storage and the Hadoop MapReduce framework [6] for data processing. The stream layer does not maintain any persistent storage component. Instead, it relies on streaming data processing infrastructure that can ingest and process data in real time. While stream processing software has been developed since the 1960s [7], there are few modern frameworks that can support the level of volume and velocity required for big data. Among these frameworks, Spark [8], Flink [9] and Storm [10] are among the most well known, but Spark stands out as the one that is widely adopted by both academic and industry. The serving layer is where users can interact with the data stored on the system using applications written in different programming languages as previously discussed. Each of these layers and their functionality within TCPS will be discussed in more detail later in this chapter.

2. Networking among data infrastructure

In TCPS, infrastructure, vehicles and people collaborate to support the application requirements of both end users and other stakeholders (e.g., automotive-related industries, motorists and public agencies). Data infrastructure, a centralised, distributed or centralised-distributed architecture, needs to communicate with data senders, data receivers and among components of the data infrastructure itself. These communications take place either wirelessly or through wired mediums. Use of one or more communication mediums will depend on several factors, such as availability of the communication mediums, application requirements, such as range, reliability, delay and bandwidth. Sources and recipients of data will include people, devices, other data infrastructure and services. Data infrastructure could include one layer or multiple layers of data storage and processors, depending on the application requirements. The number of data infrastructure layers needed is to be selected to reduce data delivery delay for the services provided by a connected cyber-physical system, to reduce the bandwidth requirement and data loss rate to support a large number of CPS elements and to run multiple diverse TCPS applications simultaneously [11].

The United States Department of Transportation (USDOT) has supported the development of the Connected Vehicle Reference Implementation Architecture (CVRIA) as a guidance for developing connected vehicle applications and infrastructures. A physical view of a connected vehicle application, traffic data collection, is shown in Fig. 6.3 [12]. A physical view of an application describes physical objects (systems and devices) and their application objects and the high-level interfaces between those physical objects. Fig. 6.3 presents the physical objects, such as traffic management center and vehicle onboard equipment (OBE), and application objects, such as vehicle situation data monitoring and vehicle safety (in the vehicle OBE physical object). Interfaces between the physical objects are shown for temporal (flow time context), spatial (flow spatial context) and security (flow security) contexts. Different colours are indicating whether they fall under center, field or vehicle category. Interfaces between physical objects are communications showing the high-level name of each flow with their temporal, spatial and security contexts. These interfaces between different physical objects, which can be referred as infrastructure, are enabled by wired or wireless communications. For example, vehicle OBE (such as a connected vehicle) and roadside equipment communicate three types of information flows (vehicle situation data parameters, vehicle situation data and vehicle location and motion for surveillance) through a wireless medium. CVRIA's application views could be useful as a reference to develop data architecture for any connected vehicle applications. CVRIA also provides enterprise, functional and communication views of different connected vehicle applications.

Fig. 6.4 shows an example of a layered architecture for the Clemson University Connected Vehicle Testbed [11]. As shown in Fig. 6.3, the layered architecture includes (1) mobile edge devices, (2) fixed edge node and (3) system edge node. Each mobile edge node, such as vehicles and pedestrians, is equipped with wireless communication devices, such as dedicated short-range communications (DSRC), Long Term Evolution (LTE) cellular or Wi-Fi−enabled device, which can collect and transmit location and mobility information. The fixed edges receive the data from the mobiles edges, usually with low latency requirements, especially if the related applications are safety critical. The fixed edges are connected to a system edge through a high-throughput, low latency and highly reliable communication option, such as fibre optic, which provides backhaul support. The system edge controls data storage, data fusion and data distribution to external entities. Although Fig. 6.4 shows a three-layer data architecture, the number of layers could vary depending on the numbers of applications to be supported by the architecture and application-specific requirements.

Different communications options are available to connect different data infrastructure layers based on the application requirements. For example, for safety-critical applications in a connected vehicle system, DSRC is recommended because of its low latency. For non−safety-critical connected vehicle applications, where low latency is not usually required, 4G LTE or Wi-Fi could be a viable option for wireless communication. Under development at the time of writing chapter, 5G LTE could be another viable option for low latency communications. These communications options are discussed in Chapter 11 in more detail.

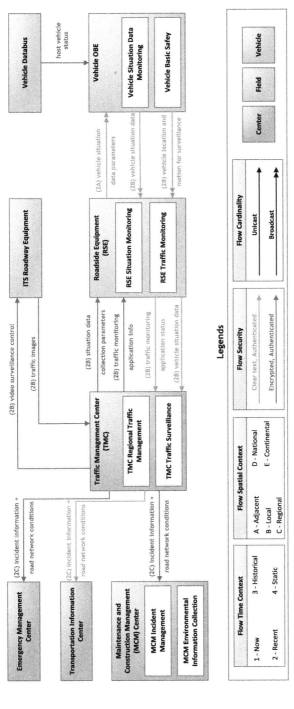

Figure 6.3 Application view of traffic data collection. *ITS*, Intelligent Transportation System; OBE, onboard equipment. Reproduced from Connected Vehicle Reference Implementation Architecture (CVRIA), USDOT, (https://local.iteris.com/cvria/html/applications/app87.html#tab-3), (accessed in May 2018).

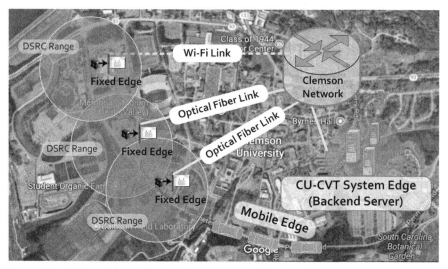

Figure 6.4 Vehicles and data infrastructure connected through different communication mediums [11].

3. Data collection and ingest

The first process that takes place within the TCPS data processing and decision support infrastructure is the collection of the data. TCPS can have a wide variety of different data sources and needs to be able to quickly and efficiently store and capture all the data from these devices. Obtaining data from these different devices in different data formats poses unique challenges that will be discussed more in this section.

Once these data are collected and stored, it needs to be ingested and sent off to perform analytics on the data to extract the meaningful data. This is typically done through a data brokering component that manages where the data are sent and how they are processed. Data brokers and their operation will be discussed in more detail in this section.

3.1 Transportation Cyber-Physical Systems data source challenges

TCPS data can come from a variety of sources such as sensors and cameras that are connected to traffic lights, connected vehicles, satellites and even travellers. Each of these sources produces different types of data that pertain to different aspects of a TCPS such as location, weather, route of travel, accident avoidance and overall infrastructure performance. These different types of data need to be processed using different methods. Some of these data collected require very little to zero processing, for example, the count of vehicles that passed a certain location during a certain period, whereas other collected data require significantly more processing such as a video feed from a CCTV camera. This wide variability in the type of data and the processing power required to obtain the required insights from the data greatly impacts the type of data infrastructure utilised by TCPS.

For those TCPS that require more processing intensive tasks, the underlying data infrastructure needs to not only be able to handle the amount of data being generated but also be able to process the same data efficiently. The amount of data being collected by the TCPS can be on the scale of petabytes which poses an issue with the storage of such a large amount of data. On top of the storage issue, there is the issue of accessing and processing the data. This requires robust processing engines and vast amounts of infrastructure to be feasible. We discuss the software systems that make this possible later in this chapter.

Users of TCPS also have some unique requirements and demand that they place on the data infrastructure. For instance, a connected vehicle needs to be able to make real-time decisions based upon data coming from its various sensors on whether to apply the brakes or not. If the data infrastructure cannot process the data and make a decision fast enough or if the data infrastructure is unavailable, the vehicle could crash resulting in physical or monetary damages. But while the data infrastructure needs to be fast and reliable, it also needs to be secure and scalable. For example, the number of connected vehicles is growing rapidly which requires the infrastructure to scale appropriately and each of these vehicles are transmitting location data that if left unsecured could lead to an unauthorised user being able to track a particular vehicle's whereabouts.

Another unique aspect of a TCPS is the way that the data are transmitted to the collection site. Some of the data collected by the TCPS come from sensors and other devices mounted on moving vehicles which poses a unique challenge. Since the vehicles are almost constantly moving, maintaining a consistent connection to transmit data can be a challenge. This combined with the high probability that some of the data will end up lost in transit to the collection device and result in the need for a robust data ingestion system that can handle this situation. This also leads to the debate on where to host the collection site, is it hosted locally close to the devices or located in the cloud? There are advantages and disadvantages to each, hosting closer to the devices eliminates some of the latency in transmitting the data but poses a larger issue for scalability and maintenance. While hosting in the cloud can introduce some extra round-trip time for the data, it helps to solve some of the scalability and maintenance issues as the infrastructure can grow and shrink based on the current demand.

3.2   Data brokering infrastructure

With various components of the batch layer and stream layer, a TCPS data infrastructure is essentially a large-scale distributed system. As a result, it faces the same challenges when scaling up the communication infrastructure. These challenges include complex environments, heterogeneity in hardware and software components, dynamic and flexible deployment and high reliability, throughput and resiliency [13]. TCPS data infrastructure can then leverage the same solution that distributed systems have, which is to implement a message-oriented middleware (MOM). In this case, messages are data elements being transferred from data sources to various data storage and processing components. With MOM, data are sent from sources, called producers, to a queue, called broker. The destination processing entities called consumers can acquire data actively by *pulling* from the broker or passively by having the data *pushed* by the broker. The consumers may or may not return an acknowledgement, another data type, to the broker, where this acknowledgement can be *pulled by* or *pushed to* the producer. In this case, the consumers play the role of producers, and the producer plays the role of consumer. Some advantages of having a MOM infrastructure instead of using remote procedure call among components are listed as follows [13]:

- Communications between producers and consumers are asynchronous and loosely coupled.
- Data losses through network of system failure are prevented due to intermediate in-memory storage on brokers.
- As participants in communication patterns are loosely coupled, it is easier to scale individual components within the data infrastructure.
- Decoupled communication also leads to reduction of failure propagation.

There exist several MOMs, many of which are open sourced. Among them, Apache Kafka stands out as the latest solution that was explicitly designed and built for the data environment of LinkedIn to provide a unified, high-throughput and low-latency platform for real-time data sources [4]. In Kafka, producers send their data to the broker layer. Data that are expected to be consumed by the same consumers are directed towards a specific and unique *topic*. Each topic can be divided into multiple *partitions*, which are maintained by different brokers inside the broker layer. Multiple producers and consumers can publish and retrieve data from the same topic or from different topics at the same time. The number of topic partitions and brokers can be scaled dynamically to cope with data demands. Benchmarked performance of Kafka demonstrated significant improvements in data throughputs over ActiveMQ and RabbitMQ, two other popular MOM frameworks [4].

In a data infrastructure like TCPS, Kafka is responsible for receiving data streams from external sources and setup so that processes from both batch and stream layers can have concurrent access to the data. For example, it is cost-effective to only purchase a single stream of Twitter firehose. By directing this stream into a single topic in Kafka, a batch consumer can acquire and archive the Twitter data in HDFS for long-term predictive analytics, while at the same time a stream consumer can analyse the data in real time for sentiment analysis, special event prediction and trend prediction.

4. Data processing engines

After the data have been collected and ingested, the next step is to perform analytics on the data to get the information required by the TCPS. There are two general classes of processing engines that can be utilised by TCPS that we will be discussing in this section: batch processing engines and stream processing engines. Each class performs different analyses which provide valuable insight into the functionality of the TCPS.

4.1 Batch processing engines for Transportation Cyber-Physical Systems

In early 2000s, researchers at Google published two papers on the topic of storing and processing big data. The first paper, published in 2003 and titled 'The Google File System (GFS)', described a file management infrastructure that is highly distributed and scalable to support data-intensive computing applications [14]. The second paper, published in 2004 with the title 'MapReduce: Simplified Data Processing on Large Cluster', talked about the design of a MapReduce programming paradigm and framework that take advantage of the GFS to operate on massive amount of data [15]. The design principles, architectures and programming practices described in these two papers quickly gained acceptance and created the foundation on which the open-source project Apache Hadoop [16] was based. Among the core components of Apache Hadoop, HDFS was based on the GFS paper, and the Hadoop MapReduce framework was based on the MapReduce paper. With Yahoo's adoption of Hadoop as its primary platform behind the Yahoo! Search engine and the company's subsequent successes in winning the terabyte (sorting 1 terabyte) and Gray (sorting more than 100 terabytes) benchmarks in 2008 and 2009, respectively, the Hadoop ecosystem has quickly gained acceptance from industry as one of the de facto platform for big data management and processing. The design and implementation of HDFS are based on the following assumptions, as described in Ref. [14]:

1. *Hardware failure is the norm rather than the exception*: As the amount of data increases, more computers are needed to store and process data. The probability of failures happening in clusters with larger number of computers will be higher comparing to that of clusters with fewer computers. For example, a Google data centre with 12,000 computers suffers more than 1000 instances of computers going offline in 1 month [17].

2. *Streaming data access*: When processing large amount of data, it is critical to avoid random access, as this will lead to performance issues in both software and hardware. In streaming data access, it is assumed that all reading and writing activities will be done in a sequential manner.

3. *Designed for batch processing rather than interactive use:* One of Google's primary sources of data is the content of the World Wide Web itself. In this environment, Google's early business model focused on indexing and searching on online contents. As a result, data operations leaned towards updating new information and generating new indices to help with the search process. While the search itself required fast response time (low latency), the preparation of data indices, which will help with searching speed and accuracy, needs to be done over the entire Google's data collection (high throughput).

4. *Large data sets:* The perspective of data changes over time as technology progresses. Typically, any data set that is larger than several hundreds of gigabytes can be considered large enough for HDFS.

5. *Simple coherency model (write once read many):* Data written into HDFS will not be modifiable. This is consistent with previous assumptions about streaming data access and batch processing.

6. *Moving computation is cheaper than moving data:* Departing from the traditional compute–storage Beowulf cluster architecture, GFS/HDFS assumes (reasonably) that the size of data processing applications is always going to be much smaller than the size of the data. As a result, it is more beneficial to move the applications to the data than the other way around.

7. *Portability across heterogeneous hardware and software platforms:* The first and fourth assumptions lead to the possibility of either gradual expansion or eventual replacements of individual computers. As hardware components from vendors are upgraded yearly, it is likely that replacement/expansion units will be under different models, resulting a heterogeneous computing cluster. It is also possible to have scenarios where it is necessary to work data stored across geographically and administratively different data centres. In this case, it is reasonable to expect the data infrastructure (GFS/HDFS) to accommodate different software platforms.

Fig. 6.5 provides an overview of HDFS' architectural design. From a user's perspective, visual observations of data stored in HDFS are like those of data stored in a standard Linux operating system. In fact, many command-line data operations in HDFS use the same keywords as their Linux counterparts. Underneath this layer of abstraction, physical contents of data are divided into individual blocks with same predetermined size. These blocks are distributed and replicated across a set of computers called DataNodes. Metadata information about which blocks belong to which original data files and where these blocks are located and replicated are stored in a master computer called NameNode. To ensure resiliency and reliability, HDFS utilises a heartbeat model in which the DataNodes must periodically contact the Name-Node to confirm their active status. If a DataNode fails to do so, the NameNode will proactively initiate the process to replicate all blocks associated with this DataNode onto other DataNodes. Fig. 6.6 shows an example of how HDFS stores a large data file. This file is 632.7 megabytes (MB) in size. The configured block size on this HDFS is 128 MB. Therefore, the file is divided into a total of five blocks, the first four are 128 MB in size and the last block is 120.7 MB in size. With a replication factor of 2, each block has its own unique identifier and is stored on two separated DataNodes. For example, the first block has ID *blk_1105960029_32233103* and is stored on one DataNode with IP address *10.125.8.221* and another with IP address *10.125.8.231*.

While users are presented with an abstracted view of the original data files, the physical contents of the data are divided among the DataNodes as data blocks. Any

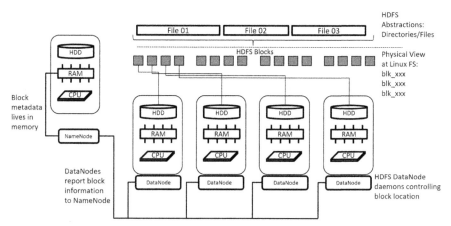

Figure 6.5 Architectural presentation of Hadoop Distributed File System (HDFS).

Figure 6.6 Example Hadoop Distributed File System' block distributions.

applications that operate on these data must consider the distributed nature of these data blocks while being aware of the sixth assumption. In other words, we want the application to be parallel and operate on individual data blocks while minimising data transfer across the network. From a traditional parallel and distributed computing perspective, some of the possible technical issues include how to spawn computing processes, how to determine which process is responsible for which data block, how to aggregate partial results and how to ensure fault tolerant and error recovery. Hadoop MapReduce, which is based on Google's published framework [6], addresses these issues by abstracting away all the underlying computing mechanisms, therefore leaving users (programmers) with only one primary responsibility: implementation of Map and Reduce phases of the data operation.

In a data processing operation on HDFS, the programming codes developed for the Map phase will be executed on all individual data blocks. The Hadoop MapReduce framework will spawn map tasks on DataNodes that physically store these blocks and effectively move computation to data. Each map task would emit intermediate data under the form of <Key, Value> pairs. We could think of a <Key, Value> pair as a data element, where Key represents a distinguishing characteristic of this data element (multiple data element can have similar distinguishing characteristics) and Value represents the actual relevant contents of this element. These intermediate data elements are stored in memory and spilt over into local hard drives as they are generated. After all Map tasks are completed, the Hadoop MapReduce framework aggregates and sorts all pairs based on their Keys. Pairs with the same Key have their

Values shuffled together and combined into a Value list, leading to a new aggregated pair: <Key, [Value0, Value1, Value2...]>. These new pairs are then distributed among a predetermined number of Reducer (default number is 1), and the programming codes developed for the Reduce phase will be applied to each individual pair to achieve the final desired results.

Behind the scene, Hadoop MapReduce framework takes care of several critical technical steps. To support parallelisation, it takes advantage of the fact that data stored on HDFS are already split and distributed across multiple DataNodes. The framework keeps track of all Map tasks in a manner like how NameNode keeps track of DataNodes. This allows automated failure recovery when a Map task fails due to hardware or system failures. In this case, a new Map task will be spawned on another replication, effectively retrying the execution in a new computing environment. In the care of failures happen on Reduce tasks, the framework will attempt to reshuffle previous intermediate data (pairs) from all corresponding Map tasks. If any intermediate data are not available (failures happen on the same nodes that run the previous Map tasks), these Map tasks will be rerun.

The Hadoop MapReduce framework and HDFS are the core components of the Hadoop ecosystem, which provide a reliable and highly scalable environment to support data processing. However, due to the complexity in algorithmic designs (everything must be mapped to Map and Reduce) and overhead costs (Hadoop components are implemented using Java Virtual Machines), it is suitable for batch jobs on massive amount of data but not for interactive jobs on smaller data sets. The Hadoop core components are among the top candidates for the batch layer of a data infrastructure based on LA.

4.2   Stream processing engines

As stated in the previous sections, the batch layer is more suitable for data processing tasks that aggregate massive amount of data, noninteractive, and do not require real-time or near-real-time response rate. Therefore, it is the responsibility of the stream layer to work on small- or medium-sized data in interactive manner to provide outputs in real time. To this end, Apache Spark, developed to address shortcomings of the Hadoop MapReduce framework, has been the most successful [8].

It should be noted that Apache Spark still utilises the MapReduce programming paradigm. That is, many core data operations in Spark are based on mapping (*flatMap, mapValues, map...*) and reducing (*reduce, reduceByKey, groupByKey...*). However, Apache Spark is implemented such that all data (original data, intermediate data and final results) are maintained in memory and reusable/accessible across different stages of interactive jobs. Prior to Hadoop major release 2.0, Spark requires a stand-alone cluster. However, with the inclusion of the new resource manager in Hadoop 2.0 called YARN (Yet Another Resource Negotiator [18]), dynamic Spark clusters can be deployed and run on the same hardware infrastructure that also supports HDFS and Hadoop MapReduce. This is shown in Fig. 6.7.

When a user initialises a Spark cluster, a SparkContext object is first created on the user side. This SparkContext represents an entry point, or a connection, to the Spark cluster to be created. At the beginning, the SparkContext contains only parameters relevant to the initialisation of this cluster (e.g., number of executors, amount of memory per executor, number of computing cores per executors…). Once the cluster is successfully deployed on the Hadoop infrastructure, the user can begin to programmatically load and operate on data. In Spark, data are loaded in as resilient distributed datasets (RDD). That is, Spark will automatically read in the data files and convert them into read-only partitioned collection of records. By default, a record is defined as one line in the data files. Spark's operations are classified into *transformations* or *actions*. Transformations include operations that are pleasantly parallel in nature and will result in a new RDD abstraction from existing RDD. Examples of transformations are *map, filter* and *reduceByKey*. Actions include operations that return actual values to the user (containing much smaller data). Examples of actions are *collect, save* and *count*. As Spark operates in memory space and reuses intermediate data, it could achieve an improvement in performance of up to two orders of magnitudes over traditional Hadoop MapReduce [8].

The real-time streaming analytic aspects of Spark is enabled by creating another data entry point called StreamingContext which is connected to the SparkContext and allows data to be continuously inserted into the Spark cluster's RDD environment over time. Unlike Flink, Spark does not work with actual continuous data streams but discretise these streams into streams of small, user-defined timing windows. These are called discretized streams (DStreams) [19]. Each timing window within a DStream is considered an RDD, and all standard Spark programming functionalities and practices are applicable on these RDD. SparkStream has been observed to achieve twice the throughput of Storm, another streaming engine developed by Twitter.

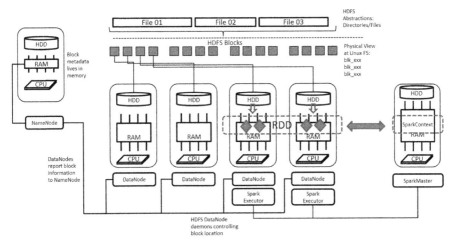

Figure 6.7 Spark deployment inside Hadoop infrastructure. *HDFS*, Hadoop Distributed File System; *RDD*, resilient distributed datasets; *HDD*, hard disk drive.

5. Serving layer

In the LA, the serving layer is where end users can interact with the data and analytical results stored within the infrastructure. As previously mentioned, this is can be done via a web-based application where a user can interact with the data via a web browser. However, there are also other software tools and options for interacting with the data at the lower levels utilising various application programming interfaces (APIs) which can also be categorised into the serving layer.

While the TCPS data infrastructure components described in previous sections are all based on Java programming language (Spark's native language is Scala, which also runs inside a Java Virtual Machine), there exist various APIs to support direct interactions with these components in different programming languages. Among these languages, Python and R stand out as top candidates for developing statistical and visual analytic tasks.

At the batch layer, the Hadoop MapReduce framework supports execution of native Python and R codes driven by the map and reduce tasks. With the Hadoop streaming library, which is part of the core Hadoop MapReduce, executable binaries (in this case Python and R programs) can be specified as map and reduce tasks and utilise Linux standard input and output to read data from HDFS' data blocks. There also exists APIs within Python and R to support more features from the Hadoop ecosystem.

As the batch layer favours large-scale noninteractive job, it is not quite appropriate for TCPS data tasks that are often interactive in nature. In these cases, the Spark framework in the stream layer becomes go-to candidate. While Spark's native language is scale, the development team maintains up-to-date API to most, if not all, of Spark's features in Java, Python and R. Users can develop Spark-based applications in Python and R natively by importing appropriate libraries and modules (packaged into Spark's standard release by default) and then submit these applications to run as Spark jobs.

There also exist database management systems that can be deployed as part of the batch layer. Examples include HBase [20], which is based on Google's BigTable paper, Cassandra [21] and MongoDB [22]. In recent years, demand for security has led to the creation of Accummulo, also based on BigTable and developed by the National Security Agency as an open-source product. These database management systems are accessible via semantics that are similar to Structured Query Language, the default syntax for all traditional RDBMS, but not as expressive.

6. Transportation Cyber-Physical Systems infrastructure as code

The TCPS data infrastructure required to collect, store, distribute and process the data generated by TCPS can be quite large and complex. Not to mention that getting the resources within the infrastructure to work at maximum efficiency and effectiveness can be a daunting and time-consuming task that can require many configuration changes, architecture iterations and debugging. The infrastructure as code (IaC) paradigm aims to change this by allowing users to create, modify and remove infrastructure through code. IaC is an approach to using cloud era technologies to build and manage dynamic infrastructure. It treats the infrastructure and the tools and services that manage the infrastructure itself as a software system, adapting software engineering practices to manage changes to the system in a structured safe way [23].

It used to be that to make large infrastructure changes or to obtain and set up new resources, a system administrator would be required to make any changes and would usually have to make them manually. Most times this meant that the changes made to the infrastructure were not well tracked. This can cause issues when trying to rollback an infrastructure to a previous working state or debug why new resources are not behaving properly as there are very few people who know the exact changes that have been made. However, IaC allows users to utilise standard software version control systems to track changes made to the infrastructure over time. IaC also allows nonsystem administrators to be able to create, modify and remove infrastructure as needed without requiring a system administrator at all.

6.1   Transportation Cyber-Physical Systems cloud infrastructure as code

Cloud computing has become increasingly popular over the past few years due in part to its flexibility. Cloud computing allows users to scale up and scale down their infrastructure based upon the amount of demand which can be particularly useful for TCPS as there are peak times where a lot of data processing is required and other times where very little data processing is required. However, this flexibility in scaling up and down does require some additional automation to be performed during the processes of creating, provisioning and removing the infrastructure to ensure that these actions are performed in a consistent and trackable manner. This is where IaC can be utilised effectively and efficiently.

Many cloud computing providers have their own IaC solutions that are designed to help users to create, modify and delete their infrastructure within the cloud. Amazon Web Services (AWS) has a service called CloudFormation that allows users to use a simple text file, written in JSON or YAML, to model and provision, in an automated and secure manner, all the resources required for the infrastructure. This file serves as the single source of truth for your cloud infrastructure [24]. A sample CloudFormation template that launches an AWS EC2 instance can be seen in Fig. 6.8. Microsoft's Azure also has its own IaC solution that is similar to AWS's CloudFormation called Azure Resource Management Templates. These templates are written in JSON format and define the infrastructure and configuration of the required Azure infrastructure [25]. Google Cloud Platform (GCP) also has a similar IaC solution available to users called the Cloud Deployment Manager that allows GCP infrastructure to be deployed using a YAML defined template file [26]. These tools are the cornerstones of a total IaC infrastructure in the cloud. However, although these services provide many useful functions, they just begin to scratch the surface of the IaC paradigm.

```
{
    "Description" : "Create an EC2 instance running the Amazon Linux 32 bit AMI.",
    "Parameters" : {
        "KeyPair" : {
            "Description" : "The EC2 Key Pair to allow SSH access to the instance",
            "Type" : "String"
        }
    },
    "Resources" : {
        "Ec2Instance" : {
            "Type" : "AWS::EC2::Instance",
            "Properties" : {
                "KeyName" : { "Ref" : "KeyPair" },
                "ImageId" : "ami-3b355a52"
            }
        }
    },
    "Outputs" : {
        "InstanceId" : {
            "Description" : "The InstanceId of the newly created EC2 instance",
            "Value" : {
                "Ref" : "Ec2Instance"
            }
        }
    },
    "AWSTemplateFormatVersion" : "2010-09-09"
}
```

Figure 6.8 Sample CloudFormation template to launch an Amazon Web Services EC2 instance [24].

Another advantage to utilising IaC for TCPS is that there are peak times, such as rush hour and during the holidays, when extra processing power is required to handle all the data being generated and collected. By utilising IaC, users can create policies that will have the infrastructure automatically create new infrastructure components based upon the demand and remove them once the demand decreases to a certain level. This allows TCPS infrastructure to automatically handle spikes in traffic and requests without the need for any user intervention. This also minimises the risk for a configuration error when standing up or tearing down new infrastructure since there is no human in the middle to forget a step or hit a wrong key. This keeps the infrastructure consistent and up to date which helps minimise the risk of outdated and unpatched servers.

Utilising IaC with cloud computing also enables the ability to iterate and change infrastructure faster and more efficiently. By being able to track the changes made to the infrastructure through the normal software version control systems, it is easier to ensure that the infrastructure is up to date and that all the changes have been applied. This also makes it easier to debug the infrastructure if something is not working properly as there is a well-documented change history in the version control system. This speed and agility is crucial for TCPS as the requirements for data storage and computation are changing rapidly and the infrastructure needs to be able to keep up.

6.2 Internet of Things infrastructure as code

Along with the lower-level compute IaC, the cloud also allows for Internet of Things device and sensor infrastructure to be created, modified and removed through code. This process is a little different than the compute infrastructure, as this process does not involve deploying actual resources, such as sensors, but rather refers to the ability to manage and update the infrastructure. One such solution is Amazon Greengrass, a software solution that allows a user run a variety of tasks including messaging, data caching, sync, machine learning, and local compute securely on connected devices. Greengrass uses familiar programming models and languages allowing users to create and test device software in the cloud first and then deploy it to the devices. [27]. This allows for the quick code and device prototyping and better change tracking regarding the software running on the sensors and devices deployed out in the field. Although these types of IaC services are still relatively new, they are already causing a shift in the traditional thinking of how data centres and devices are deployed. These types of solutions will become more prevalent as users realise the benefits that they provide.

7. Future direction

Over the next few years, the amount of data being generated by TCPS will continue to grow quickly. This will lead to an increased need for more efficient and scalable data processing of the TCPS data. This will require a tighter integration of the traditional data processing systems described in this chapter along with the flexibility and scalability provided by IaC. By utilising IaC, TCPS will be able to dynamically adjust to handle an increase in the amount of data as more vehicles and other devices connect to the system. This will keep TCPS running efficiently and effectively without the administrators of the system having to worry about the ever-changing data processing requirements.

8. Summary and conclusions

Within TCPS the data are the most important information that is produced. The data are what contains the information required to keep the TCPS operational and enable their functionality. Similarity, without the data processing infrastructure, the TCPS would not be able to obtain or produce the information required to maintain usability. As the requirements for data storage and processing change, the data infrastructure behind the TCPS will adapt with it and lead to even more efficient and effective systems. IaC will allow TCPS to automatically adapt to changes in demand and will allow for faster iteration and debugging when updating the underlying infrastructure. This will allow the people working on these systems to focus more on innovating and less on maintaining and managing the current systems.

Exercises

1. List and define the four layers of the LAMP architecture.
2. List and define the three layers of LA for data infrastructure.
3. What are the seven assumptions that the design and implementation of HDFS is based on?
4. How does a batch processing engine differ from a stream processing engine?
5. How can TCPS benefit from IaC?

References

[1] J. Lee, B. Ware, Open Source Web Development with LAMP: Using Linux, Apache, MySQL, Perl, and PHP, Addison-Wesley, 2003.
[2] Y. Demchenko, P. Grosso, C. de Laat, P. Membrey, Addressing big data issues in scientific data infrastructure, in: 2013 International Conference on Collaboration Technologies and Systems (CTS), 2013, pp. 48−55.
[3] N. Mars, J. Warren, Big Data: Principles and Best Practices of Scalable Realtime Data Systems, first ed., Manning Plubications Co., Greenwich, CT, 2017.
[4] G. Wang, J. Koshy, S. Subramanian, K. Paramasivam, M. Zadeh, N. Narkhede, J. Rao, J. Kreps, J. Stein, Building a replicated logging system with Apache Kafka, Proceedings of the VLDB Endowment 8 (12) (Aug. 2015) 1654−1655.
[5] K. Shvachko, H. Kuang, S. Radia, R. Chansler, The hadoop distributed file system, in: 2010 IEEE 26th Symposium on Mass Storage Systems and Technologies (MSST), 2010, pp. 1−10.
[6] R.C. Taylor, An overview of the Hadoop/MapReduce/HBase framework and its current applications in bioinformatics, BMC Bioinformatics 11 (Suppl. 12) (December 2010) S1.
[7] R. Stephens, A survey of stream processing, Acta Informatica 34 (7) (Jul. 1997) 491−541.
[8] M. Zaharia, M.J. Franklin, A. Ghodsi, J. Gonzalez, S. Shenker, I. Stoica, R.S. Xin, P. Wendell, T. Das, M. Armbrust, A. Dave, X. Meng, J. Rosen, S. Venkataraman, Apache Spark, Communications of the ACM 59 (11) (Oct. 2016) 56−65.
[9] A. Katsifodimos, S. Schelter, Apache Flink: stream analytics at scale, in: 2016 IEEE International Conference on Cloud Engineering Workshop (IC2EW), 2016, p. 193.
[10] A. Toshniwal, J. Donham, N. Bhagat, S. Mittal, D. Ryaboy, S. Taneja, A. Shukla, K. Ramasamy, J.M. Patel, S. Kulkarni, J. Jackson, K. Gade, M. Fu, in: Proceedings of the 2014 ACM SIGMOD International Conference on Management of Data - SIGMOD '14, 2014, pp. 147−156.
[11] M. Chowdhury, M. Rahman, A. Rayamajhi, S.M. Khan, M. Islam, M.Z. Khan, J. Martin, Lessons Learned from the Real-World Deployment of a Connected Vehicle Testbed, in: Proceeding of 97th Annual Meeting of the Transportation Research Board, Washington, D.C., 2018.
[12] Connected Vehicle Reference Implementation Architecture (CVRIA), USDOT, https://local.iteris.com/cvria/html/applications/app87.html#tab-3, (accessed in May 2018).
[13] E. Curry, Message-oriented middeware, in: Q.H. Mahmoud (Ed.), Middleware for Communications, Wiley & Sons, 2004, pp. 1−29.
[14] S. Ghemawat, H. Gobioff, S.-T. Leung, S. Ghemawat, H. Gobioff, S.-T. Leung, The google file system, in: Proceedings of the Nineteenth ACM Symposium on Operating Systems Principles - SOSP '03, vol. 37, 2003, p. 29 no. 5.

[15] J. Dean, S. Ghemawat, MapReduce: simplified data processing on large clusters, Communications of the ACM 51 (1) (Jan. 2008) 107–113.

[16] D. Borthakur, S. Rash, R. Schmidt, A. Aiyer, J. Gray, J. Sen Sarma, K. Muthukkaruppan, N. Spiegelberg, H. Kuang, K. Ranganathan, D. Molkov, A. Menon, Apache hadoop goes realtime at facebook, in: Proceedings of the 2011 International Conference on Management of Data - SIGMOD '11, 2011, pp. 1071–1080.

[17] S. Di, D. Kondo, W. Cirne, Characterization and comparison of cloud versus grid workloads, in: 2012 IEEE International Conference on Cluster Computing, 2012, pp. 230–238.

[18] V.K. Vavilapalli, S. Seth, B. Saha, C. Curino, O. O'Malley, S. Radia, B. Reed, E. Baldeschwieler, A.C. Murthy, C. Douglas, S. Agarwal, M. Konar, R. Evans, T. Graves, J. Lowe, H. Shah, Apache hadoop YARN, in: Proceedings of the 4th Annual Symposium on Cloud Computing - SOCC '13, 2013, pp. 1–16.

[19] M. Zaharia, T. Das, H. Li, T. Hunter, S. Shenker, I. Stoica, Discretized streams, in: Proceedings of the Twenty-Fourth ACM Symposium on Operating Systems Principles - SOSP '13, 2013, pp. 423–438.

[20] Mehul Nalin Vora, Hadoop-HBase for large-scale data, in: Proceedings of 2011 International Conference on Computer Science and Network Technology, 2011, pp. 601–605.

[21] G. Wang, J. Tang, The NoSQL principles and basic application of Cassandra model, in: 2012 International Conference on Computer Science and Service System, 2012, pp. 1332–1335.

[22] K. Banker, MongoDB in Action, Manning Publications Co., Greenwich, CT, 2011.

[23] K. Morris, Infrastructure as Code: Managing Servers in the Cloud, OReilly Media, Inc, Sebastopol, CA, 2016.

[24] AWS CloudFormation - Infrastructure as Code & AWS Resource Provisioning, n.d. From https://aws.amazon.com/cloudformation/. (Accessed on 09/05/2018)

[25] Azure Resource Manager, n.d. From https://azure.microsoft.com/en-us/features/resource-manager/. (Accessed on 09/05/2018)

[26] Cloud Deployment Manager - Simplified Cloud Management, Google Cloud Platform, n.d. From https://cloud.google.com/deployment-manager/. (Accessed on 09/05/2018)

[27] AWS Greengrass - Amazon Web Services, n.d. From https://aws.amazon.com/greengrass/. (Accessed on 09/05/2018)

Data Management Issues in Cyber-Physical Systems

Venkat N. Gudivada [1], Srini Ramaswamy [2], Seshadri Srinivasan [3]
[1]Department of Computer Science, East Carolina University, Greenville, NC, United States;
[2]ABB, Inc., Cleveland, Ohio, United States; [3]Berkeley Education Alliance for Research in Singapore (BEARS), Singapore

1. Cyber-physical systems: an interdisciplinary confluence

Cyber-physical systems (CPS) integrate computation with physical processes. The program solicitation #16-549 of the National Science Foundation (NSF) defines CPS as 'engineered systems that are built from, and depend upon, the seamless integration of computational algorithms and physical components' [1]. The term cyber in the NSF definition refers to a broad range of computing technologies that support decision-making computer hardware, programming, data structures, algorithms, computer networks and software engineering. The physical components can be, for example, traffic lights, vehicles, pedestrians crossing a road intersection and roads. The physical and cyber parts of CPS are interconnected by feedback control loops, and the parts affect each other.

CPS are a synergistic confluence of various subdisciplines, including model-based system design, formal methods for system specification and verification, real-time systems, embedded systems, sensors and actuators, distributed algorithms, concurrency theory, control theory, Internet of Things (IoT), cognitive computing and high-performance computing. CPS-level characteristics include system specification and verification, stability and safety, communications and interoperability, performance and scalability, reliability and dependability and privacy and security. Other facets include cybersecurity, power and energy management, human factors and system usability [2]. Thus, CPS are an exemplar of interdisciplinary fusion. CPS are also transformative given their potential for dramatically enhancing the capabilities of existing applications and ushering in innovative devices such as an artificial pancreas.

Though the genesis of CPS traces back to embedded systems and automatic process control of 1970s, the recent advances in high-performance computing and wireless sensor networks have significantly expanded CPS functional capabilities and the range of CPS applications. CPS are playing increasingly critical roles in power generation and distribution, health care, manufacturing and transportation (air, ground and sea). Since CPS-based systems communicate and respond faster than humans, their potential to provide efficiency, adaptability, autonomy and reliability is also greater [1]. For example, collision avoidance for automobiles, self-driving cars, autonomous air

Transportation Cyber-Physical Systems. https://doi.org/10.1016/B978-0-12-814295-0.00007-1
Copyright © 2018 Elsevier Inc. All rights reserved.

vehicles, intelligent transportation infrastructure and efficient operation of smart buildings are enabled by CPS.

Certain unique problems emerge in the design and operation of CPS compared to general-purpose computing applications [3]. CPS are compositions of concurrent physical processes. The time it takes to perform a task in CPS is a measure of both performance and correctness. Also, time is not an intrinsic attribute of software. Furthermore, unlike IoT, interactions between cyber and physical processes are more tightly integrated in CPS, especially for real-time control and safety-critical systems. Models and abstractions for correctly capturing the joint dynamics between cyber and physical processes are crucial for developing CPS.

Data analytics (DA), machine learning (ML) and databases play a critical role in control and decision-making on physical components/systems. Furthermore, these decisions can be made remotely and collaboratively. More specifically, the technologies that underlie the nascent discipline of data science enable collecting, cleaning, storing, retrieving and analysing large data in real time to enable decision-making in CPS.

The overarching goal of this chapter is to examine the data-related issues and opportunities in CPS. More specifically, we discuss how the ubiquity of data can be leveraged to endow CPS richer functionality. This chapter will also examine the challenged posed by the critical dependency of CPS on data and indicate approaches to overcoming these challenges.

2. Cyber-physical systems are diverse

CPS hardware and software architectures vary widely. System on a chip (SoC) is an integrated circuit (aka IC chip) which brings together all functional components of a computer. SoCs feature analog, digital, mixed signal and radio frequency functions, all on a single chip. SoCs typically include programmable processors, memory units, accelerating function units, I/O and network interfaces and software. SoCs are popular in mobile computing devices—tablets and smart phones—because of the low power consumption. SoCs abound in medicine and health care as well. For example, SoCs are used in blood pressure monitoring devices. Intel Atom, Snapdragon by Qualcomm and Tegra by Nvidia are widely used SoCs. Embedded systems are a prominent application area of SoC.

At the other end of the spectrum are embedded systems such as Nvidia Drive PX platform for autonomous vehicles. This entire platform size is no more than that of a car licence plate. The recent Drive PX model is code-named Pegasus, which has 16 dedicated inputs for cameras, radar, light detection and ranging, and ultrasonics. It also features multiple 10-gigabit Ethernet connections. Its computing performance is over 320 *Deep Learning Tera Operations* per second. Therefore, features such as computing power, size of memory, energy requirements and integration with data centres significantly differ among CPS applications.

An example of Transportation Cyber-Physical Systems (TCPS) can be given for a cybersecurity application of TCPS at an unsignalised intersection. In this example, a software-based security threat detection system, residing in a server, is overseeing one or more roadside units at a stop-controlled unsignalised intersection. Here roadside units are alerting the side street vehicles when it is safe to cross the main street traffic that has the right of way at an unsignalised intersection [4]. However, any malicious cyberattack on the roadside units could jeopardise the reliability of providing a reliable warning to side street traffic, which can result in potential crashes at that intersection. Once the software-based security threat detection software detects a security attack on a roadside unit in a connected vehicle environment at a stop-controlled unsignalised intersection, it alerts the roadside unit about the attack and instructs the roadside unit to activate preselected security protection system for such an attack. Here, the physical world, vehicles and roadside units and cyber-infrastructure such as a server and analytics such as the security detection software are connected through a wireless medium to form TCPS to thwart a cyberattack at a stop-controlled unsignailsed intersection operating a Stop Sign Gap Assist connected vehicle application [5].

3. Data management issues

CPS need a range of data management solutions depending on their on-board computing power and energy constraints. Some CPS may offload compute-intensive tasks to data centres and receive results back in near real time, while others need real-time on-board DA capability. There are four data-related issues for CPS: (1) choice of a data management system that closely matches with the functional and nonfunctional requirements of CPS, (2) dealing with data quality, (3) dealing with human cognitive biases and (4) data privacy and security issues. The economies of scale offered by cloud platforms and their ubiquity make a compelling case for using them for CPS data management and analytics.

3.1 Data management system choices

Relational database management systems (RDBMS) are the backbone of almost all software applications until recently. Underlying the RDBMS is the relational data model for structuring data and the ISO/ANSI standard SQL for data manipulation and querying. The relational data model is based on first-order predicate logic and lends itself naturally for providing a declarative method for specifying queries on the database [6]. The SQL language is originally based on relational algebra and tuple relational calculus [7].

Consider the database management needs of applications such as CPS, IoT, big data, mobile computing, Web 2.0 and location-based services. According to Gartner [8], 8.4 billion connected 'things' (i.e., IoT) will be in use in 2017. An IoT application such as *smart cities* will generate unprecedented volumes of data in real time just from temperature and humidity sensors alone. Big data applications, for example, deal with heterogeneous and sparse data. These applications require new database functionality to support tasks such as personalisation, real-time predictive analytics, dynamic pricing, fraud and anomaly detection and real-time order status through supply chain visibility.

In many of the above applications, complete database schema does not exist up front and evolves over time. Furthermore, some applications require a simple data model but fast inserts and lookups are critical. They require insert and retrieval operations on a very large scale. This entails *efficiently* supporting insert and read operations to the exclusion of update and delete operations. Updates are often implemented as a delete followed by an insert. Partial record updates are the norm for some. Yet for others, atomicity, consistency, isolation and durability (ACID)−compliant transactions are an overkill as only relaxed consistency is the norm [9]. Furthermore, the applications require multiple query languages ranging from simple Representational State Transfer (REST) application programming interface (API) through complex and ad hoc queries. Interactive processing of ad hoc queries mandates massive parallel computation using frameworks such as Hadoop and Spark. Using an RDBMS for such applications amounts to the proverbial square peg in a round hole.

Nonoverlapping data partitioning is necessary to address large data volumes. Auto-sharding refers to distributing data across computing nodes in a nonoverlapping manner by a data management system in a manner transparent to the user. Some systems provide replication − multiple copies of the same data are stored on different computers to enhance data availability and query performance. Some applications require built-in support for versioning and compression. Hardware-level fault tolerance is essential to guarantee high availability. In summary, these special needs call for a database management system (DBMS) that (1) features flexible data models that can evolve over time, (2) stores tera/petabyte scale data volumes by spreading across multiple data centres to improve locality, (3) offers high availability and *elastic scaling* without system downtime, (4) offers relaxed and user configurable consistency for situations that do not require database transactions, (5) provides near real-time query response times and (6) supports a number of concurrent users in the order of millions.

In recent years, a large number of new systems for data management have emerged to meet the above needs [9]. These new systems are referred to in the literature by various names including NoSQL, NewSQL and *Not only SQL*. The catch-all term NoSQL is used to refer to those systems that do not use SQL as their principle query language. NewSQL systems are RDBMS with new and innovative features. Some NoSQL systems may use SQL and are referred to as *Not only SQL*.

According to DB-engines [10], there are over 341 systems for data management as of January 2018. DB-engines also rank these systems based on a monthly updated score which is calculated by using several measures. They include the frequency of occurrence of the system name in Google and Bing search queries, LinkedIn and Upwork profiles, job search engines *Indeed* and *Simply Hired*, Twitter tweets, Google Trends and Q&A forums such as Stack Overflow and DBA Stack Exchange. Functional features of these systems vary widely [11].

By design, NoSQL systems do not provide all of the RDBMS features and principally focus on providing near real-time reads and writes for applications with millions of concurrent users. The term *performance at scale* is used to describe the primary feature of such systems. NoSQL systems meet the new application needs to varying degrees. Also, their functionality significantly varies from one another. For example, (1) Redis is known for its data structures and elegant query mechanisms, (2) Riak is highly scalable and available, (3) MongoDB efficiently manages deeply nested structured documents and computes aggregates on the documents and (4) Neo4j excels at managing data that is rich in relationships.

From the CPS perspective, we categorise DBMS into: (1) relational DBMS, (2) document-oriented DBMS, (3) graph-oriented DBMS, (4) column family DBMS, (5) native XML DBMS, (6) time series DBMS, (7) Resource Description Framework (RDF) stores and (8) key−value Stores. Table 7.1 summarises the salient characteristics of each DBMS class of systems and lists representative systems for each class. Some systems fall under multiple categories and are called multimodel systems. For example, Microsoft Azure Cosmos DB features functions of document, graph, key−value and column family database systems.

Table 7.1 A Taxonomy for and Classification of Database Management Systems (DBMSs)

Database Class	Salient Characteristics	Widely Used Systems
Relational DBMS	Two subclasses: row-oriented and column-oriented. Column-oriented RDBMS: optimised reads and writes for online transaction processing; enforces strong data integrity; provides transaction support, data distribution, data replication and fine-grained access control. Column-oriented: optimised reads for online analytical processing; enforces strong data integrity and provides distributed data analytics.	Oracle, MySQL, Microsoft SQL Server, PostgreSQL and DB2
Document-oriented	Ideal for managing semistructured, arbitrarily nested hierarchical document data organised in the form of key−value pairs in JSON format; support flexible schema evolution; accommodate high data variability among data records.	MongoDB, Amazon DynamoDB, Couchbase, CouchDB, MarkLogic and Microsoft Azure Cosmos DB
Graph-oriented	Ideal for efficiently storing and flexibly querying relationship-rich data; powerful operators for graph traversals and identifying subgraphs and cliques based on relationship types.	Neo4j, Microsoft Azure Cosmos DB, OrientDB, Titan and ArangoDB

Continued

Table 7.1 **A Taxonomy for and Classification of Database Management Systems (DBMSs)—cont'd**

Database Class	Salient Characteristics	Widely Used Systems
Column family	Ideal for efficiently storing sparse, nontransactional, and heterogeneous data and retrieving partial records; accommodate flexible and evolving database schema; tolerance to both network failures and temporary data inconsistency; increased processing power through horizontal scalability.	Cassandra, HBase, Microsoft Azure Cosmos DB, Microsoft Azure Table Storage, Accumulo and Google Cloud Bigtable
Native XML	Ideal for efficiently storing and retrieving sparse and hierarchically structured heterogeneous data with high variability from one record to another; all layers in an application see the same data model, and hence, there is no need for mapping of the data model between layers.	MarkLogic, Oracle Berkeley DB, Virtuoso, BaseX, webMethods Tamino, Sedna and eXist-db
Time series	Ideal for storing and retrieving time series data, which is data indexed by time; efficient execution of range queries; performance at scale; support for age-based data retention and archival.	InfluxDB, RRDtool, Graphite, OpenTSDB, Kdb+, Druid and Prometheus
RDF stores	Also called triplestores are optimised for the storage and retrieval of triples; simple and uniform data model with a declarative query language named SPARQL; import/export through standardised data interchange formats − N-triples and N-quads.	MarkLogic, Jena, Virtuoso, GraphDB, AllegroGraph and Stardog
Key−value stores	Optimised for storing key−value pairs to guarantee real-time retrieval independent of data volume; key-based lookup query mechanism; increased processing power through horizontal scalability; high availability and reliability.	Redis, Memcached, Microsoft Azure Cosmos DB, Hazelcast, Ehcache, Riak KV, OrientDB, Aerospike, ArangoDB and Caché

3.2 Data quality issues

CPS typically depend on artificial intelligence (AI) systems and ML algorithms for their operation. The terms AI and ML are often used interchangeably, though they are different. AI is concerned with developing computer systems whose performance rival that of humans. AI systems attempt to quantify uncertainty and reason with incomplete and inconsistent data. ML is a data-driven approach to developing AI systems. Focus of ML is to endow AI systems with *learning how to learn* capability. The premise is that more data generally result in better AI systems. However, the key is *more of right data* and not just more data. Data quality is a means to quantify and assess suitability of data for a given purpose [12].

Just as a chain is only as strong as its weakest link, an AI system is only as good as the data that were used to train the system. Not only there are issues of safety in mission-critical AI systems but also societal issues such as bias and exclusion are just as important. Not using the right data entails bias creeping into AI/ML systems. Bias may have significant undesirable consequences for certain segments of society. The term *algorithmic bias* is used to refer to concealed bias in computing systems. One may argue that algorithmic bias is not really a bias and it simply reflects the reality of the world manifested through the training data. In some situations, algorithmic bias is useful since the purpose of such investigation is to reveal the bias. In other situations that involve decision-making, one needs to be cognisant of the serious implications of the *algorithmic bias* and devise ways to thwart human prejudice. For this scenario, it is critical to identify and remove bias from training data. In Section 3.3, we elaborate on human cognitive biases in decision-making.

Traditionally, there are two threads of data quality research. The first one is advanced by computer science researchers and issues of interest include identification of duplicate data, resolving data inconsistencies, imputation for missing data and linking and integrating related data obtained from multiple sources [13]. Computer scientists investigate these issues using algorithmic approaches based on statistical methods [14]. The second thread of data quality research is addressed by information systems researchers [15]. Various dimensions used for data quality assessment using a data governance-driven framework are discussed in Ref. [12]. In addition to the traditional ones, these dimensions also include those that are unique to big data and ML applications. The dimensions include data governance, data specifications, integrity, consistency, currency, duplication, completeness, provenance, heterogeneity, accuracy, streaming data, outliers, dimensionality reduction, feature selection and extraction, business rules, gender bias, confidentiality and privacy and availability and access controls.

In contrast to non—machine-generated data applications, data acquisition errors can significantly degrade data quality in machine-generated data application domains such as IoT and CPS. Data acquisition errors can arise from malfunctioning sensors, sampling errors, communication errors, malicious data insertion and modification while data is in transit and data integration and aggregation errors. Detection of outliers is crucial for ensuring data quality in CPS context. Sha and Zeadlly suggest employing physical laws and multimodality data cross-verification to detect outliers and faulty data [16].

3.3 Human cognitive biases in decision-making

Given the severity of data quality in CPS and mission-critical nature of several CPS applications, *computer decision-making with human-in-the-loop* approach is essential. However, human decision-making is also subject to several cognitive biases. We use the 20 cognitive biases discussed in Ref. [17] as the basis for this section. The human cognitive biases are listed as follows:

1. **Anchoring bias** refers to the tendency of humans to use the first piece of information they receive as the standard to determine the validity of data received subsequently.
2. **Availability heuristic** is related to peoples' tendency to assign unreasonable information value to the data that are easily available to them. Convenience data sampling techniques best exemplifies the availability heuristic.
3. **Bandwagon effect** points to the fact that the degree of belief in a hypothesis is proportional to the number of people who believe in that belief. This leads to irrational reasoning and false conclusions.
4. **Blind spot bias** indicates that not being able to recognise one's own bias is a bias in itself. Surprisingly, it is easy to spot cognitive and motivational biases in others. A team decision is a powerful antidote to overcome blind spot bias.
5. **Choice-supportive bias** refers to the tendency of people to rationalise the choice they have made, though the choice may be faulty or not optimal. This bias leads to missing more optimal decisions.
6. **Clustering illusion** alludes to the tendency of humans to hypothesise nonexisting patterns in random events. Actions based on these hypotheses have no logical foundation.
7. **Confirmation bias** refers to the phenomenon exemplified by the saying birds of a feather flock together. One tends to value only that data which confirm her preconceptions.
8. **Conservatism bias** points to the fact that humans value existing evidence more than new evidence. There is implicit resistance to accepting new evidence.
9. **Information bias** refers to the tendency of humans to seek that information which does not affect action. What matters is not the size of the data but the right data.
10. **Ostrich effect** is the tendency to ignore information that is not pleasant or palatable. This effect may lead to missing important information that has significant decision-making value.
11. **Outcome bias** refers to judging the value of a decision exclusively on the outcome and ignoring the exact process involved in making the decision. This leads to not being able to identifying all the factors that affected the decision.
12. **Overconfidence** encourages greater risk taking in decision-making.
13. **Placebo effect** refers to the power of nothing – a desired outcome will happen by simply believing that it will happen.
14. **Pro-innovation bias** is overvaluing the usefulness while overlooking its limitations.
15. **Recency** is the tendency to place more prominence on newer data relative to old data.
16. **Salience** is best exemplified by the metaphor *low-hanging fruit*. It refers to the tendency to focus on statistically improbable events over probable events.
17. **Selective perception** is perceiving the world through the lens of our expectations. In other words, our expectations colour and cloud what we perceive.
18. **Stereotyping** refers to overgeneralisation, though significant differences exist in the data.
19. **Survivorship bias** refers to an incorrect decision due to biased or imbalanced data and not being cognisant about the biased data.
20. **Zero-risk bias** refers to tendency of avoiding quantifying uncertainty and reasoning with it.

3.4 Cybersecurity issues in data management

CPS are ubiquitous in smart grids, transportation, industrial control and other critical infrastructures. These systems should operate reliably in the event of malicious cyberattacks and unforeseen disturbances. While information technology (IT) infrastructures aim to secure the data from attacks, CPS have other security requirements that emerge due to its intrinsic features. The CPS pose the following key security challenges:

1. CPS applications range widely in terms of security requirements. For instance, military and nuclear power plants applications require a high degree of security compared to others such as precision weather forecasting for farmers.
2. In emerging applications such as the IoT, the computing power of the CPS components is limited. This poses serious problems to execute complex security counter measures that may require relatively more computing resources.
3. CPS are systems comprised of heterogeneous components — different computing platforms and capabilities. In these systems, hardware, software and human interactions are glued. A multitude of security issues need attention at hardware, software and human interaction levels.
4. While a CPS should secure data as in IT infrastructure environment, it should also consider security issues that span multiple systems and those that arise due to user interactions with these systems.
5. CPS have strict timing requirements on the data in addition to security. This means that *agile attack mitigation strategies* are required for CPS.
6. CPS design approaches that do not consider security issues may render such CPS vulnerable to security breaches.
7. The counteracting measures for cyberattacks on CPS should consider the interactions between the cyber and physical aspects of the systems.
8. CPS may use different networking technologies (e.g., wired and wireless) and diverse protocols, which introduces additional challenges.
9. Typically, CPS are highly autonomous systems with embedded intelligence. While this reduces manual intervention and supervision, it also necessitates protection against malicious attacks.
10. Feedback loops play an important role in CPS control. Therefore, feedback data need to be protected against tampering attempts.

Since these issues are addressed in other chapters of this volume, we turn our attention to database-centric cybersecurity issues. Databases are at the heart of most organisations and they experience the highest rate of security breaches. Through these attacks, hackers and malicious insiders gain access to sensitive data, quickly extract value, inflict damage or impact business operations. In addition to financial loss and reputation damage, breaches can result in regulatory violations, fines and legal fees. The recently introduced regulation, General Data Protection Regulation for the European Union, is the first of its kind and imposes penalties on organisations that fail to meet stringent data protection measures. One such measure requires adequate database monitoring capability to meet the audit and breach notification requirements for all personal data.

Though the computing application domains are diverse, they all share similar cybersecurity risks. The risks range from stealing credit card numbers to destabilising modern political processes and presidential elections. On 7 September 2017, Equifax stated that the personal information of as many as 143 million Americans has been compromised. In September 2016, Yahoo confirmed that data associated with at least 500 million user accounts had been stolen by an individual acting on behalf of a government [18]. This breach is believed to have occurred in late 2014 and is perhaps the largest security breach ever. Victims of major data breaches in 2016 include the US Department of Justice, US Internal Revenue Service, Verizon Enterprise Solutions, Philippine Commission on Elections, LinkedIn, Oracle, Dropbox and Cisco, among others [19]. Cyberattacks cut across private businesses, industries, government organisations and military establishments. Over 57% of organisations consider databases as the most vulnerable asset which is prone to an insider attack [20].

Comparatively speaking, data security is a major challenge for NoSQL systems compared to RDBMS. Security risks range from an assumption that NoSQL systems run in a trusted environment (hence, no authentication is required) to clear text transmission to no data encryption on disk. Authorisation and fine-grained access control is another security risk. As NoSQL systems store duplicate copies of data to optimise query processing, it is difficult to isolate sensitive data and specify access controls. Though the RDBMS security solutions apply to NoSQL systems in principle, the differences in data model, query languages and client access methods of NoSQL warrant new solutions.

Cybersecurity issues in NoSQL systems are exacerbated by data velocity, volume and heterogeneity. Also, diversity of data sources, streaming data, cloud-hosted deployments and high-volume intercloud data movements further heighten security issues. Traditional security mechanisms that are tailored to securing small-scale static data are inadequate for NoSQL systems. Shown in Table 7.2 are the critical database security threats. A recent Imperva white paper [20] lists the following as the top five database security threats: (1) excessive, inappropriate and unused privileges, (2) privilege abuse, (3) insufficient web application security/SQL injection, (4) weak audit trails and (5) unsecured storage media. In most cases, these threats can be prevented by implementing simple steps and following best practices and internal controls.

4. Database systems for cyber-physical systems

As indicated earlier, RDBMS are not ideal for CPS, big data, mobile computing and location-based services applications. In addition to the issues discussed in Section 3.1, RDBMS are principally designed to work on single-node computers. They accommodate increased workload and data volume by using faster CPUs, more memory and bigger and faster disks. This approach to increasing computing power is referred to as *vertical scaling* (aka scaling up). RDBMS vendor solutions for vertical scaling tend to require expensive hardware and often involve proprietary software.

Table 7.2 **Common Database Security Threats**

Database Threat	Description
Excessive and unused privileges	When users are granted database privileges that exceed the requirements of their job function, privileges can be used to gain access to confidential information. Also, when employee job roles change, corresponding changes to access rights to sensitive data are often not updated. Per Imperva [20], 47% of companies report that their users have excessive rights. A query-level access control is used to restrict privileges to minimum required operations and data.
Privilege abuse	Users may abuse legitimate database privileges for unauthorised purposes. Database systems administrators (DBAs) have unlimited access to all data in the database. A DBA may choose to access unauthorised, sensitive application data directly without going through the application's authorisation and access controls. Privilege abuse is an insider threat. In 2016, more than 65% of the data breach losses were attributed to privileges abuse [20]. Enforce policies restrict not only what data are accessible but also how the data are accessed.
SQL injection and insufficient application security	Hackers insert unauthorised or malicious SQL statements to get access to the data to copy or alter it. A query-level access control is effective in detecting unauthorised queries injected via web applications and database stored procedures.
Weak audit trail	Failure to collect detailed audit records of database activity represents a serious organisational risk on many levels. Fine-granular audit, unfortunately, degrades database performance. Native audit tools of the database vendors are typically inadequate to record the contextual details required to detect attacks and support security and compliance auditing. Network-based audit appliances operate independently of all users and offer granular data collection without performance penalty. Imperva notes that only 19% of companies perform database monitoring [20].
Unsecured storage media	Unprotected backup storage media is often stolen. High-privilege users such as DBAs will often have direct physical access to the database servers. Such users can turnoff native audit mechanism and copy data by issuing SQL commands. To prevent this type of data breach, all database backup files should be encrypted.

Continued

Table 7.2 **Common Database Security Threats—cont'd**

Database Threat	Description
Malware and platform vulnerabilities	Advanced attacks that blend multiple tactics such as spear phishing emails and malware are used to penetrate organisations and steal-sensitive data. Intrusion detection software and intrusion prevention software (IPS) are effective in detecting and blocking known database platform vulnerabilities and malware.
Platform vulnerabilities	Attackers exploit vulnerabilities in database management systems and the underlying operating systems. For example, attackers exploit vulnerabilities such as default accounts and passwords and database system configuration parameters to launch attacks.
Denial of service (DoS)	The attack renders the system unavailable to the authenticated and authorised users. Buffer overflows, data corruption, network flooding and resource consumption are typical DoS techniques. Resource consumption is unique to databases and is often overlooked. An attacker may rapidly open a large number of database connections. This in turn triggers the *connection rate control*, which will prevent legitimate users from consuming database server resources. DoS prevention measure should target multiple layers including the network, applications and databases. IPS and connection rate controls are effective in combating DoS.
Limited security expertise and education	Many smaller organisations lack the expertise required to implement data and application security controls and policies. This coupled with lack of user training opens doors to security breaches. Invest in security software and user training.

Horizontal scaling (aka scaling out), in contrast, refers to realising increased computing power through a compute cluster built from several inexpensive computers. The latter are typically built from commodity hardware devices or components that are relatively inexpensive, widely available and easily interchangeable with other hardware of their type. Compared to horizontal scaling, vertical scaling is more expensive and limiting.

Data consistency (all clients/users get the same response for the same query), *system availability* (all operations on a database systems will eventually succeed) and *partition tolerance* (system will continue to function normally despite network failures between system servers) are the three primary concerns that determine which DBMS is suitable for a given application. The interplay between consistency, availability and partition tolerance is formulated as the CAP theorem [21,22] — it is impossible for any distributed system to achieve all these three features simultaneously. For example, to achieve partition tolerance, a system may need to give up consistency or availability. This theorem is often misunderstood and is a topic of ongoing debates. The choice seems to be mostly between consistency and high availability. Next, we discuss basic principles of distributed computing and describe Elasticsearch (ES), a NoSQL system.

4.1 Cluster-based distributed computing

Distributed computing is a paradigm in which networked computers solve computational problems through communication and coordination by passing messages. Concurrent execution, absence of a global clock and independent failure of components characterise distributed systems. Distributed algorithms are required to solve distributed systems problems such as atomic commit, consensus, distributed search, leader election, mutual exclusion and resource allocation [23]. In the context of NoSQL systems, distributed computing is a means to provide performance at scale and achieve high availability and reliability [24].

NoSQL architectures consist of several components (e.g., storage disks, CPUs, application servers) residing on networked computers. The components communicate and coordinate their actions to achieve a common goal through mechanisms such as *shared memory* and *message passing*. In the context of NoSQL systems, we define a processing *node* as a self-contained computer comprised of a CPU, RAM and disk storage (Fig. 7.1). A logical collection of nodes is called a *cluster*. Several nodes are physically mounted on a *rack*. Some NoSQL systems run on clusters whose nodes reside in geographically separated data centres. In all the cases, the nodes are interconnected through high-speed computer networks.

Client-server architecture is a widely used computing model for distributed applications. A server provides a service which is made available to the clients through an API or protocol. Typically, the server and clients reside on physically different computers and communicate over a network. However, the server and clients may reside on the same physical computer. Workload is divided between the server and clients. NoSQL systems provide their services as servers.

A NoSQL server typically runs on a cluster in production environments. The responsibility for processing client requests and distributing and coordinating workload among various nodes can be centralised or distributed. Fig. 7.2 shows both these models. Shown on the left is the *master-worker* (aka *master-slave*) architecture. A specific node is designated as the master and is responsible for intercepting client requests and delegating them to worker nodes. In this sense, the master node acts as a load balancer. The master node is also responsible for coordinating the activities of the entire cluster. This architecture simplifies cluster management, but the master node becomes the single point of failure. If the master node fails, a *standby master* takes over the responsibility.

Shown in Fig. 7.2B is an alternative to the master-worker architecture, which is called *master-master* or *peer-to-peer*. All nodes in the cluster are treated equal. At any given point of time, a specific node is accorded the role of a master. If the master

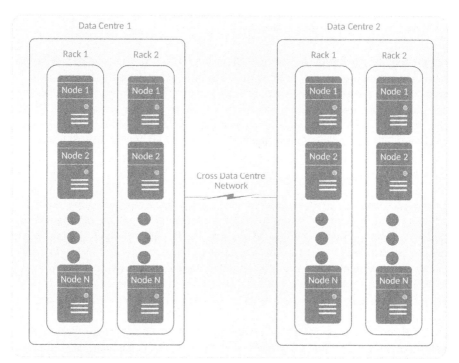

Figure 7.1 Data centre clustering.
Reproduced with permission from V. Gudivada, Cognitive Computing: Concepts, Architectures, Systems and Applications, in: V. Gudivada, V. Raghavan, V. Govindaraju, C.R. Rao (Eds.), Cognitive Computing: Theory and Applications, Volume 35 of Handbook of Statistics, Elsevier, New York, NY, September 2016, 3–38.

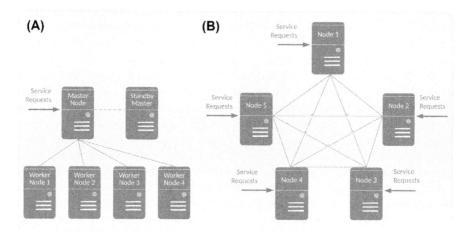

Figure 7.2 Shared-nothing cluster architecture. (A) Master-worker shared-nothing architecture and (B) master-master shared-nothing architecture.
Reproduced with permission from V. Gudivada, Cognitive Computing: Concepts, Architectures, Systems and Applications, in: V. Gudivada, V. Raghavan, V. Govindaraju, C.R. Rao (Eds.), Cognitive Computing: Theory and Applications, Volume 35 of Handbook of Statistics, Elsevier, New York, NY, September 2016, 3–38.

node fails, one of the remaining nodes is elected as the new master. Another architecture called multimaster employs a hierarchy of masters and master-worker style at the lowest level.

Master-worker and master-master configurations are called *shared-nothing architectures* since the nodes are self-contained and do not share resources. Both architectures distribute data across the nodes in the cluster to achieve performance at scale. Data are also replicated to a subset of the nodes to ensure high availability. Some NoSQL systems allow adding new nodes or removing existing ones (intentionally or due to node failure) without service interruption. NoSQL systems based on shared-nothing architecture accommodate increased workloads through horizontal scaling. Testing of NoSQL systems that use master-master architecture is easier than the ones that use master-worker architecture.

Some NoSQL systems are available as a cloud-hosted service named database as a service (DBaaS). This enables an organisation to use database services without the need for local technical expertise or local installation of NoSQL systems. The cloud operator provisions resources on demand to meet application workloads — *elastic scalability*. For example, Amazon's Simple Storage Service and DynamoDB are two examples of DBaaS.

Shared-nothing architectures achieve performance by distributing the data in a nonoverlapping manner across the nodes of a database cluster — *sharding*. The distributed data are also replicated across a subset of the nodes. Data distribution and replication are orthogonal concepts. Together they contribute to high availability — all clients of an application can always read data from and write data to the application.

4.2 Relaxed data consistency requirements

ACID is an acronym that stands for atomicity, consistency, isolation, and durability. ACID characterizes the desirable properties for transaction execution in relational database management systems. Atomicity refers to executing a database transaction as a single unit of work. Though the transaction may be comprised of several tasks, atomicity property requires that all tasks must be executed as a single unit of work — an all-or-nothing proposition. Assuming that the database is in a consistent state before the execution of the transaction, the database should remain in a consistent state after the transaction execution. Isolation property requires that multiple transactions should be allowed to execute concurrently, each progressing at its own pace and not interfering with the other concurrently executing transactions. Lastly, the durability property refers to guaranteeing that the result of a transaction execution becomes persistent despite software and hardware failures.

In contrast to ACID, NoSQL systems provide a range of options for maintaining data consistency through three design features – basic availability, soft state, and eventual consistency, which are referred to as BASE (a contrived acronym). Basic availability feature guarantees that the system is always available for read and write operations. This feature is essential for client applications to function despite network non-availability. Soft state allows for temporary data inconsistency. Given enough time, all updates will propagate through the entire system to effect data consistency eventually. It is best to think of data consistency spanning a spectrum, strict consistency at one end to eventual consistency at the other end. Strict consistency aims for immediate data consistency across the system, whereas eventual consistency will tolerate temporary data inconsistencies across the system. NoSQL systems generally offer tunable consistency, using which applications can select a right level of data consistency to match the application requirements.

Support for database transactions varies widely in NoSQL systems. Some provide support at the aggregate level. Others delegate two-phase commit required for distributed database transaction implementation to applications. Some systems use memory-mapped files and this may preclude easy application migration from one platform to another. Though strict data consistency is provided by some NoSQL systems, most embrace *eventual consistency* to support extremely fast insert and read operations.

The type of architecture (see Fig. 7.2), data partitioning and replication methods (Section 4.7) determine the degree of difficulty involved in implementing the data consistency models. Some NoSQL systems provide options for clients to choose a desired data consistency level — *tunable consistency*. For example, Cassandra provides options for choosing consistency levels for reads and writes separately.

The write consistency level specifies on how many replicas the write must succeed before returning an acknowledgement to the client application that the write is successful. The level may vary from writing to any one node, to any one node and one replica and to any one node and all replicas. The read consistency specifies how many replicas must respond before a result is returned to the client application. Assume that the data are replicated on n nodes (i.e., replication factor $= n$) and quorum is defined as $(n/2 + 1)$. The read consistency levels correspond to reading from: (1) one nearby node, (2) number of nodes equal to quorum in the local data centre, (3) number of nodes equal to quorum from each data centre and (4) all replica nodes. If the data item value from different reads are not the same, Cassandra will return the value with the most recent timestamp.

4.3 Hash functions

Hash functions and related data structures play a critical role in NoSQL systems. A hash function takes a variable length sequence of bytes and returns a fixed-length sequence of bits. The input to the function is called the *key* and the returned result is called by various names including hash, hash value, message digest (MD5) or checksum. Most often a hash function will produce unique hash for a given key. However, depending on the hash algorithm and the distribution of key values, there is a possibility that two keys may result in the same hash. This situation is referred to as *collision*.

MD5 and Secure Hash Algorithm (SHA) are widely used hash functions. MD5 algorithm produces a 128-bit hash value. SHA is designed by the US National Security Agency for cryptographic applications. SHA versions include SHA-1, SHA-2 and SHA-3. SHA-1 produces 160-bit output whereas SHA-2 and SHA-3 provide options for 224-, 256-, 383- and 512-bit hash values. For example, SHA-1 algorithm produces the hash code a5630b89be6530ae79f855ea90f218db8949ad28 (hexadecimal notation) given the string 'cyber-physical systems' as key.

Hashing is used in NoSQL systems for determining in which node of a cluster to store a new document. Randomly but uniformly distributing documents across the nodes of a cluster helps in load balancing and eliminating excessive load on any one node. The document is hashed and the value is used to determine the cluster node to store the document. Hashing is also used in caching database queries. When a query is received, it is hashed and the hash value is used to determine if the query result (from the previous execution) already exists in RAM. If so, the cached result is returned. Otherwise, the query is executed and the result is returned to the client and cached in RAM. Database query caching is implemented as (key, value) pairs, where key is the hash of the database query and the value is the result of database query execution.

4.4 Hash trees

It is helpful to think of hashing as generating a fixed-length output as a unique and shortened representation for a given piece of data. A hash tree (aka Merkle tree) is a data structure in which every nonleaf node is labelled with the hash of the labels of its child nodes. One important use for hash trees is in efficient and secure verification of data transmitted between computers for veracity. Another use is in determining whether the content files in a hierarchical directory structure are same as its backup copy (aka replica). Also, if they are not the same, hash trees provide an efficient method to determine which files are different.

Constructing a hash value for a hierarchical directory begins with the bottommost level directories (level n). Each file in this directory is hashed first and the resulting hash values are hashed again to produce another hash value — hash of the hashes. The latter is the hash value of the parent at level $n - 1$. This value is hashed again with the hash values of its siblings to produce a hash value of the parent at level $n - 2$. This process is continued until a single hash value is produced for the topmost directory. Essentially, hash values of the child nodes are used in generating the hash value of the parent. The above hash values collectively comprise the *hash tree* for the directory.

Determining whether a directory and its replica are identical simply involves computing hash values of the corresponding top-level directories. If the hash values are equal, the directory and its replica are identical. Otherwise, a node-by-node hash value comparison of the two hash trees will reveal which files are different.

NoSQL systems use hash trees to efficiently synchronise nodes that went into a disconnected state for a while from rest of the nodes in a database cluster. Hash trees enable copying only those files that have changed during the duration of the disconnected state.

4.5 Consistent hashing

One way to assign records to the nodes of a database cluster is based on the value of the *record key*. If the key values are not uniformly distributed, this assignment may lead to *hotspots* — some nodes may store a great number of records while others may receive only a few. One way to circumvent this problem is to randomly assign a record to a node. An undesirable side effect of this is that the order of keys is lost. However, it may be highly desirable to keep all records of a geographic location on one node to improve locality. Column-oriented NoSQL systems such as HBase and Google's BigTable store all records of a geographic location on one node, and the node is split into two when certain threshold is reached.

In traditional hashing, a hash algorithm is applied on the record key and the resulting hash value is used to determine the cluster node on which to store the record. The number of nodes in the cluster is a parameter to these hash algorithms. If we change the number of nodes in the cluster, nearly all keys will remap to new nodes. Consistent hashing is a technique which limits this reshuffling of records when the number of nodes in the cluster is rebalanced − when nodes are added to or removed from the cluster. If k is the number of keys and n is the number of cluster nodes, consistent hashing guarantees that on average no more than k/n keys are remapped to new nodes. In summary, consistent hashing plays a central role in minimising the amount of reshuffling when new nodes get added or existing nodes are removed from a distributed system.

4.6 Memory-mapped files, distributed file systems and vector clocks

Some NoSQL systems employ memory-mapped files to increase I/O performance especially for large files. A *memory-mapped file* is a segment of virtual memory which is associated with an operating system file or file-like resource (e.g., a device, shared memory) on a byte-for-byte correspondence. However, they may preclude easy application migration from one platform to another.

As indicated earlier, NoSQL systems are designed to run on cluster computers which are assembled using commodity hardware. Therefore, node failure rates and potential data loss are greater compared to clusters made using more expensive and noncommodity hardware. High I/O throughput is essential to deal with data volumes. Also, streaming access to file system data is needed in some cases. These requirements call for distributed fault-tolerant file systems. Such systems include Google File System and Hadoop Distributed File System (HDFS). HDFS provides interfaces for applications to enable moving computations closer to the data.

Vector clock is an algorithm for synchronising data in a distributed system. It is used to determine which version of data is the most up-to-date by reasoning about events based on event timestamps. It is an extension of RDBMS multiversion concurrency control to multiple servers. Each server keeps its copy of vector clock. When servers send and receive messages among themselves, vector clocks are incremented and attached with messages. A partial order relationship is defined based on server vector clocks and is used to derive causal relationships between database item updates. Riak, a key−value data model based NoSQL system, implements eventual data consistency using vector clocks.

4.7   Data partitioning, replication, versioning and compression

Data partitioning (aka sharding), replication and versioning are orthogonal concepts. Data partitioning and replication improve throughput of read and write operations, data availability and query performance. The range of key values of data records is called *keyspace*. In auto-sharding, data is partitioned across multiple nodes automatically using algorithmic methods such as consistent hashing or nonoverlapping keyspace regions. *Client-managed sharding* refers to data distribution specified programmatically through application logic.

Replication involves keeping multiple copies of the data on separate nodes for high availability and recoverability. The number of copies of the replicated data is called the *degree of replication*. For example, every data record may be replicated to three other nodes. In symmetric replication, if node A replicates to node B, then node B replicates to node A — bidirectional. Asymmetric replication is unidirectional. Also, replication can be synchronous or asynchronous. When a data item is updated at one node, its replicas at other nodes are either updated simultaneously (synchronous replication) or at a later time (asynchronous replication).

Intermittent versus continuous facet adds another dimension to replication. As the name implies, continuous replication involves uninterrupted replication whereas intermittent replication happens according to a time schedule. For example, continuous scheme is used for replication between the nodes of a cluster in a data centre and intermittent scheme is used for replication between cross data centre nodes during off-peak hours. Data partitioning and replication may be combined.

In *synchronous replication*, writing of a data item x to node A is not complete until the writing of x to all its replica nodes is complete. Multiple copies of the same data are stored on different computers (aka nodes) to improve data availability and query performance. Replication can be continuous or done according to a schedule. *Data sharding* refers to distributing data across the nodes in a nonoverlapping manner. When this task is done by a system in a manner transparent to the user, it is called auto-sharding.

Maintaining multiple time-stamped copies of a data item is called *versioning*. It enables retrieving the value of a data item at certain point of time in the past. Versioning combined with replication can quickly lead to enormous demands on disk space. *Data compression* data help to alleviate this problem. Some NoSQL systems also provide a feature for automatically purging the data after its expiration. This is a valuable feature for CPS applications where data have no value after certain time window.

4.8   Elasticsearch: a search and analytics engine

In this section, we focus on an NoSQL system called ES [25,26]. ES is a cluster-based distributed search and analytics engine, which offers horizontal scalability and excels in managing both unstructured and semistructured data. It enables indexing textual documents at scale and searching for them using queries specified in plain text. Also, it facilitates adding custom search features to applications. Search results can be enhanced using predictive analysis and relevancy ranking. Tasks such as identify fraud and anomaly detection are well suited for ES given its near real-time processing capability. ES does not require upfront database schema definition and the schema evolves with the application. Lastly, the advanced query language of ES enables powerful and flexible querying.

4.8.1   Elasticsearch architecture

ES logical architecture is shown in Fig. 7.3. The components shown in the left column are open source and are collectively referred to as *Elastic Stack*. *Logstash* is a full-fledged *extract, transform and load* platform for ingesting bulk data into ES. In contrast, *Beats* is a light-weight component for ingesting real-time data. The ES is the primary component which indexes documents and distributes indices across various nodes of its cluster. ES offers an Hypertext Transport Protocol (HTTP) REST interface to enable applications and users to query ES indices. It also offers several built-in algorithms for searching and scoring documents and customising the search results. Kibana turns ES into a DA platform. Kibana runs in web browser and offers an excellent user interface for querying and data visualisation.

Shown in the right column are additional components called X-Pack (extension pack), which are not open source. These additional components are essential for

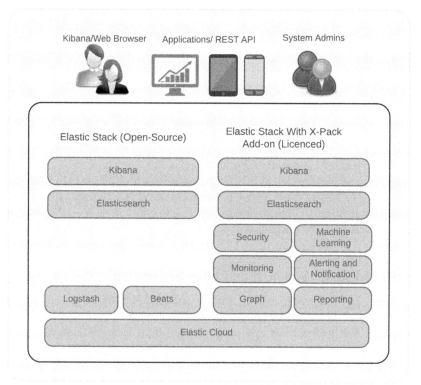

Figure 7.3 Elasticsearch logical architecture.

enterprise applications and provide various functions including authorisation and authentication via interrogation with Kerberos, for example, alerting and notification of data-driven events, monitoring, graph engine for enabling certain types of searches and ML libraries. ES and X-Pack are available on a cloud platform called *Elastic Cloud*.

ES uses sharding and replication to achieve performance at scale and high availability. Shown in Fig. 7.4 is ES's logical and physical index structures. Consider the logical index structure (Fig. 7.4 (a)). An ES index roughly corresponds to database schema in RDBMS. Just like an RDBMS database is comprised of several tables, an ES index contains one or more *types*. A *type* corresponds to a table in RDBMS. It partitions the index. Intelligent transportation systems (ITS) index (database) is stored on node 1 of a cluster. The index consists of two types (tables): traffic data and weather data. Traffic data is a collection of documents and stored under the *traffic data* type. A document is viewed as a sequence of attribute—value pairs specified in JSON format. *Mapping* (not shown in the figure) corresponds to the association between the attributes and their data types. You may explicitly specify the mapping or

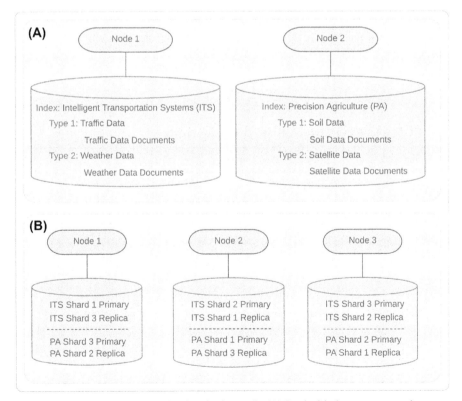

Figure 7.4 Sharding and replication in Elasticsearch. (A) Logical index structure and (B) physical index structure.

leave it to ES to figure it out automatically (implicit mapping). Node 2 stores the index with two types (soil data and satellite data) for a *precision agriculture* application.

The physical index structure of ES is shown in Fig. 7.4 (b). In contrast with logical index, physical index reveals sharding and replication details. Recall that an index is divided into fragments called *shards* for improving performance and availability. *Primary* refers to the original shard and *replica* denotes its shadow/backup version. For example, the index of the ITS application data is divided into three shards — ITS shard 1 primary, ITS shard 2 primary, and ITS shard 3 primary. Each primary shard is stored on a different node. Likewise, the corresponding replicas are also stored on different nodes such that no primary shard and its replica reside on the same node. The same three nodes are also used for storing the primary and replica shard of the *precision agriculture* application.

Though ES typically runs on a cluster for enterprise applications, it can also be installed on a single computer. We do not discuss installation details here as they change over time and also vary from one platform to another. However, we discuss a couple of configurations details. The *config* directory has three main files — elasticsearch.yml (main configuration file), jvm.options (Java VM options) and log4j2.properties (logging configuration file). ES requires Java JDK.

ES can be accessed directly through a web browser (http://localhost:9200/), command line (curl http://localhost:9200/) or through Kibana (http://localhost:5601/). Next we illustrate the creation of a simple ES database for managing scholarly publications of researchers. Some basic ES commands for this task are summarised in Table 7.3. Fig. 7.5 shows the results of executing the query 'GET/publications/journals/1' in Kibana.

Table 7.3 Basic Elasticsearch (ES) Commands

ES Command	Result Description
PUT/publications	Creates an index-named *publications*
PUT/publications/ journals	Creates a type-named *journals* for publications index PUT
PUT/publications/ books	Creates a type-named *books* for publications index PUT
PUT/publications/ chapters	Creates a type-named *chapters* for publications index
PUT/publications/ journals/1 {…}	Inserts a document of type *journals* with an *id* value of 1. The document content is specified on JSON format between { and }
GET/publications/ journals/1	Retrieves a document of type *journals* with an *id* value of 1. The document is displayed in JSON format (Fig. 7.5)

Figure 7.5 Results of executing the query 'GET/publications/journals/1' in Kibana.

5. Data analytics for cyber-physical systems

DA is the science of drawing inferences, making predictions and gaining insights into heterogeneous data which is drawn and integrated from multiple data sources. DA has its genesis in early versions of computer spreadsheets and RDBMS as online analytical processing. Its evolution and advances were referred to by various names including data mining, business intelligence, visual analytics and cognitive analytics. This evolution was primarily driven by ML, high-performance computing and big data. DA has now become a pervasive term—image analytics, video analytics, text analytics and road traffic analytics—and now refers to the processes of extracting information from unstructured data and using this information for quantitative decision-making.

For an illustration, consider the role of DA in ITS. DA integrates heterogeneous data from diverse sources — connected car networks, car navigation systems, weather sensors embedded in roadways, traffic signal control systems, among others. Cleaning, transforming and integrating these diverse data enables building ITS applications such as real-time traffic prediction and rerouting, automatic enforcement of speed limits, dynamic traffic light sequencing and vehicle-to-vehicle communication and collaboration.

5.1   Types of data analytics

Based on its intended purpose, DA is categorised into four classes — descriptive, diagnostic, predictive and prescriptive. The classes are highly interrelated and their functional overlap is significant. These classes should be viewed as facets spanning a *workflow* rather than as four distinct categories.

Regardless of the domain, DA is comprised of three activities: data acquisition, cleaning, transforming and loading; methods and algorithms and a computational platform that implicitly embodies workflows and best practices. The first activity involves preparing the input data and loading it into the computational platform. Various statistical and ML algorithms and approaches for data analysis are used to accomplish the second task. Lastly, the computational platform integrates the first two activities and provides interfaces for users and other applications.

5.2   Descriptive analytics

The goal of *descriptive analytics* is providing insights into the past leading to the present. It helps to learn from the past and use this knowledge to improve operational efficiencies and spot activities that consume disproportionate amounts of resources (aka *resource drains*). Descriptive statistics and exploratory data analysis (EDA) are the primary tools used for implementing descriptive analytics. Descriptive statistics provides tools to quantitatively describe the data in summary and graphical forms — measures of *central tendency* (mean, median and mode) and dispersion (minimum and maximum values, range, quantiles, standard deviation/variance, distribution skewness and kurtosis). EDA brings a visual dimension to descriptive analytics in the form of histograms, scatter plots, matrix plots, box-and-whisker plots, steam-and-leaf diagrams, rootograms, resistant time series smoothing and bubble charts. This visual exploration helps to gain an intuitive understanding of the data and provides scaffolding for guided inquiry. It also helps to identify research questions for further investigation.

5.3   Diagnostic analytics

Diagnostic analytics helps to identify factors that are responsible for what has been observed through descriptive analytics. In other words, it addresses the question 'why did it happen?' Several techniques including data mining and data warehousing are used to answer the question. It is exploratory in nature and requires a human-in-the-loop. Diagnostic analytics has been used in the education and learning domain for long under the name *diagnostic assessment*, which is a manual process.

5.4   Predictive analytics

Predictive analytics is about predicting the future based on the past [27]. It answers the 'what if' questions by building predictive models using inferential statistics and forecasting techniques. Predictive analytics helps to implement preventive actions or change course. Predictive models are probabilistic in nature and require substantial data for building the models.

Selecting which *variables* to use for building prediction models is referred to as *variable/feature selection*. EDA often reveals which variables are good candidates for model building. *Correlation* coefficient (r) quantifies the degree to which two variables are related. The value of r is in the range -1 to 1. If two variables are highly correlated, it means that the variables behave similarity. Therefore, only one of them should be considered for model building. Linear regression is a popular technique for predictive analytics [28]. Other regression models include discrete choice, multinomial logistic, probit, logit, time series, survival analysis, classification and regression trees and multivariate adaptive regression splines. Classification algorithms such as naive Bayes, multilayer perceptron, neural networks, radial basis functions, support vector machines and k-nearest neighbours are also used in predictive analytics.

5.5 Prescriptive analytics

Prescriptive analytics is closely associated with diagnostic and predictive analytics. While diagnostic analytics answers the question 'why did it happen?' and prescriptive analytics helps to answer the question 'what is likely to happen', prescriptive analytics is used to increase the chance of realising the desired events or diminishing the chances of occurrence of undesired events.

Prescriptive analytics is evolving into what is referred to as *cognitive analytics* [29]. Cognitive computing [30] and cognitive science are the foundation of cognitive analytics. One aspect of cognitive analytics is to compute multiple answers to questions and associate a degree of confidence with each answer. Because of the inherent complexity and nascency of cognitive analytics, very few organisations have implemented it.

5.6 Data analytics resources and tools

DA systems come in various forms with functional capabilities that vary widely. Commercial vendors include SAS, Microsoft, Oracle, Teradata and Tableau Software. Python, Java and R [31] are very popular programming languages for implementing DA. ML frameworks and libraries such as TensorFlow [32], Weka3 [33] and Keras [34] provide suitable abstraction to expedite DA applications.

The Apache UIMA project provides open-source frameworks, tools and annotators for information extraction from unstructured data [35]. Apache Hadoop and Spark are widely used open-source computing platforms for big data processing and cognitive analytics.

6. Current trends and research issues

CPS applications and their complexity are growing at an exponential rate. The behaviour of hardware and software in the cyberspace and the physical systems in the physical environment are well understood in isolation. However, the emergent properties that arise when cyber systems interact with the physical world are complex and do not lend themselves for modelling and analysis. Ad hoc approaches to CPS system design and implementation may result in systems that are brittle, are not scalable and lack design flexibility. Formal approaches to CPS design with provision for automated verification and validation is required to minimise software bugs and hardware malfunction and thwart cybersecurity attacks.

CPS-based ITS, in general, and vehicle-to-vehicle and vehicle-to-infrastructure communication, in particular, will have significant impact on people in all walks of life. CPS will have even more impact on automotive services such as testing, development, maintenance and repair. The proliferation of CPS systems calls for education and workforce development. Six foundations for a CPS curriculum have been identified [2]. They include basic computing concepts, computing for the physical world, discrete and continuous mathematics, cross-cutting applications, modelling and CPS system development.

Given the data quality and cybersecurity issues, CPS decision-making for mission-critical applications must necessarily involve human-in-the-loop. Even with this approach, one should be cognisant of the cognitive and motivational biases discussed in Section 3.3.

References

[1] National Science Foundation, Cyber-Physical Systems (CPS), March 2016. https://www.nsf.gov/publications/pub_summ.jsp?ods_key= nsf16549. (Accessed on 18/04/2018).

[2] National Academies of Sciences, Engineering, and Medicine, A 21st Century Cyber-Physical Systems Education, National Academies Press, Washington, DC, 2016. https://doi.org/10.17226/24x. (Accessed on 18/04/2018).

[3] E.A. Lee, S.A. Seshia, Introduction to Embedded Systems: A Cyber-Physical Systems Approach, The MIT Press, Cambridge, Massachusetts, 2017.

[4] M. Islam, M. Chowdhury, H. Li, H. Hu, Cybersecurity attacks in vehicle-to-infrastructure (V2I)Applications and their prevention, in: Transportation Research Board Annual Meeting, Washington, DC, 2018.

[5] Connected Vehicle Reference Implementation Architecture, (n.d.). http://local.iteris.com/cvria/html/applications/applications.html. (Accessed on 18/04/2018).

[6] E.F. Codd, A relational model of data for large shared data banks, Communications of the ACM 13 (6) (June 1970) 377–387.

[7] D.D. Chamberlin, R.F. Boyce, SEQUEL: a structured English query language, in: Proceedings of the 1974 ACM SIGFIDET (Now SIGMOD) Workshop on Data Description, Access and Control. SIGFIDET '74, ACM, New York, NY, 1974, pp. 249–264.

[8] R. van der Meulen, 8.4 billion Connected "things" Will Be in Use in 2017, up 31 Percent From 2016, February 2017. https://www.gartner.com/newsroom/id/3598917. (Accessed on 18/04/2018).

[9] V. Gudivada, D. Rao, V. Raghavan, Renaissance in database management: navigating the landscape of candidate systems, IEEE Computer 49 (4) (April. 2016) 31–42.

[10] solid IT, Knowledge Base of Relational and Nosql Database Management Systems, 2018. https://db-engines.com/en/. (Accessed on 18/04/2018).

[11] V. Gudivada, A. Apon, D. Rao, Database systems for big data storage and retrieval, in: R. Segall, N. Gupta, J. Cook (Eds.), Handbook of Research on Big Data Storage and Visualization Techniques. Advances in Data Mining and Database Management, IDG Global, Boston, MA, 2018, pp. 76−100.

[12] V. Gudivada, A. Apon, J. Ding, Data quality considerations for big data and machine learning: going beyond data cleaning and transformations, International Journal on Advances in Software 10 (1) (2017) 1−20.

[13] V. Ganti, A.D. Sarma, Data cleaning: a practical perspective, in: Synthesis Lectures on Data Management, Morgan & Claypool Publishers, 2013.

[14] J.W. Osborne, Best Practices in Data Cleaning: A Complete Guide to Everything You Need to Do Before and After Collecting Your Data, SAGE, Thousand Oaks, CA, 2013.

[15] D. McGilvray, Executing Data Quality Projects: Ten Steps to Quality Data and Trusted Information, Morgan Kaufmann Publishers Inc., San Francisco, CA, 2008.

[16] K. Sha, S. Zeadally, Data quality challenges in cyber-physical systems, Journal of Data and Information Quality 6 (2−3) (Jun. 2015) 8:1−8:4.

[17] S. Lebowitz, S. Lee, Cognitive Biases that Screw up Your Decisions, 20 August 2015. http://www.businessinsider.com/cognitive-biases-that-affect-decisions-2015-8. (Accessed on 18/04/2018).

[18] S. Fiegerman, Yahoo Says 500 Million Accounts Stolen, 2016. http://money.cnn.com/2016/09/22/technology/yahoo-data-breach/. (Accessed on 18/04/2018).

[19] IndentityForce, The Biggest Data Breaches in 2016, So Far, 2016. https://www.identityforce.com/blog/2016-data-breaches. (Accessed on 18/04/2018).

[20] Imperva, Top 5 Database Security Threats, 2016. https://www.imperva.com/docs/gated/WP_Top_5_Database_Security_Threats.pdf. (Accessed on 18/04/2018).

[21] E. Brewer, CAP twelve years later: how the "rules" have changed, Computer 45 (2) (2012) 23−29.

[22] E.A. Brewer, Towards robust distributed systems (abstract), in: Proceedings of the Nineteenth Annual ACM Symposium on Principles of Distributed Computing. PODC '00, ACM, New York, NY, USA, 2000, p. 7.

[23] W. Fokkink, Distributed Algorithms: An Intuitive Approach, The MIT Press, Cambridge, Massachusetts, 2013.

[24] M. Kleppmann, Designing Data-Intensive Applications: The Big Ideas Behind Reliable, Scalable, and Maintainable Systems, O'Reilly Media, Sebastopol, California, 2017.

[25] R. Gheorghe, M.L. Hinman, R. Russo, Elasticsearch in Action, Manning Publications, Shelter Island, New York, 2015.

[26] C. Gormley, Z. Tong, Elasticsearch: the definitive guide, in: A Distributed Real-time Search and Analytics Engine, O'Reilly Media, Sebastopol, California, 2015.

[27] V. Dhar, Data science and prediction, Communications of the ACM 56 (12) (December 2013) 64−73.

[28] G. James, An Introduction to Statistical Learning with Applications in R, Springer, New York, NY, 2013. https://doi.org/10.1007/978-1-4614-7138-7. (Accessed on 18/04/2018).

[29] V. Gudivada, M. Irfan, E. Fathi, D. Rao, Cognitive analytics: going beyond big data analytics and machine learning, in: V. Gudivada, V. Raghavan, V. Govindaraju, C.R. Rao (Eds.), Cognitive Computing: Theory and Applications. Volume 35 of Handbook of Statistics, Elsevier, New York, NY, October 2016, pp. 169−205, 978-0-444-63744-4.

[30] V. Gudivada, V. Raghavan, V. Govindaraju, C. Rao (Eds.), Cognitive Computing: Theory and Applications. Volume 35 of Handbook of Statistics, Elsevier, New York, NY, October 2016.
[31] The R Foundation, The R Project for Statistical Computing, 2018. https://www.r-project.org/. (Accessed on 18/04/2018).
[32] TensorFlow, An Open Source Software Library for Numerical Computation Using Data Flow Graphs, 2018. https://www.tensorflow.org/. (Accessed on 18/04/2018).
[33] The University of Waikato, Weka 3: Data Mining Software in Java, 2018. http://www.cs.waikato.ac.nz/ml/weka/. (Accessed on 18/04/2018).
[34] Keras, The Python Deep Learning Library, 2018. https://keras.io/. (Accessed on 18/04/2018).
[35] Apache, The UIMA Project, 2018. http://uima.apache.org/. (Accessed on 18/04/2018).

Human Factors in Transportation Cyber-Physical Systems: A Case Study of a Smart Automated Transport and Retrieval System (SmartATRS)

Paul Whittington, Huseyin Dogan
Department of Computing & Informatics, Faculty of Science & Technology,
Bournemouth University, Poole, United Kingdom

1. Introduction

Human Factors (HF), also known as 'ergonomics', are defined as the scientific discipline concerned with the understanding of interactions amongst humans and other elements of a system [1]. The rationale behind HF is to understand how a system can be designed so that it is suitable for the intended user by complimenting their abilities, as opposed to users adapting to a design that is challenging. To achieve this, it is necessary to understand the variability within the user community, including age, cognitive ability, cultural diversity [2] and physical ability. Considering HF through the involvement of the intended users results in a user-centred design, where the users can influence the design process [3]. A second benefit of this process is that the individual knowledge and expertise from the users across different disciplines can be applied to the design. The user-centred design process is highly iterative, as continual testing is required in order to ensure that the design meets the requirements of the users.

This involvement of users during project development is known as User Experience (UX) where direct user feedback is incorporated throughout the development cycle. The User Experience Professionals Association [4] defines UX as 'every aspect of the user's interaction with a product, service, or company that make up the user's perceptions of the whole'. UX determines the users' perceptions on the practical aspects of a system such as ease of use and is therefore subjective due to perceptions changing over time. There are a number of factors that affect UX, which can be classified into context, user and system factors. Contextual factors concern the social, physical and technical aspects of the experience, whereas the user factors are influenced by individuals' mood and expectations of the system, and the system factors include the functionality and interface design.

A further aspect to be considered during user-centred designed is accessibility or universal design in order to cater for human diversity, social inclusion and equality,

Transportation Cyber-Physical Systems. https://doi.org/10.1016/B978-0-12-814295-0.00008-3
Copyright © 2018 Elsevier Inc. All rights reserved.

by ensuring that the design of products should be usable for all people without the need for adaptations [5]. It is stated that to achieve universal design, the intended user community should participate in the design process and the designer should be responsible for designing which user groups should be involved. An example of an accessibility regulation is the Web Content Accessibility Guidelines [6] that provides a single shared standard for web content accessibility that meets the international needs of individuals, organisations and governments.

HF are considered by the UK Ministry of Defence as a systematic systems engineering process known as Human Factors Integration (HFI), which identifies, tracks and resolves human-related considerations, to ensure a balanced development in terms of technologies and human aspects. This concept can be applied during the development of Transportation Cyber-Physical Systems, together with user-centred design, UX and universal design, to ensure that the system meets expectations. However, there is limited research conducted into accessibility guidelines for cyber-physical systems in general.

There are many examples of cyber-physical systems in the transportation sector where the HF approach has been adopted including aircraft flight decks, air traffic control systems and the design of vehicles [7]. Within this chapter, Smart Automated Transport and Retrieval System (SmartATRS) is considered as a Transportation Cyber-Physical System where usability evaluations are conducted to assess the suitability of a system for the user community of people with reduced physical ability. SmartATRS provides an alternative modality of interaction for the Automated Transport and Retrieval System (ATRS). ATRS is a technically advanced system that autonomously docks a powered wheelchair (powerchair) onto a platform lift in a vehicle [8] using laser ranging technology originally developed for docking the Jules Verne spacecraft with the International Space Station [9].

2. Related human factors approaches

In order to develop SmartATRS, it was necessary to consider aspects of Human Computer Interaction (HCI) in terms of ergonomics of Human System Interaction(HSI), Universal Design and Design for All The ISO standard of ergonomics of HIS was originally recognised as Human-Centred Design (HCD) [10]. It can be defined as an iterative process consisting of five core stages. The first stage is to understand the context of use in order to generate user requirements. The requirements are then utilised to produce design solutions that can be evaluated against the user requirements. The iterative nature of HCD is produced by the involvement of users during the design process, which could lead to modifications to the design of the system.

2.1 Human factors integration

HFI is considered as a system engineering process that allows the human component of a system to be identified and any human-related aspects that would adversely impact the development to be traded off. The process exists within capability management that concerns the responsibilities of users in capability planning, generation and delivery roles [11]. The planning role consists of devising plans and deriving options for areas where the existing capability could be improved based on user feedback on the current gaps. This user feedback is also applied during the generation role where the new systems are integrated into the current process and evaluated. The final role is associated with the delivery of the new integration and involves initiation and acceptance of the new systems by the users.

It is stated that HFI has multiple benefits including minimising errors in the design through thorough correct analysis of HF, resulting in reduced product recalls, development costs, user training and ongoing maintenance costs. HFI consists of a framework containing seven domains to ensure that issues, risks, assumptions, constraints and requirements are captured. These domains are manpower, personnel, training, human factors engineering, system safety, health hazards and social and organisational [11]. The manpower domain relates to a number of users required to operate, maintain, sustain and provide training for systems. The considerations include comparisons with the existing systems in terms of manpower levels required and the necessary expertise of the users. The personnel domain is associated with the human characteristics of the users required to achieve optimum system performance. This can be identified through ascertaining the cognitive and physical attributes required for system operation and the skill and education levels needed for optimal effectiveness. The training domain evaluates the combination of education and on the job training required to develop the knowledge and abilities of the personnel to ensure that the systems can be operated and maintained to the required level. To determine this, the range of training required should be considered. The fourth domain consists of comprehensive integration of human characteristics into the system, where considerations need to be given, including evaluating how the user interface design suits the cognitive abilities of the users and the potential impact of the technology integration. System safety should be considered as the fifth domain to minimise risks that may occur due to normal or abnormal system operation. This includes error source identification and mitigation and the extent that unintentional errors could impact safety. Potential health hazards need to be identified and addressed by the sixth domain of HFI in order to prevent death, injury, illness, disability or a reduction in user performance. This is achieved by conforming to existing health and safety standards. The final social and organisational domain applies existing tools and techniques from psychological studies to consider the organisational environment for the system. This is concerned with managing the interoperability between components and assessing the impact that the new system has on the current cultural practices.

The HFI process can be applied to Transportation Cyber-Physical Systems to provide an evaluation of their integration with the existing processes. The manpower and personnel domains relate to the intended maintenance and end users, with the training and human factors engineering domains being assessed through usability evaluations of the cyber-physical system. The system safety domain is paramount for transportation systems that could have high levels of potential risk, causing injury or death. These risks should be mitigated in the fifth domain through the adoption of alternative techniques with higher levels of safety. Following the integration of new cyber-physical systems, assessments should be conducted to ensure that the system is not adversely affecting the performance of the users.

2.2 Human-centred design

One of the key principles of the concept is the involvement of potential users during both the design and development of the system. It is recommended by Preece et al. [3] that background interviews should be conducted at the beginning of the design process to elicit knowledge regarding the requirements and expectations of the users. Later in the design process, techniques such as walk throughs, role plays and prototypes simulations are to be conducted to evaluate designs and potentially obtain additional requirements. The process should conclude with the collection of quantitative usability data through testing and qualitative satisfaction measurements through interviews and questionnaires. These recommendations were followed during the development of the case study through eliciting the current difficulties that people with reduced physical ability encountered in their daily lives, obtaining usability data in terms of System Usability Scale (SUS) and NASA Task Load Index (TLX) and eliciting qualitative data from the users regarding their experiences.

Placing the user at the centre of the design in order to achieve the ISO Standard can be accomplished by adhering to the four recommendations stated by Norman [12]. It is imperative that a system must be easy to evaluate, the users can determine the actions that are possible at any point in time and the structure of a system must be transparent to users including any conceptual models, alternative actions and the outcomes of actions. Norman's [12] final recommendation suggests that natural mappings between intentions and required actions should be followed by a system. Norman [12] also defined seven principles of design that ensures the user is assisted when performing tasks. These principles include the creation of understandable operating manuals, simplified task structure to avoid memory overloads, planning for user errors to ensure recovery is always possible and ensuring that it is obvious which actions need to be performed to achieve the system goal. It has been demonstrated that following an HCD process enables designers to obtain a greater understanding of the social, ergonomic, organisational and psychological factors affecting technology and that system is suitable for the intended user community. There have been examples that following this approach can avoid mistakes such as poorly defined requirements, which is often the cause for failed information technology projects [13].

2.3 Usability evaluation

Usability is defined as the quality of a user's experience when interacting with products or systems that can be measured in terms of effectiveness, efficiency and satisfaction [14]. A variety of factors can contribute to usability including the ease of learning, memorability, error frequency and intuitive design, which can be evaluated through participative enquiry through the adoption of methods including focus groups, scenarios, surveys and interviews [14]. An alternative strategy to understand the learnability of a system to new or infrequent users is cognitive walk throughs where a series of tasks are conducted from the user's perspective [15]. There have been examples where this technique has been applied to evaluate smartphone messaging applications [16]. It was essential to evaluate the usability on the SmartATRS to ascertain whether the interaction modalities would be suitable for the user community of people with reduced physical ability.

The SUS and NASA TLX are two tools that can be adopted to assess intuitive design and the demands experienced by users when interacting. SUS was originally developed by Brooke [17] to provide a 'quick and dirty' reliable tool for measuring usability consisting of a 10-item questionnaire with 5 response sections from 'strongly agree' to 'strongly disagree'. NASA TLX is a subjective workload assessment tool that derives an overall usability score based on the subscales of mental demand, physical demand, temporal demand, performance, effort and frustration and thus determines the effect of each interaction modality on the user. Results from NASA TLX can be analysed through the employment of the Adjective Rating Scale [18] that defines the level of usability from 'worst imaginable' to 'best imaginable'. Other usability evaluation techniques include heuristic evaluation that review user interfaces through comparing the design against usability principles such as Nielsen's Heuristics [19]. However, these can only be successfully implemented when trained usability experts are involved in the evaluation process to apply the heuristics effectively. A further alternative technique is think-aloud testing where users are asked to think out loud when being observed interacting with a system. The Subjective Workload Dominance technique (SWORD) could be adopted instead of NASA TLX to measure workload experienced. However, SWORD rates the workload dominance of one task against another. Therefore, only a rating is provided for which tasks create greater workload than the others and not a rating of the participants' workload [20]. A similar technique to SUS is the Questionnaire for User Interaction Satisfaction (QUIS) [21] where participants rate 27 questions on a 10-point scale based on their satisfaction with specific sections on a user interface. Compared to SUS, QUIS is deemed relatively complex and more tedious for participants to complete.

2.4   Interaction modalities

Traditionally, HCI was considered as unimodal where users can only interact through a single channel, e.g., a keyboard. However, it is multimodal as users interact with a variety of devices such as the keyboard, mouse and display to perform tasks. Multimodal systems was originally defined by Oviatt [22] as systems 'that process two or more combined user input modes in a coordinated manner with multimedia outputs'. The rationale behind multimodality is to offer alternative channels for users to align with the natural method of interaction in the world (i.e., through the five major senses of sight, hearing, touch, smell and taste) [23]. Advances in hardware and software are enabling multimodal systems to emerge where humans are able to interact through natural methods including speech, touch and gesture [24]. The advent of smartphones illustrates multimodal interaction where the device can be operated via a variety of methods. There have also been examples of multimodality in assistive technologies including Kunze et al. [25] who conducted a trial of a head-mounted display with older adults and Miller et al. [26] who investigated utilisation of Google Glass to assist students in lectures who are hard of hearing. Vehicles provide a modern example of multimodal interaction where information and entertainment systems can be controlled through modalities including hierarchical menus and speech commands.

3. Case study

SmartATRS [27] can be considered as a Transportation Cyber-Physical System as it enables a user to transport their powered wheelchair in a vehicle. Furthermore, the system comprises of multiple independently operable constituent systems (e.g., the automated tailgate, platform lift and motorised driver's seat, as seen in Fig. 8.1) that can only provide the functionality of SmartATRS when combined together as a cyber-physical system. SmartATRS was developed to control an existing assistive technology called the ATRS, originally developed by Freedom Sciences Inc. ATRS is a technically advanced system first featured in *New Scientist* magazine [9] with the objective of creating a reliable, robust means for a wheelchair user to autonomously dock a powerchair onto a platform lift without the need of an assistant [8]. ATRS requires a standard multipurpose vehicle to be installed with three components; a motorised seat that rotates and exits the vehicle through the driver's door, an automated tailgate and a platform lift fitted in the rear of the vehicle.

Using a joystick attached to the driver's seat, a user with reduced physical ability manoeuvres the powerchair to the rear of the vehicle until it is adjacent to the lift

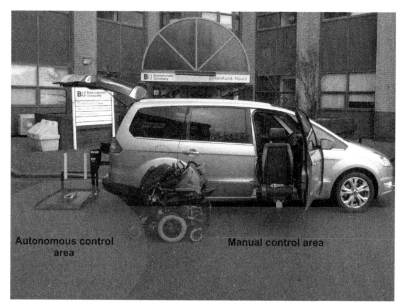

Figure 8.1 ATRS operating zones.

Figure 8.2 Wireless keyfobs used to control ATRS.

and within line of sight of two highly reflective fiducials. On an input from the user (via a button press), a laser guidance system comprising a compact Light Detection and Ranging (LiDAR) unit coupled with robotics fitted to powerchair, locates the exact position of the lift and proceeds to autonomously drive the powerchair onto the platform, as shown in Fig. 8.1. In the event of the powerchair driving outside the autonomous control area, operation will cease instantly and user intervention through the joystick is required to return the chair to this area. The small wireless keyfobs (similar to those that operate automated gates) used to control the seat, lift and tailgate have small buttons that need to be held down to interact with the system, as shown in Fig. 8.2. As they can be dropped easily, they can be problematic for a powerchair user with reduced finger dexterity, especially if they fall out of reach (e.g., under the vehicle).

3.1 Requirements

SmartATRS was developed to provide the exact functionality of the keyfobs on a smartphone interface. Demonstrations of ATRS to users with reduced physical abilities were performed at the 2011 Mobility Roadshow, a UK consumer-based event, showcasing mobility products and innovation. The demonstrations revealed that keyfobs presented a deterrent to potential users due to the finger dexterity required to operate small buttons. The keyfobs could also be dropped easily, potentially falling out of the reach of a powerchair user. Based on the demonstrations at the Mobility Roadshow, requirements were defined for SmartATRS using Volere Requirements Shells [28] and categorised in terms of Functionality (FR), Interoperability (IR), Maintainability (MR), Performance (PR), Portability (PTR), Reliability (RR), Safety (SFR) and Usability (UR). The defined requirements were as follows:

1. (SFR1) SmartATRS shall not prevent ATRS from being operated by the handheld pendants or keyfobs.
2. (FR1) SmartATRS shall be able to control the following functions: the Freedom Seat, Tracker Lift and Automated Tailgate.
3. (SFR2) SmartATRS shall ensure safe operation of all ATRS functions.

4. (UR1) The user interface of SmartATRS shall be created in a design that a user with reduced finger dexterity would be able to use.
5. (RR1) SmartATRS shall be reliable, as a user would depend on the system for their independence.
6. (FR2) ATRS shall still function as if being operated by the handheld pendants and keyfobs.
7. (PR1) SmartATRS shall minimise any additional delay to the functioning of ATRS.
8. (MR1) SmartATRS shall be easy to configure by installers.
9. (MR2) SmartATRS shall be easy to install into a standard ATRS.
10. (PTR1) SmartATRS shall be compatible with all popular smartphone operating systems that have web browsers and customisable voice control.

3.2   System architecture

SmartATRS was originally developed with two interaction methods (touch and joystick), but this was subsequently increased through the incorporation of head and smartglass-based interaction modalities.

Fig. 8.3 shows the system architecture diagram for SmartATRS including the integrated existing ATRS components, as well as the component and user interactions. In the standard ATRS, keyfobs and handheld pendants were the only interaction methods, whereas with SmartATRS, the original interaction methods are touch or joystick based. Junction boxes were manufactured to retain the operation of the existing handheld pendants as a backup method. As all of the ATRS components contained relays, a relay board comprising an embedded web server was used to interface between the components and JavaScript. The server stored the HTML and JavaScript Graphical User Interfaces (GUI) as web pages and JavaScript XMLHttpRequests (objects that transfer data between a web browser and server [29] were transmitted to access an Extensible Markup Language (XML) file). The file contains the timer durations for each ATRS function denoted as integers that represented the number of milliseconds that each function was switched on for. An XML editor was used to view and change the timer durations, therefore ensuring that the process was not visible to end users. The web server was connected to a Wi-Fi router located in the vehicle using Ethernet. The router created a secure Wi-Fi Protected Access II network whereby smartphones or other Wi-Fi—enabled devices could connect to the GUI by entering the URL or accessing a bookmark. Through the integration of iPortal [30], joystick control was achieved by communicating with the device via Bluetooth where the joystick was moved left or right for navigation and forwards for selection.

3.3   User interface design

The SmartATRS user interface (shown in Fig. 8.4) was developed based upon the views of users at the 2011 Mobility Roadshow and incorporated user feedback and safety features that were not present in the keyfobs. Seven command buttons were used to activate each ATRS function. The red emergency stop button was twice the width of the other buttons, so that it could be selected quickly in an emergency situation. The large buttons reduced the risk of incorrect selection by users with reduced

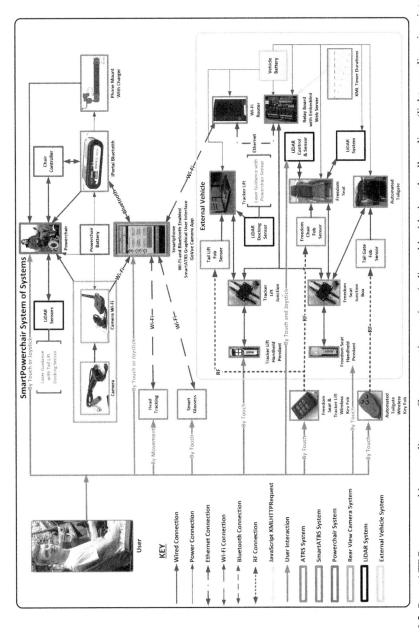

Figure 8.3 SmartATRS system architecture diagram. Component interactions indicated by black and yellow lines (light grey lines in print versions) and the user interactions illustrated in red (dark grey in print versions).

Figure 8.4 SmartATRS user interface.

finger dexterity. The command button changed colour depending on the current state of SmartATRS, with blue representing currently operating features and orange to represent a disabled function. Functions were disabled due to interlocks created to maintain safety that were not present in the standard ATRS. An example interlock was between the tailgate and the lift, where the tailgate was disabled when the lift was not stowed. This eliminated the risk of closing the tailgate onto the lift, which would result in damage to both components (which was possible in the standard system).

3.4 Risk analysis

As identified in the fifth systems safety domain of the HFI process, it is important to consider risks in order to achieve a user-centred design. Transportation Cyber-Physical Systems can present multiple risks to users due to motorised physical components. Therefore, the SmartATRS case study was used to establish potential risks that can exist with Transportation Cyber-Physical Systems technologies in a three-stage risk analysis framework for System of Systems (SoS), consisting of threat identification, risk analysis and risk evaluation [31]. In order to identify risks, an in-depth understanding of the system's structure needs to be established in terms of threat sources and vulnerable system elements. This results in identification of risks that are present within the system environment. Example system risks identified included the requirement that the smartphone must be within range of the Wi-Fi router in order for the user interface to be accessed. Consequently, the SmartATRS cannot receive commands if the smartphone is not available.

The second stage determined the consequences of the risk highlighted at the previous stage. This was evaluated using five steps comprised of likelihood analysis, impact on the system, interoperability analysis, impact level analysis and risk level analysis. The likelihood analysis step involved analysing the efficiency and probability of the risk occurring while step two or the impact on the system step formed a qualitative assessment of the effects that the risks produced on the system. The interoperability analysis step determined the effect of the risk on the interoperability of the SoS. Step four determined the impact level of the risk on the system while the final step measured the scale of the risk in terms of likelihood and impact. Table 8.1 was devised based on the system threats identified in the first stage of the risk assessment that determined the likelihood and impacts of the risks on the SmartATRS.

Stage three of the risk assessment enabled control measures to be planned in order to mitigate the risks consisting of two further steps: control measures and documentation of the risk assessment outcomes. The purpose of this stage was to identify any unacceptable risks and plan appropriate methods against them to reduce risk to an acceptable level [32] with any high-level risk given priority. One control measure employed in SmartATRS was to ensure that alternative interaction modalities were provided for users who may experience challenges operating one modality (e.g., users who cannot operate smartglasses can use a smartphone). Another example measure was to have guard timers on all functions so that if communication between the smartphone and Wi-Fi router failed (causing inoperability of the JavaScript timers), hardware timers for each relay on the board would ensure that the functions are terminated.

SmartATRS was the case study for the research where controlled usability evaluations were conducted to assess the usability of interaction modalities for people with reduced physical ability. As SmartATRS relied on the interoperability between components that could be seen as constituent systems, the case study could be viewed as a cyber-physical system. The components of both SmartATRS and the existing ATRS are considered to be constituent systems, as the components can not only function independently but only provide the functionality of SmartATRS when combined in a cyber-physical system. Example constituent systems include the LiDAR unit to provide autonomous docking, the powerchair and the smartphone. The integration with the existing ATRS is achieved through utilisation of the relay board with an embedded web server to store the SmartATRS user interface and the addition of junction boxes to enable the wireless keyfobs and handheld pendants to remain operational as a backup interaction modality.

3.5 Task analysis, usability, evaluations and workload measurements

Controlled usability evaluations were performed involving the user community to obtain an accurate assessment of usability of varying modalities. Prior to the

Table 8.1 Likelihood and Impacts of SmartATRS Risks

ID	Identified Risk	Likelihood (L, M, H)	Impact on Systems	Impact on Interoperability	Impact Level (L, M, H)	Risk Level (L, M, H)
S1	Smartphone must be in range of the router for Wi-Fi to be accessible.	L	Wi-Fi connection will not be available for smartphone. The system cannot be used.	The smartphone will not be able to connect and communicate with other systems.	H	M
S2	Vehicle cannot receive commands if the smartphone is not available.	M	The system cannot be operated without the smartphone.	System cannot operate.	H	H

L, Low; *M*, Medium; *H*, High.

conduction of the evaluations, it was necessary to perform a Hierarchical Task Analysis (HTA) to obtain an understanding of the tasks involved with operating SmartATRS.

3.5.1 Hierarchical task analysis

Adopting HTA enabled the tasks to be performed in the controlled usability evaluations to be determined. This was achieved by deconstructing the high-level parent task (i.e., departing or arriving in a vehicle) into subtasks by using a numbering system in a hierarchical structure, as shown in the extract in Fig. 8.5.

The SmartATRS HTA for departing in the vehicle consisted of six subtasks: (1) preparing vehicle, (2) activating lift and seat out of vehicle, (3) preparing powerchair, (4) autonomous docking, (5) activating lift and seat into vehicle and (6) departure. These tasks needed to be performed sequentially in order to successfully depart in the vehicle with the powerchair safely stowed. The addition of screenshots of SmartATRS to the HTA highlighted the tasks currently supported by smartphone interaction.

Task 1 involves positioning the powerchair near to the driver's door by moving the joystick in the required direction. This allows the driver to reach the door so that the seat can be driven out in Task 2. The lift and seat are activated in Task 2, using iPortal to control a smartphone via the powerchair joystick. After iPortal has been engaged using the buttons on the joystick control, it is necessary to tap the joystick in order to reach the 'Seat Out' button on the SmartATRS user interface. The 'Lift Out' button is activated via the same method using the joystick. Whist the lift and seat are being driven out of the vehicle, the driver progresses to Task 3 to prepare the powerchair for autonomous docking. This involves five further tasks: switching on the LiDAR unit which is utilised for the docking, raising the footrest to enable the powerchair to fit onto the lift, the driver transferring to the seat and folding the seat back using

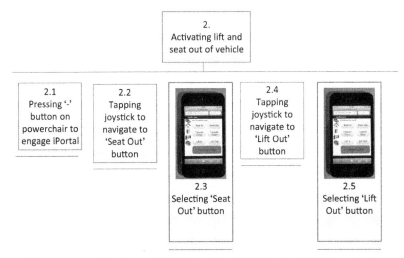

Figure 8.5 An extract of the SmartATRS Hierarchical Task Analysis for departing in a vehicle.

the joystick to ensure that the powerchair is low enough to fit into the vehicle. Task 4 uses ATRS to activate the remote control feature using the Joystick Control Module attached to the side of the driver's seat. The driver then remotely navigates the power-chair to the rear of the vehicle using the joystick on the module. Once the powerchair is in line of sight of the fiducials attached to the lift, autonomous docking is activated us-ing the button on the module. Following the docking, the lift and seat are stowed into the vehicle in Task 5 using the SmartATRS user interface via touch-based interaction. The final task consists of departing in the vehicle by closing the driver's door, fastening the seat belt, adjusting the steering wheel into the driver's preferred position and starting the ignition. The HTA for arriving in a SmartATRS-equipped vehicle would consist of an identical set of tasks in the reverse order.

Creating the HTA also contributed to the instructions that were provided to partic-ipants to ensure the safe interaction of the system and allowed a greater understanding of the processes involved within SmartATRS.

3.5.2 Evaluation 1 (keyfob, touch and joystick based interactions)

The first controlled usability evaluation was conducted to assess the usability of the interaction methods: keyfobs, touch and joystick [27]. The evaluation also provided a means to verify the GUI design of SmartATRS to ensure that it was 'fit for purpose'. The participants of the evaluation (consisting of eight males and four females between the ages of 20 and 60) operated an ATRS-equipped vehicle in an outdoor environment. The outdoor aspect of the evaluation inherently produced safety implications for par-ticipants who were unfamiliar with operating ATRS. In the subsequent evaluations, a simulation was utilised.

The participants were given a briefing prior to the commencement of the evaluation, consisting of an introduction to ATRS and SmartATRS, the purpose of the evaluation and the expectations of the participants. There was an opportunity for questions to be asked.

The participants performed a series of six tasks using keyfob, touch and joystick based interactions, before completing a questionnaire pack concerning the usability of the methods. The first section contained 10 statements adapted from SUS, where participants rated 10 statements on a 5-point scale of strength of agreement from 'Strongly Disagree' to 'Strongly Agree'. Typical statements included: (1) 'I thought using the keyfobs were easy', (2) 'I thought that the emergency stop feature of Smar-tATRS by touch was safe' and (3) 'I would imagine that most people would learn to use SmartATRS by joystick very quickly'.

The second section of the pack contained questions about the workload experienced during the tasks based on NASA TLX. The workload types measured were: physical demand, mental demand, temporal demand, performance, effort and frustration, where participants rated the workload required on scales from very low to very high. Example questions included: (1) how mentally demanding was using the key-fobs, (2) how physically demanding was using SmartATRS by touch and (3) how hurried or rushed was the emergency stop task using SmartATRS by joystick. During the evaluation, the participants performed the following six predefined tasks involving operating the ATRS components of the seat, tailgate and lift, as well as performing an emergency stop.

The component tasks were specifically chosen because they have to be performed whilst using SmartATRS, with the emergency stop task being included to evaluate safety. There were no other tasks that could be performed with SmartATRS. In the emergency stop task, the command 'Stop Lift!' was given during the simultaneous operation of the lift and seat and the participant had to stop the lift immediately. The participant was aware that an emergency stop had to be performed but was unaware of whether it would be to stop the lift or seat. A stopwatch was used to measure the time between the command being given and the lift stopping.

3.5.3   Evaluation 1 results

SUS: Analysis using the Adjective Rating Scale revealed that keyfob interaction achieved a score of 50.5 ('Poor Usability'), whereas touch based achieved 81.3 ('Good Usability') and interaction using the joystick achieved 63.8 ('OK Usability'). This clearly highlighted that touch interaction was the most usable, with most participants finding keyfob-based interaction challenging.

One of the most important results highlighted the safety of the emergency stop function and was found when 100% of participants agreed that it was safe using SmartATRS, compared with only 33% using the keyfobs. This result was supported by the results from emergency stop times for the keyfobs and touch-based interaction. Participants commented that when using the keyfobs, it was necessary to make a decision as to which button to press to stop the lift, whereas with touch-based interaction, the emergency stop button could be pressed to immediately stop all functions. The standard deviation for the keyfobs was 6.8 s, compared to only 1.2 s for touch-based interaction.

NASA TLX: The box plots in Figs 8.6 and 8.7 provide an example of the comparison of the workload experienced when using keyfob, touch and joystick-based interactions.

Fig. 8.7 illustrates the differences in the workload experienced between interaction methods and show the minimum, lower-quartile, median, upper-quartile and maximum values. It can be seen that touch- based had a significantly lower workload level in all workload types than the keyfobs.

There are greater mental and physical demands with keyfobs than touch-based interactions. As there is an increased likelihood of not successfully accomplishing the tasks with keyfobs, it was found that the temporal demand was higher, whereas with touch-based interactions, there was a low temporal demand as there is an improved chance of accomplishing tasks successfully.

A second notable observation was the higher effort and frustration levels of the joystick in comparison with touch-based interaction, likely to be caused by a steeper learning curve. It was also found that touch-based interaction had a greater discrepancy between the maximum values and the majority of the data. There was a minority of users who experienced low workload levels when using the keyfobs, but overall the

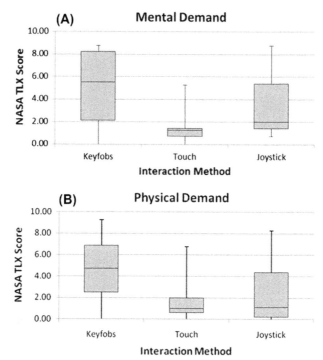

Figure 8.6 Comparing (A) Mental and (B) Physical Demand experienced.

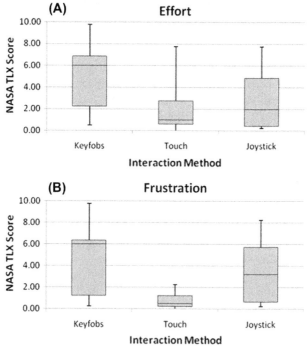

Figure 8.7 Comparing (A) Effort and (B) Frustration experienced.

box plots are fairly conclusive that touch-based interaction is the most efficient and least demanding interaction method.

The second controlled usability evaluation compared touch and head based interaction methods by integrating iOS Switch Control into SmartATRS to ascertain whether head interaction would be a feasible alternative modality for people with reduced physical ability.

3.5.4   Evaluation 2 (touch and head based interactions)

The purpose of the second control usability evaluation was to compare touch and head based interaction modalities through a simulation of SmartATRS [33]. These simulations consisted of a relay board with an embedded web server (identical to the relay board located in the vehicle), smartphone, Windows laptop and a projector. The web server on the relay board was connected to a wireless LAN module so that a smartphone could connect to the relay board wirelessly. The same user interface for SmartATRS existed in the simulation with the relays being operated from the JavaScript, but the relays were not connected to any functions. A Windows laptop also connected to the relay board wirelessly and executed JavaScript code that continuously monitored the state on the relays.

The simulation displayed video clips to represent the currently operating relays that were stored on the laptop as MPEG-4 files. Six video clips were created to represent each ATRS function and were all displayed on a single interface, as shown in Fig. 8.8.

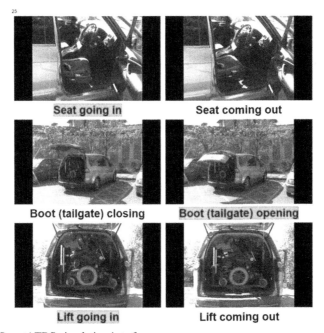

Figure 8.8 SmartATRS simulation interface.

When a relay is operated, the appropriate video played and stopped either when the function was completed or when the relay was switched off prior to completion. In the latter case, the video was paused and resumed once the relay was switched on. It was not possible for the opposite motion video (i.e., Seat In and Seat Out) to be played simultaneously, as this was impossible in the real system. Therefore, the video will pause the opposite motion video.

The user group for the evaluation consisted of 17 participants who were of both genders and who had varying disabilities requiring the use of a powerchair or wheelchair (such as cerebral palsy, Duchenne muscular dystrophy and ataxia telangiectasia) with either reduced dexterity or speech ability. The participants completed the same set of tasks as in Evaluation 1 and were provided with instructions on the methods of interaction for each modality. However, the accuracy of the emergency stop task was improved by using a video camera instead of a stopwatch. The entire task was recorded and the stopping times for each participant were elicited by analysis using video editing software and calculating the exact duration elapsed between the command being spoken and the function terminating. The usability of the interaction methods was assessed by observing whether the video clip playing on the laptop corresponded to the function that the participant intended to activate. If the video clip did not correspond, an error was made by the participant during the selection process.

3.5.5   Evaluation 2 results

SUS: Analysis using the Adjective Rating Scale revealed that touch-based interaction achieved a score of 75.7 ('Good Usability'), whereas head-based achieved 36.7 ('Poor Usability'). This clearly highlighted that touch interaction was the most usable, with most participants finding interaction with the head challenging.

A second important result identified the safety of the emergency stop function with each interaction method. The results revealed a standard deviation of 4 s for the fingers compared to 14 s for head tracking. The average stopping times were 4 and 16 s, respectively. The dramatically increased stop times for head tracking were observed to be the time taken to navigate to the emergency stop button using switch control, indicating that using the head is more unpredictable than fingers.

NASA TLX: The box plot comparisons in Fig. 8.9 illustrate the differences in the workload experienced between touch and head-based interaction.

From the minimum, lower-quartile, median, upper-quartile and maximum values, it is evident that 'fingers' showed lower mental and temporal demands, thus proving that head tracking was more mentally demanding and stressful to complete efficiently. A second important observation was the considerably higher physical demand for head tracking resulting in 65% of participants either not being able to sufficiently use switch control at all or finding it extremely challenging. The remaining 35% of participants experienced low workload levels when using the head due to having full range of neck movement. The limitations of head tracking are also reflected by the increased effort and frustration levels compared to 'fingers'. Overall the box plots were fairly conclusive that in this particular instance, touch-based interaction was more effective than head interaction.

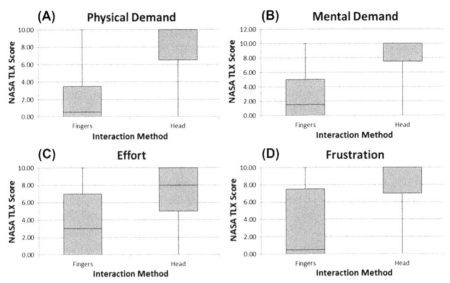

Figure 8.9 Box plot comparison of NASA Task Load Index (TLX) results in terms of (A) Physical Demand, (B) Mental Demand, (C) Effort and (D) Frustration.

3.5.6   Evaluation 3 (touch and smartglass based interaction)

The third evaluation compared touch-based and smartglass interaction mediums to ascertain whether smartglasses could potentially be useful for people with reduced physical ability. The evaluation was conducted using the Recon Jet smartglass with participants at the 2016 Mobility Roadshow. The simulation of SmartATRS, used for Evaluation 2, was applied to this evaluation to eliminate the use of a vehicle and the ATRS components. It was necessary to develop a separate SmartATRS user interface for the Recon Jet due to the small display size, as shown in Fig. 8.10.

The interface retained an identical layout as the smartphone interface, but the buttons were reduced in size so that all could be viewed on the single screen. To enable navigation using the touchpad on the Recon Jet, additional JavaScript code was developed that converted the American Standard Code for Information Interchange (ASCII) codes produced from the touchpad into *onfocus* events. Due to the poor usability of the Recon Jet previously established during a feasibility trial, it was therefore decided not to conduct a controlled usability evaluation; therefore no statistical results were obtained.

Seat In	Seat Out
Tailgate Close	Tailgate Open
Lift In	Lift Out
Emergency Stop	

Figure 8.10 SmartATRS user interface for Recon Jet.

The participants for the evaluation had varying physical conditions (including cerebral palsy, spina bifida, arthritis and poliomyelitis) resulting in the use of manual or powered wheelchairs. The Recon Jet was integrated into the SmartATRS network in order for the user interface to be displayed and participants were invited to wear the smartglass to ascertain whether they could read the display. If it was readable, the participants were instructed on the operation of the smartglass touchpad and buttons, as well as the functionality of the simulation.

3.5.7 Evaluation 3 results

The majority of the user group experienced challenges to position the smartglass on their heads due to insufficient dexterity. Further challenges were caused by the small text on the user interface resulting in the button names being unreadable and participants were consequently unable to conduct the evaluation. A further difficulty for most participants was the small buttons on the device that required significant dexterity to operate. The overall result of the evaluation was that the Recon Jet was unsuitable for use as an alternative modality for SmartATRS.

4. Discussion

The case study focused on SmartATRS that controls ATRS. This is an example of a Transportation Cyber-Physical System that consists of constituent systems that interact in order to transport a powerchair in a vehicle. SmartATRS was developed to provide an alternative modality of interaction for ATRS to replace the existing keyfobs, which were challenging for people with reduced finger dexterity to operate. The system was centred around a relay board with an embedded web server that interfaced with the ATRS functions. This produced a solution that was smartphone independent due to the user interface being accessible from any Wi-Fi—enabled device. To maintain the integrity of SmartATRS, XML was used for configuration to provide a method that was not visible to the end users. This ensured that there was no risk of users tampering with or accidentally altering the timer durations, which could result in SmartATRS becoming unsafe. The development of SmartATRS highlighted the potential difficulty that can be encountered when implementing cyber-physical system. It was important to maintain the original functionality of ATRS by ensuring that the keyfobs remained operational to use as a backup interaction modality. To ensure that the relay board successfully controlled the ATRS function, it was essential to analyse the existing wiring diagrams to ascertain the relay types contained within each component. Following the integration of SmartATRS with ATRS, it was necessary to conduct thorough testing of each function to ensure that operation was as expected and that there were no adverse safety implications created to ATRS.

The importance of safety in cyber-physical systems was the rationale behind the development of a risk analysis framework for SoS [31]. The framework considered at the three key elements of risk being HSI, interoperability analysis and emergent behaviour. HSI concerns the identification of human involvement in the cyber-physical system assisted through analysis of their relationships with the system in terms of their roles and responsibilities. The second element provides a qualitative assessment of the types of risks that can adversely impact on interoperability, with the final element considering how these risks can impact the users and systems. The result being that risks can be prioritised in terms of severity and for control measures to be devised.

The usability of the modalities of interaction for SmartATRS was measured through the conduction of controlled usability evaluations that compared keyfob, touch, head and smartglass based interaction. However, performing the controlled usability evaluations with a user community of reduced physical ability had a number of challenges. Firstly, as this can be considered as a niche user group, it can be more difficult to obtain a sufficient number of participants who have reduced physical ability but with the required cognitive ability to perform the necessary tasks. To maximise potential participants, a variety of organisations were approached who had access to user community. A second challenge was that the standard SUS and NASA TLX questionnaires were too complex for the user group to comprehend. Therefore, the language style was simplified whilst retaining the original meaning of the questions. Nevertheless, the evaluations proved to be an effective method of providing a cross comparison of the modality and of the informative statistics from SUS and NASA TLX questionnaires that enabled conclusions to be drawn.

When conductingEvaluation 1 (keyfob, touch and joystick based interactions), it became evident that the use of feedback through button colours that change dependent on the state of the system and clear text with SmartATRS was a considerable advantage of the keyfobs that provided no user feedback. Participants commented that the feedback was particularly useful when operating the lift, as it was not possible to observe the state of the lift from the driver's perspective when using the keyfobs. It was apparent that SmartATRS was less obtrusive than the keyfobs as no additional devices needed to be carried by the user in addition to a smartphone. This therefore complies with a comment by Metsis et al. [34] that assistive environments should not be obtrusive. The key findings from the first evaluation was the increased safety of the system due to having an emergency stop function that terminated all functions instantly using a single button press, instead of the keyfobs where each function could only be stopped individually. This was reflected by the difference in emergency stop times of 6.8 s for the keyfobs and 1.2 s for SmartATRS and that 100% of participants acknowledged that the stop function was safe. In relation to safety, one participant commented, 'the emergency stop button is large and clear, particularly as it is red.... It was reassuring that the stop button would stop everything at once, which reduced worry and panic'. Joystick-based interaction was viewed to have a steeper learning curve than touch interaction; however, participants remarked that through repeated use, they would be able to become accustomed. NASA TLX analysis identified noticeable increases in the mental and physical demands experienced when using the keyfobs compared to touch-based interaction through SmartATRS. The cause of the increased workload levels was summarised by a participant commenting, 'I kept forgetting which buttons to press as there is no text on the keyfobs'. It became obvious that the lack of text and the use of small, difficult to distinguish symbols was a major limitation of the keyfobs. The results of Evaluation 1 indicated that the keyfobs did not present the universal design principles of 'Simple and Intuitive Use' and 'Low Physical Effort' [35], which were apparent in SmartATRS.

Evaluation 2 (touch and head based interactions) demonstrated that, for this particular instance, touch-based interaction was less demanding that head due to a considerable discrepancy with the SUS scores of 75.7 and 36.7, respectively. The poor usability of head-based interaction was reflected by the safety of the emergency stop function that has a standard deviation stopping time of 4 s for touch based, compared to 14 s when performing the function with the head. It was realised that 14 s was an unacceptable time for an emergency situation and it was therefore concluded that using the head was not a robust means of interaction. The importance of having robust assistive technologies is acknowledged by Metsis et al. [34] who recommend that unusual situations must be supported by such technologies to cater for user error. The NASA TLX analysis of this evaluation identified that head-based interaction generated significantly increased physical, mental and temporal demands, as well as greater effort and frustration levels. From observation, it was identified that the difference in the physical demands between touch- and head-based interactions was primarily the result of participants not possessing the required neck Range of Movement (ROM) for iOS Switch Control to recognise the head movement. This finding led to a greater realisation that ROM can be seen as the determinant of whether a technology is suitable for a user, instead of their disability type.

The contribution of the final evaluation was to promote awareness of smartglasses as a potential assistive technology instead of just a product used for sports and leisure activities. Based on the participants who conducted the evaluation of the Recon Jet at the Mobility Roadshow, it was determined that the technology required good visual acuity to view the user interface and dexterity to operate the small selection buttons. Due to the required information not being communicated efficiently to the user regardless of their sensory ability, the smartglass did not satisfy the 'perceptible information' Universal Design principle [35]. An additional challenge when performing this evaluation was providing sufficient instructions on use of the smartglass, as it was not possible to view the display whilst the participant was wearing the technology.

5. Conclusions and future work

The knowledge obtained through the development of SmartATRS can be used to generate future directions for Transportation Cyber-Physical Systems. The integration of technologies to provide different interaction modalities could improve the usability and user-centred design for people with reduced physical ability. Alternative interaction modalities that could be investigated include air gesture, electroencephalogram, head and eye tracking. These would provide methods of interaction for users who do not possess the required dexterity to interact through traditional touch-based mediums. A second direction is to promote accessibility and universal design in Transportation Cyber-Physical Systems. Through literature review, it was apparent that these concepts have only been applied to web accessibility (e.g., through WCAG 2.0), but guidelines for cyber-physical systems are limited. A final directive is to establish specific guidelines for HFI for cyber-physical systems, based on the existing HFI utilised by the Ministry of Defence. Dogan et al. [36] argue the inadequacy of the methods and approaches in HF in addressing SoS aspects associated with technical and organisational complexity. The urgent need to develop HF capabilities as a key mechanism for coping with the complexity of SoS is also reiterated in this study.

SmartATRS is presented as a cyber-physical system that provides transportation of a powerchair in a vehicle and consists of a number of constituent systems including the original ATRS components of a motorised driver seat, automated tailgate, platform lift and a LiDAR unit that provides the autonomous docking of the powerchair. The system also comprises of the SmartATRS components including a relay board and junction boxes to enable the ATRS keyfobs to remain functional as a backup interaction modality. The development of SmartATRS followed the design principles of HCD, Universal Design and Design for All. This involved feedback elicited on the original interaction modality of ATRS and the limitations encountered by user community. The developed SmartATRS subsequently formed the basis for developing a risk analysis framework that can be applied to other cyber-physical systems to analyse potential risks and their impacts on the systems.

To assess the usability of SmartATRS to align with HCD, three control usability evaluations were conducted to compare the interaction modalities of keyfobs, touch, joystick, head and smartglasses. Each evaluation utilised SUS and NASA TLX to measure the usability and enable comparisons to be made. Overall it was concluded that keyfobs required significant finger dexterity due to the small buttons, touch-based interaction presented the greatest usability, joystick required coordination to simultaneously operate the device and observe a smartphone, head interaction was only suitable for users who possessed a full 80 degrees ROM of the neck and smartglasses were challenging due to a small display size accompanied by small buttons. The realisation that ROM is significant in determining whether technologies are suitable for people with reduced physical ability was the rationale for future work to develop the Smart-Ability framework.

Future evaluations are planned to assess the possibilities of other technologies being integrated into the SmartATRS cyber-physical system. It will be essential to determine whether the technologies retain the safety and existing functionality of the system to enable transportation of a powerchair in a vehicle. This case study is an example of a Transportation Cyber-Physical System that has been designed to improve the usability of ATRS through the integration of technology to provide additional interaction modalities. It is anticipated that through the implementation of these directives, as well as future developments of SmartATRS, other Transportation Cyber-Physical Systems could be implemented to further improve the quality of life for people with reduced physical ability.

Exercises

1. Why is it important to consider transportation systems as cyber-physical systems?
2. Outline the stages of the ISO standard for ergonomics of HSI with descriptions.
3. Why is it essential to involve users by adopting a user-centred design process for cyber-physical systems?
4. Describe the seven domains of HFI and provide two benefits of adopting this process.
5. What are the advantages of using the SUS as a method to evaluate the usability of a cyber-physical system?
6. Using NASA TLX, how can the workload scores be interpreted using the Adjective Rating Scale?
7. Besides the SUS and NASA TLX, name two other evaluation techniques that can be used and how these could be applied to a cyber-physical system.
8. Define HTA and provide two further examples of potential uses of the technique.
9. Based on the controlled usability evaluations described in this chapter, outline five guidelines that should be followed when conducting experimentations with cyber-physical systems.
10. Provide five examples of interaction modalities in the context of cyber-physical systems.

References

[1] International Ergonomics Association, What is Ergonomics? 2018. http://www.iea.cc/whats/. (Accessed on 18/04/2018).
[2] Chartered Institute of Ergonomics and Human Factors, Transport: Increasing Safety, Comfort and Efficiency, 2018. https://www.ergonomics.org.uk/Public/Resources/Sectors/Transport.aspx. (Accessed on 18/04/2018).
[3] J. Preece, H. Sharp, Y. Rogers, Interaction Design: Beyond Human-Computer Interaction, first ed., John Wiley & Sons, Chichester, 2015.
[4] User Experience Professionals Association, Definitions of User Experience and Usability, 2010. http://www.usabilitybok.org/glossary. (Accessed on 18/04/2018).
[5] European Institute for Design and Disability, The EIDD Stockholm Declaration, 2004. http://www.designforalleurope.org/Design-for-All/EIDD-Documents/Stockholm-Declaration/. (Accessed on 18/04/2018).
[6] W3C, Web Content Accessibility Guidelines (WCAG), 2008. https://www.w3.org/TR/WCAG20/. (Accessed on 18/04/2018).
[7] Chartered Institute of Ergonomics and Human Factors, What is Ergonomics? Find Out How it Makes Life Better, 2018. https://www.ergonomics.org.uk/Public/Resources/What_is_Ergonomics_/Public/Resources/What_is_Ergonomics_.aspx?hkey=2769db3e-4b5b-46c2-864c-dfcf2e44372d. (Accessed on 18/04/2018).
[8] A. Gao, T. Miller, J.R. Spletzer, I. Hoffman, T. Panzarella, Autonomous docking of a smart wheelchair for the automated transport and retrieval system (ATRS), Journal of Field Robotics 25 (2008) 203−222.
[9] K. Kleiner. Robotic Wheelchair Docks Like a Spaceship, 2008. http://www.newscientist.com/article/dn13805-robotic-wheelchair-docks-like-a-spaceship.html. (Accessed on 18/04/2018).

[10] D.A. Norman, S.W. Draper, User Centred System Design: New Perspectives on Human-Computer Interaction, first ed., Lawrence Erlbaum Associates, Hillsdale, 1986.

[11] Human Factors Integration Defence Technology Centre, The People in Systems TLCM Handbook: "A Guide to the Consideration of People Factors Within Through Life Capability Management", 1 September, 2009 ed., BAE Systems, London, 2009.

[12] D.A. Norman, The Design of Everyday Things, 2002 ed., Basic Books, New York, 2002.

[13] Project Management Solutions, Strategies for Project Recovery: A PM Solutions Research Report, 2011. http://www.pmsolutions.com/collateral/research/Strategies%20for%20 Project%20Recovery%202011.pdf. (Accessed on 18/04/2018).

[14] Usability.gov, Usability Evaluation Basics, 2018. https://www.usability.gov/what-and-why/usability-evaluation.html. (Accessed on 18/04/2018).

[15] Usability Body of Knowledge, Cognitive Walkthrough, 2010. http://www.usabilitybok. org/cognitive-walkthrough. (Accessed on 18/04/2018).

[16] D. Jadhav, G. Bhutker, V. Mehta, Usability evaluation of messenger applications for Android phones using cognitive walkthrough, in: The 11th Asia Pacific Conference on Computer Human Interaction, vols. 9−18, 2013.

[17] J. Brooke, SUS: a "quick and dirty" usability scale, in: P.W. Jordan, B. Thomas, B. Weerdmeester, I.L. McClelland (Eds.), Usability Evaluation in Industry, Taylor & Francis, London, 1986, pp. 189−194.

[18] A. Bangor, P. Kortum, J. Miller, Determining what individual SUS scores mean: adding an adjective rating scale, Journal of Usability Studies 4 (2009) 114−123.

[19] J. Nielsen. 10 Usability Heuristics for User Interface Design, 1995. https://www.nngroup. com/articles/ten-usability-heuristics/. (Accessed on 18/04/2018).

[20] N.A. Stanton, P.M. Salmon, L.A. Rafferty, G.H. Walker, C. Baber, D.P. Jenkins, Human Factors Methods, a Practical Guide for Engineering and Design, second ed., CRC Press, Boca Raton, 2013, pp. 315−320.

[21] Human-Computer Interaction Lab, QUIS: Questionnaire for User Interaction Satisfaction, 2018. http://www.lap.umd.edu/QUIS/index.html. (Accessed on 18/04/2018).

[22] S. Oviatt, Multimodal interfaces, in: S. Oviatt (Ed.), The Human-Computer Interaction Handbook, Lawrence Erlbaum Associates Inc., 2003, pp. 286−304.

[23] M. Turk, Multimodal interaction: a review, Pattern Recognition Letters 36 (2013) 189−195.

[24] B. Pfleging, S. Schneegass, A. Schmidt, Multimodal interaction in the car − combining speech and gestures on the steering wheel, in: The 4th International Conference on Automotive User Interfaces and Interactive Vehicular Applications, 2012, pp. 463−468.

[25] K. Kunze, N. Henze, K. Kise, Wearable computing for older adults − initial insights into head-mounted display usage, in: The 2014 ACM International Joint Conference on Pervasive and Ubiquitous Computing, 2014, pp. 83−86.

[26] A. Miller, J. Malasig, B. Castro, V.L. Hanson, H. Nicolau, A. Brandao, The use of smart glasses for lecture comprehension by deaf and hard of hearing students, in: The 2017 CHI Conference Extended Abstracts on Human Factors in Computing Systems, 2017, pp. 1909−1915.

[27] P. Whittington, H. Dogan, K. Phalp, Evaluating the usability of an automated transport and retrieval system, in: The 5th International Conference on Pervasive and Embedded Computing and Communication Systems, 2015, pp. 59−66.

[28] J. Robertson, S. Robertson. Atomic Requirements: Where the Rubber Hits the Road, 2009. http://www.volere.co.uk/pdf%20files/06%20Atomic%20Requirements.pdf. (Accessed on 18/04/2018).

[29] Mozilla Developer Network, XMLHttpRequest, 2018. https://developer.mozilla.org/en-US/docs/Web/API/XMLHttpRequest. (Accessed on 18/04/2018).

[30] Dynamic Controls, iPortal 2 Your Communication to the World: User Manual, 2013. https://dynamiccontrols.com/images/IPortalAccAdditionalInfoandLinks/GBK52983-iPortal2-User-Manual-Issue-3.pdf. (Accessed on 18/04/2018).

[31] D. Ki-Aries, H. Dogan, S. Faily, P. Whittington, C. Williams, From requirements to operation: components for risk assessment in a pervasive system of systems, in: The 4th International Workshop on Evolving Security and Privacy Requirements Engineering, 2017.

[32] G. Stoneburner, A.Y. Goguen, A. Feringa, Sp 800−830. Risk Management Guide for Information Technology Systems, 2002.

[33] P. Whittington, H. Dogan, Improving user interaction through a SmartDisability framework, in: The 30th International BCS Human Computer Interaction Conference, 2016.

[34] V. Metsis, L. Zhengyi, Y. Lei, F. Makedon, Towards an evaluation framework for assistive technology environments, in: The 1st International Conference on PErvasive Technologies Related to Assistive Environments, 2008, p. 12.

[35] H. Snider, N. Takeda. Design for All: Implications for Bank Operations, 2008. http://siteresources.worldbank.org/DISABILITY/Resources/Universal_Design.pdf. (Accessed on 18/04/2018).

[36] H. Dogan, S.A. Pilfold, M. Henshaw, The role of human factors in addressing systems of systems complexity, IEEE SMC (2011) 1244−1249.

Transportation Cyber-Physical System as a Specialised Education Stream

Michael Henshaw[1], Lipika Deka[2]
[1]School of Mechanical, Electrical, and Manufacturing Engineering, Loughborough University, Loughborough, United Kingdom; [2]School of Computer Science and Informatics, De Montfort University, Leicester, United Kingdom

1. Introduction

Cyber-Physical Systems (CPSs) are often highly complex, and sometimes mission-critical systems comprising physical components monitored and controlled by embedded computational cores usually requiring real-time responses (e.g., autonomous collision avoidance in driverless cars). They could comprise hundreds of embedded control units in a single system (such as an automobile) or many heterogeneous systems, each with hundreds of thousands of embedded control units, such as a city transport management system. Such systems are networked frequently (but not always) through internet protocols, when they are referred to as the Internet of Things (see Ref. [1]). These are already complex systems, but one must also consider the frequent and multimodal interactions of human beings (as originators, developers, operators, end users and possibly as malicious hackers) with the CPS, which adds a further layer of complexity and a significant quotient of non-engineering specialist knowledge needed for design and operation of CPS. In 2009, Ebert and Jones remarked that [2] 'embedded systems heavily influence design and engineering constraints of their respective surrounding systems — and vice versa'; coupled with the human interaction and social sciences knowledge required for effective development of Transportation Cyber-Physical System (TCPS), it becomes apparent that there is a need to reconsider the knowledge and skills taught to science and engineering graduates. This is the theme of this chapter.

Helen Gill of the National Science Foundation of the United States coined the term 'cyber-physical system' in the year 2006 [3]. It is debateable whether it is a discipline or a domain, but it is an important area for study and it is a relatively new one. As Cheng [4] rightly says, it is 'not a union but an intersection' of several disciplines (engineering and societal) such as control theory, embedded systems, signal processing, sensors and communication networks, cybersecurity, data analytics, human factors, ethics, law, etc., together with the domain-specific knowledge of automotive engineering, instrumentation, avionics, power engineering, civil engineering, etc. The concept map of CPS [5] refers to CPS as a 'discipline' and we will adopt that description here,

Transportation Cyber-Physical Systems. https://doi.org/10.1016/B978-0-12-814295-0.00009-5
Copyright © 2018 Elsevier Inc. All rights reserved.

always remembering that it is a discipline created from the combination of many disciplines. To some extent, its scope has been defined by research initiatives; funding bodies from both the European Union (EU) and United States have initiated major commitments towards accelerated growth of CPS R&D. Over €15 billion funds have been allocated by the European Union (EU) under its Vision 2030 initiative [6] and the United States National Science Foundation (NSF) has also invested heavily. As a strategic industrial and societal endeavour, other nations have also funded development very significantly, and transportation is a major domain for innovation and growth with respect to CPS.

For some years there has been an increasing emphasis on the necessity for engineers to take an holistic and collaborative approach [7] to the creation of systems and this need is exemplified, and possibly extended, by CPS. Indeed, Wilkinson has cited CPS as a driver for new thinking in the traditional integrative discipline of systems engineering [8]. It has always been the case that engineers from one traditional engineering discipline must collaborate with those from others to produce a useful system, but the partitioning of contributions is becoming blurred and it is necessary for engineers to have a much more highly developed knowledge of a wider range of disciplines. In particular, all engineers must now have a much stronger command of software knowledge than in the past. For example, aerospace engineers, educated according to traditional aerospace degree curricula, are not likely to have a substantial knowledge of computer science concepts such as object-oriented abstractions and model-based real-time system design principles that are core concepts in modern aerospace systems [9].

Developing an effective higher education curriculum in any interdisciplinary domain should be addressed through a 'fundamental purposes of the inquiry' [10], and in the context of this book, the purpose of this chapter is to look into higher education in the specific CPS domain of TCPS. However, a TCPS includes many smart technologies (i.e., CPS units and networks) besides vehicles, and so the distinction due to the transport-specific domain is somewhat nebulous. The discussion will, therefore, mostly concern CPS in general. Furthermore, the need for education/training in CPS goes beyond academic study; the EU ROAD2CPS project [11] makes a distinction between customers and developers/operators, commenting that both groups will need suitable training. Customer training is out of scope for this chapter, but consideration of developer/operator training and education provides a contribution to the scoping of academic curricula and will inform this discussion.

A 2016 report of capability assessment carried out by the UK Transport Catapult indicated a short-term skills gap of 742,000 people in Intelligent Mobility by 2025 [12]. These are primarily in science, technology, engineering and mathematics (STEM) subjects but also include about 8000 in management and psychology. This is illustrative of the skills shortage in TCPS experienced elsewhere in the world. The report suggests that the shortage could be addressed through various educational interventions, but a significant number depend on academic courses, especially at masters' level. Besides curriculum development, this report also recommends much closer ties between industry and academia to meet the skills gap, emphasising the need for practical work-based learning as a part of academic study. The need for change is highlighted by the World Economic Forum [13], which not only identifies skills shortage for the fourth industrial revolution (i.e., CPS) but also an inadequacy in higher education worldwide, highlighting the 'dichotomy between Humanities and Sciences and applied and pure training'. The conclusion must be that to service the skills needed for TCPS, even in the short term, universities and colleges must change from traditional knowledge delivery to broader curricula with a greater emphasis on practical (real-world) experience. The rapidity with which TCPS is developing exacerbates the shortage of skills as most nations are already experiencing a skills gap.

The chapter begins by considering the nature of academic disciplines (Section 2) and then discusses the disciplines needed for TCPS (Sections 3 and 4). Different types of educational offerings are considered in Section 5 and some conclusions complete the chapter in Section 6.

2. Background

2.1 Academic disciplines

Academic disciplines traditionally focused on a well-defined body of knowledge as a distinguishable branch of a faculty (e.g., science, humanities, social sciences, engineering...); Becher and Trowler [14] describe them as tribes distinguished primarily through discipline-specific language. The disciplines are areas for both research and education. There is significant international variation in the breadth of study, what one might term the 'purity' of the disciplines that are taught to degree level. In recent decades, two developments have been added to the breadth of courses offered by universities: firstly, joint honours degrees gained some popularity, although the two subjects were often within the same faculty; secondly, courses began to reflect types of application (e.g., mechatronics). Ref. [15] classified academic disciplines along the dimensions of hard or soft (i.e., material-centric or human-centric), nonlife systems or life systems and pure (typically theoretical) or applied, as shown in Fig. 9.1. Interestingly, this classification from 1973 might be challenged in 2018 because of the broadening of curricula for a number of the disciplines. But this broadening and combining of disciplines has given rise to new disciplines. Ref. [16] has suggested that the development of disciplines is governed by similar laws to the process of natural evolution.

Cohen and Lloyd [16] identify the following four processes that can be applied metaphorically to the development of disciplines and give an example of each:

- Heredity: whereby the same features get passed on from generation to generation
- Variation: whereby new and more adaptable species (hence disciplines) evolves through mutation, recombination and natural selection
- Speciation: whereby new species are formed
- Extinction: whereby there is a loss of species.

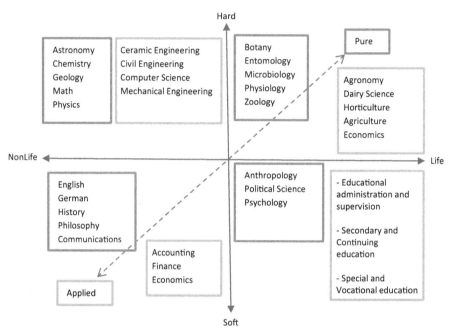

Figure 9.1 Classification of academic disciplines due to Anthony Biglan [14].

But more interesting for the purposes of this chapter is their consideration of heterosis and hybrid disciplines. Heterosis (sometimes called hybrid vigour) implies that hybrid offspring have improved function of any biological attribute, and in the case of disciplines, Cohen and Lloyd imply that disciplines that draw on research beyond their individual discipline silo become superior [16]. The core disciplines such as mathematics, physics and biology came into being because of the need to understand the workings of the world and its environment and evolved partly due to pure academic inquisitiveness, whereas disciplines such as agriculture, with initial concepts such as crop rotation, irrigation, etc., to modern day concepts such as genetically modified crops, arose because of the need for advancements of methods for greater economic productivity. Many of the relatively modern disciplines, particularly in science and engineering, have evolved as a result of technological advancements in quest of better quality of life as mankind adapts to global challenges such as climate change, energy crises, population growth, higher life expectancy and immigration.

In terms of strategies for enquiry, researchers can be broadly divided into positivists (science and engineering) and constructivists (social sciences and humanities), but recent years have seen a significant increase in the use of mixed-method approaches [17]. A mixed-method approach is very challenging for the researcher because positivists and constructivists have fundamentally different worldviews, but for many complex endeavours in engineering (for instance), an appreciation of the social perspective is essential. Mixed-method approaches cannot simply be the arbitrary application of methods from the positivist and constructivist methodological canons but must be a disciplined and thoroughly understood triangulation of methods to provide verifiable results. The discipline of systems of systems engineering, which is similar to CPS [1], is notable for adopting a multiepistemological approach to enquiry [18], using combinations of positivist and constructivist methods to understand the development and operation of systems within the complex human environment [19].

Horlick-Jones and Sime [20] have argued that a transdisciplinary approach is needed to tackle complex societal problems; they note, in particular, its relevance to transport. Transdisciplinary suggests an holistic approach, as opposed to multidisciplinary (additive) and interdisciplinary (interactive). The significance of the distinction concerns the adoption of appropriate methodologies and, as we shall see below, the manner in which many disciplines are handled in studying and teaching TCPS may be significant.

In principle, curricula and teaching methods are defined by the research that underpins and evolves a discipline. The discussion above has focused on research as the means through which a discipline is defined; the task now is to understand how the scope of the discipline of CPS, defined by research, should be translated into a curriculum and philosophy of teaching.

2.2   Transportation systems

The ambition of humankind to travel further, faster and safer has led to increasing sophistication in terms of transportation systems and a concomitant increase in the complexity of those systems. At its most basic, a transportation system comprises simply the ability to be mobile and the ability to navigate and control (Fig. 9.2). A next step is the use of a vehicle (in early times these might be beasts of burden[1]), and different means of propulsion were developed for different domains and terrains. As the means of transport became more widespread and numerous, a level of coordination is required and even in early times regulation became an essential aspect of coordinating vehicles [21]. At the time of writing, TCPS is enabling new methods of coordination and there is significant attention and effort being devoted to development of appropriate regulation (see Chapter 10).

As transportation systems have evolved in the industrial age, new academic disciplines have come into being, such as transportation engineering, highway engineering, urban transportation, etc., as subdisciplines of civil engineering and transport domain–specific disciplines such as aerospace engineering, maritime engineering, automotive engineering, space systems, etc. Those described as subdisciplines are often taught at masters' level, building on more general science or engineering degrees. Rapid advancement in computing, sensing, data analytics and communication technology

---

[1] It seems that in law, horses are generally treated as vehicles when ridden on the highway (e.g., https://www.gov.uk/guidance/the-highway-code/rules-about-animals-47-to-58 or https://law.justia.com/codes/north-carolina/2011/chapter20/article3/section20-171).

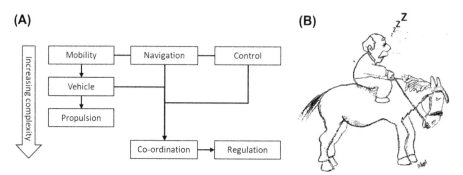

Figure 9.2 (A) Evolution of transportation systems and (B) early autonomous transport. Cartoon by Miles J de C Henshaw.

in the latter half of the 20th century has given birth to a new discipline of intelligent transportation system (ITS). ITS is concerned with providing better coordinated and safer transport solutions and services without necessarily incorporating 'intelligence'. But recent years have seen transportation systems become truly 'intelligent', with the ability to sense, analyse and act; communicate with each other and with the infrastructure via networking mediums such as vehicle to anything using technology such as direct short-range communications [22]. TCPSs include a wide variety of automated and autonomous functionality, ranging from driver assistance to fully autonomous vehicles and automated signalling to autonomous traffic management.

2.3 The need for Transportation Cyber-Physical System engineers

CPSs have evolved from the discipline of embedded systems, for which there was a clear demarcation between hardware, software and firmware design to the present state where hardware, software and firmware are intricately integrated with each aspect impacting the other [23]. The demarcation defined three distinct groups of designers, but the degree of integration means that each group must now be intimately knowledgeable about the other two. The evolution can be mostly attributed to advancement in computer science (resulting in system functionalities shifting from hardware to software), advancement in communications technology (particularly wireless technology facilitating connection of the computational cores) and an increase in the number of transistors per integrated circuit in accordance to Moore's law (leading to miniaturisation). Not only is the prediction of emergent behaviour significantly more difficult for CPS but also there are new risks associated with safety and cybersecurity, and new design approaches are needed [24]. As a result, education programmes in CPS are beginning to emerge [23,25–28]; furthermore, it is recommended by the US Academy of Sciences that CPS education be incorporated into undergraduate courses in engineering and computer science [29].

3. A cyber-physical system workforce

As CPS considerations become urgent, it has been suggested that the future CPS workforce will comprise three types [23,28]:

1. Engineers from traditional disciplines such as electrical engineering, mechanical engineering, systems engineering, control engineering, computer science, etc.
2. Engineers trained in particular application areas or in subdisciplines, such as aerospace, civil engineering, vehicle engineering, transportation engineering, etc.
3. Specially trained CPS engineers (specialising in its various domains such as TCPS) whose realm of knowledge will lie at the cusp of 'cyber' and the 'physical' world.

The US National Academy of Sciences [28] strongly recommends that CPS educational programmes should emphasise the interaction between the cyber and physical aspects of the CPS system and that this should be within the primary domain knowledge of the CPS engineer.

Because virtually all systems of relevance are now CPS [8], at this time (2018), equal emphasis should be given to curriculum development for continuous professional development of the existing workforce and for the future workforce. Undergraduate curricula should ensure understanding of the complete CPS life cycle, including concept generation, design, development, verification, validation, deployment and maintenance/support. For some of these developmental life cycle stages, notably verification and use of models in design, it should be anticipated that the curriculum will be frequently updated with new approaches and techniques in the coming years [30].

However, the recommendations above concern only the engineering aspects, and it is clear that CPS requires consideration of societal and environmental aspects [5]. Furthermore, human factors and ethical aspects must also be considered [30–32].

4. Required knowledge and skills

This section begins by reviewing a variety of sources that have proposed CPS curricula and then maps the knowledge required based on these and other considerations.

4.1 Proposed cyber-physical system curricula

In 2016, the US National Academy of Sciences conducted a study on the need for CPS education and prepared guiding CPS education content. Based on workshop feedback from academia and industry, the report [28,29] strongly promoted the introduction of university programmes in CPS, recommending three broad areas of content: (1) principles of CPS, (2) foundational skills and (3) system characteristics. The first area concerns physics, mathematics, sensor technology, data/signal analysis and control theory as the basis for the components of cyber and physical. Foundational skills are mostly associated with the principles above but concerned with practical implementation; they focus strongly on the numerical and computational aspects, although do include modelling of dynamic, heterogeneous systems as an important element. System characteristics are largely concerned with aspects that systems engineers would more generally refer to as speciality engineering [33]: safety, security, stability, human factors, etc.

It is interesting to contemplate the degree to which existing systems engineering curricula address CPS needs. In broad terms, the content areas (as defined in the systems and software engineering life cycle ISO15288 [33]) provide good coverage of the engineering aspects, though not necessarily the societal considerations, but there are specific processes for which current tools and approaches are inadequate, most notably, verification, architecting and aspects of speciality engineering [30]. The Stevens Institute has reverse engineered the problem of devising a CPS curriculum by starting with the deliverables a student would need to submit to demonstrate adequate knowledge and skills. From this, they have constructed a curriculum for 'systems engineering of CPS'; their analysis resulted in a programme that includes four courses [23]:

- Course 1 - Conception of CPS: Deciding What to Build and Why?
- Course 2 - Design of CPS: Ensuring Systems Work and Are Robust?
- Course 3 - Implementation of CPS: Bringing Solutions to Life?
- Course 4 - Sustainment of CPS: Managing Evolution

In essence, the programme uses traditional systems engineering techniques (e.g., Quality Functional Deployment) but with specific CPS considerations. The focus is on the existing workforce (i.e., primarily groups 1 and 2 in Section 3) and therefore is set at the masters' level.

In a domain-specific study, Ref. [9] reviewed existing aerospace engineering and computer science and engineering curricula and discovered knowledge gaps, for example, in the integration of control theory concepts into optimisation and online regulation of real-time computing resources, leaving recent graduates 'unfit for purpose'. Aerospace curricula typically remained traditional, focussing mainly on structures (physical), gas dynamics and dynamics and control, without fostering 'computational thinking' in the graduates. They consulted within the aerospace industry and found that industry experts, and particularly those involved in managing aircraft and spacecraft programs, believed that aerospace beginners must be educated in embedded systems programming and/or software engineering and trained in the general 'computational thinking'. They concluded, however, that it was not possible to have a course in CPS because of the breadth and depth of what must be covered. Instead of introducing new programs from scratch, they recommend that current undergraduate aerospace curricula should incorporate 'computational' and 'calculus-based' thinking through topics such as real-time computing, control systems and co-modelling and design. Recognising modelling as being a key issue for CPS, [34] presents a modelling language and toolset that can be used to teach students CPS through modelling activities. The focus of the course is cyber and control modelling and simulation.

A NIST (National Institute of Standards and Technology, US) workshop report of 2013 [35] has inspired a number of educational developments; the report suggested a number of radical ideas for delivery of training but all towards the objective of ensuring 'an academic CPS environment is available that is interdisciplinary and dynamic, provides laboratory experience, and covers human behaviour as well as the business side of CPS' [35]. It is suggested that degrees in CPS would need to be multi-department, to provide the breadth required. Inspired by this report, the University of California, Irvine, initiated a graduate-level degree program in embedded and CPSs in 2013 [27]. They report on a market survey that indicates a significant interest (commercially) in CPS education. The course covers theoretical elements in the first year, and in the second (final) year, the education shifts to practical aspects, associated with design, case studies and project work. There is a strong emphasis placed on the practical skills that will be acquired.

The practical aspects of curricula have been emphasised by [36] who describe the creation of an educational laboratory as a service for teaching CPS. An important feature of the testbeds is that they are actually physical, not simulations, but with virtualisation available to cope with large numbers of students. Anticipating significant demand, the authors suggest that the laboratory should be available through a MOOC (massive open online course), although this is a future plan rather than an implemented training offer. Similarly, [37] also turns to a MOOC to deliver CPS training through the development of automated exercise generation. The focus of this paper is on the training method, rather than CPS, which is simply used as an exemplar. Nevertheless, the need to train people who are already practising engineers (categories 1 and 2 in Section 3) has clearly encouraged the use of online learning, in contrast to face-to-face teaching, a view supported by the market research of [27].

The CPS workforce clearly relies on sufficient numbers being educated in STEM subjects. To encourage children to take these subjects up at degree level and as career choices, [26] developed a programme targeting high school students as part of their NSF-funded project on 'Autonomous Driving in Mixed Environment'. The programme introduces children to CPS through a hands-on engineering project on *Obstacle Avoidance by Autonomous and Driverless Cars*. To be able to complete the task, students are trained in relevant topics such as C/C++ programming, physics, mathematics and tools used by CPS researchers such as the various sensors like GPS, laser range finder and radar systems.

The initiatives summarised above indicate that there has been substantial activity during the last five years in the development of CPS education and establishing the appropriate content, although this has been predominantly in the United States. There is some level of consensus about the approach that should be taken; the key points are:

- Curricula must be broad, taking in several engineering disciplines, computer science and social sciences, with a strong emphasis on the integration of the various diverse elements.
- Hands-on practical experience is essential, with activities (e.g., projects) being conducted in real-world or nearly real-world contexts.

4.2 Cyber-physical system education: knowledge mapping

The report [28] provides a detailed curriculum map for CPS and lists the US degree programmes that comply with it to some extent. The subjects presented focus on technical systems and only partially address societal matters. The following draws on and expands the curriculum map proposed by the US National Academy of Sciences.

The skills for engineering CPS are summarised in Fig. 9.3: these are broadly the skills that one would expect to meet in a systems engineer [38] but with a particular focus on the integration of cyber and physical aspects. The four skills are broken down further in Figs 9.4—9.7. However, these are not sufficient to cover all required areas, and Fig. 9.8 indicates additional areas about which the CPS developer must have some knowledge.

The highly connected nature of CPS, and especially the embedded intelligence, means that the CPS engineer must think beyond straightforward functionality to long-term implications. The deployment of learning systems makes it particularly important to consider the possibility of future behaviours that may be unethical in

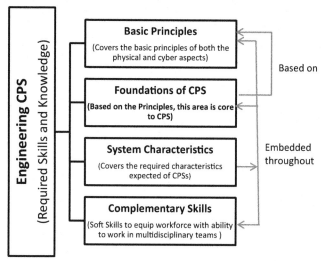

Figure 9.3 Four interdependent subject areas for engineering cyber-physical system (CPS). Based on Ref. [28].

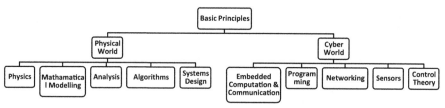

Figure 9.4 Basic principles for engineering cyber-physical system (CPS). Based on Ref. [28].

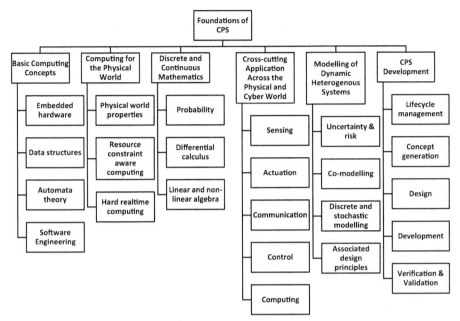

Figure 9.5 Foundations of cyber-physical system (CPS). Based on Ref. [28].

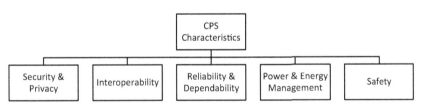

Figure 9.6 Cyber-physical system (CPS) characteristics. Based on Ref. [28].

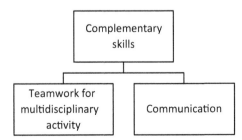

Figure 9.7 Complementary skills. Based on Ref. [28].

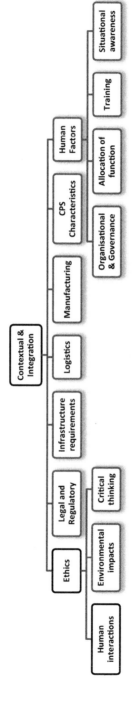

Figure 9.8 Contextual and integration considerations for cyber-physical system (CPS).

certain situations [31]. Curricula must, therefore, contain ethics and legal/regulatory aspects. Both the effect on humans and the effect of systems on the natural environment must be considered. This is of particular importance for TCPS, where the interactions are with the general public and the environmental impact may be significant.

CPS may be designed to operate within specified infrastructure characteristics, but life cycle considerations mean that continued operation following infrastructure development or upgrade, and the effect of individual CPS on other systems that rely on infrastructure, must be considered. Similarly, for TCPS especially, logistics must be considered as a key element of effective design and should, therefore, be included in the curriculum. All systems must be designed for manufacture, and some knowledge of manufacture should be included; furthermore, another environmental consideration will be the availability of materials so that design for sustainability both in terms of environmental sustainability and business sustainability is a concern. The CPS characteristics (Fig. 9.6) as defined by [28] can be considered to be a subset of the contextual and integration matters. Although human factors are implied in several themes, it is considered appropriate to specifically identify the areas of importance (Fig. 9.8). Organisational matters are of relevance to TCPS, as systems will interact with enterprises of various sizes; governance is an important consideration, because responsibility for deployed TCPS must be properly understood and defined; this is linked to regulatory matters. Allocation of function works at a more detailed level and concerns the sharing of tasks between human operators and TCPSs; these have significant implications for design and may need to take into account adaptability and future changes to the system. For TCPS, training of operators, maintainers, etc., will be required and the way in which different stakeholders should be trained in the use of TCPS should be an item on the curriculum. Finally, situational awareness is of major significance for safety (see Chapter 10) [30].

The disciplines and subjects identified above as CPS relevant have been placed on the framework of [15], as reconfigured by [16], in Fig. 9.9. For specific entities in a TCPS, additional disciplines might include propulsion, aerodynamics, stability, materials, etc. It becomes clear that the CPS curriculum would include subjects in three major discipline areas of applied sciences, natural sciences and social sciences. It is possible, but not essential, that the aesthetics of design could also be relevant, in which case all four quadrants would be occupied. This begs the question whether such a dense curriculum is really plausible, as it requires the students to appreciate significantly different philosophical viewpoints and a diverse mixture of methods and techniques. It is more reasonable to speak of a curriculum that has core elements and a level of flexibility so that students may develop a T-shaped CV; one in which there is a broad appreciation across all the disciplines but a deep specialisation in one or two. This emphasises the importance of teamwork and ensuring an appreciation of other members of the team to the overall goal of creating or operating TCPS.

4.3 Wicked problems

Except for the simplest systems, CPSs are generally classified as a subset of a class called systems of systems [1] and these are very often described as posing 'wicked

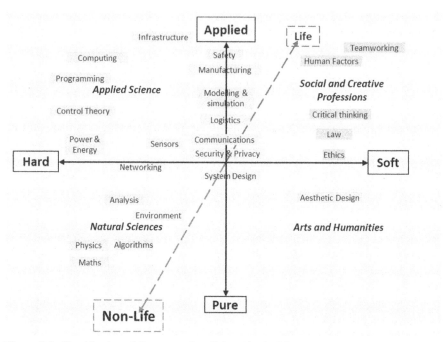

Figure 9.9 Classification of Transportation Cyber-Physical System disciplines using [15] framework as reconfigured by [16]; shading indicates nonlife, life or both along the third axis.

problems' [39]. Originally posed by [40], wicked problems are complex, they have no definitive formulation, no stopping rule, and very often the solutions cannot be described as good or bad. There is no template, since each problem is a one-off. A TCPS can be considered at many levels of abstraction, but if we assume that it involves multiple interacting elements, then it has many of the characteristics of a wicked problem. There is no curriculum for wicked problems, but there are personal attributes that equip an individual better or worse for managing a wicked problem. In particular, a tolerance of ambiguity is an asset when trying to deal with such problems. The education and training for TCPS should, therefore, encourage students to develop a mindset that can appreciate and manage wicked problems; this mindset is likely to be particularly engendered through appreciation of the social and creative professions quadrant in Fig. 9.9.

4.4 Key disciplines for Transportation Cyber-Physical System curriculum

Having explored the TCPS curriculum in some detail, based largely on that defined by [28], but with additional consideration mainly from the social sciences, it is helpful to express this at a higher level of abstraction, as depicted in Fig. 9.10. Here, we consider the components of CPS to include networks as an essential element for TCPS. Each

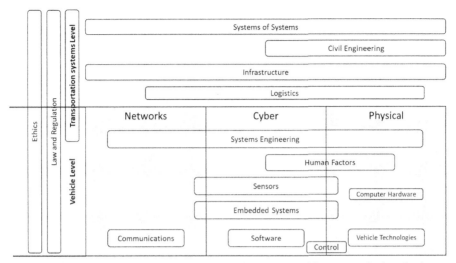

Figure 9.10 Key components of a Transportation Cyber-Physical System curriculum for degree and graduate-level study.

discipline or area of interest identified will contain within it several additional disciplines and subdisciplines. But the student working to this curriculum would achieve the vertical part of the T-shaped CV from detailed study of one of the areas shown, and the horizontal part from an understanding of each. Because TCPS requires transdisciplinary working, the approach to teaching the elements shown in Fig. 9.10 should be to teach wherever possible in multidisciplinary teams and in a genuinely transdisciplinary manner. Projects with students from different disciplines are a way to achieve this [25].

5. Curriculum delivery mechanism

Sections 3 and 4 have considered the curriculum content in some detail; for the most part, it has been assumed that this would be the curriculum for degree or masters' level qualification. However, the curriculum can be delivered through a variety of mechanisms and these are summarised below:

- **Short courses**: Such courses can be delivered over a few days or a few weeks depending upon breadth and depth each course is designed to cover. For example, there may be a short course introducing TCPS to high school students designed in the form of a summer school of 2–4 weeks duration, during which students learn and develop a very simple TCPS model. On the other hand, a short course may comprise in-depth knowledge of TCPS modelling and simulation delivered as an intensive weeklong course. Such a course can be attended by participants from academia or industry. Short courses can be offered by industry and academia and are usually a commercial endeavour. Short courses may offer a course completion certificate but usually do not have an assessment component.

- **Undergraduate degrees**: Most of the currently available courses in TCPS (as well as those being planned) fall into this category. Ideally, an undergraduate course in TCPS should cover the entire life cycle of systems development, including idea generation, design, modelling and simulation, verification and validation, development and deployment. Such a course must also include complementary skills such as those shown in Figs 9.7 and 9.8. Undergraduate courses can be developed as engineering courses with introductory or optional modules, including human—computer interface, human factors, ethics and law. TCPS can also be offered as a module within a CPS engineering undergraduate degree or at the other end of the spectrum, as part of a dual-degree program such as in aerospace engineering and computer science as offered by the University of Michigan [25]. Undergraduate degrees will be the most effective mechanism for increasing the size of the skilled workforce, as most of the entry-level recruitment in relevant industries is from the cohort of recent graduates.
- **Postgraduate degrees**: Such degrees are from first level to doctoral level and are either offered as full time or part time; most generally, they are masters' level by teaching. Curricula within these programmes may include research and development projects further advancing the field of TCPS and should preferably be in collaboration with relevant industry.
- **Apprenticeships**: Apprenticeship is a form of on-the-job training which may include an element of classroom study leading to a recognised qualification. An apprentice must be above 16 years of age and the duration of an apprenticeship is usually between 1 and 5 years. Apprenticeships are highly specialised training courses and suitable for the existing workforce [12].
- **Continuing professional development**: This is a means by which employees continue to learn and develop either formally or informally as they work. This could include academics, people working in TCPS industry and administration undergoing short courses, workshops or trainings in order to gain lacking TCPS skills. Continuing professional development can be self-directed or can be delivered as short courses or workshops by academia, industry or consultancies.
- **Certificate courses**: Certificate courses can be developed and offered by academia with or without collaboration with relevant industry. Such courses do not offer a full degree qualification but provide formal recognition to a student acknowledging that the student has understanding of the delivered knowledge component. Embedded systems programming or modelling and simulation of TCPS could be examples of such a knowledge component.
- **Distance learning or remote learning**: This form of education delivery does not require students to be physically present in a traditional educational setting. Learners can schedule their own learning while teachers and trainers deliver their material online and schedule assessments online as well. Though an effective way of learning for working professionals who wish to make career progress or even career change, TCPS skills and knowledge is best acquired through hands-on experience which can be a challenge for distance learning courses. Nevertheless, there has been a recent surge in MOOC (see Section 4.1), that takes traditional distance learning a step further through open access. A very relevant example is the Self-Driving Car Engineer Nanodegree program offered by Udacity[2].
- **Secondments**: Given the clear need for hands-on experience, secondments from universities into relevant industries (and vice versa) provide an essential part of curriculum delivery.
- **On-the-job training**: Staff can gain new skills and knowledge through in-house or on-the-job training. Such training can be delivered by instructors from within the same organisations or delivered by consultancies.

---

[2] See https://eu.udacity.com/course/self-driving-car-engineer-nanodegree–nd013.

This is just a sample of knowledge delivery mechanism. Within each mechanism, the level of knowledge delivery can vary depending on the skills required. Furthermore, skills required at the various levels of an organisation can vary significantly, and courses will be needed to cater for each.

Whichever mechanism is chosen, it is widely acknowledged that CPS education must primarily follow the kinaesthetic learning or a hands-on approach.

6. Conclusions

This chapter has primarily focused on education relevant at degree or masters' level; other educational needs exist, but these have not been considered in detail herein.

TCPS comprises complex systems, the development and operation of which rely on skills from many different disciplines. It has become evident that many engineers working in TCPS have inadequate software skills to satisfactorily address the needs of current systems, which have significant embedded software. Although there has been a considerable amount of work to define engineering curricula for CPS, it seems that ethical and legal aspects have not been adequately addressed within engineering degrees. Analysis indicates that the CPS engineers of the future must have relevant knowledge in pure science and in social sciences, as well as in applied knowledge.

The highly connected nature of TCPS means that modern developers must have a wide knowledge of the contributing disciplines, because failure to have breadth of understanding will likely lead to faults or unintended emergent behaviours. Ideally, students educated in TCPS will have a T-shaped CV, which implies that they will have competent broad knowledge across a range of relevant topics, together with an in-depth knowledge of one or two areas.

Teamwork will be an essential part of delivering and operating a TCPS, and so teamwork should be explicitly included in the curriculum. It is also clear that any programme of study for TCPS must include a substantial amount of hands-on practical study.

Universities have traditionally taught in single disciplines or in domains in which few disciplines need to be studied in depth. CPS challenges that approach by requiring curricula that include many disciplines, but to be taught effectively, a transdisciplinary approach—in which every team member has a competent understanding of all relevant disciplines—is needed. There is considerable scope for pedagogic research to develop new approaches for teaching transdisciplinary skills.

Most importantly, students should develop an holistic view of the system to be engineered and so the degree and masters' course for TCPS must go beyond the imparting of knowledge only, but develop the outlook and holistic appreciation of the students.

Much of the discussion has concerned CPS education in general; aspects specific to TCPS are mostly the specific domain aspects associated with vehicles of different types.

TCPS holds the prospect of significant benefits to humankind and the possibility to manage transport in a way that reduces the impact on the environment. It also offers considerable commercial opportunities to organisations and nations able to exploit TCPS. These benefits will only be realised if there is a TCPS workforce educated to degree level in relevant natural, applied and social sciences in an integrative fashion.

References

[1] M.J.D.C. Henshaw, Systems of systems, cyber-physical systems, the internet-of-things…whatever next? Insight 19 (3) (2016) 51−54.

[2] C. Ebert, C. Jones, Embedded software: facts, figures, and future, Computer 42 (2009) 42−52, https://doi.org/10.1109/MC.2009.118. (Accessed on 14/04/2018).

[3] E.A. Lee, S.A. Seshia, Introduction to Embedded Systems − A Cyber-Physical Systems Approach, 2017, p. xi.

[4] A.M.K. Cheng, An undergraduate cyber-physical systems course, in: Proceedings of the 4th ACM SIGBED International Workshop on Design, Modeling, and Evaluation of Cyber-Physical Systems − CyPhy'14, 2014, pp. 31−34, https://doi.org/10.1145/2593458.2593464. (Accessed on 14/04/2018).

[5] P. Asare, D. Broman, E. Lee, M. Torngren, S. Sunder, Cyber-Physical Systems − A Concept Map, 2012. Available at: http://cyberphysicalsystems.org/. (Accessed on 14/04/2018).

[6] AICC, ITEA Artemis-IA High-Level Vision 2030, 2013. Brussels.

[7] The Royal Academy of Engineering, 'The Royal Academy of Engineering Creating Systems that Work: Creating Systems that Work', Engineering, (293074), 2007, p. 17. Available at: www.raeng.org.uk/education/vps/pdf/RAE_Systems_Report.pdf. (Accessed on 14/04/2018).

[8] M. Wilkinson, Discussion Paper: An Architect's Manifesto for the Development of Systems Engineering INCOSE UK Architecture Working Group, V1.1, 5th June 2016, (can be requested from president@incoseonline.org.uk).

[9] E.M. Atkins, J.M. Bradley, 'Aerospace Cyber Physical Systems', in Guidance, Navigation, and Control, AIAA, Boston, 2013, pp. 1−26.

[10] S. Nikitina, Three strategies for interdisciplinary teaching: contextualizing, conceptualizing, and problem-centring, Journal of Curriculum Studies (2006), https://doi.org/10.1080/00220270500422632. (Accessed on 14/04/2018). Boston, MA.

[11] M. Reimann, et al., ROAD2CPS Deliverable 2.3-Technology and Application Roadmap, 2016. Brussels. Available at: http://road2cps.eu/events/wp-content/uploads/2016/03/Road2CPS_D2_3_TechnologyandApplication_Roadmap.pdf. (Accessed on 14/04/2018).

[12] Transport Systems Catapult, Intelligent Mobility Skills Strategy, Report, 2016. Milton Keyenes. Available at: https://s3-eu-west-1.amazonaws.com/media.ts.catapult/wp-content/uploads/2016/10/03103255/3383_IM-Skills_Business-Case_Brochure1.pdf. (Accessed on 14/04/2018).

[13] World Economic Forum, The Future of Jobs − Employment, Skills and Workforce Strategy for the Fourth Industrial Revolution, World Futures Review, Cologne/Geneva, 2016. Available at: http://www3.weforum.org/docs/WEF_FOJ_Executive_Summary_Jobs.pdf. (Accessed on 14/04/2018).

[14] T. Becher, P.R. Trowler, Academic Tribes and Territories, second ed., Open University Press, 2001. Available at: https://books.google.co.uk/books?id=7GlEBgAAQBAJ&printsec=frontcover&source=gbs_ge_summary_r&cad=0#v=onepage&q&f=false. (Accessed on 14/04/2018).

[15] A. Biglan, The characteristics of subject matter in different academic areas, Journal of Applied Psychology 57 (3) (1973) 195−203.

[16] E.B. Cohen, S.J. Lloyd, Disciplinary evolution and the rise of the transdiscipline, Informing Science: The International Journal of an Emerging Transdiscipline 17 (17) (2014) 189−215.

[17] J. Cresswell, Research Design: Qualitative, Quantitative, and Mixed Methods Approaches, third ed., SAGE, Thousand Oaks, CA, 2008.

[18] A.S. Poza, S. Kovacic, C. Keating, System of systems engineering: an emerging multi-discipline, International Journal of System of Systems Engineering 1 (1/2) (2008) 1, https://doi.org/10.1504/IJSSE.2008.018129. (Accessed on 14/04/2018).

[19] E.N. Urwin, et al., Through-life NEC scenario development, IEEE Systems Journal 5 (3) (2011) 342−351, https://doi.org/10.1109/JSYST.2011.2158680. (Accessed on 14/04/2018).

[20] T. Horlick-Jones, J. Sime, Living on the border: knowledge, risk and transdisciplinarity, Futures 36 (4) (2004) 441−456, https://doi.org/10.1016/j.futures.2003.10.006. (Accessed on 14/04/2018).

[21] B. Lucas, Which Side of the Road Do They Drive On? TSM-Resources, 2004. Available at: http://www.tsm-resources.com/left/Which side of the road do they drive on.htm. (Accessed on 14/04/2018).

[22] H.J. Miller, S.-L. Shaw, Geographic Information Systems for Transportation, OUP, Oxford, 2001.

[23] J.P. Wade, et al., Systems engineering of cyber-physical systems: an integrated education program, in: 123rd ASEE Annual Conference and Exposition, 2016−June, 2016. Available at: https://www.scopus.com/inward/record.uri?eid=2-s2.0-84983288456&partnerID=40&md5=75887e49f3b620f408bfd5ff1ac405ac. (Accessed on 14/04/2018).

[24] E.A. Lee, Cyber physical systems: design challenges, in: 2008 11th IEEE International Symposium on Object and Component-Oriented Real-Time Distributed Computing (ISORC), 2008, pp. 363−369, https://doi.org/10.1109/ISORC.2008.25. (Accessed on 14/04/2018).

[25] M. Chowdhury, K. Dey, Intelligent transportation systems-a frontier for breaking boundaries of traditional academic engineering disciplines [Education], IEEE Intelligent Transportation Systems Magazine 8 (1) (2016) 4−8, https://doi.org/10.1109/MITS.2015.2503199. (Accessed on 14/04/2018).

[26] V. Gadepally, A. Krishnamurthy, U. Ozguner, A hands-on education program on cyber physical systems for high school students, Journal of Computational Science Education 3 (2) (2012) 11−17, https://doi.org/10.22369/issn.2153-4136/3/2/2. (Accessed on 14/04/2018).

[27] F. Kurdahi, et al., A Case Study to Develop a Graduate-Level Degree Program in Embedded & Cyber-Physical Systems, Newport.Eecs.Uci.Edu, 2016.

[28] National Academies of Sciences, A 21st Century Cyber-Physical Systems Education, 2016, https://doi.org/10.17226/23686. (Accessed on 14/04/2018). Washington, DC.

[29] National Academies of Sciences, A 21st Century Cyber-Physical Systems Education, HIGHLIGHTS, 2017.

[30] S. Hafner-zimmermann, M.J.D.C. Henshaw, The Future of Trans-Atlantic Collaboration in Modelling and Simulation of Cyber-Physical Systems a Strategic Research Agenda for Collaboration, Steinbeis-Edition, Stuttgart, 2017. Available at: http://www.tams4cps.eu/wp-content/uploads/2017/02/TAMS4CPS-SRAC-publication_2017.pdf. (Accessed on 14/04/2018).

[31] European Parliament Research Service, Ethical Aspects of Cyber Physical Systems, 2016, https://doi.org/10.1007/978-0-387-09834-0. (Accessed on 14/04/2018). Brussels.

[32] J. Sztipanovits, S. Ying, Foundations for Innovation in Cyber-Physical Systems, Workshop Report, Energetics Incorporated, Columbia, 2013, https://doi.org/10.1007/s13398-014-0173-7.2. (Accessed on 14/04/2018).

[33] ISO/IEC/IEEE, Systems and Software Engineering — System Life Cycle Processes, London, 2015.

[34] K. Bauer, K. Schneider, Teaching cyber-physical systems, in: Proc. Workshop on Embedded and Cyber-Physical Systems Education — WESE'12, 2012, pp. 1—8, https://doi.org/10.1145/2530544.2530547. (Accessed on 14/04/2018).

[35] Energetics Incorporated, Foundations for Innovation in Cyber-Physical Systems, Columbia, Maryland, US, 2013, https://doi.org/10.1007/s13398-014-0173-7.2. (Accessed on 14/04/2018).

[36] A. Gokhale, G. Biswas, M. Branicky, CPS laboratory-as-a-service: enabling technology for readily accessible and scalable CPS education, in: First Workshop on Cyber-Physical Systems Education (CPS-Ed 2013), 2013.

[37] D. Sadigh, S. Seshia, M. Gupta, Automating exercise generation: a step towards meeting the MOOC challenge for embedded systems, in: Proceedings of the Workshop on Embedded and Cyber-Physical Systems Education, 2012, pp. 2—9, https://doi.org/10.1145/2530544.2530546. (Accessed on 14/04/2018).

[38] SEBoK, Systems Engineering Overview, SEBoK, 2016. Available at: http://sebokwiki.org/w/index.php?title=Systems_Engineering_Overview&oldid=52119. (Accessed on 14/04/2018).

[39] C. Siemieniuch, M.A. Sinclair, Extending systems ergonomics thinking to accomodate the socio-technical issues of systems of systems, Applied Ergonomics 45 (10) (2013) 1016.

[40] H.W.J. Rittel, M.M. Webber, Dilemmas in a General Theory of Planning, Policy Sciences 4, no. 2 (1973) 155—169. http://www.jstor.org/stable/4531523. (Accessed on 14/04/2018).

Research Challenges and Transatlantic Collaboration on Transportation Cyber-Physical Systems

Michael Henshaw
School of Mechanical, Electrical, and Manufacturing Engineering, Loughborough University, Loughborough, United Kingdom

1. Introduction

There is an intense interest worldwide in the development of autonomous transport, with much attention focused on autonomous cars in particular. The rapid advances in cyber-physical systems (CPS), due to improvements in sensor technologies, computing and control algorithms, have meant that the possibilities associated with self-driving vehicles have appeared to outpace the regulatory frameworks needed for their introduction. However, governments have recognised the economic opportunities that these technologies offer and are endeavouring to provide environments in which these may be realised. Germany, for instance, produces approximately 70% of premium vehicle brands worldwide [1] so that the maintenance of a conducive regulatory environment for the operation of new models is also a commercial imperative.

To a large extent, the research challenges for Transportation Cyber-Physical Systems (TCPS) are associated with meeting regulatory and economic requirements (and the interplay between these two considerations). These aspects will be considered within this chapter.

Although autonomous cars has been the most immediate concern, it is important to note that freight transportation has already incorporated significant levels of autonomous operation [2], and that shipping and aviation are also domains of significant opportunity and challenge. There are, thus, specific domain and application areas of research challenge, which must be considered.

The Trans-Atlantic Modelling and Simulation for CPS (TAMS4CPS) Horizon 2020 project (grant agreement no 644821) ran from February 2015 until January 2017; its purpose was to identify collaborative research opportunities between the European Union (EU) and the United States of America in the area of modelling and simulation to support CPS [3]. This project identified seven key research themes of mutual interest and discussed the collaboration context and opportunities. This project has broadly defined the research challenges that are elaborated below; models and

Transportation Cyber-Physical Systems. https://doi.org/10.1016/B978-0-12-814295-0.00010-1
Copyright © 2018 Elsevier Inc. All rights reserved.

model testing are a fundamental part of all technical developments and so many of the general challenges for TCPS can be related to the modelling challenges.

In this chapter, transatlantic should be understood to mean collaboration between the United States and EU and/or United Kingdom.[1] It must also be appreciated that a common interest in solving a particular problem by research does not necessarily translate into an opportunity for collaboration, because commercial and/or political considerations may predominate. Nevertheless, the areas where there appears to be a consensus regarding the benefits of collaboration are highlighted.

2. A context of predictions

There are a great many, diverse predictions for how mobility will develop in the future; all are predicated on the expectation that autonomy is a significant component of future transport systems. Intel has proposed that by 2050 the 'Passenger Economy' will be worth $7 trillion [4]. This assumes a shift from vehicle ownership to mobility as a service, which is motivated by increased urbanisation and the need to reduce congestion, ever-growing connectedness, a continued blurring of work and personal life and more ad hoc living arrangements in both. Major factors influencing this change, they believe, will be pollution and safety concerns leading to regulation that makes other travel modalities more expensive (e.g., through tolls and congestion charges). This implies a significant reduction in the number of cars: 80%−90% fewer according to The Economist [5]. However, this view is disputed by other commentators; Toyota, for instance, believes this prediction is premature and does not take account of other circumstances [6].

Litman [7] has outlined some of the additional influences, such as passenger comfort and anxiety, that imply a multimodal manner of autonomous vehicle use, including personal and shared vehicles, as well as shared rides. He further indicates the additional equipment that will be needed in autonomous vehicles, such that the prices for autonomous transport could be considerably higher than conventional transport, at least for the next 10−30 years. Nevertheless, for some [8], smart cities already exist and the first signs of shared mobility are already evident.

Regardless of the modalities, there are a number of benefits that encourage the use of driverless vehicles, not least of which is the time freed up for users to pursue other activities while travelling, although it is noted that this will require changes in trust of the vehicles and in regulation [4]. Furthermore, Lanctot [4] also asserts that there will be a significant reduction in traffic accidents and that even a modest reduction of 5% would save nearly 60,000 lives per year. However, Litman [7] argues that pilotless vehicles introduce additional risks associated with hardware/software failures, hacking, increased risk taking, platooning issues and increased total vehicle travel. Indeed, the cybersecurity of autonomous vehicles could pose a very significant risk [9],

---

[1] At the time of the TAMS4CPS project, the United Kingdom was part of the European Union, but it will be a separate entity from March 2019.

with the intensity depending on the extent to which they require network services. Examples of vehicle hacking have been reported in which control of the vehicle has been acquired via navigation or entertainment systems [10]. The marked increase in cyberattacks on infrastructure and services during 2017 [11] indicates that coordinated attacks could pose massive threats to CPS at national and international scale. CPS, of necessity, employ many sensors so that capture of large quantities of data is inevitable. There are also risks associated with the capture and use of personal data that must be considered and the EU, at least, considers that new laws will be needed to protect users in this respect [10].

It is generally assumed that adoption of autonomous vehicles will benefit the environment; this is due both to changing use patterns (as noted above) and to increased use of electric (and hybrid) vehicles. This latter is a trend that could occur without adoption of autonomous vehicles but is happening simultaneously [8]. Estimates of carbon reduction (for instance) vary widely because of the assumptions made in changing transport patterns of use. Indeed, Thomopolous and Givoni [12] insist that carbon reduction can only be achieved by a radical shift to shared mobility and that, even so, this may cause a shift away from other forms of transport, which are more space efficient, to increased use of cars, so undermining the benefits. Using a mixture of vehicles types and assumptions about driving behaviour and control, for example, Shladover et al. [13] have estimated improvements in lane capacity of up to 80%, but there are so many different scenarios that could be considered that it is not clear, yet, what environmental improvement can reasonably be expected. Thomopoulos and Givoni [12] comment with respect to autonomous cars that 'research and debate on this topic largely focus on the "autonomous" and not adequately on the "car" element', and it is certainly true that models of car use as facilitated by autonomy or, more importantly, models of overall transport systems that include both autonomous and human-operated vehicles are an essential research need in order to better understand how autonomy may be environmentally, socially and commercially beneficial.

Although rules regarding liability, etc., are adequate to enable lawyers to advise on the risks associated with driverless vehicles [1], most authors appear to agree that a consistent regulatory framework does not yet exist. This is also true for flying vehicles, where the safety requirements are more stringent than for other forms of transport and there is also a concern about the recreational flying of small vehicles that will require restrictions in some countries (e.g., [14]).

The Society of Automotive Engineers has defined five levels of automation for automobiles [15], of which levels 4 and 5 are the highest: these are (respectively) some human driver modes and no human driver modes. Some authors (e.g., [7]) believe that many of the benefits of autonomous vehicles will only be realisable at these higher levels (4 and 5); this is likely to lead to significant testing costs and poses some difficult regulatory and operational challenges [16]. Sivak and Schoettle [16] also make the interesting point that it will be relatively straightforward to programme an autonomous system to follow rules (e.g., traffic regulations), but that too literal an interpretation could be disadvantageous (basically, the point of Asimov's 'I, Robot' stories [17]).

Clark et al. [18] have pointed out that the Vienna Convention on Road Traffic [19] provides explicit requirements (Article 8) that all vehicles shall have a driver who shall remain in control of the vehicle. Whilst broad interpretation of this requirement has enabled many countries to proceed to testing autonomous vehicles on public roads, nevertheless, there has had to be a human driver present capable of taking over control. On September 2015, the G7 nations and the EU agreed a declaration on automated and connected driving [20] that recognised the need to establish a harmonised regulatory framework and the need for sustained cooperation in the areas of the following [10]:

- coordinating research, promoting international standardisation within an international regulatory framework,
- evolving technical regulations and
- ensuring data protection and cybersecurity.

Development of regulatory frameworks is required for all TCPS and it is likely that this will evolve over many years (a topic to which we return at the end of this chapter). Research is required to address the formulation of regulation, the tests and metrics for compliance and the development of technologies that will meet the requirements. Demonstrating that TCPS will operate safely in all situations to the satisfaction of the public is one of the foremost challenges facing the introduction of widespread autonomous transportation; many of the research challenges are associated with aspects of this need.

3.   Dynamic and complex systems

There are numerous definitions of CPS, many of which are concerned with specific applications. Furthermore, there has emerged a confusion of terms to describe the complex, dynamic and software-intensive systems that are now a characteristic of modern life. Henshaw [21] has distinguished between CPS, Systems of Systems (SoS) and Internet of Things (IoT); he concludes that the most helpful definition is due to [22] that CPS is 'the fundamental intellectual problem of conjoining the engineering traditions of the cyber and physical worlds'. Henshaw distinguishes between four classes of system (see Fig. 10.1):

- An unnetworked CPS: standalone physical system with significant levels of embedded software; typically, this will have appropriate sensors to interact in some way with the external environment in order to complete its operations.
- SoS (independent of cyber components): characterised as a network of systems in which individual component systems have managerial and/or operational independence.

Then combinations of the above two:

- IoT: interacting CPS that are networked (in an SoS sense) via the internet.
- Interacting CPS that are connected by non-Internet technologies (or phenomena).

Unnetworked systems may be complicated but are generally determinant systems that are well understood, but interaction (i.e., networking) introduces new levels of complexity that may even behave in a nondeterministic way, particularly when interacting with human beings. Typically, the problems to be resolved in design and

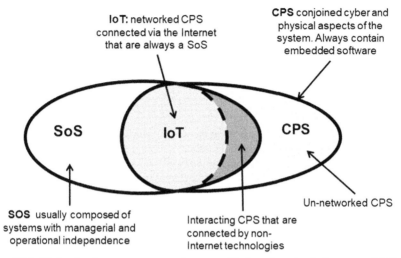

Figure 10.1 Distinction between systems of systems (SoS), cyber-physical systems (CPS) and the Internet of Things (IoT).
After Henshaw [21].

operation of CPS are due to the characteristics of being networked and having levels of autonomous decision-making capability. They will almost always have the SoS characteristic of being developed in an evolutionary manner [23], but perhaps a more accurate description (in this case) is that they are constantly reconfiguring due to individual systems joining or leaving, or the network structure changing. Gartner has, apparently, decreased its estimate of the number of connected devices by 2020 from 20.8 to 20.4 billion! [24]; no doubt the estimates will have changed several times by the time this chapter is published. It does not matter how many − there are a lot. Just because devices are connected, it does not mean that they are interoperating or even interacting, but it does mean that they could be, and this is an unfathomable level of complexity to be modelled and understood. The shared mobility paradigm (and even shared vehicle) described above is predicated on individuals being able to access information and send instructions to TCPS entities using their smartphones. As individual consumers move around, they generate packets of data that form a thread defining their travel, according to William Goodall (Director of transport technology at Deloitte, UK). The implication of this is that a typical journey may be multimodal. Thus, mobility implies many different CPS interacting with millions of users, operated by transport companies for which data is their primary asset [8].

TCPS are, then, a dynamic and complex system in which there are high levels of uncertainty. The variety within such a system provides many of the benefits that may be sought by operators and consumers: it is this that provides flexibility. Indeed, variety is generally considered to be an attribute of resilience. But the inability to model this variety may also allow catastrophic failure to be unpredicted or unpredictable. Thus, the main research challenges are associated with coping with uncertainty.

4. Key research challenges

As demonstrated by the foregoing discussion, predictions about future operation of TCPS are many and diverse. However, the discussion helpfully identifies the top-level challenges (or objectives) for TCPS by focussing attention on the parameters that constitute the predictions.

In essence, TCPS must:

- Be acquired and operated in a paradigm that is commercially beneficial and offers better financial and societal value than extant systems
- Reduce the environmental impact of transportation
- Operate safely and, in particular, offer improvements in safety
- Operate within a regulatory framework that protects humans from physical, psychological, and cyber hazards
- Offer individual travellers an improved service over current methods (in terms of cost and/or comfort and/or convenience and/or reliability and/or usable time for work or recreation)

Against these top-level objectives, a set of key research challenges have been formulated [3]. Mostly, these challenges were identified by the TAMS4CPS project through a series of bilateral workshops (EU and US) held during 2016.

4.1 Security of cyber-physical systems

In 2015, Chrysler issued a voluntary recall on 1.4M vehicles following a cyberattack on a Jeep, that used the entertainment software as an access point to other more critical functions [25]. This is one example of a risk to TCPS that is likely to grow, according to Loukas [26], who defines a cyber-physical attack as 'a security breach in cyberspace that adversely affects physical space'. Loukas draws a distinction between cyber-physical attacks that originate in cyberspace and physical cyberattacks that originate in the physical world but then lead to software or data being compromised. In fact, for TCPS, both types of attack are of concern and likely to become dominating concerns in the future. The highly networked nature of TCPS means that whatever mode of operation is considered, an attack could bring cities to a complete standstill and in an extreme case cause significant destruction and loss of life. Cyberattacks, in any form, are the ultimate asymmetric threat, costing very little to instigate, but demanding huge resources for protection; furthermore, it is very difficult to identify or inhibit the attackers. Of all the research challenges, security of TCPS appears to be the highest priority and possibly the most intractable problem both from the risks that cyber threats represent and also as an inhibitor to adoption of CPS, particularly by small- and medium-sized enterprises [27].

There has been a considerable level of research activity in IoT security and, especially, there are numerous assessments of the security of energy systems. Sajid et al. [28] have examined the risks associated with industrial systems; they listed no fewer than 11 research directions to be addressed.

Incorporation of security architectural features into models: one area in which progress may be made to positively influence design in the near term is to identify architectural features related to TCPS security and to develop metrics for secure TCPS. Security architecture patterns exist for software systems, but these are not yet proven for CPS, which should also incorporate the physical aspects [3]. The objective of this research would be to incorporate security features as standard into CPS design and integration models, at least for TCPS component systems in the short term.

4.2 Cyber-physical systems testing

Whilst it is possible to test the functionality of individual systems, in performance terms, the testing of combinations of CPS, particularly when embedded in their operational environment, which in the case of TCPS is the city or nation that they serve, becomes a significant challenge, because the performance of individual devices does not give an insight into the behaviour of interoperating systems [29]; in fact one could conceive SoS as being described by the property that the overall behaviour cannot be adequately determined from any of the individual component systems. There are several reasons for needing to improve testing:

Verification: verification means testing the system of interest to ensure that it performs as it was designed to perform. Colloquially, this is often expressed as testing that 'we built the system right' [30]. It is a research challenge in its own right (see below), but conventional approaches, in which a representative (or even the complete) set of conditions are tested to ensure that the outputs of the system are as designed, are not feasible. The inclusion of autonomy in individual CPS leads to an unmanageable number of possible system states, but more particularly, if the system is highly networked, as in the case of a TCPS, then even defining the system of interest is a complex and ambiguous task.

Interoperability: TCPS are predicated on the ability of different CPS to interoperate (i.e., work together), which requires exchanges of information and possibly energy or material. The IoT is clearly concerned with exchange of information, but TCPS may require physical interoperability (e.g., for freight, smart containers may need to be physically interoperable with vehicles). There are many interoperability frameworks; the Net-Centric Operations Industry Consortium (NCOIC) framework [31] considers nine levels clustered in threes as: network transport, information services and people, processes and applications. At the network transport level, interfaces are relatively easily specified, but at the higher levels there is greater uncertainty and ambiguity about the interactions between different CPS. If we consider unwanted emergent behaviour to be due to lack of knowledge about interactions (either individually or as a consequence of too many simultaneous interactions to model effectively), then it is clear that testing interoperability to establish behaviours in advance of deployment is an important aspect of predicting overall system behaviour. Testing across the spectrum of interoperability is important for design and qualification of systems to be used in TCPS. Interoperability is also a commercial requirement for the introduction of new systems; although this is mainly dealt with through adherence to standards or protocols, verification of interoperability requires tests to be conducted. Interoperability test beds already exist (e.g., [32]), but an expansion of test beds and the associated testing methods is required to support the advancement of TCPS.

Large-scale test beds for TCPS: TCPS will require the embedding of autonomous systems within the human environment, and this poses numerous safety and security challenges (as discussed above), including long-term consequences for the people involved in the tests. There is a need to understand the likely behaviour of such systems when deployed and also the behaviour of humans when interacting with these systems. Experimentation is an important aspect of validating models of complex, multimodal behaviours and also demonstrating new technologies in controlled but realistic environments. Large-scale test beds are an essential means through which realistic data can be acquired to build and/or check models, but they are expensive to develop and operate. The test beds are, of course, models themselves and must be planned to ensure that they adequately address scale effects. MCity (https://mcity.umich.edu/our-work/mcity-test-facility/) is a purpose-built proving ground for testing connected and automated vehicles. Built on a 32-acre site at University of Michigan, at a cost of $10M, MCity is a mock-up urban and semi-urban environment with many facilities for testing automated vehicles, but its projects go beyond technology to consider commercial and societal issues as well [33]. Access to facilities such as this is an important utility for researchers in TCPS and will accelerate the development of technologies and operational paradigms. This type of facility encourages multidisciplinary research, by default, and provides insight into all levels of system maturity from concept to deployment.

Evaluation of cross-domain architectures: the development of cross-domain architectures is an important area for research with respect to TCPS, but testing the architectures for assurance purposes also poses a significant challenge. TCPS include many different system owners or operators and it is necessary to share data, especially during a crisis [34]; the CPS architecture may include different software domains but could also be situated in different physical domains. The different domains may have different security levels, which makes effective sharing difficult. Software test beds are required to enable architectures to be assured for regular operational and crisis situations.

Testing for resilience: resilience is an entity's *ability to resist, or achieve timely recovery from, adversity*[2]; it is an essential property of TCPS. During operation, a TCPS monitors its environment through a range of sensors and makes decisions to ensure its continued operation; adverse conditions or situations must be detected in order to take appropriate action. However, the metrics to identify potentially adverse emergent behaviours and the appropriate resilience actions must be known in advance. Virtual testing environments are needed in which the emergent behaviours can be studied and visualised and the responses to various actions intended to mitigate adverse behaviours predicted reliably. Experimentation and testing for resilience have not so far received significant attention. Kumar et al. [35] have developed a test bed for resilience and security, but this focuses primarily on identification of faults and their impacts, rather on the more general problems of failure due to emergence.

---

[2] Definition by Henshaw, as used by Loughborough University UK, Global Challenge in Secure and Resilient Societies.

The properties of resilient TCPS and the means through which they may be monitored should be a high priority for future research that will lead to more resilient designs and inform other research concerned with modes of operation.

4.3 Human–Transportation Cyber-Physical Systems interaction

Traditionally, humans have been kept safe from robots by keeping them separate, e.g., by putting the robot in a cage; but this is changing across a range of applications [36]. Although logistics systems can (and do) have high levels of automation with little human interaction, for TCPS intended for mobility, this cannot be the case. This creates a variety of important research challenges, many of which concern the development of appropriate models; in particular, there is an urgent need to include competent models of human behaviour within TCPS models for both design and operation [37]. This includes models of individual human behaviour and societal behaviour (particularly with respect to forecasting technology acceptance and modes of operation). Whilst much research has focused on the behaviour of the TCPS, attention must also be paid to the behaviour of humans in the presence of TCPS [38].

Situation awareness: as early as 1995, Endsley [39] identified situation awareness as a 'predominant concern in systems operation' and drew particular attention to the concomitant vulnerabilities due to system complexity and automation. Situation awareness is considered in three levels: perception of current situation, comprehension of current situation and projection of future status. Humans of vastly different knowledge and experience of TCPS interact with it, and so the manner in which different individuals understand the current system state of the CPS is also likely to be vastly different. Furthermore, it is not clear whether the same cues will alert all humans to the system's state in the same way (probably not). However, it is the third level (projection of future status) that most frequently causes accidents; humans find it difficult to foresee what a robot will do next. Situation awareness is notoriously difficult to measure experimentally [40] and research is needed to instrument useful models of situation awareness to inform design and, potentially, to include within the control algorithms for TCPS.

One could also speak of the situation awareness of the TCPS itself. The TCPS use sensor data to build a model of its environment algorithmically, which then enables the systems to take decisions to carry out actions. The competence and appropriateness of the decisions are directly related to the quality of the model: does it include all the relevant parameters? Are the sensor measurements sufficiently comprehensive, accurate, frequent, etc.? However, in the case of interaction between the TCPS and humans, a model of human behaviour is required and that must reliably enable the third part of situation awareness (projection of future status with respect to decision horizons). The lack of satisfactory models of human behaviour for inclusion within SoS and CPS control has been a strong research requirement in two projects soliciting priorities from the EU and US researchers [3,41] and is regarded by many as a significant barrier to the deployment of CPS from a safety point of view.

The development of simulation environments to study and test the various aspects of situation awareness should be a high priority; these environments will form test beds that could be used for assurance purposes for TCPS components.

Governance: because SoS, by definition, contain systems operated by different entities, some have considered that there are implicit ambiguities with regard to decision-making and liability [42]. For TCPS, there appears to be ambiguity with respect to liability [43], but it is anticipated that the human must retain responsibility. Regulations for road vehicles are formulated around the concept of the driver, but it is suggested that the concept of driver may need to change [1,44]. Most likely, these issues will be determined through case law, rather than by a priority research. However, the situation under which cases may be brought will be shaped, to some extent, by allocation of function (i.e., the partitioning of tasks between CPS and human). Research should address the role of humans within a TCPS, from the perspectives of safety, assuring trust, maintenance of human skills, etc.; however, it is recognised that this is likely to be a matter of evolutionary changes as the TCPS develop and human expectations and capabilities change. The implications of allocation of function in different scenarios need to be understood.

4.4   Verification of Transportation Cyber-Physical Systems

For the software engineering community, formal verification concerns proof of the correctness of mathematical formulations within the software, but for CPS, the physical aspects (which are described differently) must also be verified. As Mosterman and Zander have commented [45], 'the physical configuration of a CPS may be determined only at runtime'. TCPS are composed of hybrid systems in a dynamic environment: at some high level of abstraction, such a system can be represented architecturally as a set of system types and interactions, but verification is usually considered to be relevant at the specific level. Verification is, therefore, a major and unresolved challenge. Indeed, it is likely that the traditional view of verification cannot even be considered relevant to a large TCPS, and so research is needed to define what verification means in this context. The problem for verification of TCPS is twofold: firstly, the system boundary is ill-defined and so the system of interest to be verified is difficult to define and will generally be too large (in terms of number of entities) for traditional verification approaches to be applied; secondly, traditional verification assumes a static system configuration within a changing environment, but for TCPS, the system itself is changing.

Zheng and Julien [46] reviewed verification approaches currently being undertaken by CPS developers and concluded there is little commonality between various communities about the problem of verification, but recommended that a future research trajectory would integrate simulation tools and fuzzy models into verification approaches.[3]

---

[3]   In fact, these authors used the terms verification and validation somewhat interchangeably; however, from a systems engineering perspective, verification is the major issue and the recommendations of Zheng and Julien are applicable to it.

Combining formal verification and simulation technology: although simulation-based verification is input driven (i.e., an input stimulus is needed in order to simulate the systems output) and formal verification starts from an output (property) and searches for inputs that would lead to failure [47], combining these approaches is seen as a possible strategy for verifying highly complex systems [3]. It is suggested that formal test beds (Section 4.2) could reduce the cost of design checking, if carried out sufficiently early in the design cycle. The use of federated test beds and reusable simulation components could lead to economic methods for verification using a combined approach.

Co-modelling and co-simulation: a corollary of the combination of formal models and simulation is the need for co-simulation, with a wider applicability than verification and especially as a requirement for development of the design process. The nature of CPS means that some models will be discrete event, and some will be continuous time; co-simulation combines these different models (or simulations) by exchanging information between them. In fact, for TCPS, there are likely to be many different models that must somehow be combined in a reliable and consistent way [48]. Co-modelling and co-simulation are important areas of development for TCPS in which some frameworks for combining simulations are emerging [49].

Evolutionary approach to testing and evaluation: a more radical change is to consider continuous testing of the TCPS. Model-based design and testing have been in use for some time; a potential development is to use data-driven models instead so that the systems analyses streaming data to update models and predict future behaviour. Thus, control actions are taken based on current status and this could be developed to provide run-time verification of the system. The research required would address models and data analytics.

4.5 Big data analytics for control and machine learning

As noted in Section 4.4, big data analytics can be developed for TCPS control purposes; indeed analysis of big data is already used to identify trends for commercial or societal purposes and, increasingly, to provide situation awareness for command and control purposes, so that the basis for TCPS control has been established through Information and Communication Technologies (ICT) endeavours (i.e. purely cyber endeavours). A further benefit of effective data analytics is with regard to machine learning so that the TCPS situation awareness is continually improved (or updated) using data-driven models to describe its environment and even the human behaviours that it may encounter. There is a massive research effort in data analytics [50], but the specific methods through which it can benefit TCPS require research. Sharma and Ivančić [51] have suggested that big data could completely change the models used in CPS and they suggest areas for future research; of particular interest for TCPS is an application such as comparing data from a specific vehicle with many (all) other vehicles, instead of a predefined model, in order to determine interventions such as maintenance.

4.6   Transportation Cyber-Physical Systems operational paradigms

As described in Section 2, there is a wide range of prediction concerning the value of TCPS in terms of the benefits to operators, customers, the environment, etc., because each prediction makes assumptions about the model of operation of the TCPS (either at local or national level). For urban transport, Lanctot [4] has suggested a variety of business/operational models tending towards mobility as a service, which actually represents a stark change in human−vehicle relationship, not just in terms of operation but as a mark of social status and financial investment or commitment. Most models of future transport are motivated by an increasingly urbanised population and although an Organisation for Economic Co-operation and Development (OECD) estimate of urbanisation put the likely proportion at 60% by 2030 [52], that still leaves 40% of the population not included within these models of mobility. It is reasonable to assume that the motivations for new mobility paradigms are more significant in urban environments, but nevertheless, a much better understanding of the pros and cons of different mobility models is required.

The discussion above has focused on automotive vehicles, but when other modalities are included, such freight delivery by air, sea and rail or last mile delivery by drone [53], then the number of possibilities in terms of TCPS paradigms becomes very large. Ultimately, the models adopted will be determined by largely political considerations, but the different paradigms drive different infrastructure requirements and different business models, and so research is needed into the trade space for TCPS to provide decision makers with the most reliable information possible to create the TCPS that most accurately reflects their strategic purposes.

4.7   Summary of research challenges

One of the difficulties in identifying research challenges for TCPS is that there are so many! The massive increase in systems complexity due to autonomy and connectedness offers huge opportunities but also invalidates some traditional engineering approaches. Similarly, the technology has the potential to be disruptive by enabling new business models for transport. In terms of the challenges that must be overcome to ensure safe and reliable TCPS, the priorities are creating systems that are cyber secure and the tools and techniques to verify systems for safety, security and performance. In all cases, the development of suitable models of various kinds and in combination is a priority for research.

5.   Skills for Transportation Cyber-Physical Systems researchers

The research challenges described in Section 4 cover a wide range of disciplines in science, engineering and social sciences. Questions about regulatory aspects of TCPS indicate that law is also a relevant subject (for some institutions, law is within social sciences). Researchers cannot be specialists in every subject, but Damm and Sztipanovits [54] have suggested that in Europe and the United States, current education in computer science will be inadequate for future CPS engineers and that curricula that include a much wider range of disciplines, especially those relevant to human—CPS interaction, will be needed. More generally, they state that computer science and engineering courses must incorporate knowledge about the physical world and traditional engineering courses should incorporate more knowledge of the cyber world. Given that there are almost no systems built, nowadays, that do not include substantial amounts of software, the inclusion of more cyber knowledge within engineering courses should be an imperative.

TCPS researchers must, then, develop a broader knowledge alongside their specialism, but more generally, they should be educated to have a holistic viewpoint in order to appreciate the implications of design decisions on the wider CPS. A practical understanding of systems engineering is an essential capability that a TCPS researcher should acquire and the attributes of a systems engineer [55] should also be those of a TCPS researcher.

6.   Regulatory environments

A prerequisite for collaborative research is that there is a shared objective; it is important, therefore, to understand differences between the EU and United States in terms of the likely regulatory environment into which autonomous vehicles are deployed. In fact, there is currently a lot of similarity in the regulatory environment [1] on either side of the Atlantic, but there are some risks of divergence. Governments are alert to the need and are active in the development of regulation in the automotive sector. In Europe, work is proceeding on an update to the Vienna Convention [56] to ensure that autonomous vehicles are adequately covered. The convention will incorporate levels of automation, so the regulation can be established for various levels of TCPS maturity. This is a fast-moving activity, and the reader is advised to consult the United Nations Economic Commission for Europe website (unece.org) to keep abreast of the current status. The US Government is aware of the need for harmonious regulation across state boundaries, and work is proceeding on federal regulation. Similarly, although Germany and the United Kingdom are probably leading the development of regulation in Europe, it is recognised that differences across borders will not be wise.

Currently, it is a common regulation that requires a human driver to be able to take over if necessary, but this will likely become inappropriate in the future and does not affect the research endeavours identified in this chapter.

Maritime vessels are generally subject to two sets of regulations (national and international). Although development of autonomous ships is proceeding rapidly (for instance, Norway intends to deploy manned autonomous ships in 2018 and unmanned ships in 2020 [57]). Although there has not so far been development of regulations that accommodate autonomy, the International Maritime Organisation is engaged in an activity to do so.

Air vehicles are regulated by national aviation authorities, and although the issues of autonomous flight have been discussed for some years, a satisfactory regulatory environment for civilian operations is still some way off. Hitherto, restrictions have been placed on weight and size of privately owned vehicles, and in some countries (e.g., UK) it is a requirement that the vehicle can only be flown within visual range. Governments recognise both the commercial benefits and the safety risks of unmanned air vehicles and work is afoot to develop appropriate, national, regulatory frameworks. Of the three domains (land, sea and air), it is air that the risk of different regulatory requirements is most significant.

Overall, although it is likely that there will be different regulatory requirements between the United Kingdom, EU and United States, they are unlikely to be of a nature to affect the research agenda put forth in this chapter or to have a significant impact on the research carried out in TCPS, with the exception of operational paradigms (Section 4.6).

7. Opportunities for collaboration

The research priorities in this chapter have been largely derived from two Horizon 2020 projects: ROAD2CPS (grant agreement No. 644164) [37] and TAMS4CPS (grant agreement No. 644821) [3], both of which concerned identification of research priorities and the latter specifically sought to identify a collaborative research agenda between the EU and United States. It had been predetermined that the most prominent opportunities for collaboration were in modelling and simulation for CPS and the following seven research themes were identified:

- CPS test beds
- Inclusion of human factors in modelling and simulation for CPS
- Open framework for model interoperability
- Incorporation of security architectural features into models for CPS
- Combining formal verification and simulation technology
- An evolutionary approach to testing and evaluation of adaptive/resilient CPS
- Big data analytics modelling via machine learning

Full details of these themes are available in the project e-book [3].[4]

With respect to TCPS, though, one project emerged that would be of especial significance and that would fully exploit the benefits of transatlantic collaboration. The culture of transportation varies between Europe and the United States. Traditionally, Europe has tended to have greater emphasis on public transport, compared to the United States where private transport is more significant, particularly in cities. Potentially, this could lead to different approaches to governance, regulation and integration for TCPS systems. An area of fruitful collaboration will be the comparison of case

---

[4] It should be noted that the political situation in both Europe and the United States changed significantly during 2016/17 towards the end of this project. The collaborative opportunities identified are based only on common technical ground. Mechanisms for collaboration are not considered in this chapter.

studies, particularly of smart cities (as they develop) between Europe and the United States. This will also generate a richer set of data with which to instrument models of TCPS.

8.   Conclusions

There is a huge amount of research being conducted worldwide into CPS, and TCPS receives significant attention as an underpinning aspect of the development of smart cities. This review has necessarily considered a very narrow set of references and has been mostly focused on automotive transport, with only a few comments on air and maritime vehicles. It has considered infrastructure aspects very slightly and ignored space assets entirely, even though they are an essential capability to enable many aspects of TCPS.

Several key research challenges are identified in Section 4, but the priority research projects are those that address cyber-physical security, CPS verification and the inclusion of competent human models within CPS models. This is because the characteristics of TCPS cause most significant gaps in capability, compared to less-complex systems, in these areas. The SoS nature (in which individual systems are independently operated), high levels of connectedness (many to many) through internet and other links, high levels of autonomy in individual systems and deployment within the human environment that requires direct interaction, all lead to significant uncertainty and a level of complexity that exceeds the capabilities of existing modelling techniques. The challenges identified must be addressed in the short term for current levels of autonomy and in the long term as greater levels of autonomy are deemed deployable.

There has been much speculation about the operational structure of future mobility; new structures will undoubtedly arise because of CPS and it is by no means certain that universal structures will emerge. The research challenges identified herein will be relevant to any future structure; however, the specific implementation of research outputs could be very different, depending on the TCPS models adopted.

Acknowledgements

The author acknowledges the contributions made by the TAMS4CPS and ROAD2CPS project members and especially Dr. Sabine Hafner-Zimmermann, Dr. Luminita Ciocoiu, Dr. Lipika Deka, Dr. Sofia Ahlberg-Pilfold and Dr. Zoe Andrews. Some of this work was supported by the European Commission (grant nos. 644821 and 644164).

References

[1] Norton Rose Fulbright Whitepaper, Autonomous Vehicles. The Legal Landscape in the US and Germany, 2016.
[2] N. Vickery, Autonomous Vehicles in Logistics: What Are the Impacts? Cerasis, 2017. Available at: http://cerasis.com/2017/05/24/autonomous-vehicles-in-logistics/. (Accessed on 14/04/2018).

[3] S. Hafner-zimmermann, M.J.D.C. Henshaw, The Future of Trans-Atlantic Collaboration in Modelling and Simulation of Cyber-Physical Systems a Strategic Research Agenda for Collaboration, Steinbeis-Edition, Stuttgart, 2017. Available at: http://www.tams4cps. eu/wp-content/uploads/2017/02/TAMS4CPS-SRAC-publication_2017.pdf. (Accessed on 14/04/2018).

[4] R. Lanctot, Accelerating the Future: The Economic Impact of the Emerging Passenger Economy Autonomous, 2017. Autonomous Vehicle Service. Available at: www. strategyanalytics.com. (Accessed on 14/04/2018).

[5] Economist Leader, Uberworld - The World's Most Valuable Startup is Leading the Race to Transform the Future of Transport, The Economist, 3rd September 2016. Available at: https://www.economist.com/news/leaders/21706258-worlds-most-valuable-startup-leading-race-transform-future. (Accessed on 03/04/18).

[6] T. Bindi, AV Predictions Premature: Toyota, ZDNet, 25 October 2017. http://www.zdnet. com/article/autonomous-vehicle-predictions-are-premature-toyota/. (Accessed on 03/04/18).

[7] T. Litman, Autonomous vehicle implementation predictions: implications for transport planning, in: Transportation Research Board Annual Meeting, 2014, https://doi.org/ 10.1613/jair.301. (Accessed on 14/04/2018).

[8] D. Talbot, The Shape of Things to Come: Experts on Future Transport in 2017, InMotion: Insight & Vision, January 2017. Available at: https://www.inmotionventures.com/experts-predict-future-transport-2017/. (Accessed on 03/04/18).

[9] J. Kornwitz, The Cybersecurity Risk of Self-Driving Cars, 2017. Available at: https://phys. org/news/2017-02-cybersecurity-self-driving-cars.html. (Accessed on 14/04/2018).

[10] S. Pillath, Automated Vehicles in the EU, 2016. Brussels. Available at: http://www. europarl.europa.eu/RegData/etudes/BRIE/2016/573902/EPRS_BRI(2016)573902_EN.pdf. (Accessed on 14/04/2018).

[11] G. Corera, If 2017 Could be Described as "Cyber-Geddon", What Will 2018 Bring? BBC News Website, 30 December, 2017. Available at: http://www.bbc.co.uk/news/technology-42338716. (Accessed on 31/12/17).

[12] N. Thomopoulos, M. Givoni, The autonomous car—a blessing or a curse for the future of low carbon mobility? An exploration of likely vs. desirable outcomes, European Journal of Futures Research 3 (1) (2015) 14, https://doi.org/10.1007/s40309-015-0071-z.

[13] S. Shladover, D. Su, X.-Y. Lu, Impacts of cooperative adaptive cruise control on freeway traffic flow, Transportation Research Record: Journal of the Transportation Research Board (2012) 63–70, https://doi.org/10.3141/2324-08.

[14] UK DfT, 'Unlocking the UK's High Tech Economy: Consultation on the Safe Use of Drones in the UK Government Response Government Response, July 2017.

[15] Society of Automotive Engineers, Taxonomy and Definitions for Terms Related to Driving Automation Systems for On-Road Motor Vehicles, 2014. Available at: http://standards. sae.org/j3016_201609/. (Accessed on 03/04/18).

[16] M. Sivak, B. Schoettle, Should We Require Licensing Tests and Graduated Licensing for Self-Driving Vehicles?, 2015. Michigan. doi: Report No. UMTRI-2015-33.

[17] I. Asimov, I, Robot, Gnome Press, US, 1950.

[18] B. Clark, G. Parkhurst, M. Ricci, Understanding the Socioeconomic Adoption Scenarios for Autonomous Vehicles: A Literature Review Ben, 2016. Bristol. Available at: http:// eprints.uwe.ac.uk/29134/1/Venturer-LitReview-5-1-Report-Final.pdf. (Accessed on 14/ 04/2018).

[19] Economic Commission for Europe, Convention on Road Traffic, 1993. Available at: http:// www.unece.org/fileadmin/DAM/trans/conventn/crt1968e.pdf. (Accessed on 14/04/2018).

[20] EU, G7 Declaration on Automated and Connected Driving, European Commission Announcements, 2015. Available at: https://ec.europa.eu/commission/commissioners/2014-2019/bulc/announcements/g7-declaration-automated-and-connected-driving_en. (Accessed on 14/04/2018).

[21] M.J.D.C. Henshaw, Systems of systems, cyber-physical systems, the internet-of-things...whatever next? Insight 19 (3) (2016) 51−54.

[22] E. Lee, The past, present and future of cyber-physical systems: a focus on models, Sensors 15 (3) (2015) 4837−4869, https://doi.org/10.3390/s150304837. (Accessed on 14/04/2018).

[23] M.W. Maier, Architecting principles for systems-of-systems, Systems Engineering 1 (4) (1998) 267−284, https://doi.org/10.1002/(SICI)1520-6858(1998)1:4<267::AID-SYS3>3.0.CO;2-D. (Accessed on 14/04/2018).

[24] Which-50 Staff Authors, IoT Connected Devices to Reach 20. 4 Billion by 2020, Says Gartner, Which-50, February 2017. Available at: https://which-50.com/iot-connected-devices-reach-20-4-billion-2020-says-gartner/. (Accessed on 03/04/18).

[25] L. Mearian, Update: Chrysler Recalls 1.4M Vehicles After Jeep Hack, Computerworld, July 2015, pp. 2014−2016. Available at: https://www.computerworld.com/article/2952186/mobile-security/chrysler-recalls-14m-vehicles-after-jeep-hack.html. (Accessed on 03/04/18).

[26] G. Loukas, Cyber-Physical Attacks − A Growing Invisible Threat, Elsevier, Kidlington, 2015.

[27] C. Ruckriegel, Report on the Road2CPS Roadmapping Workshop − Paris 24th June 2015, 2015. Stuttgart. Available at: http://road2cps.eu/events/wp-content/uploads/2015/12/Road2CPS-WP2_Roadmapping-WS-Paris_2015-06-24-Report-V11-Public-Version.pdf. (Accessed on 14/04/2018).

[28] A. Sajid, H. Abbas, K. Saleem, Cloud-assisted IoT-based SCADA systems security: a review of the state of the art and future challenges, IEEE Access 4 (2016), https://doi.org/10.1109/ACCESS.2016.2549047. (Accessed on 14/04/2018). Special Section on the Plethora of Research in Internet of Things (IoT).

[29] C.B. Keating, Emergence in system of systems, in: M. Jamshidi (Ed.), System of Systems Engineering, John Wiley & Sons, Hoboken, NJ, USA, 2008, https://doi.org/10.1002/9780470403501.ch7. (Accessed on 14/04/2018).

[30] B.S. Blanchard, W.J. Fabryscy, Systems Engineering and Analysis, fifth ed., Pearson Education, 2013.

[31] NCOIC, NCOIC Interoperability Framework NCOIC Patterns Overview, 2008. Available at: https://www.ncoic.org/images/technology/NIF_Pattern_Overview.pdf. (Accessed on 14/04/2018).

[32] European Commission ISA2, Interoperability Test Bed, 2017. Available at: https://ec.europa.eu/isa2/solutions/interoperability-test-bed_en. (Accessed on 14/04/2018).

[33] J. Mervis, Not so fast, Science 358 (6369) (2017) 1370−1374. Available at: http://science.sciencemag.org/content/358/6369/1370. (Accessed on 14/04/2018).

[34] V. Gowadia, et al., Secure cross-domain data sharing architecture for crisis management, in: Proceedings of the Tenth Annual ACM Workshop on Digital Rights Management − DRM'10, 2010, p. 43, https://doi.org/10.1145/1866870.1866879. (Accessed on 14/04/2018).

[35] P.S. Kumar, W. Emfinger, G. Karsai, A testbed to simulate and analyze resilient cyber-physical systems, in: Proceedings − IEEE International Symposium on Rapid System Prototyping, RSP, February 2016, pp. 97−103, https://doi.org/10.1109/RSP.2015.7416553. (Accessed on 14/04/2018).

[36] T.M. Anandan, The Shrinking Footprint of Robot Safety, RIA Robotics Online, 2014. Available at: https://www.robotics.org/content-detail.cfm/Industrial-Robotics-Industry-Insights/The-Shrinking-Footprint-of-Robot-Safety/content_id/5059. (Accessed on 14/04/2018).

[37] M. Reimann, et al., in: M. Reimann, C. Ruckriegel (Eds.), Road2CPS Priorities and Recommendations for Research and Innovation in Cyber-Physical Systems, Steinbeis-Edition, Stuttgart, 2017.

[38] European Parliament Research Service, Ethical Aspects of Cyber Physical Systems, 2016, https://doi.org/10.1007/978-0-387-09834-0. (Accessed on 14/04/2018). Brussels.

[39] M.R. Endsley, Toward a theory of situation awareness in dynamic systems, Human Factors: The Journal of the Human Factors and Ergonomics Society 37 (1) (1995) 32−64, https://doi.org/10.1518/001872095779049543. (Accessed on 14/04/2018).

[40] P.M. Salmon, N.A. Stanton, G.H. Walker, Measuring situation awareness in complex systems: comparison of measures study, International Journal of Industrial Ergonomics 39 (3) (2009) 490−500, https://doi.org/10.1016/j.ergon.2008.10.010. (Accessed on 14/04/2018).

[41] M. Henshaw, et al., The Systems of Systems Engineering Strategic Research Agenda Systems of Systems Engineering, 2013. Brussels. Available at: https://www.tareasos.eu/docs/pb/SRA_Issue2.pdf. (Accessed on 14/04/2018).

[42] C. Siemieniuch, M.A. Sinclair, Extending systems ergonomics thinking to accomodate the socio-technical issues of systems of systems, Applied Ergonomics 45 (10) (2013) 1016.

[43] Digital Transformation Monitor, Autonomous Cars: A Big Opportunity for European Industry, January 2017, p. 6. Available at: https://ec.europa.eu/growth/tools-databases/dem/monitor/sites/default/files/DTM_Autonomous cars v1.pdf. (Accessed on 03/04/18).

[44] Department of Transport, The Pathway to Driverless Cars, 2015. Available at: https://www.gov.uk/government/uploads/system/uploads/attachment_data/file/446316/pathway-driverless-cars.pdf. (Accessed on 03/04/18).

[45] P.J. Mosterman, J. Zander, Cyber-physical systems challenges: a needs analysis for collaborating embedded software systems, Software and Systems Modeling 15 (1) (2015) 5−16, https://doi.org/10.1007/s10270-015-0469-x. (Accessed on 14/04/2018). Springer Berlin Heidelberg.

[46] X. Zheng, C. Julien, Verification and validation in cyber physical systems: research challenges and a way forward, in: 2015 IEEE/ACM 1st International Workshop on Software Engineering for Smart Cyber-Physical Systems, 2015, pp. 15−18, https://doi.org/10.1109/SEsCPS.2015.11. (Accessed on 14/04/2018).

[47] W.K. Lam, Simulation-based verification versus formal verification, in: Hardware Design Verification: Simulation and Formal Method-Based Approaches, Prentice Hall, 2005.

[48] J. Fitzgerald, K. Pierce, P.G. Larsen, Co-modelling and co-simulation in the engineering of systems of cyber-physical systems, in: Proceedings of the 9th International Conference on System of Systems Engineering: The Socio-Technical Perspective, SoSE 2014, 2014, pp. 67−72, https://doi.org/10.1109/SYSOSE.2014.6892465. (Accessed on 14/04/2018).

[49] L. Guo, et al., Metronomy: a function-architecture co-simulation framework for timing verification of cyber-physical systems, in: International Conference on Hardware/Software Codesign and System Synthesis, CODES+ISSS 2014, ACM Special Interest Group on Design Automation, 2014, https://doi.org/10.1145/2656075.2656093. (Accessed on 14/04/2018).

[50] U. Sivarajah, et al., Critical analysis of Big Data challenges and analytical methods, Journal of Business Research 70 (2017) 263−286, https://doi.org/10.1016/j.jbusres.2016.08.001. (Accessed on 14/04/2018). The Authors.

[51] A. Sharma, F. Ivančić, Modeling and analytics for cyber-physical systems in the age of big data, ACM Sigmetrics 41 (4) (2014) 74−77, https://doi.org/10.1145/2627534.2627558. (Accessed on 14/04/2018).

[52] OECD, OECD Environmental Outlook to 2030, 2008. Available at: https://doi.org/10. 1787/9789264040519-en. (Accessed on 14/04/2018).

[53] D. Wang, The economics of drone delivery, Guest Post, IEEE Spectrum, 5 (January 2016). Available at: https://spectrum.ieee.org/automaton/robotics/drones/the-economics-of-drone-delivery. (Accessed on 03/04/18).

[54] W. Damm, et al., CPS Summit: Action Plan: Towards a Cross-Cutting Science of CPS for Mastering All-Important Engineering Challenges, 2016, p. 2016.

[55] NASA, The Art and Science of Systems Engineering, 2009. Available at: https://www. nasa.gov/pdf/311199main_Art_and_Sci_of_SE_SHORT_1_20_09.pdf. (Accessed on 14/ 04/2018).

[56] L.S. Lutz, Automated Vehicles in the EU: Proposals to Amend the Type Approval Framework and Regulation of Driver Conduct, Casualty Matters International, 2016, p. 8.

[57] M.F. Merlie, Autonomous Ships: Are Regulations Being Left in Their Wake? Int. Inst. of Marine Surveying, 2017. Available at: https://www.iims.org.uk/autonomous-ships-regulations-left-wake/. (Accessed on 14/04/2018).

Future of Transportation Cyber-Physical Systems — Smart Cities/Regions

Kakan Dey[1], Ryan Fries[2], Shofiq Ahmed[1]

[1]Department of Civil and Environmental Engineering, West Virginia University, Morgantown, WV, United States; [2]Department of Civil Engineering, Southern Illinois University, Edwardsville, IL, United States

1. What is a Smart City?

The 'Smart City' paradigm enables integrated operations of digitally connected city infrastructure and service systems (e.g., mobility systems, healthcare, energy infrastructure, public safety) by deploying different communication technologies, real-time data collection infrastructure and data analytics and intelligence platforms to improve the efficiency of city services and to improve quality of life. In a Smart City, communication infrastructure, computing resources, sensing infrastructure and data analytics infrastructure (known as the Internet of Things) build the backbone of the cyber-physical system (CPS) and enable synchronised operations of economic, political, social, cultural and urban activities [1]. Fig. 11.1 depicts an example overview of various systems, including transportation in a Smart City environment. Depending on the deployment cost, funding availability and maturity of technologies, any combination of various Smart City infrastructure systems and service systems can be implemented [2]. The success of Smart City deployments is largely dependent on an emphasis on adoption of innovative technology-based infrastructure and service systems, broader community engagement in the development—deployment—operations of such systems, dynamic leadership and efficient management of resources [3,4]. Depending on the resources available, numerous cities around the world can begin implementing Smart City concepts at different scales. Fig. 11.2 summarises the Smart City infrastructure and service systems deployed at several cities around the world. With private sector innovations as the major driving force in Smart City domain, public and private sectors have developed partnerships to accelerate deployment and innovation in Smart City frontiers, such as the 'Smart City Challenge' program initiated by the US Department of Transportation (USDOT) and described further in Section 5.4 of this chapter [5].

Transportation Cyber-Physical Systems. https://doi.org/10.1016/B978-0-12-814295-0.00011-3
Copyright © 2018 Elsevier Inc. All rights reserved.

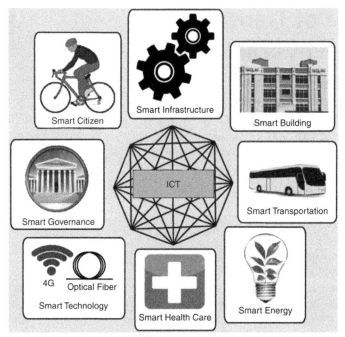

Figure 11.1 Illustration of Smart City components [2].

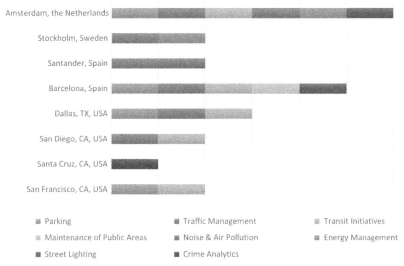

Figure 11.2 Smart City features at selected cities [6].

2. Major characteristics of a Smart City

As evident from earlier section, the functions of different Smart City infrastructure and service systems are different. However, all of them have many common characteristics. A few of the major characteristics are discussed in the following subsections.

2.1 Smart/intelligent infrastructure sensors

Smart infrastructure sensors are the key components of almost every Smart City system such as energy, transportation, building, healthcare, environmental, and public safety. There are wide ranges of sensor technologies which have been used in a Smart City environment. These sensors are primarily used to monitor the state of certain system characteristics in real time. Data from distributed sensor networks are used to determine the current operational condition of any system such as traffic conditions along a corridor or the whole network within a city.

In the transportation system, various sensors have been used to perform diversified tasks. Here we list common sensor technologies in smart transportation systems.

- *Loop detectors* are used to measure traffic volume, vehicle presence, speed, vehicle classification and detect traffic incidents [7].
- *Microwave radar* can be used to detect vehicle flow, speed and presence. Vehicle-mounted radar also supports obstacle detection and automatic cruise control [8].
- *Infrared sensors* measure the reflected energy from a vehicle and can identify vehicle type and vehicle characteristics [8].
- *Dedicated short-range communication (DSRC) radio* is a two-way vehicle-to-vehicle (V2V) communication technology which can share safety-critical vehicle information to nearby vehicles [9].
- *Cameras* are used with traffic signals to monitor traffic (e.g., presence detection and red light compliance). Modern vision technology-supported cameras are used to detect vehicles and are even used in automated vehicles for obstacle detection.
- *Light Detection and Ranging (LiDAR)* is used in autonomous vehicles to detect obstacles (i.e., other vehicles, pedestrians, roadway-fixed objects) and navigate safely through complex roadway environments [10].

Other smart sensors used in different Smart City systems:
Sensors in smart building systems:

- *Electrochromic glass* which is controlled by electricity to vary the amount of sunlight penetration through windows [11].
- *Lighting control* uses automated shading system to sense the available natural light and reduce use of artificial light when it is not needed. There are many lighting control solutions such as Gamma lighting control [12] and automated lighting and a shade control system [13].

Sensors in a smart energy grid:

- *Automatic smart meters* transmit unusual consumption and usage data to the control centre for appropriate response [14].

- *Tollgrade device* has been installed on power lines and send a detailed status message in the case of any detected disruptions [15].
- *Weather sensors* are used to monitor weather conditions and the temperature of the transmission line [14].

Sensors in a smart water distribution system:

- *Automatic smart meters* are similar to those described for the energy grid. These meters can monitor water consumption and notify control centres of unusual consumption.
- *Pressure gauges* are used to monitor the condition of a pipeline to identify preventive maintenance and prevent disruptions [16].
- *Temperature sensors* have been used to monitor water temperature to detect possible line breaks and notify control centres [16].

2.2 Big data infrastructure and data analytics capability

As smart systems are equipped with numerous sensors to monitor the performance of different system components, large amounts of data in different formats (such as text data, video data, structured or unstructured data) will be generated by these sensors. Thus, big data infrastructure and data analytics tools are the critical components of any Smart City infrastructure to develop intelligence from the collected data. The major functions of a big data framework and data analytics system can be divided into three stages [17]: (1) data generation and acquisition, which involves collecting heterogeneous data with different spatial and temporal characteristics, (2) data management and processing, which involves analysing data and making decisions using data analytics solutions, and (3) application, which involves initiating actions based on the knowledge gained. Many cities have been implementing cloud infrastructure to store, process and develop intelligent decisions using a massive amount of data from multiple Smart City infrastructure systems.

Artificial intelligence (AI)—based data analytics solutions have been used extensively in analysing big data. AI methods develop data-driven models and discover significant patterns in the available data. Many companies dealing with big data (e.g., online shopping sites, credit card companies, finance and investment companies) are using AI to analyse big data and develop real-time decisions. For example, INRIX Population Analytics, a data-driven analytical technique, uses millions of anonymised mobile phone and global positioning system (GPS) device data points to develop traffic movement insights. Transport for London uses this analytics platform to analyse real-time traffic flow and traffic density across the London traffic network for real-time traffic management and planning decisions [18]. While, all Smart Cities have to deal with big data challenges, not all have sufficient expertise and resources. Multiple private services have been providing big data storage and analytics platforms known as 'cloud computing'. For example, Amazon Web Services [19] and Microsoft Azure [20] are two of the most renowned and widely used cloud service providers, which could be used for Smart City deployments. For a more detail review of big data infrastructure and data management tools, the readers are referred to Chapter 6.

2.3 Communication technologies

Smart Cities are characterised by numerous and different types of sensors installed in a distributed network to monitor traffic, to collect weather data or to monitor the energy grid. Reliable communication and networking infrastructure is critical to connect thousands of sensors to collect infrastructure condition data. Depending on the distance, throughput and latency requirements between sensors and key infrastructure components, different communication technologies have been used in Smart City environronment. These technologies could include combinations of wired and wireless communication options. The key communication technologies are briefly explained next.

2.3.1 Fibre optic networks

Fibre optic is the most widely used backbone communication infrastructure for any communication network. Fibre optic uses light pulses to send information from one place to another [21]. The key benefits of using fibre optic networks are high bandwidth, low attenuation, low interference, high security and high reliability over long distances [21].

2.3.2 Wi-Fi communication

Smart Cities have been deploying Wi-Fi communication infrastructure to connect their infrastructure. For example, New York City's Linknyc initiative will install 500 gigabyte free Wi-Fi kiosks at old phone booths, which will also serve as charging stations for citizens [22]. However, Wi-Fi communication has limited coverage, and the bandwidth widely varies between 25 and 200 Mbps. In smart transportation infrastructure systems, Wi-Fi networking has been used to connect vehicles with other vehicles and connect smart infrastructures (e.g., streetlights, traffic signals).

2.3.3 Cellular communication

Due to the proliferation of smartphone technologies and the evolution of cellular communication technologies (3G->4G->LTE->5G), cellular communication infrastructure plays a critical role in a Smart City environment [23]. Because of wide cellular network coverage and large bandwidth, many innovative transportation services such as ride sharing services (e.g., Uber, Lyft), routing support and entertainment services rely on cellular communication and tracking of smart devices. As connected and automated vehicles (CAV) will rely on V2V communication for many functions, a fast, reliable, low latent and high-range network system such as 5G could become a key communication platform in future transportation system. Although 5G technology is under development for CAV applications, performance in the experimental tests is promising. The communication latency in 5G varies between 0.001 and 0.01 seconds, which satisfies latency requirements of 0.02−1 seconds for most CAV applications [24].

2.3.4 Dedicated short-range communication (DSRC)

DSRC is a short-to-medium range wireless communication technology exclusively created for intelligent transportation system (ITS) applications [25]. It is one of the key communication technologies adopted to enable low latency and high data transmission critical communications for V2V communication—based connected vehicle safety applications. Designated licenced bandwidth, fast network acquisition, low latency, high reliability and interoperability are some key features of DSRC communication.

Smart City agencies must evaluate available communication options considering different performance measures (e.g., communication range, bandwidth, latency, cost) and Smart City application requirements. A comparative analysis of these different communication technologies is presented in Table 11.1.

3. Smart City as a systems of systems

Although the Smart City idea originated with the goal of providing smart transportation services, other city infrastructure and service systems have become an integral part of the broader Smart City platform and formed a true 'systems of systems (SoS)' paradigm. According to Popper et al. [36], an SoS is 'a collection of task-oriented or dedicated systems that pool their resources and capabilities together to obtain a new, more complex "metasystem" which offers more functionality and performance than simply the sum of the constituent systems'. Because of numerous interactions of different SoS components, a Smart City is explained in this section in the context of an SoS by reviewing major infrastructure and service systems.

3.1 Transportation systems

Transportation Cyber-Physical System (TCPS) is the most critical and distributed infrastructure in a Smart City's CPS. To provide safe, efficient and reliable mobility services for goods and people, modern transportation systems have been transforming to a smart and intelligent platform supported by V2V, vehicle-to-human (V2H) and V2I communications, as well as different levels of vehicle automations and underlying communication and computing infrastructure. A general illustration of this smart transportation system is shown in Fig. 11.3. Major components of this smart transportation system are discussed next.

3.1.1 Smart vehicles

Although conventional vehicles are equipped with hundreds of electronic devices and form in-vehicle CPS, they do not communicate with other vehicles or transportation infrastructure. Advanced vehicle models are equipped with multiple sensors to support safety and mobility features. These features include automatic emergency braking system, blind spot warning system, adaptive cruise control system, rear cross-traffic

Table 11.1 A Comparative Characteristics Analysis of Different Communication System

Communication Type		Range	Bandwidth	Data Transfer Rate	Remarks
Fibre optic communication		Not applicable (connected through wire)	190 ~ 200 THz [26]	10 ~ 1000 Gb/s [26]	Fastest network
Wi-Fi		46 ~ 92 m [31]	2.4 ~ 60 GHz [30]	0.011 ~ 1 Gb/s [30]	Relatively faster and user friendly
Cellular Communication	3G	Depends on the strength of carrier network	1 ~ 5 MHz [27]	3 ~ 15 Mb/s [27]	Older version
	4G		10 ~ 20 MHz [27]	50 ~ 100 Mb/s [33]	Better than 3G in terms of data rate and latency
	LTE		Up to 100 MHz [27]	>300 Mb/s [27]	Advanced version
	5G	>5 km	100 GHz [32]	1 ~ 10 Gb/s [34]	Going to be the most reliable wireless communication network of the future [35]
Dedicated short-range communication		30 ~ 300 m [29]	5 ~ 6 GHz [29]	3 ~ 54 Mb/s [28]	Efficient medium to be implemented in vehicle to infrastructure (V2I) and V2V

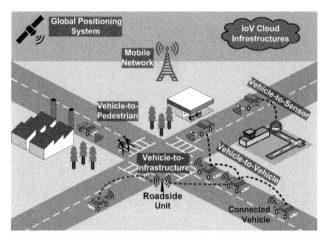

Figure 11.3 A general illustration of smart transportation system [37]. *IoV*, Internet of Vehicles.

warning system, and lane departure warning system. These features provide the vehicle with significant safety and mobility benefits [38]. In addition to these features, several high-end vehicle models use cloud services to support advanced drivers' assistance systems [39,40]. For example, the *BMW Connected* application uses cloud-based real-time traffic information to provide predictive travel time data for scheduling and trip planning [41]. This application also automatically stores the drivers' mobility patterns (e.g., daily trip to work at 8 a.m., pickup the kids at 2 p.m.), origins and destinations to maximise user experience.

With the rapid progress in research and development, experts predict that automated vehicles will be ready for mass deployment within the next decade [42]. Automated vehicles combine multiple sensing technologies (e.g., LiDAR, camera), navigation systems, motion planning algorithms and control systems for driverless transportation of passengers and goods [43]. Sensing technologies can identify any obstacles on a vehicle's path. Navigation systems conduct path planning to reach the trip destination from an origin. Motion planning systems use sensor outputs and path planning outputs to develop detailed vehicle paths in the next time steps. For example, path planning could recommend details such as stay in the lane, lane change, brake, accelerate and turn, depending upon the position of other vehicles, sensed obstacles and route to the destination. While contemporary automated vehicle concepts do not rely on V2V and V2I communication, it is expected that these features will provide critical information about a vehicle's surroundings that cannot be collected using automated vehicle-sensing systems alone. Beyond vehicle-based advanced technologies, transportation infrastructure has also been transformed by installing technologies to sense, collect and develop transportation system−level conditions and predictions to improve safety, mobility and environmental performance as detailed in the next subsection.

3.1.2   Smart transportation infrastructure

Beyond vehicle-based advanced technologies, transportation infrastructure also has been transforming. Agencies operating transportation infrastructure have been deploying technologies to sense, collect and provide transportation system—level condition assessments and predictions to improve safety, mobility and environmental performance. Smart transportation infrastructure will accelerate the deployment of automated and connected vehicles. Several approaches have been taken by many cities and regions to deploy smart transportation infrastructure such as automated toll collection systems, adaptive signal control, smart streetlights and more. Electronic toll collection systems have been deployed throughout the world to lessen congestion by allowing vehicles to move fast through toll collection facilities. Fig. 11.4 illustrates a typical example of electronic toll collection infrastructure, which includes six major components (numbered 1 to 6). When a vehicle breaks the first laser beam (1) entering the toll zone and triggers the transceiver (2), the transceiver communicates with the vehicle's onboard transponder and captures the date, time and toll charge. Simultaneously, a camera (3) takes photos of the vehicle's front licence plate. Next, the vehicle passes through the second laser beam (4), it triggers the second camera (5) and then the second camera takes photos of the vehicle's rear licence plate. The final step is payment deduction from driver's account or paid via other options such as a website or bank (6).

3.1.3   Smart cloud services

Cloud-based transportation services have been used in many applications (e.g., Waze, routing planning) and will play a critical role in all Smart City infrastructure and service systems. Massive amounts of data collected from sensors in smart vehicles and infrastructure will require huge computing resources and could be supported by cloud services. Cloud computing has been used to store, process and analyse diverse traffic data (e.g., vehicle condition data, weather and roadway condition data, real-time traffic

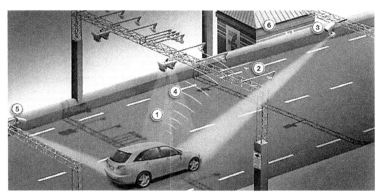

Figure 11.4 Example Electronic toll collection system [44].
From https://www.pcb.its.dot.gov/eprimer/module8.aspx#fn10.

signal phasing data, social media data) [45]. Currently, cloud services have been used for numerous transportation applications, such as adaptive signal operations, real-time traffic condition assessment and prediction applications [46]. For example, BMW has launched the smartphone application (app) 'Enlighten' to communicate real-time corridor traffic signal information to the drivers of selected vehicle models. This app combines data from a city's traffic management system (i.e., signal data) in a cloud infrastructure and shares route-specific traffic signal data with drivers [47]. Using the GPS on a smartphone, this application pinpoints any upcoming signals and analyses the distance between the vehicle and signal. With this information, the application notifies the driver whether he/she can maintain the same speed or if they need to slow down. 'Enlighten' enables stress-free driving by using cloud service−based data collection, processing and analytics tools.

3.1.4   Next generation air transportation system

Apart from the surface transportation system, air and water transportation systems are two major transportation modes for long-distance passenger and freight movement. Because of the high speed, reliability and safety record of air transportation, millions of people use air transportation for long-distance travel. Due to an unprecedented increase in air transportation demand, major airports around the world have been experiencing capacity issues. In the last century, the modernisation in the air transportation system was not sufficient to serve growing demand. To address this issue, the United States has been leading the development and deployment of the Next Generation Air Transportation System (NextGen) and related CPS infrastructure. The Joint Planning and Development Office (JPDO) of the USDOT started the initiative to develop the NextGen concept of operations in 2003 [48] to provide the required flexibility in terms of air transportation system capacity including security management and mitigation of the impacts of environment such as air quality and aircraft noise. NextGen has set a target to achieve its vision by 2025 and their major objectives are (1) reducing cost, (2) reducing travel time and increasing reliability, (3) fulfilling the future demand and expectation, (4) improving air safety and security of the United States and worldwide air transportation system, (5) mitigating the impacts of weather and other disruptions, (6) reducing noise, fuel consumption and emissions and (7) preventing future threats.

According to JPDO, the NextGen system will have nine main capabilities [48]: (1) air transportation security, (2) collaborative flow contingency management, (3) efficient trajectory management, (4) collaborative capacity management, (5) flexible separation management, (6) improved environmental performance, (7) improved safety operations, (8) flexible airport facility and ramp operations and (9) integrated NextGen information. To achieve these capabilities, NextGen program's operational CPS has been divided into five subsystems and each subsystem has several functions to support all objectives of the NextGen program [49]. The key functions are presented in Fig. 11.5.

Development and deployment of the NextGen CPS is largely dependent on the coordination and communication between aircraft operations and services, airport

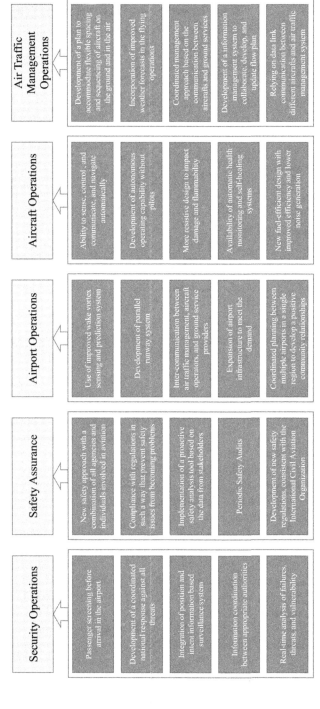

Figure 11.5 Operation of Next Generation Air Transportation System program including the subsections and functions [49].

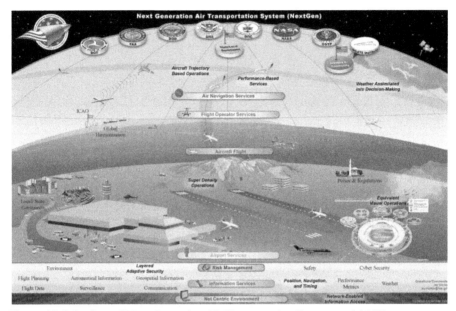

Figure 11.6 Services of Next Generation Air Transportation System model [48].

services, a safety management centre, an air traffic management control centre and overall security services. Fig. 11.6 shows these different service domains and components of the NextGen system.

3.2 Energy infrastructure

Energy infrastructure is one of the most critical systems that enables operations of all other Smart City infrastructure. Thus, the importance of transforming energy CPS to be smart, resilient and efficient is vital for prosperity of the Smart City paradigm. Emerging smart microgrid technology will help in achieving improved energy efficiency [50]. The smart energy microgrid in Wildpoldsried, Germany, is a showcase of such a smart energy system. With the collaboration of diverse energy sources (e.g., solar panels, windmills and biogas), this energy system is capable of producing more than five times the energy needs of Wildpoldsried [51]. In the United States, Arizona Public Service (APS) has started a pilot project to install two-way microgrid solar panel systems on the roofs of 1600 homes to generate 10 MW of renewable energy. This program was a partnership between APS and Siemens where every household will be credited for giving back excess electricity to the utility system [52].

Because the transportation sector has been considered as one of the major energy consumers, it has a significant contribution to greenhouse gas emissions [53]. To reduce the environmental impacts of the transportation sector, the concept of transportation electrification is a major trend in many industrialised nations. For instance, the United Kingdom (UK) has proposed a ban on the sale of new gasoline and diesel-powered vehicles by 2040 [54]. Similar proposals have been considered in other countries such as France, India, Germany and China. Electrification of transportation promotes deployment of environmentally friendly electric vehicles that can reduce vehicle carbon emission at a large scale. Though electric vehicles do not emit any greenhouse gas during operation, the power generation plants should be more energy efficient and use green energy sources in a smart energy grid system to reduce overall transportation sector's carbon footprint.

Smart energy grid technology will bring new dimensions to Smart City systems through communication with other infrastructure (e.g., wireless charging infrastructure for electric vehicles). Some cities and states are even considering to implement the idea of using streetlights as charging stations for electric vehicles [55,56]. Innovative concepts such as vehicle-to-grid two-way energy flow could be an emerging service. This service could consist of electric vehicles not only being recharged by the grid but also surplus energy being fed back into the grid for short-term energy needs during unexpected peaks in demand. For example, Oncor, the largest distribution and transmission company in Texas, has launched a smart solar power−based microgrid. Oncor's smart microgrid platform has four microgrid components, which operate independently. This smart power generation and distribution platform can self-diagnose any problem in the event of any failure (e.g., generators breaking down) and can reconfigure it momentarily and automatically notify users [57]. For smooth management operation, distribution management system has been incorporated to connect all the subdomains of this grid. In the smart grid concept, the communication network is the backbone of smart energy infrastructure. Fig. 11.7 illustrates an example architecture of networking within a smart electric grid.

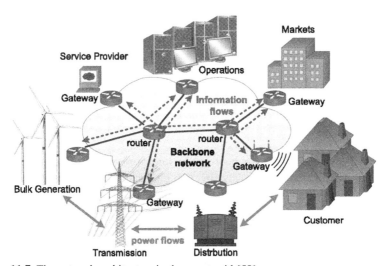

Figure 11.7 The network architecture in the smart grid [58].

3.3   Public safety

It is essential that cities can deliver core safety services to the public. These services could include safety monitoring and patrols, ticketing, crime investigation and criminal detention, among others. Smart City concepts present several opportunities to improve how each of these services is provided to the public. Opportunities exist in the integration of real-time information, improving security monitoring and surveillance and managing disasters and the city's recovery.

Smart Cities should leverage real-time information from multiple sources to enable timely responses to emergencies [59]. These information sources could include first responder networks, field personnel reports, video surveillance networks, traffic management centers (TMCs), dispatch centres, public service answering points (PSAPs), Geographic Information System (GIS) databases and other control and command centres [59]. An early example of such integration and information synthesis was reported to reduce crime in New York City by 27%. These gains were realised by integrating public safety information from across the city at one place. This integration allowed the development of a '911 real-time dashboard' displaying emergency needs and resources side by side and allowing dispatchers to make more-informed decisions. In turn, responders in the field were better informed by dispatchers or through access with their mobile devices [59].

Surveillance systems have become quite pervasive in urban areas. Transportation agencies monitor roads, intersections and transit stations; law enforcement agencies monitor public locations, police vehicle dashboard cameras and officer body cameras; private sector businesses monitor their stores and other assets and residents use surveillance in their homes and apartments. Previous research has identified that the purpose of surveillance differs and data were not commonly shared [60].

Surveillance continues to be the focus of much investment [61] and combining surveillance with data analytics and network technology hold much promise. For example, synthesising videos from many sources (such as stores, trains, social media) could help identify potential crimes and make key public safety insights [61]. Surveillance will likely remain a key area of focus because some of the infrastructure already exists and the synthesis tools continue to advance.

One example of surveillance efforts in Seoul, South Korea includes monitoring school children to prevent kidnapping, using radio-frequency identification (RFID) tags and closed-circuit television in Seoul, South Korea [62]. Another example is the monitoring of social workers or police officer locations in real time [63]. The latter has already been used in court cases in the United States.

Disaster management and recovery can be improved through implementation of Smart City concepts [64], namely by communication and surveillance. With respect to communication during disaster response, first responders are of particular importance. Fire services, police, emergency medical services and other responders can be challenged by the inability to communicate with each other while in the field. Also, many responders communicate using the same commercial networks the public does, which may become congested during large disasters. At the time of this writing, efforts were underway to create a broadband network dedicated to first responders throughout the United States. As these efforts continue, perhaps these limitations will be overcome [64].

Surveillance is an important tool to provide responders situational awareness, allowing fast and appropriate responses to events [65]. For example, surveillance could improve emergency response by identifying specific equipment that is needed or relaying best streets for those en route.

3.4 Healthcare

Improving quality of healthcare is an important function of Smart City services. To cope with limited resources while facing increasing demand, healthcare services must adopt advanced technologies to maximise the efficiency of the healthcare system by integrating traditional healthcare with innovative technologies such as smart bio-sensors, wearable devices, remote operation and information and communication technology [2]. Smart transportation infrastructure could benefit healthcare, enabling many smart healthcare services. For example, Luxembourg has become the first European Union state ready to deploy the eCall emergency-responsive Medicare system. Transportation is a critical factor for this system to function [66]. eCall is a new automatic emergency call system which will use the Pan-European '112' emergency number to receive a call either manually or automatically using vehicle sensors activated after any vehicle crash. In the eCall system, after the automatic detection of any crash by in-vehicle sensors, the vehicle unit immediately sends emergency messages to a call centre, also known as a PSAP 112. An operator at the PSAP 112 reviews the crash data and vehicle location information to develop a response plan. Smart transportation system supports the response effort by providing real-time traffic forecasting (e.g., congestion) so that the emergency units can reach the crash scene in the shortest possible amount of time. Moreover, the operator can talk to the occupants of the vehicle for additional information (e.g., severity of crash, the number of occupants) and provide comfort by ensuring that help is on the way to the accident location.

Smart healthcare has many other benefits as well. For instance, using assisted living technology (e.g., smart wearable devices and smart sensors), senior citizens can live independently at their residences without compromising their social activities and healthcare necessity [67]. According to Vecchia et al. [68], RFID and photo sensors can be used to build an intelligent infrastructure for future smart hospitals. The prototype of the system will consist of a set of clients, a centralised server and a positioning system which will integrate RFID and photo sensors. Through the server, medical staff can check with their patient's clinical reports, location and movement. With RFID and photo sensor technology, hospital authorities can also restrict information access by any unauthorised persons. An overview of this future smart healthcare platform is illustrated in Fig. 11.8.

3.5 Environment

The environment affected by the transportation system could include the roadside environment, the society it serves and the financial well-being of the region. When

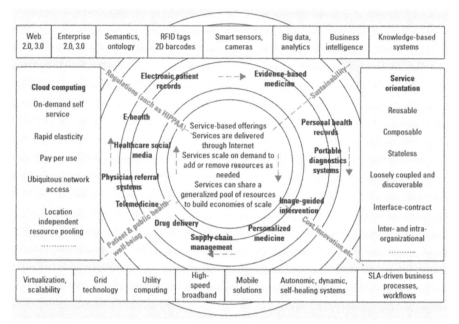

Figure 11.8 Integration of different smart services in a healthcare system [69].

considering the roadside environmental impact, pollution control, smart energy use, waste generation and resource use are all of concern. Pollution control could include reducing emissions, reducing the quantity of runoff while maintaining acceptable runoff water quality and addressing the urban heat island effect. When considering emissions, research has shown that efficient operations could have a larger effect than several 'green' construction techniques. For example, Tupper et al. illustrated that traffic incident management along an urban freeway could reduce carbon dioxide emissions five times more than construction alternatives such as recycling pavement, locally sourcing materials and using warm mix asphalt [70]. Improving the operation of local city streets by optimising traffic signal timing has the potential to reduce a variety of harmful vehicle emissions. It is important to note that these engineering solutions must also be complimented by public policies that help manage demand, ensuring that additional vehicles do not immediately negate the benefits of improved efficiency. In the UK, studies have identified that recent efforts yielded limited reductions in greenhouse gas emissions like CO_2 [71]. Also, despite speculation that ridesharing providers, such as Uber and Lyft, reduced the need for private vehicle ownership, some findings suggest these services also shifted ridership from public transit. Thus, ridesharing providers might not provide the environmental benefits originally thought [72]. Overall, it remains unseen if Smart City approaches to improve surface transportation efficiency will reduce emissions and fuel use or merely be usurped by additional personal vehicle trips.

Figure 11.9 Example real-time streamflow information [73].

As scientists continue to observe more unpredictable weather patterns, storm intensity, storm water quantity and quality design assumptions will inevitably change. In the meanwhile, cities will need to leverage available data and forecasts. For example, the Missouri Department of Transportation in the Midwest United States has learnt from several periods of heavy rainfall. High river levels required the closure of interstate bridges in both December 2015 and May 2017. During the latter, operations engineers leveraged a system of real-time stream gauge data and forecasts (see Fig. 11.9) to improve their operations and their communication with the travelling public.

Many have engaged citizens to become a part of the improvement in their city's environmental quality. As part of a project from MIT's Senseable City Lab, citizens in Hong Kong and Shenzhen have agreed to wear sensors to help report the air quality around their cities [74]. Similar efforts are underway across Europe and in Africa using apps downloaded to citizens' mobile phones [75]. It is envisioned that efforts such as these can help evoke passion among citizens towards improving their home cities.

Some agencies have even published guidelines for smart cities development with respect to the environment. For example, the small island nation of Mauritius developed such a guide because of their high value on land [76]. In addition, practitioners could use established methods of measuring environmental sustainability such as envision [77]. Last, other guides focus on the steps that city leaders should take when transforming their cities to become smarter [78].

3.6 Other Smart City infrastructure

Though the transportation system is the largest smart infrastructure system, it does not stand alone as the most important (e.g., water supply system, gas supply system,

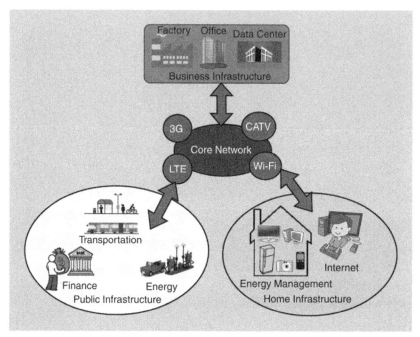

Figure 11.10 Smart infrastructure system [2].

building system). Fig. 11.10 depicts an example overview of different smart infrastructure systems and their interaction through different communication technologies.

3.6.1 Smart building system

Smart buildings maintain communication between different intelligent building components to improve occupants' comfort and safety and to reduce energy consumption [79]. Moreover, smart buildings interact with the external environment and systems (e.g., environmental condition, electrical grids) to provide critical smart building services. For example, smart glass windows turn transparent to translucent to block the glass visibility and control light, reducing heat transmission during summer days [80]. Siemens' Desigo Insight, management system for buildings, is one of the most widely used technologies in smart building infrastructure. In Tornado Tower, Doha, sensors activate diverse building system components (e.g., heating, ventilation, air conditioning), fire safety, security, video surveillance, control of the smart sensors and control light luminance, all managed by Siemens' Desigo Insight [81].

3.6.2 Smart water distribution system

Smart water grids integrate with Smart City infrastructure through smart sensors, smart meters, digital controllers and analytic tools. Real-time monitoring of asset condition (e.g., pipeline condition), pressure and water quality, water consumption and automated meter readings collection are some key benefits of smart water grid system [16].

Many cities have already implemented smart water grid systems to maximise economic and service benefits. For example, Panama City, Florida, has upgraded almost 25,000 existing water meters with smart sensors to address the issue of unaccounted-for water usage. Implementing these smart sensors has aided the tracking of lost water and identifying system leaks. In addition, this system has improved customer service and efficiency of the system significantly [82].

3.7 Stakeholders

Similar to the early days of intelligent transportation systems, there remains a need for strong leadership and champions to motivate the changes for truly improving our cities. Some argue that these changes are perhaps part of a larger trend towards reinventing cities [83] and suggest significant potential for change in medium and small cities as well.

The other part of the challenge in developing Smart Cities is there are so many different stakeholders involved. These could include transportation engineers, city administrators, law enforcement, fire and rescue, sanitation services, transit agencies, taxi companies, freight companies and many more. Each has different uses for and needs from our transportation system. Each has different data to offer and could benefit in different ways from Smart City initiatives. Smart Cities' activities in the European Union have grouped stakeholders into six action clusters [84]. Most notably, transportation CPS stakeholders would engage in the sustainable urban mobility cluster. Within that stakeholder group, some argue that public sector stakeholders must rethink how their organisations can become more customer focused rather than function focused [78]. For example, transportation agencies in smart cities should focus on moving people instead of maintaining roads. In that essence, transit and road departments would share the same focus.

Beyond each stakeholder cluster, it is essential that barriers are removed and the theoretical silos of different agencies and industries are broken down. History has shown again and again that information sharing is a challenge, particularly between disparate stakeholders. To address these challenges, some suggest that we need new ways of engaging stakeholders if smart cities will help improve stakeholder access and inclusion and/or empower agencies or companies towards being a catalyst in a city's transformation [85].

4. Emerging transportation services in the Smart City context

TCPS has been used as the enabling platform for many emerging transportation services (e.g., smartphone app—based services, smart sensors—based services) which were not imagined before. In this section, a few major emerging transportation services are discussed.

4.1   Real-time winter road conditions

In much of the world, winter weather creates maintenance needs to keep transportation facilities in operation. Improving assessment of road conditions has long been a topic of interest for transportation agencies. First, agencies are interested in optimising their response, such as when and where to dispatch ploughs. Second, providing accurate real-time information to the travelling public is also important.

To make operational decisions about how to maintain roads during winter weather, transportation agencies and cities can rely on a variety of data sources. These sources can be categorised based on the type of information: existing conditions and forecasted conditions. Sources of existing conditions could include road weather information systems (RWIS), traffic camera images and reports from maintenance vehicles. RWIS have been deployed along road networks in many parts of the world. These systems usually collect several types of existing weather conditions information, such as air temperature, pavement temperature, precipitation, wind speed, etc. When agencies maintain these stations, they can provide valuable sources of information to support operations decisions and might also be useful to travellers as well. Although previous efforts have attempted to integrate RWIS between states and regions, opportunities exist in the context of Smart Cities. Weather sensors operated by different public agencies (DOTs and the National Weather Service) and private companies should be integrated to provide the best value to citizens.

Traffic cameras along road facilities can also capture key details about winter weather, such as existence of precipitation and coverage/clearance of a road. Unfortunately, reviewing camera images for operational purposes is not efficient when scaled to the number of traffic cameras in larger cities. The travelling public might find value in this source of information, if access is simple and available online.

Instrumented winter maintenance vehicles can also provide valuable real-time information about winter road conditions. Transportation agencies have studied different ways of collecting, processing and communicating winter weather information from vehicles. Some used multiple sensors, reporting that data transfer between field vehicles and databases was a common issue, but that operational systems could yield significant savings in salt use [86]. Other agencies have focused their road sensor efforts towards cameras [87]. The camera images provide value both to the operational managers and the travelling public. Continued research suggests that machine learning algorithms show much promise for reviewing road images and identifying/categorizing road surface conditions, such as snow covered or clear [88]. Similar advances could allow connected vehicles with dash cameras also to assist in these reporting efforts.

Transportation agencies also purchase weather forecasts from private companies. For example, the Illinois Department of Transportation purchased weather service from Schneider Electric in 2015 [89]. Because such arrangements usually preclude the sharing of forecasts with the public, these sources are strictly for internal use supporting operations decisions.

For current practices in winter weather road operations to mesh with the envisioned Smart Cities paradigm, several changes need to take place. Most notably, integration should take place between the variety of weather sensors operated by different agencies and companies. These include information static stations such as RWIS, mobile sensors on maintenance vehicles and forecasted information. These types of integration are already evident in some private sector apps. The Smart Cities applications discussed in this section should enhance the capability of both weather information service providers and those tasked with maintaining our transportation facilities during winter weather events. These enhancements are expected with more accurate reports of existing conditions and a richer network of weather sensors.

4.2   Smartphones and traveller information

Personal computing and communication devices are ubiquitous in today's world and show no signs of fading. These devices provide two primary uses for Smart Cities: information dissemination and data collection. Applications in these two areas are well developed but the roles of public and private participants are overlapping.

Recent research has found that smartphones have become so pervasive that they are shifting the needs of public transit riders. Although this shift suggests smartphone users are making better use of their transit ride time by working, studying or playing on their mobile devices; these activities have also increased the passenger demand for seating and tables [90].

Many smartphone users can already receive alerts based on their location, their preferences and the applications they install. Specific to traveller information, both private and public sector apps are available in many regions. For example, travellers in the Chicago metropolitan area could choose to use the Travel Midwest mobile app [91] or a variety of private sector apps such as Google Maps or Waze. Each collects traveller information from different sources and might have different recommendations.

Smartphones and other personal computing devices also play a valuable role in data collection. The most common application is using mobile phones to identify the travel time along a specific section of roadway. This application can be accomplished in a variety of ways. A mapping app could track the user's progress with cellular communication and use that information to update recommendations for upstream users. Roadside devices could detect the Wi-Fi or Bluetooth signals from travellers, identifying the device media access control addresses (MAC) and estimating the travel times. Although data are normally anonymised, travellers are not always aware of their role in the processes.

On the contrary, some travellers enroll to become participants in such data collection. For example, Waze allows users to input and/or confirm information such as roadway debris or stalled vehicles. Thus, travellers with smartphones can be both sensors and information consumers. Many cities already collect and disseminate notable amounts of traveller information. But for these efforts to truly be impactful transportation stakeholders should identify what is the public sector role in collecting and disseminating real-time traveller information for Smart Cities? This question has several parts.

- Should the public sector only collect road sensor information (e.g., travel times) and simply share it online? The accuracy of traveller information is important for the efficiency of our transportation networks. Public agencies have requirements to meet; for example, the accuracy, availability and timeliness requires of 23 CFR 511 in the United States. Although private companies are not required to meet these thresholds, they must provide information of adequate quality for their users.
- Should agencies abandon their installation and maintenance of freeway sensors and simply let the private sector provide such information from participating travellers and commercial vehicles? There are examples of each of these options from around the world, demonstrating that both options are feasible.
- Is it important that public agencies take the lead in recommending alternative routes during traffic incidents? When traffic incidents reduce the capacity of a roadway in an urban area, there are commonly many routes for traffic to choose instead. The difference would arise when public agencies suggest all diversion traffic use higher-capacity routes, but private apps might suggest some drivers use local roads through adjacent neighbourhoods. This difference identifies a policy constraint facing public agencies and illustrates that optimising the transportation network utilisation seldom requires all vehicles choose the same route.

Transportation engineers working on traveller information for Smart Cities should guide stakeholders towards answering these and other questions. Although a certain level of redundancy is beneficial, it is unclear how much and what types of information that the public sector should focus on.

4.3   Smart streetlights

Traditionally, smart streetlights refer to lights, which would make roadway sections or parking lots brighter by detecting a person/vehicle and/or dim after vehicles and people leave. The concept of smart streetlights has evolved. For instance, different companies have been experimenting with streetlight systems that are smart and efficient and could provide services such as music, sound and display features [92]. These systems can be used to disseminate emergency warnings (e.g., news on upcoming hurricane) or display important information (e.g., status of approaching signal through a connected display unit). Smart streetlights can reduce energy consumption significantly by demand-based utilisation of energy [93]. For example, LED streetlights in Texel, the Netherlands, are equipped with twilight wireless controller systems and capable of controlling lighting levels of streetlights. Through this system, Texel cut their lighting energy consumption by more than 60% and became the first Dutch municipality where public lighting is 100% energy neutral [94]. A networked LED streetlighting system can connect with emergency services such as 911 and could promote safer highways through video surveillance of pedestrian movements [95]. Some cities are implementing the concept of smart streetlights with diverse functions. For example, Shanghai, China, has installed 15 lamp posts fitted with touch screens and surveillance cameras. These streetlights are capable of providing free Wi-Fi, collecting traffic conditions and acting as a charging station for electric vehicles [96]. Moreover, every one of those 15 lamp posts is equipped with an emergency button, providing immediate access to the city's public services, including police and firefighters. In the case of any hazards (e.g., hurricane/cyclones), the system can broadcast emergency warnings to pedestrians, drivers and local residents.

4.4 Smart parking services

Vehicles looking for a parking spot in a downtown business district account for a significant portion of congestion. According to Shoup [97], the amount of vehicles that are cruising for parking account for almost 40% of total traffic volume. This additional traffic causes traffic congestion, wasted time and wasted energy in the form of fuel. For example, in Los Angles, California, searching for parking spots creates around 730 tons of CO_2, 95,000 lost work hours and wastes 47,000 gallons of gasoline annually [97]. Providing motorists timely information about available parking spaces could reduce congestion. There are various smart parking concepts that are deployed in many cities around the world. An overview of several of the prominent concepts is presented in following subsections.

4.4.1 CoPark approach

This smart parking system uses V2V and V2I communication to locate any unoccupied parking spaces within the shortest possible travel time. This decentralised system uses wireless communication among smart agents (e.g., smart Wi-Fi sensors) installed in a vehicle to inform others about any unoccupied parking space [98]. In this system, a roadside unit installed at the parking entrance informs and guides approaching vehicles to the nearest vacant parking spaces. Fig. 11.11 illustrates a sensor-based parking system that uses wireless communications to detect the presence of vehicles and send the information to a server. Other vehicles can communicate with the server to identify available/empty parking spaces and their locations.

Figure 11.11 Smart parking system using sensors [99].
From New Smart Parking by Libelium includes Double Radio with LoRaWAN and Sigfox, 2016. http://www.libelium.com/smart-parking-surface-sensor-lorawan-sigfox-lora-868-900-915-mhz/. (Accessed on 29.09.17), © Libelium Comunicaciones Distribuidas S.L. - http://www.libelium.com.

4.4.2   Park and ride approach

In the suburbs of San Francisco, California, Rockridge Bay Area Rapid Transit is the first smart park and ride system in the United States. In this smart parking system, anyone can park at strategically placed parking facilities and ride on a fixed route commuter bus or a train to reach their destinations. It typically provides real-time traffic information to users through message signs about vacancy of parking spaces in each lot, departure of the next bus or train and downstream traffic condition [100]. Based on the real-time parking and traffic congestion information, one can easily decide whether to use park and ride or drive their own vehicle.

4.4.3   Crowdsourcing-based approach

Crowd Park is a social networking application that allows individual drivers to book a parking space and prepay the parking fee. Using the sensors of a smartphone, it is possible to detect a driver's transportation mode, such as whether they are driving or walking [101]. If a transition pattern is identified, such as driving → stopped → walking, the system could conclude that the vehicle is parked. The application can also detect whether the traveller is walking towards the parking lot and inform others of a prediction that a parking spot could be available soon. Moreover, drivers can upload information at their own will to let other drivers know when their parking spot is going to be available again.

4.5   Smart intersections

The smart intersection concept is enabled by real-time communication between motor vehicles, public transport, traffic signals, emergency vehicles, cyclists and pedestrians for safe and efficient operation of multimodal conflicts at intersections [102]. As future CAV will communicate with each other with V2V and with traffic signal systems through V2I, legacy traffic control systems at intersections need to be modernised. In particular, upgrades should include capabilities to create an integrated vehicle intersection control system for effective intersection operation and management [103]. Important features of smart intersections include smart optimisation of signal phase and timing (SPaT) applications, information sharing with approaching vehicles about safe speed, eco-friendly signal operations, intersection safety warning and collision avoidance [104,105]. Though CAV technologies are mostly under development, many large cities have been demonstrating the idea of smart intersections to improve mobility performance. Pittsburgh, Pennsylvania, US, is one of the first cities implementing this smart intersection idea. A pilot project of 18 intersections at East Liberty and Shadyside, the smart traffic control system concept was implemented through the use of a intersection camera and radar detection system. Based on the approaching vehicle volume detection, the SPaT optimisation was conducted. It was found that corridor travel time was reduced by 24%, vehicle wait time was reduced by 42% and vehicle emissions were reduced by 21% [106] after the implementation of the smart intersection concept. Fig. 11.12 illustrates

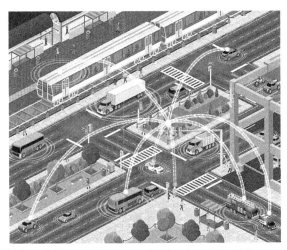

Figure 11.12 Vehicle-to-infrastructure communication in multimodal transportation systems [107].

V2I communication between traffic signal systems and different modes of transportation that enables this smart intersection concept.

5. Smart City developments around the world

In this section, few major Smart City deployments around the world including their key smart features are presented. These include London, England; Seoul, South Korea; and Singapore.

5.1 London, England

London, England, has made noteworthy efforts towards the Smart City concept. Strong leadership, combined with public involvement, has been the key to this success. Examples of these efforts include the London Dashboard, the London Datastore initiative, the Freight Electric Vehicles in Urban Europe (FREVUE) electric freight demonstrator project and the 2050 Infrastructure Plan. The London Dashboard provides a wealth of information about the city, with a notable emphasis on real-time transportation information. This includes Tube status, the current and forecasted bike availability, bus service status, open-source street maps and a variety of traffic cameras [108]; see Fig. 11.13.

Next, the London Datastore provides a data-sharing resource for public officials, citizens and businesses alike. Information includes transport performance data, school placement maps, house pricing information, forecasted growth scenarios, infrastructure mapping and a series of blogs. This abundance of available and useable data has led to the development of approximately 400 smartphone apps to further enhance

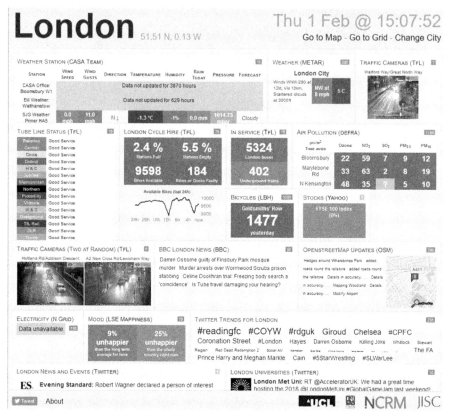

Figure 11.13 Example city dashboard, London, UK [108].

the public's use of this resource. The London Datastore was recognised with the Open Data Publisher Award in 2015 [109]. It is noteworthy that the live traffic camera pages were among the most popular on the site in the first year [110].

Like many urban centres, London suffers from poor air quality and high traffic congestion. In response, the FREVUE demonstrator project was implemented. A core concept in this project is to rethink how urban deliveries are made. Instead of individual shippers using diesel trucks to make deliveries throughout London, a 'consolidation centre model' was developed. This model establishes warehouses for urban deliveries to certain neighbourhoods. The deliveries are then consolidated and transported on the last leg of the journey using electric-powered trucks, reducing both truck traffic and emissions [111]. This and other efforts are part of *an Ultra Low Emission Vehicle Delivery Plan for London*. Part of this ambitious plan could require hybrid vehicles entering certain parts of the city, zero-emission zones, and to switch to all-electric power. This type of system might use vehicle GPS which would recognise their entrance into these areas using a concept called a geofence. Although these details are still being discussed, they show promise for continuing to address the urban air quality issues caused by gas-powered vehicles [112].

London's 2050 infrastructure plan recognises that providing quality transportation services is a priority to maintaining population growth near the city centre. The goals included reducing emissions, shifting mode choices and reducing fatal and serious crashes. Planning elements of this document include densifying land use and urban infill near the centre of the city. The infrastructure elements notably focus on shifting public travel towards more sustainable options. These include several public transport service improvements, increasing radial public transport capacity and transforming surface streets for walking, public transit and biking. Despite this emphasis on public transit, the plan does recommend upgrading some existing roads, adding a tolled circumferential route, constructing a second airport and acknowledging the need for rail freight to support London's appetite for goods [113]. The road investments total £4 billion over 10 years, including £200 million for the bus network [114].

5.2 Seoul, South Korea

South Korea has been pursuing Smart City concepts for some time. Songdo, South Korea, is considered as the world's first Smart City [115], built from the ground up with this concept in mind. Although the final results are still unclear, nearby Seoul has also made strides towards the goal of becoming a Smart City. They planned to reach their goal in three steps: building the Smart City infrastructure, providing Smart City services to citizens and travellers and continue advancing smart services from 2015 and beyond [116].

Services to the public now include free Wi-Fi at many public spaces, including subways trains, parks and government buildings. Approximately 10,000 free Wi-Fi locations were initially planned. To help low-income and vulnerable populations benefit from these services, plans were developed to distribute used mobile phones to 200,000 citizens per year. To improve access to city services, projects were started to make all administrative services accessible online and also available to mobile devices. These changes were also combined with a streamlining of reservation requests for city services, all to one location available online [117]. In addition, real-time monitoring of trash cans around the city helps prevent littering while optimising waste pickups [118].

To improve public safety and security, Seoul officials increased surveillance monitoring and implemented automated monitoring of the videos, which enabled all videos to be reviewed instead of only 30% (when done manually). There was also a notable focus on surveillance and monitoring for school safety [116].

More specific to transportation, Seoul has engrained Smart City concepts into virtually all modes of transportation. For example, an integrated public transit payment system allows travellers to use the same method for all transportation services in/around the city [119]. This change improves convenience for commuters and visitors alike. Next, the transportation operation and information service provide travellers with information about the city's transportation network. That could include real-time information about buses, subway, car sharing, biking and road traffic [120]. In addition, electric buses can charge their batteries while they drive across certain sections of the road [121]. Only time will tell if these initiatives improve the efficiency and quality of life in and around the city.

5.3 Singapore, Singapore

Singapore is a unique case because the government is striving for not just a Smart City but a smart nation. In addition, it is unique because of the overwhelming government ownership of housing, nearly 80% [122]. These two factors lead to many interesting challenges and opportunities for Smart City projects.

Singapore was named the smartest city in the world in 2016 by Juniper Research [114]. Advanced transportation played a significant role in earning this recognition. Reviewers coined Singapore as a 'world leader when we look at [the] transport network'. Many of their efforts included both infrastructure and mobility policies [123]. For example, the city has implemented mileage-based vehicle user fees, integrating a system of GPS to charge tolls based on more accurate distances. This system adds ease to the implementation of different toll rates, allowing congestion charging of private vehicles [122]. Singapore has also heavily invested in a network of sensors and communication systems for traffic signal optimisation and smart parking. These sensors inform traffic signals of approaching traffic demand and inform drivers of parking locations with available spaces. Together these systems have reduced congestion enough that travel speeds have improved significantly [114].

Best practices learnt from Singapore's implementations suggest using pilot projects before implementing anything citywide [122]. The city has implemented at least a dozen pilot projects [123]. One such project was testing a system that would detect potholes and rough roads using smartphones during bus rides [123]. Unfortunately, pilot projects can be costly, time-consuming and might only yield site-specific findings. To develop and test ideas faster and with less costs than in the real world, Singapore officials are making a digital model of the city called Virtual Singapore. This model will include real-time information about the population, the climate and much more. Although opponents of this project claim too much data and computing will be needed, the rewards of success could be great. When completed, Virtual Singapore can help city planners, engineers and decision makers select the most effective solutions and implement them faster than pilot projects and trial-and-error approaches [124].

Other findings from Singapore's efforts include the challenges of integrating multiple city agencies. Each collects different types of information at different intervals and with varying accuracy. To leverage these different resources, certain pieces of information should be integrated. Because different types of information require different levels of security, it is not reasonable that everything merges onto a single system. However, it is important to identify a common platform with which different applications and selected information can be merged [122]. As the technologies and policies implemented in Singapore continue to mature, researchers and planners will be interested in learning from this Smart City's journey.

5.4 Columbus, Ohio, USA

The city of Columbus, Ohio, is located in the Midwest of the United States. This city was included as an example of Smart City development because they were chosen as the winner of the USDOT's 2016 Smart City Challenge. The Challenge attracted applications from 78 cities throughout the United States and helped shape a picture of how Smart City concepts could address the urban mobility needs of midsized US cities. Common themes among these applications included the need to provide better first and last mile services for public transit riders; improving the movement of goods into and within cities; coordinating data collection between systems, agencies and market sectors; improving parking efficiency; reducing CO_2 emissions and optimising freeway and arterial traffic [125].

The proposed developments that were keys to the Columbus Smart Cities proposal were strong public—private relationships, accessibility and sustainability. The city of Columbus worked closely with private companies in their region and was able to transform the USDOT's $40 million award into a $140 million commitment. Companies such as Vulcan pledged support of this proposal with both funding and expertise. This demonstration of support for their proposed Smart Cities vision was surely one key to its success [126].

Another key element to the Columbus Smart Cities proposal was accessibility for all. Their plan targeted specific challenges to their region, including high infant mortality, limited access to jobs for the socially and economically disadvantaged and limited travel options for visitors. These challenges were addressed by improving mobility options, payment options and information access about those options. To access both healthcare and employment, the proposal included a connected transit line, Wi-Fi hotspots, first and last mile bike sharing and a notable improvement to traveller information [126].

Sustainability was also a focus area of the Columbus Smart City vision. The stakeholders were adept in recognising that transitioning their vehicle fleet towards electric power sources would not improve their carbon footprint without efforts to shift to renewable energy sources. Thus, their plans included decarbonising their power sources while simultaneously increasing the number of and information about available electric vehicle charging stations [126].

The journey towards the Columbus Smart City success did not start with the announcement of the USDOT's announcement. They were able to demonstrate how their city and surrounding region had already made great strides in addressing each of their goals [126]. For example, they were already recognised as one of the top 30 Greenest Local Governments by the US Environmental Protection Agency [127]. This recognition, and several others, helped demonstrate the city's dedication towards the goals proposed in their Smart City applications. In addition, the overwhelming support from local companies also provided evidence of broad support for their initiatives.

At the time of this writing, Columbus was issuing rebates for installing electric vehicle charging stations at apartment and condo complexes [128], installing solar power to support electric vehicles [129] and holding electric vehicle public outreach events [130]. Local companies also started some of their initiatives including a microtransit system serving employees of JPMorgan Chase [131]. As cities throughout the United States learn from the experience of Columbus, these and other initial deployments could accelerate deployment of Smart City ideas in the United States and abroad.

6. Future research directions

Though the deployment of Smart City concept is progressing, still a few major concerns and challenges need to be addressed with extensive research efforts. In this section, those future research directions are discussed.

6.1 Technology

To realise the anticipated benefits of Smart City, several technologies must come to maturity through continued research and development. These include DSRC devices, SPaT transmission systems and automated vehicle sensor processing.

There are a variety of wireless communication options available for vehicle manufacturers and transportation agencies to consider. These include 5.9 GHz DSRC, Wi-Fi, Bluetooth, RFID systems, cellular communication systems and worldwide interoperability for Microwave Access. Although many of these are well established and commercially available, they might not have low enough latency to meet the safety needs of automated or connected vehicle applications. DSRC appears to meet the latency requirements [132], but there are limitations requiring availability of clear line of sight [133]. Future research should continue identifying best practices for using this communication platform.

Another key area for future research is the dissemination of traffic SPaT information. Traffic signals control an overwhelming proportion of intersections within cities. Many have studied congestion and safety improvements when SPaT information is available to drivers and vehicles, but future research is needed to address implementation issues. For example, many transportation agencies have limited funding to maintain their existing signals, so installing SPaT communication devices is a low priority. Future research could identify best practices in funding, design, installation and maintaining SPaT communication devices.

Last, future research should continue investigating ways to make automated vehicles safer for the public. It is noteworthy that several automated vehicle designers have demonstrated their prototypes on a variety of roads under different conditions; however, crashes such as the 2016 Tesla crash [134] have also illustrated the need for further efforts. In particular, it is essential that drivers have a better understanding of their responsibilities during automated driving.

6.2 Interdependency

Different systems in a Smart City environment rely on the integration of modern technologies to provide efficient services to enhance the quality of citizens' lives. Implementation of a Smart City ecosystem consists mainly of changes to the transportation system. This system includes CAV, deployment of smart parking systems, execution of smart streetlight systems and other Smart City services. These systems are largely dependent on smooth integration with communication and data analytics infrastructure and developing interdependencies between system components and between systems. With the increase in interdependencies, interoperability issues could arise because of the inability of legacy infrastructure to interconnect with modern technologies. Smart City design and deployment must address these issues and reduce failure risk due to complex system interdependency [135]. Security risks for communication infrastructure, such as phishing, data falsification and spoofing, could compromise the quality of Smart City services and users' privacy. Such events could even shut down the whole system [136]. For example, Equifax, one of the three major consumer credit reporting agencies in the United States, had become a victim of a cyberattack that potentially compromised sensitive information of 143 million American citizens. Hence, ensuring cybersecurity of a cloud database will remain a major challenge in the future. In many cases, embedded software in Smart City infrastructure (e.g., car devices, medical devices, traffic control devices) can make them susceptible to hacking [137]. However, developing a comprehensive Smart City architecture considering interdependency is a major challenge [138].

6.3 Resiliency of interconnected systems

Natural disasters and man-made disasters have been testing resilience characteristics of modern transportation system and other Smart City systems. With the deployment of modern technologies and their performance during extreme weather events, modelling and study of smart systems' resilience characteristics have become more critical. According to Bruneau et al. [139], resiliency of a system is defined with the following three features. (1) failure probabilities, (2) consequences of failures and (3) recovery time. As the interdependencies between various smarty city components are becoming more complex, this resiliency feature has become more consequential. Recognising the importance of resiliency, the Fixing America's Surface Transportation Act required transportation planning organisations to consider resiliency in the planning process [140]. Many other governments around the world are taking similar initiatives to address the resiliency issues of critical infrastructure systems such as the Joint United States−Canada Electric Grid Security and Resilience Strategy [141]. However, there are several major research challenges on resilience modelling of complex and coupled CPS of smart infrastructure systems [142]. Most of the times, natural/man-made hazards cause immediate impacts (e.g., deaths, loss of property) and less frequently cause long-term system failure (e.g., loss of power, scarcity of drinking water, healthcare degradation). For example, because of hurricane Sandy in 2012, more than 8.5 million people lost power in 21 states [143], degraded the air and water quality [144], which led to public health risks. In future Smart City deployments, every system (e.g., transportation system) will be connected to one or more other systems (e.g., energy, infrastructure) through core communication infrastructure and CPS technologies. Eventually, failure of one system can lead to stress and even failure of other systems. Hence, the study of resiliency in the Smart City context is a great challenge ahead for researchers.

6.4   Workforce development

Perhaps today's college students are training for careers that do not yet exist. That adage might hold true for careers supporting tomorrow's Smart Cities. Some suggest best practices including mentoring young leaders with a combination of teachers and working professionals, as well as including activities in and out of the classroom [145]. Based on the Smart City case studies to date, future workforces will likely need a blend of hard and soft skills. For example, hard skills might include using GIS data, applying quantitative analysis methods, using simulation software or communications systems analysis. Soft skills might include communicating with a various stakeholders using different face-to-face and digital methods, applying urban planning theories and considering impacts of Smart City policy options. To address these needs, some are starting to offer a graduate degree in this exciting area, the University College of London among the first [146].

7.   Conclusions

Major innovations in the CPS domain have been transforming Smart Cities through numerous emerging smart services to citizens. Recognising the potential of CPS-supported Smart City infrastructure and services, both public and private entities have been partnering to experiment and deploy many Smart City applications. In this chapter, the authors reviewed diverse aspects of the Smart City paradigm, including basic characteristics, enabling technologies and emerging technologies. One key challenge facing future implementations of Smart City concepts is development of reliable communication technologies and data analytics platforms that could process massive heterogeneous sensor data in real time and provide intelligence to diverse stakeholders to initiate action that achieve higher efficiency from limited resources. As cybersecurity is a major concern in ever increasingly connected Smart Cities, development of reliable security solutions is critical. Another big challenge is resilience against disruptive events such as natural disasters. A resilient Smart City vision can be achieved by developing management strategies and technological solutions that focus on resiliency against climate changes, transportation system resiliency, energy system resiliency and communication and analytics system resiliency. To achieve maximum benefits from Smart City applications, they must be designed with a variety of considerations and include guidance from a wide range of stakeholders.

Exercises

1. Investigate the urban centres in your region to find if any have a city dashboard? If not, choose London, England's. Describe five ways you could use this tool for research that could improve the city.

2. Investigate your nearest city with more than one million in population (whole metropolitan area). Report on and discuss the following:
   a. What types of air pollutants are measured?
   b. What actions have been taken?
   c. Have these actions led to any improvements?
   d. What future plans do you recommend?
3. Visit your local transit agency's website and choose a bus route that appears to be important to the overall system. If you were tasked with organising a stakeholder meeting to integrate transit and road congestion along that corridor, identify which agencies you would invite. For each agency, list the types of information or questions you would like to learn about.
4. Investigate how road operation information is relayed to the public in your area.
   a. What types of real-time information are available?
   b. How is it relayed to the public?
   c. How recently was it updated?
   d. Is winter weather a recurring concern in your area?
5. Visit a popular transit stop and collect information from waiting passengers.
   a. Is real-time information available about when the next bus arrives? If so, how is the information available? What sensors are used to predict bus positions?
   b. What proportions are multitasking while they wait?
   c. Does the transit agency offer an app for smartphones? If so, does that app track the location of passengers while using it?
6. Choose a Smart City discussed in Section 5 and investigate the most recent developments. Write a half- to one-page summary of what you find about transportation improvements or projects in that city. Be sure to include results, if reported.
7. Find a journal article or conference proceeding related to SPaT information. Read the article and provide a one-page summary. In your summary, be sure to include the methods used and the key findings and recommendations made.
8. What courses have you taken or plan to take, that could prepare you for a career supporting Smart City development?
9. Identify a Smart City CPS in any nearby city and identify the key features of that CPS. Discuss the ways to improve the performance of that system.
10. Explain resiliency of Smart City infrastructure using the impacts of the Hurricane Harvey in 2017 in Houston, Texas, as a case study.
11. What are the major challenges the world is facing in terms of developing resilient infrastructure?
12. Identify a smart infrastructure project deployed in any major city and draw a system architecture showing its various components, interconnections and key technical features.
13. Find a journal article related to one or multiple applications of smart transportation systems and summarise the paper including your thoughts on the methods and limitation of the research.

References

[1] R.K.R. Kummitha, N. Crutzen, How do we understand smart cities-an evolutionary perspective, Cities: The International Journal of Urban Policy and Planning 67 (2017) 43—52.

[2] S.P. Mohanty, U. Choppali, E. Kougianos, Everything you wanted to know about smart cities: the internet of things is the backbone, IEEE Consumer Electronics Magazine 5 (3) (2016) 60−70.

[3] S.B. Letaifa, How to strategize smart cities: revealing the SMART model, Journal of Business Research 68 (7) (2015) 1414−1419.

[4] C. Colldahl, S. Frey, J. Kelemen, Smart Cities: Strategic Sustainable Development for an Urban World, School of Engineering, Blekinge Institute of Technology, 2013 (M.Sc. thesis).

[5] Smart City Challenge, U.S. Department of Transportation, 2017. https://www.transportation.gov/smartcity. (Accessed on 18/04/2018).

[6] FHWA, Integrated Corridor Management and the Smart Cities Revolution: Leveraging Synergies, 2017. https://ops.fhwa.dot.gov/publications/fhwahop16075/ch2.htm. (Accessed on 18/04/2018).

[7] W. Guo, Z. Wang, W. Wang, H. Bubb, Traffic incident automatic detection algorithms by using loop detector in urban roads 8 (1) (2015) 41−48.

[8] L.E.Y. Mimbela, L.A. Klein, P. Kent, J.L. Hamrick, K.M. Luces, S. Herrera, Summary of Vehicle Detection and Surveillance Technologies Used in Intelligent Transportation Systems, The Vehicle Detector Clearinghouse, FHWA, 2007 (Technical Report).

[9] ITS JPO, DSRC: The Future of Safer Driving. https://www.its.dot.gov/factsheets/dsrc_factsheet.htm. (Accessed on 18/04/2018).

[10] S. Taranovich, Autonomous Automotive Sensors: How Processor Algorithms Get Their Inputs, 2016, in: https://www.edn.com/design/analog/4442319/Autonomous-automotive-sensors−How-processor-algorithms-get-their-inputs. (Accessed on 18/04/2018).

[11] C. Hoberman, C. Schwitter, Adaptive Structures: Building for Performance and Sustainability, 2008. https://www.di.net/articles/adaptive-structures-building-for-performance-and-sustainability/. (Accessed on 18/04/2018).

[12] Gamma Lighting Control. https://w3.usa.siemens.com/buildingtechnologies/us/en/building-automation-and-energy-management/siemensgamma/pages/siemensgamma.aspx?sp_source=usbt100214. (Accessed on 18/04/2018).

[13] Residential Application. http://www.lutron.com/en-US/Residential-CommercialSolutions/Pages/Residential-Solutions/Residential-App/ResidentialApplications.aspx. (Accessed on 18/04/2018).

[14] Smart Grid Sensor, 2011. http://internetofthingsagenda.techtarget.com/definition/smart-grid-sensor. (Accessed on 18/04/2018).

[15] D. Cardwell, Grid Sensors Could Ease Disruptions of Power, 2015. https://www.nytimes.com/2015/02/04/Business/energy-environment/smart-sensors-for-power-grid-could-ease-disruptions.html?mcubz=3. (Accessed on 18/04/2018).

[16] P.J. Khuan, Managing the Water Distribution Network with a Smart Water Grid, Public Utilities Board Singapore, 2016.

[17] B.N. Silva, M. Khan, K. Han, Big data analytics embedded smart city architecture for performance enhancement through real-time data processing and decision-making, in: Wireless Communications and Mobile Computing, 2017.

[18] Movement Analytics Key to Unlocking Big Data Revenue for Mobile Operators, 2016. http://inrix.com/press-releases/movement-analytics-key-unlocking-big-data-revenue-mobile-operators/. (Accessed on 18/04/2018).

[19] Amazon Web Services. https://aws.amazon.com/. (Accessed on 18/04/2018).

[20] Microsoft Azure. https://azure.microsoft.com/en-us/?v=17.34c. (Accessed on 18/04/2018).

[21] F. Idachaba, D.U. Ike, O. Hope, Future trends in fiber optics communication, in: Proceedings of the World Congress on Engineering, Volume: 1, London, U.K, 2014.

[22] K. Robinson, Wi-Fi and the Rise of Smart Cities, 2015. https://www.wi-fi.org/beacon/kevin-robinson/wi-fi-and-the-rise-of-smart-cities. (Accessed on 18/04/2018).

[23] A. Brydon, Opportunities and Threats from LTE Device-to-Device (D2D) Communication, 2014. http://www.unwiredinsight.com/2014/lte-d2d. (Accessed on 18/04/2018).

[24] Z. Xu, X. Li, X. Zhao, M.H. Zhang, Z. Wang, DSRC versus 4G-LTE for connected vehicle applications: a study on field experiments of vehicular communication performance, Journal of Advanced Transportation 2017 (2017), https://doi.org/10.1155/2017/2750452. Article ID 2750452, 10 pages.

[25] H.J. Miller, S.-L. Shaw, Geographic Information Systems for Transportation: Principles and Applications, Oxford University Press, 2001.

[26] N. Massa, Fiber optic telecommunication, in: Fundamentals of Photonics, 2000. Module 1.8.

[27] The Evolution of Mobile Technologies, Qualcomm, 2014 (Technical Report).

[28] Standard Specification for Telecommunication and Information Exchange between Roadside and Vehicle Systems-5 GHz Band Dedicated Short Range Communications (DSRC) Medium Access Control (MAC) and Physical Layer Specifications, 2010. https://compass.astm.org/EDIT/html_annot.cgi?E2213+03(2010). (Accessed on 18/04/2018).

[29] R. Bera, J. Bera, S. Sil, S. Dogra, N.B. Sinha, D. Mondal, Dedicated Short Range Communications (DSRC) for Intelligent Transport System, IEEE, 2006.

[30] IEEE 802.11 Wi-Fi Standards. http://www.radio-electronics.com/info/wireless/wi-fi/ieee-802-11-standards-tutorial.php. (Accessed on 18/04/2018).

[31] B. Mitchell, The Range of a Typical Wi-Fi Network, 2017. https://www.lifewire.com/range-of-typical-wifi-network-816564. (Accessed on 18/04/2018).

[32] A. Zaidi, Developing MMWAVE Mobile Radio Interface, 2017. https://www.ericsson.com/research-blog/developing-mmwave-mobile-radio-interface/. (Accessed on 18/04/2018).

[33] R.N. Mitra, D.P. Agrawal, 5G mobile technology: a survey, ICT Express 1 (3) (2015) 132—137.

[34] M. Agiwal, A. Roy, N. Saxena, Next generation 5G wireless networks: a comprehensive survey, IEEE Communications Surveys and Tutorials 18 (3) (2016) 1617—1655.

[35] P. Poppvski, Ultra-reliable communication in 5G wireless systems, in: 1st International Conference on 5G for Ubiquitous Connectivity (5GU), Levi, Finland, 2014.

[36] S. Popper, S. Bankes, R. Callaway, D. DeLaurentis, System-of-Systems Symposium: Report on a Summer Conversation, Potomac Institute for Policy Studies, 2004. Arlington, VA.

[37] M.A. Javed, E.B. Hamida, W. Znaidi, Security in intelligent transport systems for smart cities: from theory to practice, Sensors 16 (6) (2016).

[38] Consumer Reports, Cars with Advanced Safety Systems, 2017. https://www.consumerreports.org/car-safety/cars-with-advanced-safety-systems/. (Accessed on 18/04/2018).

[39] A. Ahdoot, How Big Data Drives Tesla, 2016. https://www.colocationamerica.com/blog/how-big-data-drives-tesla. (Accessed on 18/04/2018).

[40] BMW Launches Digital Mobility Experience Based on the Open Mobility Cloud Using Microsoft Azure, 2016. https://blogs.microsoft.com/transform/2016/03/31/bmw-launches-new-digital-mobility-experience-based-on-the-open-mobility-cloud-using-microsoft-azure/. (Accessed on 18/04/2018).

[41] BMW Connected Drive. https://www.bmw.com/en/topics/fascination-bmw/connected-drive/Connected.html. (Accessed on 18/04/2018).

[42] NHTSA, Automated Vehicles for Safety. https://www.nhtsa.gov/technology-innovation/automated-vehicles#issue-overview. (Accessed on 18/04/2018).

[43] M.N. Hasan, S.M.D.A. Alam, S.R. Huq, Intelligent car control for a smart car, International Journal of Computer Applications 14 (3) (2011).

[44] https://www.pcb.its.dot.gov/eprimer/module8.aspx#fn10. (Accessed on 18/04/2018).

[45] R. Lea, Smart Cities: An Overview of the Technology Trends Driving Smart Cities (Technical Report), IEEE, 2017.

[46] K. AshokKumar, B. Sam, R. Arshadprabhu, Britto, Cloud based intelligent transport system, Procedia Computer Science 50 (2015) 58−63.

[47] BMW Compatible Apps. https://www.bmw.com/en/topics/offers-and-services/bmw-compatible-app/mobility-and-services.html. (Accessed on 18/04/2018).

[48] Concept of Operations: For the Next Generation Air Transportation System, Joint Planning and Development Office, 2011.

[49] Next Generation Air Transportation System, Joint Planning and Development Office, 2014.

[50] M. Ford, Can a 'Smart Grid' Turn Us on to Energy Efficiency?, 2009. http://www.cnn.com/2009/TECH/03/01/eco.smartgrid/. (Accessed on 18/04/2018).

[51] The New Core of the Energy System, 2016. https://www.siemens.com/customer-magazine/en/home/energy/renewable-energy/the-new-core-of-the-energy-system.html. (Accessed on 18/04/2018).

[52] Solar Power to the People. https://partneredcontent.time.com/siemens/intelligent-energy-equation/economy/economy-spotlight1. (Accessed on 18/04/2018).

[53] Monthly Energy Review, U.S. Energy Information Administration, September 2017. https://www.eia.gov/totalenergy/Data/monthly/pdf/mer.pdf. (Accessed on 18/04/2018).

[54] A. Asthana, M. Taylor, Britain to Ban Sale of All Diesel and Petrol Cars and Vans from 2040, 2017. https://www.theguardian.com/politics/2017/jul/25/britain-to-ban-sale-of-all-diesel-and-petrol-cars-and-vans-from-2040. (Accessed on 18/04/2018).

[55] M. Brown, 3 Types of Solar Street Light Systems, 2014. http://www.genproenergy.com/genpro-energy-blog/3-types-of-solar-streetlight-systems.html. (Accessed on 18/04/2018).

[56] L.M.E. Smith, London Street Lamps Are Being Turned into Electric Car Charging Points, 2017. http://www.independent.co.uk/environment/london-street-lamps-electric-car-charging-points-ubitricity-tech-firm-hounslow-council-richmond-a7809126.html. (Accessed on 18/04/2018).

[57] A. Burger, Oncor Launches Paradigm-Breaking Microgrid in Texas, Renewable Energy World, 2015. http://www.renewableenergyworld.com/articles/2015/04/oncor-launches-paradigm-breaking-microgrid-in-texas.html. (Accessed on 18/04/2018).

[58] W. Wang, Z. Lu, Cyber security in the smart grid: survey and challenges, Computer Networks 57 (5) (2013) 1344−1371.

[59] D. Washburn, U. Sindhu, Helping CIUs Understand "Smart Cities" Initiatives, Forrester, 2010.

[60] R. Fries, M.A. Chowdhury, A. Dunning, Transportation security framework for a medium-sized city, European Journal of Transport and Infrastructure Research 8 (2008) 1−16.

[61] Hitachi Data Systems, Can Smart Cities Also Be Safer Cities?, 2015. https://www.hitachivantara.com/en-us/pdf/white-paper/hds-public-safety-whitepaper.pdf. (Accessed on 18/04/2018).

[62] J.H. Lee, M.G. Hancock, M.C. Hu, Towards an effective framework for building smart cities: lessons from Seoul and San Francisco, Technological Forecasting and Social Change 89 (2014) 80—99.

[63] A.S. Elmaghraby, M.M. Losavio, Cyber security challenges in smart cities: safety, security, and privacy, Journal of Advanced Research 5 (2014) 491—497.

[64] D. Peeples, Big News for Cities: First Responders to Get the Tools They Need to Save More Lives, 2017. http://smartcitiescouncil.com/article/big-news-cities-first-responders-get-tools-they-need-save-more-lives. (Accessed on 18/04/2018).

[65] M. Hamblen, Smart Cities: In Atlanta, Smart City Plans Aim for Safety, Computer World, 2016.

[66] Harmonised ECall European Deployment, 2017. https://iheero.eu/. (Accessed on 18/04/2018).

[67] M. Vitali, B. Pernici, Interconnecting processes through IoT in a health-care scenario, in: IEEE International Smart Cities Conference (ISC2), 2016.

[68] G.D. Vecchia, L. Gallo, M. Espasito, A. Coronato, An infrastructure for smart hospitals, Multimedia Tools and Applications 59 (1) (2012) 341—362.

[69] H. Demirkan, A smart healthcare systems framework, IT Professional 15 (5) (2013) 38—45.

[70] L.L. Tupper, M.A. Chowdhury, L. Klotz, R.N. Fries, Measuring sustainability: how traffic incident management through intelligent transportation systems has greater energy and environmental benefits than common construction-phase strategies for "Green" roadways, International Journal of Sustainable Transportation 6 (2012) 282—297.

[71] The Environmental Industries Commission, Getting the Green Light: Will Smart Technology Clean up City Environments? Environmental Industries Commission, London, 2015.

[72] L. Rayle, S. Shaheen, N. Chan, D. Dai, R. Cervero, App-based, On-Demand Ride Services: Comparing Taxi and Ridersources Trips and User Characteristics in San Francisco, University of California Transportation Center (UCTC), 2014.

[73] US Geological Survey, USGS Current Water Data for Missouri, 2017. https://waterdata.usgs.gov/mo/nwis/rt. (Accessed on 18/04/2018).

[74] One Country Two Lungs, Senseable City lab, 2017. http://senseable.mit.edu/twolungs/. (Accessed on 18/04/2018).

[75] Breath Easy. http://cs.everyaware.eu/event/airprobe. (Accessed on 18/04/2018).

[76] Mauritius Ministry of Environment, Sustainable Development, and Disaster and Beach Management, Environmental Guideline for Smart Cities. Mauritius, 2015.

[77] American Society of Civil Engineers, (n.d.), Envision. http://www.asce.org/envision/. (Accessed on 18/04/2018).

[78] BSI, PAS 181 Smart City Framework, 2014. https://www.bsigroup.com/en-GB/smart-cities/Smart-Cities-Standards-and-Publication/PAS-181-smart-cities-framework/. (Accessed on 18/04/2018).

[79] Intelligent Infrastructure: How to Make a Smart Building More Profitable, 2016. https://www.siemens.com/content/dam/internet/siemens-com/us/home/company/topic-areas/intelligent-infrastructure/buildings/documents/bt-cpp-intel-infrstrrctr-wp.pdf. (Accessed on 18/04/2018).

[80] AIS Swytchglas-Smart Glass. https://www.aisglass.com/swytchglas. (Accessed on 18/04/2018).

[81] Our Future Depends on Intelligent Infrastructures. https://www.siemens.com/digitalization/public/Pdf/siemens-intelligent-infrastructure.pdf. (Accessed on 18/04/2018).

[82] O. Martyusheva, Smart Water Grid, Department of Civil and Environmental Engineering, Colorado State University, 2014 (Technical Report).

[83] Booz and Company, Reinventing the City, 2010 (WWF Report), http://assets.panda.org/downloads/wwf_reinventing_the_city_final_3_low_resolution.pdf. (Accessed on 18/04/2018).

[84] Market Place of the European Innovation Partnership on Smart Cities and Communities, 2016. https://eu-smartcities.eu/. (Accessed on 18/04/2018).

[85] M.P. Rodriguez-Bolivar, Transforming City Governments for Successful Smart Cities, Springer, 2015.

[86] B. McCullough, M. Leung, W. Kang, Automated Vehicle Location (AVL) for Road Condition Reporting, Indiana Department of Transportation, Indianapolis, 2009.

[87] Iowa Department of Transportation, Plow Cams Now Online for All to See, 2014. http://www.news.iowadot.gov/newsandinfo/2014/02/plow-cams-now-online-for-all-to-see-iatraffic.html. (Accessed on 18/04/2018).

[88] Linton, Fu, A connected vehicle solution for winter road surface condition monitoring, in: Transportation Research Board Annual Meeting and Conference, National Academies, Washington, D.C., 2016.

[89] R.N. Fries, A. Fadoul, M.T. Niloy, V. Vyas, M. Atiquzzaman, Real-T2ime Information Dissemination Requirements for Illinois Per New Federal Rule: Project Extension (Phase II), Illinois Center for Transportation, Rantoul, 2016.

[90] T.E. Julsrud, J.M. Denstadli, Smartphones, travel time-use, and attitudes to public transport services. Insights from an explorative study of urban dwellers in two Norwegian cities, International Journal of Sustainable Transportation 11 (8) (2017) 602−610.

[91] Gateway Traveler Information System, (n.d.). from Travel Midwest.com, http://www.travelmidwest.com/lmiga/announcements.jsp?type=siteNews. (Accessed on 18/04/2018).

[92] D. Duggan, A light that's bright: illuminating concepts develops system of "smart" streetlights, Crain's Detroit Business 26 (1) (2010).

[93] A. Kovacs, R. Batai, B.C. Csaji, P. Dudas, B. Hay, G. Pedone, T. Revesz, J. Vancza, Intelligent control for energy-positive street lighting, Energy 114 (2016) 40−51.

[94] Starry Nights on Texel: Through Intelligent Lighting to Energy Neutrality, 2017. https://www.tvilight.com/2017/02/10/starry-nights-on-texel/. (Accessed on 18/04/2018).

[95] D. Jin, C. Hannon, Z. Li, P. Cortes, S. Ramaraju, P. Burgess, N. Buch, M. Shahidehpour, Smart street lighting system: a platform for innovative smart city applications and a new frontier for cyber-security, The Electricity Journal 29 (10) (2016) 28−35.

[96] World's Best City Projects for Smart Street Lights, 2017. https://cityos.io/Worlds-Best-City-Projects-for-Smart-Street-Lights. (Accessed on 18/04/2018).

[97] D.C. Shoup, Cruising for parking, Transport Policy 13 (2006) 479−486.

[98] A. Aliedani, S.W. Loke, A. Desai, P. Desai, Investigating vehicle-to-vehicle communication for cooperative car parking: the co-park approach, in: IEEE International Smart Cities Conference (ISC2), 2016.

[99] New Smart Parking by Libelium Includes Double Radio with LoRaWAN and Sigfox, 2016. http://www.libelium.com/smart-parking-surface-sensor-lorawan-sigfox-lora-868-900-915-mhz/. (Accessed on 18/04/2018).

[100] C.J. Rodier, S.A. Shaheen, Transit-based smart parking: an evaluation of the San Francisco bay area field test, Transportation Research Part C: Emerging Technologies 18 (2) (2010) 225−233.

[101] K.C. Lan, W.Y. Shih, An intelligent driver location system for smart parking, Expert Systems with Applications 41 (5) (2014) 2443−2456.

[102] Smart Intersection. http://urban-online.org/en/networked-traffic-system/smart-intersection/index.html. (Accessed on 18/04/2018).

[103] J. Lee, B. Park, Development and evaluation of a cooperative vehicle intersection control algorithm under the connected vehicles environment, IEEE 13 (01) (2012) 81–90.

[104] C.H. Cho, H. Su, Y.H. Chu, W.Y. Chang, F.C. Tsai, Smart Moving: A SPaT Advanced Driving Assistance System, Network and Operations Management, 2012.

[105] Service Package. http://local.iteris.com/arc-it/html/servicepackages/servicepackages-areaspsort.html. (Accessed on 18/04/2018).

[106] Pittsburgh Expands 'Smart' Traffic Signal Network. http://www.traffictechnologytoday.com/news.php?NewsID=58709. (Accessed on 18/04/2018).

[107] Vehicle-to-Infrastructure (V2I) Resources. https://www.its.dot.gov/v2i/. (Accessed on 18/04/2018).

[108] City Dashboard, London. http://citydashboard.org/london/. (Accessed on 18/04/2018).

[109] London Datastore, Greater London Authority, 2017 [Online], London.gov, https://www.london.gov.uk/what-we-do/business-and-economy/science-and-technology/smart-london/london-datastore-smart-london. (Accessed on 18/04/2018).

[110] Datastore 1st Birthday, London Datastore, 2017 [Online], https://data.london.gov.uk/datastore-1st-birthday/. (Accessed on 18/04/2018).

[111] London. FREVUE, [Online]. [Cited: 9 20, 2017.] https://frevue.eu/cities/london/. (Accessed on 18/04/2018).

[112] Mayor London and Transport for London, An Ultra Low Emission Vehicle Delivery Plan for London. London, 2015.

[113] Mayor of London, London Infrastructure Plan 2050. London, 2015.

[114] B. Buntz, The World's 5 Smartest Cities, Internet of Things Institute, 18 May 2016 [Online], http://www.ioti.com/smart-cities/world-s-5-smartest-cities. (Accessed on 18/04/2018).

[115] M.T. Bilotta, Songdo, South Korea: the world's first smart city - in pictures, The Guiardian (December 22 2014) [Online], https://www.theguardian.com/cities/2014/dec/22/songdo-south-korea-world-first-smart-city-in-pictures. (Accessed on 18/04/2018).

[116] Smart Seoul, Basic Strategic Plan for Information of Seoul Metropolitan City, 2015.

[117] ITU-T, Smart Cities Seoul: A Case Study, 2013.

[118] Ecube Labs, Case Study: City of Seoul, Smart Cities Council. [Online]. [Cited: 9 20, 2017.] http://smartcitiescouncil.com/resources/case-study-city-seoul. (Accessed on 18/04/2018).

[119] M.J. Rowley, Smart City Seoul, Cisco Newsroom, January 14 2014 [Online], https://newsroom.cisco.com/feature-content?articleId=1309662. (Accessed on 18/04/2018).

[120] TOPIS, Seoul Topis, 2014 [Online], http://topis.seoul.go.kr/eng/english.jsp. (Accessed on 18/04/2018).

[121] R. van Hooijdonk, 6 of the Smartest Smart Cities in the World, March 10 2017 [Online], https://www.richardvanhooijdonk.com/en/6-smartest-smart-cities-world/. (Accessed on 18/04/2018).

[122] S.K. Lee, H.R. Kwon, H. Cho, J. Kim, D. Lee, International Case Studies of Smart Cities, Inter-American Development Bank, Singapore, Republic of Singapore, 2016.

[123] J.M. Watts, N. Purnell, Singapore is taking the 'smart city' to a whole new level, Wall Street Journal 24 (2016).

[124] K. Ebi, Singapore at 50: City Grows up, Reinvents Itself, Smart Cities Council, August 5 2015 [Online], http://smartcitiescouncil.com/article/singapore-50-city-grows-reinvents-itself. (Accessed on 18/04/2018).

[125] US Department of Transportation, Smart City Challenge: Lessons Learned, 2016. https://www.transportation.gov/policy-initiatives/smartcity/smart-city-challenge-lessons-building-cities-future. (Accessed on 18/04/2018).

[126] City of Columbus, Beyond Traffic: Smart Cities Challenge Phase 2, 2016 (Technical Application), https://www.transportation.gov/policy-initiatives/smartcity/smart-city-challenge-columbus-oh-final-application. (Accessed on 18/04/2018).

[127] City of Columbus, Columbus Ranks No. 13 on EPA's Top 30 Local Government List of Green Power Users, 2015. https://www.columbus.gov/Templates/Detail.aspx?id=76855. (Accessed on 18/04/2018).

[128] J. Fening, Smart Columbus Offering $170,000 in Rebate Funding for Electric Vehicle Charging Stations for Apartment and Condominiums, 2017. https://www.columbus.gov/WorkArea/DownloadAsset.aspx?id=2147498403. (Accessed on 18/04/2018).

[129] City of Columbus, Smart Columbus Deploys Over $3.6 Million Worth of Mobile Solar Technology, 2017. https://www.columbus.gov/Templates/Detail.aspx?id=2147498725. (Accessed on 18/04/2018).

[130] J. Fening, Smart Columbus Launches Ride and Drive Roadshow to Encourage Columbus Commuters to Drive Electric and Drive Less, 2017. https://www.columbus.gov/WorkArea/DownloadAsset.aspx?id=2147499767. (Accessed on 18/04/2018).

[131] City of Columbus, Chariot and JPMorgan Chase Team up to Ease Employee Commutes as Part of Smart Columbus Initiative, 2017. https://www.columbus.gov/WorkArea/DownloadAsset.aspx?id=2147501441. (Accessed on 18/04/2018).

[132] F. Perry, K. Raboy, Z. Huang, D. van Duren, Dedicated Short Range Communications Roadside Unit Specifications, FHWA, Washington, 2016.

[133] R. Robinson, F. Dion, Multipath Signal Phase and Timing Broadcast Project, Michigan Department of Transportation, 2013.

[134] W. Knight, Tesla crash will shape the future of automated cars, MIT Technology Review 7 (1) (2016).

[135] ITS JPO, Interoperability. https://www.its.dot.gov/research_areas/interoperability.htm. (Accessed on 18/04/2018).

[136] A. Aldairi, L. Tawalbeh, Cyber security attack on smart cities and associated mobile technologies, Procedia Computer Science 109 (2017) 1086–1091.

[137] Privacy Implications of the Internet of Things. http://resources.infosecinstitute.com/privacy-implications-internet-things/. (Accessed on 18/04/2018).

[138] M. Quyang, Review on modeling and simulation of interdependent critical infrastructure systems, Reliability Engineering and System Safety 121 (2014) 43–60.

[139] M. Bruneau, S.E. Chang, R.T. Eguchi, G.C. Lee, T.D. O' Rourke, A.M. Reinhorn, M. Shinozuka, K. Tierney, W.A. Wallace, D. von Winterfeldt, A framework to quantitatively assess and enhance the seismic resilience of communities, Earthquake Spectra 19 (4) (2003) 733–752.

[140] FHWA, Fixing America's Surface Transportation Act, 2017. https://www.fhwa.dot.gov/fastact/. (Accessed on 18/04/2018).

[141] Governments of the United States and Canada, Joint United States-Canada Electric Grid Security and Resilience Strategy, 2016 (Technical Report).

[142] S. Hosseini, K. Barker, J.E.R. Marquez, A review of definitions and measures of system resilience, Reliability Engineering and System Safety 145 (2016) 47–61.

[143] Responding to Hurricane Sandy: DOE Situation Report, 2012. https://energy.gov/articles/responding-hurricane-sandy-doe-situation-reports. (Accessed on 18/04/2018).

[144] The Long Road to Recovery: Environmental Health Impacts of Hurricane Sandy. https://ehp.niehs.nih.gov/121-a152/. (Accessed on 18/04/2018).

[145] Smart Cities Council, Developing the Smart City Workforce: It Doesn't Always Happen in the Classroom, Smart Cities Council, October 16 2016 [Online], http://smartcitiescouncil.com/article/developing-smart-city-workforce-it-doesnt-always-happen-classroom. (Accessed on 18/04/2018).

[146] University College London, UCL Graduate Degrees: Smart Cities and Urban Analytics, University College London, 2017 [Online], http://www.ucl.ac.uk/prospective-students/graduate/taught/degrees/smart-cities-urban-analytics-msc. (Accessed on 18/04/2018).

Index

Note: 'Page numbers followed by "f" indicate figures, "t" indicate tables and "b" indicate boxes'.

Printed in the United States
By Bookmasters